D1308245

Understanding
Gay and Lesbian Youth

LESSONS FOR STRAIGHT
SCHOOL TEACHERS, COUNSELORS, AND ADMINISTRATORS

David Campos

Rowman & Littlefield Education
Lanham, Maryland • Toronto • Oxford
2005

Published in the United States of America
by Rowman & Littlefield Education
A Division of Rowman & Littlefield Publishers, Inc.
A wholly owned subsidiary of The Rowman & Littlefield Publishing Group, Inc.
4501 Forbes Boulevard, Suite 200, Lanham, Maryland 20706
www.rowmaneducation.com

PO Box 317
Oxford
OX2 9RU, UK

British Library Cataloguing in Publication Information Available

Library of Congress Cataloging-in-Publication Data
Campos, David.
  Understanding gay and lesbian youth : lessons for straight school teachers, counselors, and
administrators / David Campos.
      p. cm.
  Includes bibliographical references and index.
  ISBN 1-57886-267-1 (hardcover : alk. paper) — ISBN 1-57886-290-6 (pbk. : alk. paper)
  1. Homosexuality and education—United States. 2. Gay students—United States.
  3. Lesbian students—United States. I. Title.
  LC192.6.C265 2005
  371.826'64—dc22

                                                                    2005004685

⊖ ™The paper used in this publication meets the minimum requirements of
American National Standard for Information Sciences—Permanence of
Paper for Printed Library Materials, ANSI/NISO Z39.48-1992.
Manufactured in the United States of America.

Contents

Preface and Acknowledgments

Nearly three years ago I stumbled onto the topic of gay and lesbian youth in schools. Throughout the nineties I grew to believe that this group of students was accepted and supported in schools, because I was witnessing an increasing number of gay and lesbian characters and storylines in sitcoms and dramas, more celebrities publicly acknowledging they were gay and lesbian, and widespread media coverage of gay and lesbian issues. I inaccurately assumed that the (seemingly) increasing social acceptance of gay and lesbian persons had made its way into school campuses nationwide. I could not have been more mistaken. I began to research this population for an earlier book, and in my interviews with gay, lesbian, bisexual, and transgender youth, I learned that some were accepted in their learning communities (e.g., classmates at one high school voted two lesbian students as the "sweetest couple"), but most of them were not. I heard one distressing story after another.

One student, who was perceived to be gay, was chased by a group of boys and threatened with physical harm. When he found shelter in a classroom, his assistant principal laughed at his ordeal and told him that he was making a big deal out of nothing. Another teacher ridiculed a lesbian student, and another assistant principal demanded that a boy act more like a man. One North Carolina high school principal even took down the campaign posters of an openly gay student and would not explain why he tried to stop the youth from running for student body president. Countless stories were recounted to me of school personnel who would not let gay and lesbian students discuss matters associated with their sexuality, but allowed heterosexual students to raise relationship and dating issues in class; who ignored the epithets associated with homosexuality, but rebuked students who used other contemptuous words or phrases; who refused to discuss gay and lesbian issues in class, but debated other politically controversial issues.

Many students sought solace and safety in teachers, counselors, and administrators, but these students' concerns were brushed off as a trivial matter. Imagine how horrible these students felt. They had challenges and needs that were unmet, their peers had not accepted them, they were being harassed, they had no support network or outlet of any kind, and they had no access to information on gay and lesbian issues. They had nowhere to turn to. Many gay and lesbian youth (and those presumed to be such) continue to attend schools where they meet similar circumstances. It should be no surprise that this population of youth is at an increased risk for suicide compared to their heterosexual counterparts.

Discussion of gay and lesbian matters can make the best of school personnel nervous and uncomfortable because what they know about homosexuality is often based on inadequate or inaccurate information (i.e., myths and stereotypes). This book is designed to help teachers, counselors, and administrators better understand gay and lesbian youth by (1) introducing this population of youth—the first four chapters describe these unique students and their challenges; (2) teaching about the gay and lesbian community—the second set of four chapters is a gay and lesbian primer of associated terms, myths, history, and so on; and (3) offering recommendations for supporting these youth in their learning communities—the last set of four chapters discusses how school personnel can become allies of gay and lesbian students. I invite you to learn about this population of youth and how to safeguard their well-being so that they are no longer alienated, ostracized, harassed, or left behind.

Acknowledgments

I could never have published this book without the help and support of a number of valuable people. A special thanks to Dr. Lori K. Condie and Dr. Charles R. Middleton, who took time from their busy schedules to share their stories with me. I am certain that your narratives will enable others to better understand gay and lesbian youth. You two are excellent role models. I also want to thank the many people who shared their experiences with me but chose not to be recognized. All of you contributed to the spirit of the book, and each of you provided me with special insight into working with this population of youth.

Thank you to Michael W. E. Edwards and the folks at The Advocate for allowing me to use the "Generation Q" stories. I am also indebted to the wonderful people who granted me permission to use some of their copyrighted material: Lisa Neff from Chicago Free Press, Andrew Marcks from the Austin American-Statesman, Carroll Macke from Kansas City Kansas Public Schools, Martha Kempner from SIECUS, Kathleen Rakestraw from the American School Counselor Association, and Alan Horowitz from Out for Equity.

I hold much gratitude to the professionals at Rowman & Littlefield Education. My editor, Thomas Koerner, was unfailingly encouraging and believed in this book from the very beginning. Thank you for allowing me to deliver the message that these youth can be understood and helped. I extend a special thank-you to the team who brought this book through production, especially Cindy Tursman, who was very patient with me. I am also grateful to Milburn Taylor for his wonderful illustrations; you were unfailingly positive and a pleasure to work with.

It would be an oversight if I failed to acknowledge my colleagues for their support and encouragement. I am grateful to Dr. Kathy Fad and Dr. Gail Ryser, who inspired me to write the book in the first place. Thank you, Gail, for giving me feedback on the two surveys. I also want to thank Dr. Valerie Janesick for offering me much guidance and support as a mentor.

You always look out for my professional well-being and growth. A special acknowledgment is due to Dr. Kenneth A. Perez for his early critique on the manuscript; to Allison Conn-Cafaro for her valuable feedback on the chapter for school counselors; and to Dr. Koran Kanaifu, Simon Chow, and Alex Clemenzi for keeping my spirits up as I wrote the many drafts of this manuscript.

Finally, I would be remiss if I did not extend my deepest appreciation to my family. I am privileged to have such loving parents and brothers. My mother and father, Guadalupe and Agapito, are steadfast pillars in my life, and Ernie and John are incredible sources of support. Thank you for so much.

David Campos

Introduction: You're Straight, Not Narrow

"THEY WEREN'T ABOUT TO CHANGE MY MIND"

Mrs. Kendall teaches freshman and sophomore English in a suburban Chicago school. She is a veteran teacher of 27 years with elementary, middle, and high school teaching experience. She loves to teach but becomes distressed with professional development that deals specifically with gay and lesbian youth. She explains, "I'm a nice lady. I work hard, and I do the best job that I can. I love all of my students. But I cannot get myself to feel good about or even comfortable about gay people and kids. I've gone through diversity and sensitivity training, but it's not right that we allow kids and adults to be gay or lesbian."

Mrs. Kendall's strong Catholic background is the basis for her sentiment, and she is adamant that homosexuality is wrong. "I don't believe in homosexuality. The Bible clearly says that homosexuality is wrong. My priest says to love the sinner and hate the sins. That's what I try to do." Teachers at her school were mandated to attend professional development on this topic when a gay boy attempted suicide. The student had been harassed in classes and hallways despite the fact that the school had a sexual harassment policy. The district feared a lawsuit, so teachers were asked to attend the workshop.

Mrs. Kendall and many of her colleagues were apprehensive about participating in the training. "I listened. I was quiet. I just didn't see the point of having to approach this subject. We didn't do it in the seventies, eighties, or nineties. Why now? I think all these discussions are turning kids gay." She became frightfully nervous during one exercise. "I'm sure that I blushed. I was so uneasy. I had to hold a gay magazine during an activity, and I must have been beet red. I just felt that the energy from the magazine was going to run through me and turn me gay. I listened to what they had to say, but they weren't about to change my mind."

Mrs. Kendall does an excellent job of creating a safe and nurturing classroom environment, and she has applied some elements from the professional development into her classroom. She never allowed for teasing of any kind, and she learned to admonish students for using sexual orientation as banter. "I don't allow my kids to curse. I don't care what the words are; that's not an option. And they cannot make fun of each other. I did learn that you should stop whatever may be offensive to certain groups of people. I've gotten better at explaining why they shouldn't do that. In that sense, I protect gay and lesbian youth."

Mrs. Kendall is becoming hesitantly accepting of gay and lesbian persons. "My husband is much better about this whole gay and lesbian thing. He works with some gay folks, and he's gotten used to it, I guess. Sometimes we talk about it, and I've started adjusting my attitude toward them. I guess we're all the same, really." She suggests the idea of retiring soon so that younger, more accepting teachers will better attend to gay and lesbian youth. "I'm not going to be doing this much longer. I guess it's better that way. Gay kids need someone younger, someone more open to the idea of doing more for these kids. That's why God created new teachers."

Overview

Mrs. Kendall is like many teachers across the country. She is good-natured and hardworking, and she cares about her students. Mrs. Kendall is also uneasy about gay and lesbian youth. In her lifetime, she has not had to contend with such youth and is consequently uncomfortable about preparing herself and her learning community for what seems unnecessary. Little does Mrs. Kendall know that she is an excellent candidate for becoming an ally to gay and lesbian youth. She is aware of her convictions, she is adamant about having a safe and nurturing classroom for all students, and she recognizes that gay and lesbian persons are nothing to fear.

You may identify with Mrs. Kendall, as she has no intention of ever becoming an advocate (i.e., participating in marches, wearing pink-triangle T-shirts, and so forth), but she is willing to better understand how to accept, tolerate, and include gay and lesbian youth in her classroom. This book is for schoolteachers, counselors, and administrators like Mrs. Kendall who seek to prepare themselves and their learning communities for gay and lesbian youth. Before we delve into the topics of gay and lesbian youth, the community, and how to become an ally, the following questions are addressed in this chapter:

- Why does the gay and lesbian topic make me feel uncomfortable?
- Why is it important for me to read this material?
- Do I have to be an advocate for gay and lesbian youth?

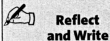

Reflect and Write

Do you think it is important that schools support gay and lesbian youth? Why? What is the most challenging aspect of supporting gay and lesbian youth?

Why Does the Gay and Lesbian Topic Make Me Feel Uncomfortable?

You must admit that when you picked up this text you were a little uncomfortable. The title made you nervous, and now you are somewhat anxious about the content. Rest assured that all of those feelings are perfectly normal. You are among the thousands of school personnel who are uneasy about confronting gay and lesbian issues, especially when it comes to youth. In 2002 alone, some school personnel and parents exhibited behavior indicating that they were apprehensive about diverse sexual orientations in their schools:

- One school board in Florida called homosexuality a sin and emphasized that they would oppose any curriculum that promoted or condoned a "homosexual lifestyle."

- Some Hayward, California, teachers refused to participate in sensitivity training, "Safe Schools for All: Supporting Gay, Lesbian, Bisexual, Transgender and Questioning Youth and Families," claiming that their religion objected to it.
- After a gay principal in Maple Grove, Minnesota, wrote a letter to parents informing them of his sexual orientation, a mother withdrew her daughter from his school.
- A student in Fort Worth, Texas, a member of his school's Christian prayer club, revealed that he was gay. His high school principal asked him to resign from the club and warned him not to start a Gay–Straight Alliance.
- A conservative faction in Cleveland, Citizens for Community Values, filed suit against the Ohio public school system because its members believed that district policies had caused physical and emotional harm to students. They wrote, "We have a responsibility to advise parents that with the approval of school officials, organizations such as GLSEN and PFLAG have been allowed to sponsor clubs, programs and activities through which students are being lured into a behavior pattern that threatens their physical, mental and emotional well-being" (Resnick, 2002).
- Some California parents filed suit against the Novato School District for allowing elementary children to a see a play on discrimination and prejudice, *Cootie Shots: Theatrical Inoculations against Bigotry for Kids, Parents and Teachers*. The play contained references to homosexuality.

Youth-serving personnel and parents have varied reasons for feeling discontent around gay men and lesbian women. Some believe that being gay or lesbian is sinful because they assert that the Bible emphasizes that homosexuality is unnatural and immoral. Essentially, most people are uneasy because the gay and lesbian issue is foreign and seemingly contrary to the normal, heterosexual way of life.

We live in a heterosexist society. In other words, we live in a society where everyone is assumed to be heterosexual. If you think for a moment, everyone in your community—your family, your neighbors, your friends, your coworkers, your students, and so forth—are assumed to be heterosexual. You also assume that people who serve you—at the mall, church, or doctor's office—are all heterosexual. While glancing through mainstream magazines or flipping through cable channels, you see pervasive images of heterosexuals. Rarely do you see two men holding hands while walking down the aisles at your local grocer, a female-to-male transgender person in church, or a lesbian principal and her partner dancing at the high school prom.

Schools, in particular, are breeding grounds for heterosexism. Most school personnel and students, for instance, expect to see heterosexual couples in the hallways, talk openly about their heterosexual relationships, assume that students will conform to gender-appropriate clothes and behavior, assume that only girls will try out to become twirlers, expect students to participate in gender-appropriate sports teams, and so forth. (Box 1.1 illustrates some other ways heterosexism is manifested in campuses across the country.)

BOX 1.1. EXAMPLES OF HETEROSEXISM IN SCHOOLS

Heterosexism is the assumption that all persons naturally behave according to their birth-assigned gender. Heterosexism is any form of bias against gay, lesbian, bisexual, or transgender persons as a result of believing that heterosexuality is omnipresent or superior to homosexuality, which is psychologically, spiritually, or morally wrong.

- No one expects homosexual couples at the prom.
- Everyone assumes that boys will run for prom king, and girls will run for prom queen.
- School policies do not address gay and lesbian youth.
- Professional development for teachers rarely addresses gay and lesbian youth.
- School personnel rarely intervene when youth call one another "fag," "faggot," "lesbo," and so forth.
- There is no mention of gay and lesbian issues in the curriculum.
- There is no support for gay and lesbian youth, and there are no Gay–Straight Alliances.
- No magazines for and about the gay and lesbian community are found in the school library.

For most of your life you have been groomed in heterosexism. Your parents, siblings, friends, teachers, and religion reinforced the idea that you and everyone else around you were interested in the opposite sex. They assumed you would date and marry the opposite gender, and you held the same expectation of them. No matter what your ethnicity, family constellation, economic or social status, or culture may be, you were inculcated into heterosexism. And, anytime anyone mentioned homosexuality, it was discussed in the pejorative. Early in your life, you heard words like *fag, queer, dyke,* and *sissy.* You may not have known what these words meant, but you knew they were not flattering. As you grew older, you learned that adults used these epithets to deprecate someone or to make contemptuous remarks about his or her apparent sexual orientation, and you learned that youth used these terms as banter or verbal assaults in scuffles and to humiliate one another. Not one time in your life would you have appreciated someone calling you a "fag," "queer," "dyke," "sissy," or even "gay" or "lesbian." In our society, these words are razor sharp and score deep. They are not unique to particular regions of the country, and their prevalence does not vary according to school size or type. These words are commonplace throughout schools today.

Most people are taught to believe that gay men and lesbian women are heinous. Why would you think otherwise when reputable persons like Jerry Falwell blame the World Trade Center tragedy on gay and lesbian persons? Or when politicians like Ronald Reagan and his wife Nancy publicly claim they cannot find any merit in gay and lesbian pride? Or when General Colin Powell announces that gay and lesbian military personnel will "demoralize and jeopardize the military's effectiveness" (Baker, 2002)? In fact, you are likely to believe that

- gay men are child molesters;
- lesbians hate men, are manly themselves, and are likely to become truck drivers and construction workers;
- gay men are weak, feminine, and can only become hairdressers, florists, and fashion designers;
- gay and lesbian persons are lonely and unhappy;
- gay and lesbian persons can make heterosexuals gay or lesbian; and
- gay and lesbian persons intentionally choose their sexual orientation.

These widely held stereotypes have no hint of accuracy whatsoever, and whenever people talk about the gay and lesbian community in disgust, they perpetuate these false images. One disturbing urban legend about the gay and lesbian community started soon after the advent of AIDS. As the legend goes, an attractive, sincere woman vacations in an ideal city, where she meets and falls in love with an equally handsome, debonair man. The two spend the final days of the vacation in romance, which leads to a seemingly fulfilling sexual encounter. On the last day of the vacation, the man gives the woman a card, which she later reads: "I am a gay man, and I have given you the gift of AIDS. Now you straight people know what it feels like." This is an urban legend in the truest sense and *never* happened. But imagine how you and others would perceive gay men after hearing that this happened to a distant friend or relative.

You have probably been taught that homosexuality is wrong, immoral, and sinful. Organizations such as the Christian Coalition and the Family Research Council have advertised in major newspapers that the "alternative lifestyle" is a choice and that any gay, lesbian, bisexual, or transgender person can be cured. In church or prayer groups, religious leaders use the Bible to reference God's wrath against homosexuals, and some public figures (e.g., Dr. Laura Schlesinger, Senator Trent Lott, Judge Connie Wilkerson) have been outspoken about their negative impressions of homosexuality. Moreover, people who matter most in your life have probably denounced gay, lesbian, bisexual, and transgender persons.

In all, you and thousands of others have every right to feel uncomfortable, uneasy, and disturbed while reading the

 Critical Thinking

Others have influenced your perceptions about gay and lesbian persons. What have been some of the disparaging remarks you have heard about gay and lesbian persons? Who said them, and in what context?

material in this book. Undoubtedly, this is new and uncharted territory for you, and this controversial topic is sure to evoke a range of upsetting emotions.

Why Is It Important for Me to Read This Material?

Many teachers, counselors, and administrators are not sure how to approach gay and lesbian youth. Some believe that these youth are other schools' problems. Others believe that we should ignore the population altogether and that these problems will go away, and others believe that we should combat gay and lesbian propaganda lest we lose more youth to the gay and lesbian recruitment scheme. The fact is we need to do what we can so that all differences among youth are tolerated and accepted, regardless of their academic and social prowess, their ethnic or economic background, their gender and sexual orientation, and so forth. Let's consider Erik Erikson's words: "Some day, maybe, there will exist a well-informed, well-considered and yet fervent public conviction that the most deadly of all possible sins is the mutilation of a child's spirit" (Rofes, 1989, p. 444). If we do not make an attempt to understand gay and lesbian youth, they will continue to have their spirits mutilated each day in schools across the country.

Gay and lesbian youth are in your school. They may not come running to you with information about their sexual orientation, and they may not wear the symbols commonly associated with the population, but they are in your classrooms. The size of this population is difficult to determine, and it varies because most gay and lesbian youth are quiet about their sexual orientation. Estimates, nonetheless, are significant. Ginsberg (1996), for instance, estimates that 6% of all adolescents are gay or lesbian, while Marinoble (1998) believes that 10% of adolescents eventually identify themselves as nonheterosexual. The National Education Association (GLSEN, 2002), on the other hand, estimates that 1 in 20 youth has same-sex attractions, and YouthPride (1997) claims that 1 to 3 youth of every 10 are nonheterosexual or have a family member who is. Applying a conservative 2% to the 40.7 million youth between 10 and 19 years old living in the United States (U.S. Department of Census, 2002) would mean that nearly 814,959 youth are gay, lesbian, bisexual, or transgender. Given this figure, these youth are likely to thrive in your school.

You may not know of any openly gay or lesbian youth at your school because most have been socialized to conceal their sexual orientation. Some keep this information secret from their closest friends, fearing the repercussions of disclosing their sexuality. But why

 Application

Think about how many gay or lesbian persons you know. If you do not know of any, think about some gay or lesbian characters on TV, in movies, or in the media. What are some of their qualities? How do they reinforce or dispel stereotypes?

Some teachers are uncomfortable around gay and lesbian students.

should we expect more youth to be open about their sexuality? The fact remains that adolescents are critical of one another, and there is a social stigma attached to homosexuality. These facts combined have proven to make openly gay and lesbian youth into targets of harassment, bullying, ridicule, assault, or teasing. For instance, in the following vignette, Kurt had mannerisms that led others to believe he was gay. This was enough for other youth to wage a prejudice attack against him.

KURT, 15, GAY IN DES MOINES, IOWA

My story sucks, really. I'm judged wherever I go. People hate me just because of the way I walk and talk. I don't mean to be the way I am. I just am. I wish I were more straight acting.

The earliest I can remember being teased was like when I was eight. I was at the playground across the street from my house, and some boys kept calling me "little girl," and they wouldn't stop. I remember thinking, "But I'm not. Why are they being that way?" I grew up in a house where I was the only child, and the only other kid I played with was the girl next door. She was never mean to me, and she never judged me. She and I would play house, and she was cool. Even when we got older, she still was cool. But these mean boys were calling me "little girl, little girl, little girl." I didn't say anything to them. Two of them started to pull me, like to take me somewhere, but I resisted. I was so scared. I thought they were going to beat me up. The girl called my mom, and then the boys left me alone.

Then, by middle school, it started getting worse. All the kids would call me "queer" and "fag" and "butt pirate." And I never did anything to them. They were just mean. Last year my mom bought be me a sweater, and I tied it around my neck just like the guys in *GQ*, and the kids just laughed and laughed and told me I was nothing but a big queer and that I was going to get AIDS. Then this guy came up to me and started to hit the sleeves around me. I told him to stop, but he didn't. Then this other guy came up from behind and started to pull the sleeves really hard, and I started to choke. He says he didn't do it hard, but he did. I couldn't breathe, and I started to cry. Everyone around was laughing. Some girls were telling him to stop, but he didn't. That's when Mrs. Morrison came in and told them to stop. She told me to go splash some water on my face and get something to drink. She started class, and she didn't tell the kids anything.

She sent a girl for me like 30 minutes later, and I didn't want her to look at me. She was cool, though. She told me those guys were stupid, and she put her arm around me. Nobody apologized to me. Nobody even asked if I was OK. And some guys whispered "cry baby." I just ignored them. What could I do?

I don't understand it, sometimes. It seems like I never do anything right. Everybody made fun of me when I wore my Justin Timberlake button. And like everybody loves MTV, and I made a book cover with construction paper with an MTV design, and they told me so many mean things. In English, we have to keep a journal. Everybody else's is plain and dumb, but I cut pictures out of magazines of things I like and pasted them on the cover. They made fun of me again. One boy even took it from me and wrote in there, "Dear God: Why am I big fag?" I ripped the page out, and the teacher didn't even say anything.

KURT, 15, GAY IN DES MOINES, IOWA (Continued)

Nothing I do is right. I told my mother and father that I wanted to play the clarinet, and they told me no. They said I had to play the trumpet. I told my homeroom teacher I wanted to start a drama club, and she told me it was a bad idea and I should just focus on Spanish. Sometimes I just want to run away to Los Angeles or San Francisco. Then maybe everybody would be happy that I was gone.

For what reasons would Mrs. Morrison ignore Kurt and the choking incident? Were her actions right or wrong? Was Kurt entitled to an apology? What could she have done differently? What kind of support are Kurt and others like him entitled to?

Studies confirm that learning communities are hostile toward gay and lesbian youth. Human Rights Watch (2001); the American Association of University Women (2001); the Gay, Lesbian and Straight Education Network (GLSEN) (2002); and a host of other organizations have consistently reported that gay and lesbian youth are victimized more often than heterosexual youth, and teachers often dismiss, trivialize, or ignore the plight of these youth. Some gay and lesbian youth are victimized in ways unimaginable. Adam Colton of California, for instance, had some students assault him and carve the word *fag* into his stomach. A group of students jumped and lassoed Derek Henkle of Nevada and then threatened to pull him from a car. One youth was spit on, another was urinated on, one was chased home, and another was mock raped by a group of boys. If that were not enough, many of these youth risk rejection from their peers. Research has found that some gay and lesbian youth lose close friends soon after informing them of their sexual orientation. Such consequences are enough to scare the bravest of youth into staying in the proverbial closet, depressed, withdrawn, suicidal, truant, or failing in academics.

Despite these obstacles, a record number of youth are disclosing their sexual orientation in schools. In fact, research finds that gay and lesbian youth are disclosing their sexual orientation to others ("coming out") at earlier ages than prior generations. Studies of adults in the 1970s, for instance, found that most gay and lesbian persons would come out between the ages of 19 and 23; studies of youth in the 1990s, however, revealed that they were coming out between the ages of 14 and 16. Reasons for this recent phenomenon vary, but sexuality experts seem to believe that youth in general witness the following:

- More social acceptance of gay and lesbian persons. Since the Stonewall Riots of 1969 (discussed in chapter 7), popular surveys have indicated a growing approval of gay and lesbian persons.
- More discussions about the gay and lesbian community in mainstream news. Heated debates in the media have occurred regarding whether gay and lesbian

persons should serve openly in the military, be allowed to adopt children, be allowed to marry, be allowed domestic-partner benefits, and so forth.

- More gay and lesbian images on TV and in movies. Gay and lesbian characters and storylines are found in prime-time sitcoms, premium cable channels, and cinema. Documentary reality shows (e.g., *The Real World, Survivor, Big Brother, Teen Idol*); sitcoms (e.g., *Ellen, Will & Grace, Friends*); dramas (e.g., *Dawson's Creek*); soap operas (e.g., *Undressed*); cartoons (e.g., *South Park*); cable-produced dramas (e.g., *Six Feet Under, Sex and the City, Queer as Folk*); and mainstream movies (e.g., *My Best Friend's Wedding, In and Out, The Mexican*) have featured gay and lesbian persons as characters.
- More celebrities living openly as gay or lesbian. Talk show host Rosie O'Donnell, ABC news correspondent Jeffrey Kofman, musician Melissa Etheridge, tennis player Amelie Mauresmo, New York Senator Tom Duane, actor Christopher Sieber, and so forth have all publicly acknowledged their sexual orientation.
- More schools sponsoring Gay–Straight Alliances (GSA). GLSEN (2002) reports that the number of GSAs in schools across the country has increased to over 1,000.
- Easier access to information about the gay and lesbian community via the Internet. In a matter of minutes, youth can locate information about gay and lesbian persons or connect with gay and lesbian persons in chat rooms.
- Successful lawsuits by gay youth against their school districts for failing to protect them from harassment.

In all, these unprecedented events are paving the way for youth to publicly acknowledge their sexual orientation even though their learning communities may not be prepared for or accepting of them.

The time has come to prepare yourself for gay and lesbian youth. You may not be thrilled with the idea, but the fact remains that you are morally and legally obligated to ensure that all youth have a safe school environment. Failing to do so leaves you likely to be named in a lawsuit if others believe that you intentionally chose to ignore the plight of a gay or lesbian youth, failed to act on their behalf, or participated in their denigration. Jamie Nabozny, for instance, was awarded nearly a million dollars after he sued his former Wisconsin high school principal for failing to protect him from the repeated verbal and physical assaults he endured at school. Timothy Dahle settled for $312,000 from his Pennsylvania district. Other youth have prevailed in their lawsuits against school districts that denied them the opportunity to form Gay–Straight Alliances or similar clubs. School districts have lost thousands of dollars simply because they believed they were right in denying students the opportunity to start such clubs.

You need to read this material because it is the right thing to do. You may not agree with what you believe gay and lesbian persons represent, but all youth should see that,

"The principal said he wanted allies, not advocates."

despite your misgivings about gay and lesbian persons, you have respect and tolerance for all groups of people enough to learn how to accept, protect, and include gay and lesbian youth in your learning community. Nationality, gender, learning style, and so forth do not influence how you treat your students. Sexual orientation should not either.

Do I Have to Be an Advocate for Gay and Lesbian Youth?

The purpose of this text is to transform you into an *ally*, not necessarily an *advocate*, for gay and lesbian youth. The *American Heritage College Dictionary* (2002) defines *ally* as

- *n.* One in helpful association with one another, and
- *v.* To place in a friendly association. (p. 38)

The overarching goal is to get you to become a friendly associate of gay and lesbian youth. They rightfully deserve to thrive without fear in your learning community, and they should feel comfortable enough to come to you for guidance. Whether you stand to counsel them or not, at the very least you should know what they are going through, how to respond to their disclosure, and where to direct them for additional support.

Becoming an ally involves knowing more about the following: the unique challenges presented to gay and lesbian youth, gay and lesbian history and community, legal standards, and ways to include gay and lesbian youth in your learning community. No one is forcing you to advocate for the gay and lesbian community, march in the next gay-pride parade, or join a local PFLAG (Parents and Friends of Lesbians and Gays) group. For now, hold on to whatever convictions you have regarding gay and lesbian persons, but as you read keep an open mind and remind yourself that all youth need your respect and a safe learning community. Just begin to accept that some youth are gay, lesbian, bisexual, or transgender, that they are entitled to respect from you and their peers, and that they should be free from harm.

 Reflect and Write

What is the value for a youth to live as openly gay or lesbian? Why would a youth disclose his or her sexuality to peers?

Put Yourself in the Picture

You overhear some students in a classroom discussing that gay men and lesbians go to hell because their "lifestyle" is a sin. Another mentions that God hates gays and lesbians and that that is why there are earthquakes in San Francisco. One student in the classroom is gay. What would you tell the group so that no one is offended by the remarks?

Summary

Gay and lesbian youth do not fit neatly into the heterosexist paradigm, and consequently they are sure to make some people uncomfortable. These youth are here to stay, and as society becomes more accepting of them, you will witness a growing number of openly gay and lesbian youth in your school. Some learning communities are unprepared for this trend, and gay and lesbian youth are therefore subject to relatively hostile environments. The purpose of this text is to transform you into an ally of these youth so that they can realize their academic and social potential in a safe learning environment. As former U.S. Surgeon General David Satcher (Associated Press, 2001) said, "We have a responsibility to be more supportive and proactive than judgmental" of gay and lesbian youth. You are not forced to adapt your convictions and become an advocate, making signs and wearing buttons, freedom rings, or rainbow jewelry. Simply put, schools, parents, and communities must teach youth and one another to approach sexual orientation with a mature and considerate attitude. Failing to do so leaves far too many youth unnecessarily anguished. In the ensuing chapters, you will read about the challenges that gay and lesbian youth have in their lives, some background information about the community, and how to become an ally. Keep an open mind and remember that just because you are straight does not mean you have to be narrow.

Idea File

1. Watch a mainstream movie that features a gay or lesbian theme or character (e.g., *And the Band Played On, As Good as It Gets, Beautiful Thing, The Birdcage, Boys Don't Cry, Chasing Amy, Doing Time on Maple Drive, Flawless, The Mexican, My Best Friend's Wedding, The Next Best Thing, The Object of My Affection, Philadelphia, The Talented Mr. Ripley*). Identify a gay or lesbian character's strengths and weaknesses. Determine how the character is portrayed in stereotype and contrast him or her with a heterosexual character.

2. Interview an openly gay or lesbian youth. Ask the youth what school is like for him or her. What could teachers and counselors do to make life easier for the youth? What are some things that school personnel simply do not understand? If a youth is unavailable, adapt your questions and ask an openly gay or lesbian adult to reflect on his or her experiences.

3. Create a support group for teachers who are having a hard time approaching this topic. Have a counselor facilitate the meetings. Discuss what is so difficult about becoming an ally and how to overcome some of the discomfort. Invite an openly gay or lesbian adult to share his or her experiences and suggest what teachers can do differently for gay and lesbian youth.

References

American Association of University Women. (2001). *Hostile hallways: Bullying, teasing, and sexual harassment in school.* Washington, DC: Author.

American heritage college dictionary (4th ed.). (2002). Boston: Houghton Mifflin Company.

Associated Press. (2001, June 28). Surgeon general issues "call to action" on sexual health. CNN.com. Retrieved June 30, 2001, from http://cnn.health.

Baker, J. M. (2002). *How homophobia hurts children: Nurturing diversity at home, at school, and in the community.* New York: Harrington Park Press.

Ginsberg, R. W. (1996). Silenced voices inside our school. *Initiatives, 58,* 1–15.

GLSEN. (2002). *The 2001 national school climate survey: The school related experiences of our nations lesbian, gay, bisexual and transgender youth.* New York: Office for Public Policy of the Gay, Lesbian, and Straight Education Network.

Human Rights Watch. (2001). *Hatred in the hallways: Violence and discrimination against lesbian, gay, bisexual, and transgender students in U.S. schools.* New York: Author.

Marinoble, R. M. (1998). Homosexuality: A blind spot in the school mirror. *Professional School Counseling, 1*(3), 4–7.

Resnick, E. (2002, July 19). Group threatens to sue schools for "gay agenda." *Gay People's Chronicle.* Retrieved August 23, 2002, from http://www.glsen.org/templates/news/record.html?section= 12&record=1383.

Rofes, E. (1989). Opening up the classroom closet: Responding to the educational needs of gay and lesbian youth. *Harvard Educational Review, 59*(4), 443–53.

YouthPride Inc. (1997, April). *Creating safe schools for lesbian and gay students: A resource guide for school staff.* Retrieved July 20, 2001, from http://members.tripod.com/~twood/guide.html.

U.S. Department of Census. (2002). *2000 Census.* U.S. Department of Census. Retrieved August 10, 2003, from http://www.census.gov.

Triangle Pegs for Round Holes:
A Unique Population of Youth

Facts and Statistics about Gay and Lesbian Youth

"YOU'RE NOT GOING TO HAVE THAT CLUB HERE."

Ms. Lori Condie teaches geometry and algebra in one of the largest high schools in Chicago. Even though she is not the faculty sponsor of her school's Gay–Straight Alliance (GSA), she garnered the support it needed to be recognized as an official school club. In 2002, an openly lesbian student approached a teacher about sponsoring a gay and lesbian club. The teacher was amenable to the idea and consequently asked the principal what had to be done to start the club. The principal asked for a petition of student signatures, and within weeks the student had acquired over 700 signatures. The student submitted the petition but was denied permission, with the excuse that the school already had a multicultural club. The faculty sponsor asked the principal what additional information was needed to alter her decision. The principal purportedly responded, "You're not going to have that club here."

The students and the faculty sponsor recognized this as an unjust and callous decision, so Ms. Condie solicited help from the Chicago mayor's office, particularly from the gay and lesbian community liaison, who eventually asked the superintendent to intervene. In a matter of days, the students had their GSA. As a whole, the club and its members are well received by the students. Ms. Condie adds,

> The GSA did a Day of Silence, which was a pretty big deal. There was some resistance from certain teachers, but for the most part it went fine. There's no resistance from kids. It's totally from the faculty. . . . It's kind of interesting, now, how you see girls holding hands or guys holding hands in the hallways, kissing. They kiss just like everybody else does. It's totally out there now. Not one kid gets harassed. They're popular kids. We even had two same-sex couples go to the prom this year.

Some faculty and staff remain unsupportive of the club, often going to the extent of denouncing its initiatives.

> I have teachers come up to me and say, "You know, your people were kissing over here." And I'm like, "My people? Who?" And that's the way they address them, as "my people." I get these issues all the time. I'm like, "Did I become the token lesbian of the school?"

Even though she is an advocate for gay and lesbian youth, as a math teacher, Ms. Condie does not get regular opportunities to discuss gay and lesbian issues. She does, however, enforce the rule that students cannot call each other gay or lesbian epithets.

(Continued)

"YOU'RE NOT GOING TO HAVE THAT CLUB HERE." (Continued)

The only times I get the opportunity to talk about anything remotely gay or lesbian are when kids are calling each other "faggot" or they're saying, "that's gay." Any student who knows me knows that's the forbidden thing to do. I had a girl in my division whose uncle is gay, and she called someone a "faggot." I screamed at her and told her not to come back to my room until she could tell me why she used that word. When I hear "faggot" and "that's gay," I'll stop them and say, "Explain to me what gay is. What does that mean? Why are you using that word?" And they're like, "You know," and I'm like, "No, I don't know."

Overview

Ms. Condie has been a teacher for over 20 years and has witnessed an increase in the number of gay and lesbian youth appealing for safe and supportive school climates. Many gay and lesbian youth want a school climate that accepts or tolerates them, not to make the lives of teachers, counselors, and administrators uncomfortable, but because they want and need a social supportive mechanism from which they can draw strength. Adolescent researcher Susan Morrow (1997) analogized that contemporary youth in general traverse a rocky road to adulthood, but gay and lesbian youth hike through a minefield to get to the same destination.

Imagine how overwhelmed one of Ms. Condie's students must have felt to have taken his own life. He was considered a troubled student and was an active gang member. He had apparently made a pass at another boy. The boy did not reciprocate, and this scared him. Ms. Condie recalled,

> This was before we had the GSA we have here at school. This was probably something that he should have kept to himself. As horrible as that sounds, he was not in a position to make passes at anybody. It certainly was not the right boy to be making a pass at. Ultimately, he was afraid of what was going to happen to him. . . . On that day, something was really troubling him, and he was really trying to talk to me. He kept coming back and telling me that something was wrong. I was like, "Just tell me what it is," but he couldn't get it out. He was sputtering, trying to say something. He must have decided that this was the easy way out, because he left school that day and shot himself.

Make no mistake about it; this student was experiencing some challenges in his life, some of which were likely attributable to his being gay. Perhaps if his school personnel had understood some of the risks commonly associated with growing up gay and how to reach out to him, this fatal event could have been avoided. In this chapter, you will learn how gay and lesbian youth are at an increased risk for academic and social problems. In particular, this chapter addresses the following issues:

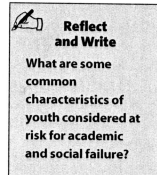

Reflect and Write

What are some common characteristics of youth considered at risk for academic and social failure?

- Why are gay and lesbian youth considered "at risk"?
- What is homophobia?
- How does homophobia affect gay, lesbian, and heterosexual youth?
- Could my school have a homophobic or hostile learning climate toward gay and lesbian youth?

Why Are Gay and Lesbian Youth Considered "At Risk"?

Gay and lesbian youth are an at-risk population because they have additional challenges and burdens in their lives that increase the likelihood of developmental failure. Not only do they contend with the normal demands of adolescence such as wanting to be popular, wanting to fit in, and wanting to succeed, but they must contend with a sexual orientation that is contrary to those around them and that is often the direct target of intolerance. Gay and lesbian youth are at risk because they have a higher-than-usual chance of developing academic and social problems. Moreover, hostile environments pose a potentially harmful influence on their mental health that hinders optimal development.

Some researchers believe that no other group of youth suffers more than gay and lesbian youth (Marino, 1995). Indeed, the list for their potential risks is long. Imagine the psychological distress they experience when their peers use gay and lesbian epithets to humiliate one another, or when gay and lesbian issues are discussed in a pejorative way. Being gay or lesbian is a stigma in society, and gay and lesbian persons are rarely affirmed in schools. A boy who scribbles his name with another boy's name on his book cover to signify a romance is bound to be condemned, ridiculed, and ostracized at best, and verbally and physically assaulted at worse. A transgender female-to-male student who attends a school formal sporting a crew cut and a traditional tuxedo is likely to be harassed.

Gay and lesbian youth's psychological distress is further impacted when there is no accurate information about the gay and lesbian community in their libraries, the curriculum rarely addresses gay and lesbian issues or discusses them in a complimentary style, health and sex education fail to include information about diverse sexuality, there is no social outlet or support for gay and lesbian youth, and there are no openly gay and lesbian role models in the faculty or staff. These circumstances make some gay and lesbian youth feel marginalized, denigrated, and worthless to the point that they become self-destructive (Vare & Norton, 1998).

Unsurprisingly, gay and lesbian youth are more likely than their heterosexual counterparts to experience depression and feelings of isolation and fear. The context is simple, really. If youth are rejected, alienated, or victimized or feel that they may be if others find out about their sexual orientation, they are likely to experience psychological distress that leads them to attempt and commit suicide, drop out of school, run away, abuse substances, and so forth (see box 2.1). The following sections demonstrate exactly how gay and lesbian youth are at risk for academic, social, and emotional failure.

BOX 2.1. THE CONTEXT THAT LEADS SOME GAY AND LESBIAN YOUTH TO SELF-DESTRUCTIVE BEHAVIORS

1. Gay and lesbian youth in hostile learning environments are likely to feel alienated, ridiculed, condemned, harassed, and ostracized.
2. As a result, they begin to feel anxiety, fear, worthlessness, stress, isolation, and depression.
3. This leads them to engage in self-destructive behaviors such as attempting/committing suicide, dropping out, running away, skipping classes, and abusing substances.
4. This reinforces feelings of 2.

Suicide

Youth suicide is a serious social problem. From 1950 to 1980, the incidence of suicide among all youth between 14 to 24 years old increased 170%, while other age groups increased 20% (Centers for Disease Control, 1986). In 1996, suicide was the leading cause of death among 15 to 19 years olds, and currently about 9% of all youth report a suicide attempt. Nearly 5,000 young adults commit suicide each year (Bailey & Phariss, 1996). The suicide rate among gay and lesbian youth is unsettling. Studies consistently confirm that the leading cause of death for gay and lesbian youth is suicide. A comprehensive national study on suicide conducted in 1989 established that gay and lesbian youth constitute a disproportionate percentage of annual suicides. The study found that gay and lesbian youth were two to three times more likely to attempt suicide than their heterosexual counterparts (Gibson, 1989). Moreover, 30% of adolescent suicides were committed by gay and lesbian youth, even though they compose a small percentage (estimates range up to 10%) of all youth.

About 1,500 gay and lesbian youth intentionally end their lives each year (Cook & Palwoski, 1991, cited in Vare & Norton, 1998; Maguen, 1992), and a third of these suicides happen before the age of 17 (Gibson, 1989). Jennings (cited in Macgillivray, 2000) estimates that every five hours and 48 minutes a gay, lesbian, bisexual, transgender, or questioning youth succeeds with a suicide, and every 35 minutes such youth attempt suicide. One gay and lesbian youth hotline indicated that 60% of their calls were about suicide attempts. This is critical, considering that suicide attempts by these youth are more serious and lethal than the attempts made by their heterosexual counterparts (McFarland, 1993). Regardless of the sample size or their demographics, ideas of suicide or suicide attempts are common among gay and lesbian youth. Consider the following results from studies about gay and lesbian youth:

- 44% of a Rhode Island sample had contemplated suicide (Rhode Island Task Force on Gay, Lesbian, Bisexual and Transgendered Youth, 1996).
- 45.1% of 110 Seattle youth who had been harassed had seriously considered suicide, and 43.1% had made suicide plans (Seattle Youth Risk Behavior Survey, 1995, cited in Safe Schools Coalition of Washington, 1999).
- 53% of a Seattle street-youth sample had attempted suicide (Kruks, 1991).
- A Massachusetts sample suggested that gay and lesbian youth were six times more likely to attempt suicide (Massachusetts Youth Risk Behavior Survey, 1997, cited in Safe Schools Coalition of Washington, 1999).
- Half of a Vermont sample of students who had had same-gender sexual experiences had seriously considered suicide, and 34% had attempted suicide within the year (Vermont Youth Risk Behavior Survey, 1997, cited in Safe Schools Coalition of Washington, 1999).
- A third of a Minnesota sample mentioned that they had attempted suicide (Minnesota Adolescent Health Survey, 1987, cited in Safe Schools Coalition of Washington, 1999).
- In a sample of 221, 40.3% had attempted suicide, and 25.8% had thought about it at least once (Proctor & Groze, 1994).
- 37% of school counselors reported that the gay and lesbian youth they had seen had attempted or contemplated suicide (Fontaine, 1998).
- In a sample of 137 gay and bisexual male youth, a third had attempted suicide, and half of these had attempted multiple times (Remafedi, Farrow, & Deisher, 1991).
- Of a sample of gay and lesbian youth who had suffered a physical attack, 34% of the gay youth and 42% of the lesbian youth had attempted suicide (Gay, Lesbian and Straight Education Network of Colorado, 2002).

Many school personnel incorrectly assume that gay and lesbian youth have a sexual identity crisis or cannot resolve an internal conflict and that this is the reason they consider suicide. Others wrongly believe that gay or lesbian youth are inherently weak and prone to suicide ideation. The fact is that most gay and lesbian youth consider suicide as a means to escape the pain of prejudice, rejection, and isolation. Simply put, the stress that gay and lesbian youth endure from society's negative attitudes and pressures cause many to consider suicide—some youth believe that an end to their life will be an end to the misery of intolerance. McFarland (1993) explains, "The experience of growing up different than society expects contributes to the suicidal risk. Lacking positive adult models, skills, and support systems, gay and lesbian youths can easily conclude that there is little hope of becoming happy or productive" (p. 19).

ROBBIE KIRKLAND

Robbie Kirkland, a 14-year-old gay youth, ended his life in January 1997. A poem that he had written two years prior to his death captured the extent of his unhappiness:

> I'm dying and no one cares,
> I try to stand and walk,
> I fall to the hard cold ground,
> It feels as if to life I'm no longer bound,
> The others look and laugh at my plight.
> (Mallett, 1997, cited in Stevens & Morgan, 1999, p. 241).

He must have been under unbearable pressure and pain to believe that his only option for peace was to take his life. His suicide note read, "I am sorry for the pain that I have put everyone through. I hope I can find the peace that I couldn't find in life" (Stevens & Morgan, p. 241).

What response would you write if one of your students gave you this poem? What other actions would you take?

Concerned adults should be mindful of the warning signs found among youth contemplating suicide. Such youth tend to

- talk about committing suicide—"I wish I were dead," "No one would even care if I died;"
- show patterns of death or suicide in assignments—ideas of suicide conveyed in poetry, images of death consistently displayed in artwork;
- appear sad, depressed, or anxious—sometimes have no affect, cannot tolerate praise;
- be apathetic about their appearance—hair disheveled, clothes soiled or mismatched;
- experience a marked decline in academic performance—appear inattentive, have no concentration, have no regard for assignments, refrain from school and social activities;
- experience changes in sleep patterns—sleep too much or too little;
- give away personal property;

- experience changes in weight or appetite—sudden weight loss or gain, little or voracious appetite;
- lose interest in school and social activities once found pleasurable;
- withdraw from friends—drastic change in personal relationships;
- have sudden personality changes—moody, no sense of humor;
- mutilate self—use of sharp objects to score images onto their body;
- engage in reckless, risk-taking behaviors—driving at high speeds, playing with guns.

Academic Interruptions

Schools can be frightening and oppressive places for some gay and lesbian youth, and this can interrupt their academic courses. Some youth have reported that being at school or en route is so dangerous for them that avoiding school altogether is the only option they have for their safety. Other gay and lesbian youth have mentioned that their school environment made them so uncomfortable that they did not want to establish friendships and would decline to partake in extracurricular and social activities. But why should these youth be expected to enjoy school, learn, and stay in schools where they have a hard time making friends or fear for their lives? Rarely do schools contribute positively to gay and lesbian youth's sexual-identity development, and a lack of safety, acceptance, and tolerance is sure to prevent some of them from earning a quality education.

Schools can distress many gay and lesbian youth to the point of academic failure. One study found that as many as 80% of a sample had experienced declined school performance (Elia, 1993). Various factors account for such circumstances, and combined these prove challenging for gay and lesbian youth's ability to attend to school and homework. These youth are often consumed with fear or are preoccupied with concerns that they will be condemned, ridiculed, or harassed if others find out about their sexuality. One Wisconsin study compared the safety and well-being of youth who had experienced antigay harassment with those who had not. Only half of the harassed sample agreed with the statement, "At school I try hard to do my best work." Nearly 78% of their nonharassed counterparts answered in the affirmative. Moreover, about a third of the harassed youth agreed with the statement, "My teachers really care about me and give me a lot of encouragement," compared to 53.2% of the nonharassed youth. Indeed, gay and lesbian youth often lack enthusiasm about school and often report that their school environment is troubling (Russell, Serif, & Dricoll, 2001).

In addition, heterosexual adolescents have peers to consult with when they cross adolescent milestones (first crush, first dates, first kiss, and so forth), but gay and lesbian youth have no one and are likely to be mentally overwhelmed as they orchestrate sexual-orientation milestones in isolation. No one would disagree that adolescence is a turbulent period in human development. All youth want to fit in. All youth want to be liked, and they expect conformity from one another. They typically worry about being overweight, too short, too tall, too thin, or having to wear glasses or braces, and the added burden of being gay or lesbian is destined to make academics a low priority.

Having few friends, having no one to consult with, fearing harassment, and performing poorly in academics are precursors for truancy, thus making gay and lesbian youth likely to skip classes and school (Taylor, 2000; Tharinger & Wells, 2000; Stevens & Morgan, 1999). The Gay, Lesbian and Straight Education Network (2002) study found that 31.9% of gay, lesbian, bisexual, and transgender youth skipped a class at least once in the previous month and that 30.8% had skipped at least one full day because they felt unsafe at school. Another study found that 40% had problems with truancy (Elia, 1993), and one study of 4,159 high school students found that gay, lesbian, and bisexual youth are five times more likely than their heterosexual counterparts to miss school because they are fearful in their school environments (Garofalo, Wolf, Kessel, Palfrey, & DuRant, 1998). Other studies have obtained similar results suggesting that these youth are up to five times more likely to skip school because of safety issues (Safe Schools Coalition of Washington, 1999).

Gay and lesbian youth are also at risk for dropping out of school. The national average for dropping out of school is 11%, but one gay and lesbian youth sample found that 28% had dropped out because they were uneasy in their high schools (Gibson, 1989, cited in Gill, 1998). Nearly a third of another sample had dropped out of school because of harassment, low self-esteem, or fear that others would discover their sexual orientation (Elia, 1993).

Substance Abuse

The mental anguish caused by feelings of low self-worth, inferiority, isolation, and condemnation lead many gay and lesbian youth to use or abuse substances. Studies have reported that substance abuse is far more frequent and severe among gay and lesbian youth than it is among their heterosexual counterparts. Gay and lesbian youth turn to alcohol, marijuana, and so forth to comfort them and relieve them from their internal conflicts. As early as the late eighties, research suggested that gay and lesbian youth were three times more likely to abuse substances (Gibson, 1989). Among a gay and lesbian sample, Remafedi (1987) found that 58% had regularly abused substances. Another study of gay and bisexual males found that 77% had used alcohol, 42% had used marijuana, 25% had used crack, and 15% had used hallucinogens (Rotheram-Borus et al., 1992). A Columbia University study (1992, cited in Todd, 1999) found that 68% of gay youth reported alcohol use, with 26% using alcohol on a weekly basis, and 44% had used other drugs (8% reported feeling drug dependent). The rates were higher for the lesbian sample, as 83% of them had used alcohol, 56% had used other drugs, and 11% had used crack or cocaine (Todd, 1999). Box 2.2 shows how gay and lesbian youth compare to heterosexual youth in their substance usage.

THE ADDED CHALLENGE OF BEING GAY OR LESBIAN

"Everyone will make fun of me because I have to wear glasses."

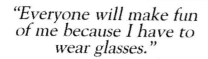

"I just can't gain another pound!"

"Oh no, not another pimple!"

"I wish I had a deeper voice."

"But all of the kids have Air Jordans."

"Just let me get to my next class without 'faggot' this and 'faggot' that."

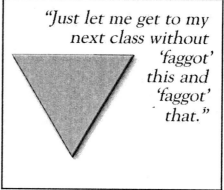

The added challenge of being gay or lesbian.

BOX 2.2. STUDIES UNFAILINGLY SUGGEST THAT GAY AND LESBIAN YOUTH ARE MORE LIKELY TO ENGAGE IN SUBSTANCE ABUSE		
The 1995 Seattle Teen Health Risk Survey	Heterosexual sample %	Gay, lesbian, and bisexual sample %
Engaged in high–risk or heavy drug use (including alcohol, marijuana, inhalants, depressants, and so forth)	21.7	33.2
The 1997 Vermont Youth Risk Behavior Survey	Youth with opposite-gender experience %	Youth with same-gender experience %
Smoked cigarettes in past 30 days	55	64
Drank alcohol every day for past 30 days	2	16
Had at least one drink on school property every day for past month	1	11
Smoked marijuana 40 or more times in past 30 days	10	22
Smoked marijuana on school property 40 or more times in past 30 days	1	12
Used cocaine in past 30 days	7	29
Injected illegal drugs two or more times (ever)	3	19
The 1997 Massachusetts Youth Risk Behavior Survey	Other respondents %	Gay, lesbian, bisexual, or have had same-gender experiences %
Had ever used hallucinogens	16	46
Had ever used marijuana	50	77
Had ever used cocaine	7	33

Source: Adapted from Safe Schools Coalition of Washington. (1999). *Eighty-three thousand youth: Selected findings of eight population-based studies as they pertain to anti-gay harassment and the safety and well-being of sexual minority students.* Seattle: Author.

Runaway/Throwaway Circumstance

Street youth in general leave their homes because of some sort of physical, emotional, or sexual abuse, or they are cast out because of one conflict or another. Gay and lesbian youth are no exception. In fact, a high incidence of runaway or throwaway youth are gay or lesbian. This should come as no surprise because families rarely support the sexual identity of their gay or lesbian members. Many parents are devastated by the news that their child is gay or lesbian, and their moral and religious convictions or shame compel them to reject their children. Other youth, full of despair, flee to urban cities to escape condemning or violent family members and to seek out supportive friends and family substitutes.

These youth are attracted to cities that have large gay and lesbian communities, which they assume will accept them more readily (Kruks, 1991). The actual number of gay and lesbian street youth is unknown (about 1.2 million youth run away from home each year), but studies of street youth in Seattle, Los Angeles, and Philadelphia suggest that as many as 40% are gay or lesbian. One state department of health estimated that as many as 50% of street youth left home because of the sexual identity conflicts with their families (Bailey & Phariss, 1996). Remafedi (1987) found that about a quarter of gay youth were forced out of their homes because their families could not cope with their sexual orientation, and more than half of a New York City gay and lesbian youth sample said they felt safer on the streets than living in group or foster homes (Mallon, 1994, cited in Ryan & Futterman, 1998).

Other Vulnerabilities: Exploitation, Prostitution, HIV/AIDS Infection

Gay and lesbian youth are vulnerable when they are displaced from their homes to the streets of large urban areas. These cities often have unique dangers unlike those of smaller cities or rural communities. Arriving in cities like Los Angeles, San Francisco, Chicago, or New York City with very little or no money forces some youth to do whatever it takes to sustain themselves, including prostitution. Kruks (1991), for instance, found that 77% of the Los Angeles street hustlers identified themselves as gay or bisexual. Some youth even believe that living on the streets or having sex for money was all they were worth. Other youth are manipulated by adults who eventually exploit them. These youth fall prey to adults who promise them warm meals, a cozy home, and a safe future, but they only find constant threats of emotional abuse, physical and sexual assault, and exposure to sexually transmitted diseases.

Drugs, alcohol, and sex are far more available in urban areas, and youth who indulge in these things are likely to acquire sexually transmitted diseases (STDs). Worse yet, youth who are drunk or high on drugs or who simply do not care about their well-being are likely to have unprotected sex, putting them at high risk to acquire HIV, the virus that causes AIDS. There is a higher incidence of HIV/AIDS in urban areas. Macgillivray (2000) found that 20% of the reported AIDS cases in Los Angeles and Miami are among adolescents, that 35% of the cases in Newark are among adolescents, and that 2% of 15 to 17 year olds in San Francisco have HIV. Nearly a third of the young gay and bisexual males in one California study had engaged in unprotected anal intercourse, 12% had used intravenous drugs, and 70% of those infected with HIV did not know they were infected (Grossman, 1997).

STDs and HIV infection among gay and lesbian youth is a serious problem altogether, and they do not have to be displaced from their homes to be at risk. These youth often feel compelled to explore their sexuality so as to affirm or deny that they are gay or lesbian or to deceive others into believing that they are heterosexual. Other youth go looking for the physical affection they lack in their lives. Because some communities are intolerant of open same-sex behavior, the only means for same-gender sexual exploration are ones that are secretive. Often these secretive or clandestine sexual encounters (found mostly among males)—with other youth or adults—occur in parks and bathhouses, and they more often than not involve risky sex with complete strangers (Macgillivray, 2000). These encounters may be the only outlet for same-gender affection, and some youth will develop negative feelings about themselves, believing that the secretive, clandestine, risky sex is all they are good for.

Gay and lesbian youth have been found to engage in sex earlier and more often than their heterosexual counterparts. Saewyc, Bearinger, Heinz, Blum, and Resnick (1998, cited in Stevens & Morgan, 1999), for instance, found that gay, lesbian, and bisexual youth were three times more likely to experience onset of heterosexual intercourse before 13 years of age. In an earlier study, Saewcy, Bearinger, Blum, and Resnick (1995, cited in Stevens & Morgan, 1999) found that, of sexually active girls, the lesbian and bisexual sample had more heterosexual sexual intercourse, more pregnancies, and were more likely to have unprotected sex. All of this experimentation among gay and lesbian youth increases their risk for sexually transmitted diseases and HIV infection.

The percentage of youth who are HIV positive is not fully known, but the Office of National AIDS Policy (1996) has reported that 25% of new HIV cases occur in youth between the ages of 13 and 20. Moreover, about 20% of the latest reported cases of AIDS occur among persons who are 20 to 29 years old. This percentage is disconcerting because the latency period between HIV infection and the onset of AIDS is considerable, which strongly suggests that an adolescent could become HIV infected and not manifest AIDS itself until early adulthood.

What Is Homophobia?

The term *homophobia* was originated in the 1970s by Smith (1971), Weinberg (1972), and Freedman (1975). Weinberg coined the term to describe the "dread of being in close quarters with homosexuals" and a "revulsion toward homosexuals." The term later developed to include "extreme rage and fear reaction to homosexuals" (Freedman, p. 19). Today, the term most commonly refers to the unreasonable hatred, fear, and prejudice against and negative attitudes toward people who are gay, lesbian, bisexual, and transgender; the qualities they embody; or their community. The word *unreasonable* is added to this definition because there is no sound basis for hating, fearing, or discriminating against such persons. In fact,

- you cannot become gay, lesbian, bisexual, or transgender just by talking to or befriending someone who is;
- you cannot get AIDS just by shaking hands with, nodding hello to, smiling at, talking to, or hugging someone who is gay, lesbian, bisexual, or transgender;
- there is no scheme to recruit children into becoming gay or lesbian;
- gay and lesbian persons are not members of an evil or satanic cult (in fact many of them are active members of Christian churches); and
- gay and lesbian persons do *not* molest children.

In short, gay and lesbian persons are no different than you are. They come in all shapes, sizes, and colors. They are found in all ethnicity groups, religious sectors, and social-class constellations. Some are wealthy; others are middle class. Some are white-collar professionals; others are blue-collar. Some are hardworking; others are idle. These persons have experienced happiness and sadness, love and hate, and ambition and apathy, and they desire the same comforts of life and freedoms as you do. Most importantly, as with all groups, one person does not define the whole group. As the saying goes, there are good and bad qualities in all people. The same holds true for gay and lesbian persons.

Historically, society has not been very kind to gay and lesbian persons. In the last century, numerous stories recount how gays and lesbians have been persecuted. They have been killed, beaten, tormented, tortured, harassed, imprisoned, raped, and ostracized. Many people find it hard to believe that homophobia is commonplace in contemporary society. Some homophobic incidents receive national attention: the kidnapping, torture, and killing of Matthew Shepard; the injuries sustained by Caitlin Meuse for participating in Day of Silence; and the killing of Fred Martinez Jr., a transgender youth in New Mexico. Most incidences of homophobia, however, do not draw such widespread attention.

Homophobia is exemplified in a variety ways on a sort of continuum molded by the dominant culture through the heterosexist paradigm discussed in chapter 1. Essentially, the dominant culture holds that homosexuality is wrong, that it is contrary to the normal way of living, and that gay and lesbian persons are not worthy of validation. Consequently, some places of worship, schools, or workplaces are intolerant of gay and lesbian persons; some families do not accept homosexuality; and some friends or loved ones reject persons because of their sexual orientation. Homophobia is sometimes considered institutionalized because government laws, cultural rules, social expectations, religious beliefs, and other mandates strongly forbid gay and lesbian persons from enjoying some of the benefits inherently available to heterosexuals. Gay and lesbian persons cannot get married, adopt children in every state, serve openly in the armed forces, or become an Eagle Scout. They are not always entitled to their partner's health- or life-insurance benefits, they do not receive tax benefits afforded to married couples, and they can sometimes be fired from their jobs because of their actual or perceived sexual orientation.

On one end of the spectrum are the more subtle and indirect forms of homophobia. These occur whenever a person uses slurs—*faggot, lesbo,* or *butt pirate*; whenever anyone tells or encourages jokes about gays and lesbians; whenever someone perpetuates stereotypes about gay and lesbian persons—"All gay men want to be women" or "Lesbians hate men"; or whenever anyone uses gay or lesbian epithets to denounce someone—"You're nothing but a big fag," "You act so queer," or "Why do you have to be so gay about it?" Homophobia becomes increasingly direct and severe whenever a person publicly proclaims that homo- or bisexuality is disgusting or abnormal or that gays and lesbians deserve to die of AIDS. When the derision turns to verbal harassment toward a person, homophobia is considered violence, which is closely followed by physical assault. As expected, the most heinous of homophobia occurs when someone is murdered simply because of his or her sexual orientation. Box 2.3 illustrates how homophobia is manifested in schools.

BOX 2.3. HOMOPHOBIA MANIFESTS IN SCHOOLS IN A VARIETY OF WAYS

Slurs, Jokes, and Stereotypes
    "Fag"
    "Lesbo"
    "Did you hear the one about . . ."
    "What do you call . . . ?"
Epithets
    "She's nothing but a . . ."
    "What a flamer!"
    "You sure do act queer."
Verbal Harassment and Threats
    Hurtful insults, teasing, and gossip
    Obscene notes or conversations
    "I'm going to get you, you little AIDS faggot."
    "Just wait, you little dyke."
Psychological Assaults
    Intentionally defaming, extorting, humiliating, isolating, manipulating, ostracizing, rejecting, or terrorizing
Physical Assaults
    Beating, kicking, punching, pushing, shoving, or strangling

Some people have an immense hatred toward gay and lesbian persons and thrive on harassing them for no apparent reason other than to mutilate their spirit. Jeffrey Swinford, for instance, is fulfilling a 20-year sentence for killing a gay man. As early as eighth grade, he wrote a report on homosexuality, clearly stating that he did not approve of it and that he believed "nothing good could come out of [homosexuality]." From his prison cell, he mentioned, "I just don't see how [homosexuality] can happen. It just pisses me off. . . . I don't have any opinion whatsoever for homosexuals except that they should all be taken care of."

Whenever you ponder the modern-day homophobe, you are likely to imagine someone like Jeffrey Swinford or an extremely conservative, beer-drinking, pickup-driving, Southern white male. Given that homophobia is constant in society, however, it manifests itself in all kinds of people—doctors, senators, celebrities, teachers, attorneys, students, and so forth. Most individuals would never consider making a negative remark or joke about an ethnic or religious group, and they would not treat someone differently based on the person's racial background. In fact, very few people would call someone a "nigger" or a "spic," but some people see nothing wrong with calling someone a "faggot," a "dyko," a "transy," or the like. Moreover, whenever a student uses a racial or ethnic epithet or a statement that denounces women or people with disabilities, a rebuke and censure are likely to follow. Teachers, however, rarely intervene when students use characteristics about gay and lesbian persons to humiliate one another.

 Critical Thinking

What have been some homophobic comments you have made in the past? Why did you say them, and in what context? What repercussions do you think your comments had?

How Does Homophobia Affect Gay, Lesbian, and Heterosexual Youth?

Homophobia can have a devastating effect on youth. The most apparent effect is the victimization of gay, lesbian, and other sexual-minority youth. Studies on school climates consistently confirm that openly gay and lesbian youth (or those perceived to be) are verbally and physically harassed more often than their heterosexual counterparts. In fact, gay and lesbian youth are more likely than their heterosexual peers to report being threatened with a weapon, skipping school because they feel unsafe, or dropping out because of harassment or threats of harm. FBI crime files suggest that reported hate crimes—violent, intentional attacks on people or their property because of their race, ethnicity, religion, gender, disability, sexual orientation, and so forth—occur nearly 10,700 times per year. Of these attacks, gay and lesbian persons are the most frequent targets, with schools being a primary setting for the violence (Callahan, 2001). Many hate-crime victims are at the hands of males under the age of 20, as statistics reveal that nearly 29% of antigay offenders are under the age of 18 (National Education Association, 2001) and that youth under the age of 17 commit 17% of all antigay hate crimes (Todd, 1999). These statistics leave many professionals to speculate that some adolescents have extreme difficulty accepting persons who do not conform to "normal" social behavior and that these adolescents often assume for themselves the role of social enforcer.

Research on gay and lesbian youth and the discrimination they encounter at school reveals the following:

1. Gay and lesbian youth feel unsafe at school.
   - A sample of 4,159 freshmen through senior youth found that gay, lesbian, and bisexual youth are five times more likely to miss school because they fear for their safety (Garofalo et al., 1998).
   - The Gay, Lesbian and Straight Education Network (2002) study of 904 gay, lesbian, bisexual, or transgender youth revealed that nearly 70% said they felt unsafe in their school because of their sexual orientation, and 45.7% mentioned they felt unsafe because of their gender expression.
   - The Massachusetts Governor's Commission on Gay and Lesbian Youth (1993) study of 4,000 high school students found that gay and lesbian students were five times more likely that their heterosexual peers to skip school because they feared for their safety.
   - In a Wisconsin study, gay and lesbian youth who mentioned that they had experienced antigay harassment were seven times more likely than their peers who had no such experiences to have missed at least one day of school out of fear for their safety (Safe Schools Coalition of Washington, 1999).
2. Antigay slurs are a daily routine in schools.
   - Over 90% of the youth in the GLSEN (2002) study had heard frequently (or often) the expressions "That's so gay" or "You're so gay," which conveyed "dumb" or "stupid"; nearly 85% had heard homophobic remarks including "faggot" or "dyke" just as frequently.
   - Over 97% of students in a Massachusetts high school reported hearing frequent homophobic comments made by peers (Massachusetts Governor's Commission on Gay and Lesbian Youth, 1993).
   - Thirty-six percent of 2,064 students in grades 8 through 12 indicated that they had been called "gay" or "lesbian" often or occasionally; the majority of these students indicated that they would become "very upset" if someone said they were gay or lesbian (American Association of University Women, 2001).
   - Human Rights Watch (2001) cited two studies in which 28% of 11th-grade respondents admitted to making antigay remarks, and in which Des Moines high

schools students reported hearing antigay comments every seven minutes, on average.

3. Gay and lesbian youth are targets of offensive comments.
   - Pilkington and D'Augelli (1995) found that 80% of gay, lesbian, and bisexual youth reported being verbally abused.
   - Thirty-four percent of self-identified gay, lesbian, or bisexual Seattle youth indicated that they had been verbally harassed or attacked because of their perceived sexual orientation (Safe Schools Coalition of Washington, 1999).
   - The majority of the youth in the GLSEN of Colorado (2002) survey indicated that they had experienced some verbal harassment because of their sexual orientation, and 26.2% of them reported that the harassment happened frequently.
   - Gross and Aurand (1992) found that 60% of gay males and 30% of lesbians reported being verbally or physically assaulted at least once between middle school and college because they were gay or were perceived to be.
   - According to the National Education Association (2001), 45% of gay and 20% of lesbian high school students had experienced some form of verbal or physical assault from their peers.
   - A study of gay male youth found that 69% had experienced verbal abuse at school (Remafedi, 1987).

4. Gay and lesbian youth are physically injured or threatened with physical harm.
   - A 1997 Wisconsin Youth Risk Behavior study found that youth who had experienced antigay harassment were four times more likely than their heterosexual counterparts to have been threatened or injured by someone with a weapon at school (Safe Schools Coalition of Washington, 1999).
   - Studies of sexual-minority youth in Seattle and Vermont revealed that gay and lesbian youth were more likely to report having been threatened with or injured by a weapon at school (Safe Schools Coalition of Washington, 1999).
   - About a third of the GLSEN (2002) respondents reported being victims of physical harassment due to their sexual orientation, and 10% reported that the harassment occurred frequently.
   - About 40% of gay and lesbian youth in one study indicated that they experienced violent physical assaults, most of which was perpetrated by their peers (Hunter, 1990, cited in Rhode Island Task Force on Gay, Lesbian, Bisexual and Transgendered Youth, 1996).
   - Pilkington and D'Augelli (1995) found that 44% of gay, lesbian, and bisexual youth had been physically threatened, 29% of girls and 22% of boys had been physically injured, and 10% had been assaulted with a weapon.

These numbers should not overshadow the fact that these are real students, some of whom have endured intense emotional and physical anguish. To better understand their plight, consider what some youth have described they encounter at school:

- "We were picked on. We were called "queer" and "faggot" and a host of other homophobic slurs. We were also used as punching bags by our classmates, just for being different" (Massachusetts Governor's Commission on Gay and Lesbian Youth, 1993).
- "I was harassed a lot. Some people would push me down in the halls. Only one person would talk to me. Nobody sat with me at lunch, but I got over it pretty soon. I became the loner" (Campos, 2002).
- "When I was 15, a sophomore at East Providence High School, I came out to a few of my friends. Eventually it got around the school. One day, on the second-to-last day of school, I went out to the parking lot, and the captain of the football team met me in the hallway and said, "You can't go by me, faggot." I dropped the art project I was carrying, and he beat the crap out of me" (Rhode Island Task Force on Gay, Lesbian, Bisexual and Transgendered Youth, 1996).
- "Beginning in the fifth grade, I had problems. I was transferred to a new school. The kids there called me "fag" and "homo." I looked up what these meant and found that they were right. In sixth grade, they beat me up several times. There were four or five of them together at the same time. I wasn't learning anything" (Remafedi, 1987).
- "I was chased all the way to my house by a mob of people as things were thrown at me and I was kicked and hit" (Campos, 2002).

Homophobic behavior that is not addressed or censured also leads heterosexual youth to believe that gay and lesbian persons are heinous and undeserving of acceptance or tolerance. Essentially, youth who witness or engage in homophobia that goes unchallenged learn that the mistreatment of gay and lesbian persons is permissible and justifiable (Baker, 2002). Moreover, befriending, supporting, or defending a gay or lesbian youth is risky for a nonviolent heterosexual youth, who could potentially be labeled as gay or lesbian and face potential harassment as well. The mistreatment sends the powerful message to gay and lesbian youth that their sexual orientation is a disgrace and a dishonor and that it is devalued—they have deviated from the normal, preferred sexual orientation. A homophobic climate, once

Reflect and Write

How often do you hear homophobic comments in your school? What have been some of the homophobic comments your students have made? What response did you have? How could you have challenged their comments?

again, leaves many of them feeling anxious, fearful, humiliated, stressed, isolated, and depressed. Some gay and lesbian youth will go to great lengths to hide their sexual orientation and will partake in homophobic behavior just to avoid the stigma associated with being gay or lesbian. In short, these youth are left depleted of their social, emotional, and physical well-being, causing them to have very little self-worth.

Could My School Have a Homophobic or Hostile Learning Climate toward Gay and Lesbian Youth?

Your school could have a hostile or homophobic learning climate for gay and lesbian students. The literature strongly suggests that such climates are not totally attributable to the student body; school personnel can also harbor negative attitudes and feelings toward gay and lesbian persons. As many as half of student samples indicate that they have heard staff make homophobic comments, and that rarely do teachers or staff intervene when homophobic comments are made. One Iowa study reported that teachers who heard antigay slurs failed to respond to them 97% of the time (Carter, 1997). In fact, teachers and staff were less likely to challenge students when homophobic remarks were made than when sexist or racist comments were made (Gay, Lesbian and Straight Education Network of Colorado, 2002).

Evidence also suggests that school personnel can have strong homophobic attitudes. For instance, eight out of ten preservice teachers reported having negative attitudes toward gay and lesbian persons, and nearly a third of these were classified as "high grade homophobes" (Sears, 1992). This figure may very well account for students' reports that when teachers discuss homosexuality, it is usually in the pejorative, and it is usually handled negatively (Telljohann & Price, 1993). Such discussions are rare in schools, but it would seem that the most appropriate class in which to discuss diverse sexual orientation would be health education. In one national study, however, it was found that only 46% of secondary school health teachers teach about this topic, and of those who do, 87% devote only one or two class periods to the topic (Telljohann, Price, Poureslami, & Easton, 1995). Less than half of this sample reported that their administrators would support a club for gay and lesbian youth.

Understandably, when teachers and administrators fail to reach out to gay and lesbian youth, school counselors would seem to be a likely source of support. A national study of school counselors, however, found that only 27% felt it was in their responsibility to counsel students who were gay and lesbian, and only 25% felt "very competent" to counsel gay and lesbian students (Price & Telljohann, 1991). In short, it seems that teachers and staff are uncomfortable dealing with gay and lesbian matters.

The survey in box 2.4 is designed to help you determine whether your school has a homophobic or hostile climate and to whom it can be attributed—teachers and staff, students, or both. While the survey is not scientifically valid, and though a host of factors that contribute to a hostile environment have certainly been omitted, the primary goal is for you to contemplate some of your school's areas of weakness or strength in supporting and safeguarding gay and lesbian youth. Ultimately, you and your colleagues should work toward improving the areas that need the most attention. As a secondary goal, you should begin to ponder your own attitudes and beliefs toward gay and lesbian youth; how these contribute to the school climate; and how these can be adjusted so that all students, regardless of their sexual orientation, feel included in your classroom.

BOX 2.4. SCHOOL CLIMATE TOWARD DIVERSE SEXUAL ORIENTATIONS

This survey is designed to measure your school climate toward gay, lesbian, bisexual, or transgender youth. There are no right or wrong answers. Rate each statement as carefully and as accurately as you can by writing the appropriate number beside each statement.

1 = Strongly agree
2 = Agree
3 = Neither agree nor disagree
4 = Disagree
5 = Strongly disagree

To the best of my knowledge, I find that . . .

	TEACHERS and STAFF at my school believe:					STUDENTS at my school believe:				
1. Sexual orientation should be included in diversity tolerance or multicultural curricula and taught to the student body.	1	2	3	4	5	1	2	3	4	5
2. The gay and lesbian community should be included in multicultural fairs.	1	2	3	4	5	1	2	3	4	5
3. Students are reprimanded whenever they use words such as *faggot, dyke,* and *queer* in the school hallways, classrooms, locker rooms, and so forth.	1	2	3	4	5	1	2	3	4	5
4. Students should know where to go for resources on gay, lesbian, bisexual, and transgender issues.	1	2	3	4	5	1	2	3	4	5
5. Their peers refrain from using words such as *faggot, dyke,* and *queer* in school.	1	2	3	4	5	1	2	3	4	5

(Continued)

BOX 2.4. SCHOOL CLIMATE TOWARD DIVERSE SEXUAL ORIENTATIONS (Continued)

6. Sexual orientation should be discussed in health or sex education classes.	1	2	3	4	5	1	2	3	4	5
7. Teachers and staff should make a concerted effort to challenge all sexual-orientation slurs.	1	2	3	4	5	1	2	3	4	5
8. Famous gay and lesbian persons and their contributions to society should be included in social science courses/topics.	1	2	3	4	5	1	2	3	4	5
9. Literature on or by gay and lesbian persons or inclusive of such characters should be included in English classes.	1	2	3	4	5	1	2	3	4	5
10. A "safe person" should be designated at school who counsels students with sexual-identity issues, if any should arise.	1	2	3	4	5	1	2	3	4	5
11. A Gay–Straight Alliance or similar club should be (is) supported by faculty and staff.	1	2	3	4	5	1	2	3	4	5
12. A Gay–Straight Alliance or similar club should be (is) supported by the student body.	1	2	3	4	5	1	2	3	4	5
13. Gay Pride Month should be acknowledged and discussed with the student body.	1	2	3	4	5	1	2	3	4	5
14. Teachers should receive in-service training on how to support gay and lesbian youth.	1	2	3	4	5	1	2	3	4	5
15. The school policy should include the protection of gay and lesbian students from harassment.	1	2	3	4	5	1	2	3	4	5
16. Teachers and staff should consider families headed by same-gender parents whenever there is school-and-home communication.	1	2	3	4	5	1	2	3	4	5
17. Teachers are comfortable teaching gay and lesbian students.	1	2	3	4	5	1	2	3	4	5
18. Students are comfortable going to school with openly gay and lesbian students.	1	2	3	4	5	1	2	3	4	5

(Continued)

BOX 2.4. SCHOOL CLIMATE TOWARD DIVERSE SEXUAL ORIENTATIONS (Continued)

19. Teachers and staff should attend social gatherings sponsored by the Gay–Straight Alliance.	1	2	3	4	5	1	2	3	4	5
20. Students should attend social gatherings sponsored by the Gay–Straight Alliance.	1	2	3	4	5	1	2	3	4	5
21. Their peers should feel comfortable talking with members of the school community about diverse sexual orientations.	1	2	3	4	5	1	2	3	4	5
22. Their peers should feel comfortable if a faculty or staff member was gay or lesbian.	1	2	3	4	5	1	2	3	4	5
23. Their peers should be happy to learn that a varsity football player was gay.	1	2	3	4	5	1	2	3	4	5
24. Their peers should be happy to learn that the head cheerleader was a lesbian.	1	2	3	4	5	1	2	3	4	5
25. Their peers should feel comfortable knowing that same-gender student couples were holding hands or showing affection in the hallways.	1	2	3	4	5	1	2	3	4	5
26. Same-gender couples should be able to attend the prom.	1	2	3	4	5	1	2	3	4	5

Teachers and staff total score: _____   Students total score: _____

1. Accepting and supportive climate   26–52
2. Moderately hostile climate   52–78
3. Hostile climate   78–104
4. Severely hostile climate   104–130

Climate attributed to teachers and staff is:
____ Accepting and supportive
____ Moderately hostile
____ Hostile
____ Severely hostile

Climate attributed to students is:
____ Accepting and supportive
____ Moderately hostile
____ Hostile
____ Severely hostile

Summary

Gay and lesbian youth have complicated lives filled with challenges and hardships that occur largely in their schools. The fundamental norm for all youth is to grow up hetero-sexual. Youth who do not conform to this standard are sure to encounter the dominant group's system of social enforce-ment—rejection, avoidance, alienation, harassment, and so forth. The odds are certainly stacked against most gay and lesbian youth, as they are likely to be victims of verbal and physical mistreatment. In fact, one in six gay students is beaten so badly that he or she requires medical attention (Bart, 1998).

Homophobia, manifested in an array of forms, from subtle to direct, is commonplace in our schools. A New York study of high school juniors and seniors, for instance, found higher levels of hostility toward gays than toward racial or ethnic minorities (Fontaine, 1998). Research findings such as these should come as no surprise considering that homo-phobia is embedded and enforced in our social rules and government mandates. Homophobia has devastating effects on heterosexual and sexual-minority youth alike. Heterosexual youth learn that gay and lesbian persons should be mistreated, and because of this, sexual-minority youth are sure to experience an array of untoward and unhealthy emotions that leave many of them at risk for academic, social, emotional, and physical prob-lems. Homophobia will not miraculously disappear. Some effort on your part is needed to transform a hostile learning environment into an inclusive, tolerant one. In the next chap-ter, you will learn how gay and lesbian youth are a heterogeneous population and yet have some common developmental patterns, and you will learn how to comport yourself if such a youth should seek your help and support.

> **Reflect and Write**
>
> What leads you to believe that gay and lesbian students in your school are safeguarded from harassment?

Idea File

1. Create and display a poster that shows students where a "safe place" is to talk about sexual-orientation issues. The poster could include catchy phrases like, "You're gay and that's OK" or "It's not the end of the world if you're gay or lesbian." The poster should include the names of faculty members who are "safe" people to talk to and who convey a level of trust.
2. Have teachers (or students) brainstorm as many examples of heterosexism as they can.
3. Have a counselor come talk to your students to ensure that they know where they can go to talk to someone about sexual-orientation issues. Make a list of local and elec-tronic resources for gay and lesbian youth, and distribute it after the discussion.

4. Adapt the *School Climate toward Diverse Sexual Orientation* survey so that students can rate each item according to their own beliefs. Have the students complete the survey and tally up their responses. Review each item and have students debate why gay and lesbian youth need certain safeguards.

References

American Association of University Women. (2001). *Hostile hallways: Bullying, teasing, and sexual harassment in school.* Washington, DC: American Association of University Women.

Bailey, N. J., & Phariss, T. (1996). Breaking through the wall of silence: Gay, lesbian, and bisexual issues for middle level educators. *Middle School Journal, 27*, 1–14. Retrieved September 19, 2002, from http://www.glsenco.org/Educators/Teachers/NMSA%20article.html.

Baker, J. M. (2002). *How homophobia hurts children: Nurturing diversity at home, at school, and in the community.* New York: Harrington Park Press.

Bart, M. (1998). Creating a safer school for gay students. *Counseling Today, 26*, 36–39.

Callahan, C. J. (2001). Protecting and counseling gay and lesbian students. *Journal of Humanistic Counseling, Education and Development, 40*(1), 5–10.

Campos, D. (2002). Personal interviews with openly gay and lesbian youth, Walt Whitman Community School, Dallas, TX, May 9–10.

Carter, K. (1997, March 7). Gay slurs abound. *Des Moines Register*, p. B1.

Centers for Disease Control, Center for Environment Health. (1986). *Youth suicide surveillance report.* Atlanta: Department of Health and Human Services.

Cook, A. T., & Palwoski, W. (1991). *Youth and homosexuality: Issue paper 3.* Washington, DC: Federation of Parents and Friends of Lesbian and Gays.

Elia, J. (1993). Homophobia in the high school: A problem in need of a resolution. *The High School Journal, 77*(1/2), 177–85.

Fontaine, J. H. (1998). Evidencing a need: School counselors' experiences with gay and lesbian students. *Professional School Counseling, 1*, 8–14.

Freedman, M. (1975). Homophobia: The psychology of a social disease. *Body Politic, 24*, 19.

Garofalo, R., Wolf, R. C., Kessel, S., Palfrey, J., & DuRant, R. (1998). The association between health risk behaviors and sexual orientation among a school-based sample of adolescents. *Pediatrics, 101*, 895–902.

Gay, Lesbian and Straight Education Network. (2002). *The 2001 national school climate survey: The school related experiences of our nations lesbian, gay, bisexual, and transgender youth.* New York: Gay, Lesbian and Straight Education Network.

Gay, Lesbian and Straight Education Network of Colorado. (2002). *Just the facts: A summary of important statistics about gay and lesbian youth.* Retrieved September 19, 2002, from http://www.glsenco.org/Educators/Administrators/just_the_facts.htm.

Gibson, P. (1989). *Alcohol, drug abuse, and mental health administration: Report of the Secretary's Task Force on Youth Suicide* (DHHS Publication No. ADM 89-1623). Washington, DC: U.S. Department of Health and Human Services.

Gill, K. (1998). Maintaining the dignity and rights of gay and lesbian students. *Reclaiming Children and Youth, 7*(1), 25–27.

Gross, L, & Aurand, S. (1992). *Discrimination and violence against lesbian women and gay men in Philadelphia and the Commonwealth of Pennsylvania.* Philadelphia: Philadelphia Lesbian and Gay Task Force.

Grossman, A. (1997). Growing up with a "spoiled identity": Lesbian, gay, and bisexual youth at risk. *Journal of Gay and Lesbian Social Services, 6*(3), 45–56.

Human Rights Watch. (2001). *Hatred in the hallways: Violence and discrimination against lesbian, gay, bisexual, and transgender students in U.S. schools.* New York: Author.

Hunter, J. (1990). Violence against lesbian and gay male youths. *Journal of Interpersonal Violence, 5*(3), 295–300.

Kruks, G. (1991). Gay and lesbian homeless/street youth: Special issues and concerns. *Journal of Adolescent Health, 12*, 515–18.

Macgillivray, I. K. (2000). Educational equity for gay, lesbian, bisexual, transgendered, and queer/questioning students: The demands of democracy and social justice for America's schools. *Education and Urban Society, 32*, 303–23.

Maguen, S. (1992). Teen suicide: The government's cover-up and America's lost children. *The Advocate, 597*, 40–47.

Mallet, E. (1997, April 6). Suicide of gay youth. *Cleveland Plain Dealer,* p. 1.

Mallon, G. (1994). Counseling strategies with gay and lesbian youth. In T. DeCrescenzo (Ed.), *Helping gay and lesbian youth: New policies, new programs, new practices* (pp. 75–91). New York: Haworth Press.

Marino, T. W. (1995). To be young and gay in America. *Counseling Today, 37*, 1–8.

Massachusetts Governor's Commission on Gay and Lesbian Youth. (1993). *Making schools safe for gay and lesbian youth: Breaking the silence in schools and in families: Education report.* Boston: Massachusetts Governor's Commission on Gay and Lesbian Youth.

McFarland, W. P. (1993). A developmental approach to gay and lesbian youth. *Journal of Humanistic Education and Development, 32*, 17–29.

Morrow, S. L. (1997). Career development of lesbian and gay youth: Effects of sexual orientation, coming out, and homophobia. *Journal of Gay & Lesbian Social Services, 14*, 1–5.

National Education Association. (2001). *Understanding gay and lesbian students through diversity.* Washington, DC: Author.

Office of National AIDS Policy. (1996). *Youth & AIDS: An American agenda.* Washington, DC: Author.

Pilkington, N. W., & D'Augelli, A. R. (1995). Victimization of lesbian, gay, and bisexual youth in community settings. *Journal of Community Psychology, 23*(1), 33–56.

Price, J. H., & Telljohann, S. K. (1991). School counselors' perceptions of adolescent homosexuality. *Journal of School Health, 61*(10), 433–38.

Proctor, C. D., & Groze, V. K. (1994). Risk factors for suicide among gay, lesbian, and bisexual youths. *Social Work, 39*, 504–13.

Remafedi, G. (1987). Homosexual youth: A challenge to contemporary society. *Journal of the American Medical Association, 258*, 222–25.

Remafedi, G., Farrow, J. A., & Deisher, R. W. (1991). Risk factors for attempted suicide in gay and bisexual youth. *Pediatrics, 87*, 869–75.

Rhode Island Task Force on Gay, Lesbian, Bisexual and Transgendered Youth. (1996, March). *Schools shouldn't hurt: Lifting the burden from gay, lesbian, bisexual and transgendered youth.* Rhode Island: Author. Retrieved July 20, 2001, from http://members.tripod.com/~twood/safeschools.html.

Rotheram-Borus, M., Rosario, M., Meyer-Bahlburg, H., Koopman, C., Dopkins, S., & Davies, M. (1992). *Sexual and substance use behavior among homosexual and bisexual male adolescents in New York City.* New York: HIV Center for Clinical and Behavioral Studies, New York State Psychiatric Institute.

Russell, S., Serif, T, & Dricoll, A. (2001). School outcomes of sexual minority youth in the United States: Evidence from a national study. *Journal of Adolescence, 24*, 111–27.

Ryan, C., & Futterman, D. (1998). *Lesbian and gay youth: Care and counseling.* New York: Columbia University Press.

Saewyc, E. M., Bearinger, L. H., Blum, R. W., & Resnick, M. D. (1995). Heterosexual behaviors and pregnancy among nonheterosexual adolescent girls. *Journal of Adolescent Health, 16*, 161.

Saewyc, E. M., Bearinger, L. H., Heinz, P. A., Blum, R. W., & Resnick, M. D. (1998). Gender differences in health and risk behavior among bisexual and homosexual adolescents. *Journal of Adolescent Health, 23*, 238–47.

Safe Schools Coalition of Washington. (1999). *Eighty-three thousand youth: Selected findings of eight population-based studies.* Seattle: Author.

Sears. J. T. (1992). Educators, homosexuality, and homosexual students: Are personal feelings related to professional beliefs? In K. M. Harbeck (Ed.), *Coming out of the classroom closet: Gay and lesbian students, teachers, and curricula* (pp. 29–79). New York: Harrington Park Press.

Smith, K. T. (1971). Homophobia: A tentative personality profile. *Psychological Reports, 29*, 1091–94.

Stevens, P. E., & Morgan, S. (1999). Health of lesbian, gay, bisexual, and transgender youth. *Journal of Child and Family Nursing, 2*, 237–49.

Taylor, H. E. (2000). Meeting the needs of lesbian and gay young adolescents. *Clearing House, 73*, 221–25.

Telljohann, S. K., & Price, J. H. (1993). A qualitative examination of adolescent homosexuals' life experiences: Ramifications for secondary school personnel. *Journal of Homosexuality, 26*(1), 41–56.

Telljohann, S. K., Price, J. H., Poureslami, M., & Easton, A. (1995). Teaching about sexual orientation by secondary health teachers. *Journal of School Health, 65*(1), 18–22.

Tharinger, D., & Wells, G. (2000). An attachment perspective on the developmental challenges of gay and lesbian adolescents: The need for continuity of caregiving from family and schools. *School Psychology Review, 29*, 158–72.

Todd, C. (1999). *How school administrators can provide the leadership necessary to creating schools where all people are valued, regardless of sexual orientation.* Retrieved July 18, 2002, from http://www.glsen.org/templates/resources/record.html?section=14&record=384.

Vare, J. W., & Norton, T. L. (1998). Understanding gay and lesbian youth: Sticks, stones, and silence. *Clearing House, 71*, 327–28.

Weinberg, G. (1972). *Society and the healthy homosexual.* New York: St. Martin's Press.

Developmental Milestones You Should Know

"WHAT YOU FEEL LIKE IS LIKE YOU'RE THE ONLY ONE IN THE WORLD"

Dr. Charles R. Middleton is the first openly gay president of a major university—Roosevelt University (Chicago). The 60-year-old British history scholar grew up in the 1950s in conservative Miami where there was a conspicuous agenda to rid the city of undesirables, including gay and lesbian persons. This social attitude, compounded by the fact that his father was homophobic and often made critical remarks about the gay and lesbian population, made lasting impressions on Middleton—and they were not favorable. "I knew about gay people, but everything I knew about them was all negative. If you were gay, you kept it hidden and didn't do anything about it." Despite the fact that the adolescent Middleton had crushes on other boys, he had no working knowledge of what being gay was. "I had my eye out for some handsome men, but I didn't do anything about it. I was scared to death. And I didn't know anyone who was gay."

Middleton spent years denying his sexual orientation, which caused him to experience feelings of isolation. He recalls,

> You know how high school guys are; they're out watching high school girls. The guys are talking about how this one is attractive and that one is. I used to think, "Alright, well, okay, uh, what am I missing here?" I used to think, "Well, I know them . . ." and "Well, she's nice and I like her. I don't get it. . . . They're obviously dealing with something that I'm not privy too." I now know that that's desire because I would see guys I knew and think, "Well, he's nice looking. He's more than nice." That's lonely because what you feel like is that you're the only one in the world, and you really are alone because you've made yourself the only gay person in the world. And it's scary, and there's a lot of risk at stake, and you don't have any role models. I don't think it's any easier to come out today than it ever was. I'm not one of those people who think that today's kids are really fortunate. I don't think that it's ever easy for you to come to a level of self-awareness that allows you to be comfortable with yourself.

To dodge the repercussions of having same-gender attractions, Middleton immersed himself in academics.

> In everything I did I was an overachiever. I didn't want to have these "gay" feelings, so I denied them and I suppressed them. I did everything I could to keep busy. So I became an overachiever. In essence it actually helped. I probably got more done than I would have gotten done relying upon native abilities because I was always out there: "I'm okay. I'm fine. Look at all these things that I can do." But there was a lot of loneliness.

(Continued)

"WHAT YOU FEEL LIKE IS LIKE YOU'RE THE ONLY ONE IN THE WORLD" (Continued)

Middleton underscores that accepting one's own same-gender orientation is never easy. He analogizes,

> To want to be able to run very fast and to do everything you could to run very fast, practicing, but basically your body doesn't run fast. It just doesn't. You can make it a little faster than if you didn't practice, but you are never going to run fast. That's a disappointment. . . . It's like, "Who am I? Because once I become okay with who I am, then I can get on with doing things that take advantage of who I am," be that "I am a musician" or "I'm not a musician"; "I'm not an athlete" or "I am an athlete"; "I am not particularly adept at certain academic things" or "I am adept at certain academic things"; "I'm gay" or "I'm straight." All of those things are self-awareness issues. And self-awareness is not a natural state of being. People have to come to it. And they come to it in their own time, and through their own route, and it is never easy.

Overview

Dr. Middleton grew up in a conservative era where he never had opportunities to explore his sexuality. As an adolescent and young adult, Middleton had same-gender attractions, yet he learned to avoid all affairs associated with his sexual orientation. For a number of years, Middleton suppressed his homosexual feelings, and he eventually got married and had three children. His marriage ended in divorce when he later developed a self-awareness regarding his sexuality and became comfortable with who he was. He recalls, "In the late 1970s, I began to realize that I was okay. I started rejecting stereotypes and saying, 'This is who I am.' That's when I began to say and feel that." He and his partner have been together for over 20 years.

Middleton's history is quite common among gay and lesbian persons of his generation. Essentially they would not and did not explore their sexual orientation until later in their adult lives. You may be inclined to believe that one's sexual orientation should only be explored as an adult (as Middleton did), when the person is wiser and can handle a same-gender relationship in a discrete manner. Undoubtedly, thousands of youth in the United States will follow a similar path, and it will take them years to come to an ultimate acceptance of their sexual orientation. Some will never reach that level of comfort and will live in denial for the rest of their lives.

The drastic divide between Middleton's generation and the youth of today is 40 years, and today's gay and lesbian youth know about openly gay and lesbian celebrities (e.g., Rosie O'Donnell, Billy Bean); watch gay and lesbian characters on sitcoms (e.g., *Will & Grace*, *It's All Relative*), premium-channel dramas (*Queer as Folk*, *Six Feet Under*), and reality TV shows (*Queer Eye for the Straight Guy*, *Boy Meets Boy*, *The Real World*); know the gay and lesbian issues readily debated in the media (e.g., the July 7, 2003, Supreme Court decision affirming privacy for gay and lesbian persons); and are beginning to have Gay–Straight Alliances in their schools. Society can safely assume that the voices of today's gay and lesbian youth are stronger than in previous generations and will become stronger in the future. This is not to say that a strong voice is immune to emotional setbacks. The strongest of gay youth will work hard to overcome the inherent challenges associated with being gay or lesbian. This chapter discusses some of the developmental milestones commonly traversed by gay and lesbian persons. In particular, this chapter seeks to answer the following questions:

- How does the development of gay and lesbian youth differ from that of heterosexual youth?
- What is the Kinsey Scale and what should I infer from it?
- What do I do if a student tells me he or she is gay or lesbian?

Reflect and Write

Reflecting on your adolescence, what were some common milestones that you and your peers experienced? How do these differ from the milestones of contemporary youth? How might gay and lesbian youth have additional challenging or complex milestones?

How Does the Development of Gay and Lesbian Youth Differ from That of Heterosexual Youth?

Gay and lesbian youth navigate through the same developmental stages expected of their heterosexual counterparts, including the formation of a sexual identity. These youth experience the same range of emotions traditionally ascribed to the adolescent—they are thinking about careers and life after high school, they seek their independence from parents, they desire relationships and seek intimacy (as appropriate for the age group), and so forth. For gay, lesbian, and heterosexual youth alike, developing physically, psychologically, morally, and socially in today's era is no small feat.

For youth with same-gender attractions, their psychosocial development is compounded by the fact that they have a whole range of complex developmental tasks to resolve in their lifetime—tasks that persons can begin to undertake any time in childhood, adolescence, or adulthood. Contrary to popular belief, a person does not wake up on a given day and decide that he or she is gay. Persons no more choose to be gay, lesbian, bisexual, or transgender than they choose to be heterosexual. Instead, persons with same-gender attractions gradually form their sexual identity at their own unique pace.

Seminal research on the identity development of gay and lesbian persons has been reported by Eli Coleman (1982), Vivienne C. Cass (1984), Richard Troiden (1989), Arthur

Lipkin (1999), and many others. Rather than digress and discuss each of their contributions, which can be found in *Lesbian, Gay, and Bisexual Identities and Youth* by D'Augelli and Patterson (2001), a sketch of the developmental milestones that emerged from the adult sampling in their work will be described instead. Think of these milestones, sometimes referred to as pivotal moments, as steps taken by most gay and lesbian persons in their lifetime. (A continuum of these is found in box 3.1.)

BOX 3.1. CONTINUUM OF PIVOTAL MOMENTS COMMONLY TRAVERSED BY GAY AND LESBIAN PERSONS

Continuum of pivotal moments	Some messages likely to resonate in a person's mind
Awareness of stigma	"It's bad and wrong to be 'gay or lesbian.'" "Persons will make fun of you if they think that you are 'gay or lesbian.'" "You can get beat up for being 'gay or lesbian.'" "You will go to hell for being 'gay or lesbian.'" "I have to conform. I have to follow gender-appropriate rules."
Realization that "I am different"	"I'm not like the others." "I'm not particularly fond of playing with toys or games that children of my gender play with." "There's something different about me."
Sexualization of the sense of difference	"I'm attracted to persons of my gender." "I have crushes on persons of my gender."
Denial and resistance	"I'm not like the gay and lesbian people/characters I've seen." "I'm not gay, and I can prove it." "I'll focus all of my energy and invest all of my time in so many other things."
Realization of sexual orientation	"Even though I'm not like those other gay and lesbian persons, I know that I have same-gender attractions."
Acceptance of sexual identity	"I'm gay." "Maybe I can meet others who are gay or lesbian." "I think I'll 'come out' to my best friend."
Exploration of GLBT community	"I'll try to find places where other gay and lesbian persons hang out—clubs, Internet sites, church groups, and so on." "I'll start dating."
Opening up and recognizing that sexuality is one part of the whole person	"Being gay is part of who I am." "I am comfortable being openly gay in all settings, and I do not let the opinions of others affect how I regard myself."

Keep in mind that gay and lesbian persons, despite their commonalities, are a heterogeneous group of persons. Consequently, each person contends with a pivotal moment in a unique way, and the steps taken toward the next is at a pace contingent upon a variety of factors (e.g., support from family, level of comfort with peers) central to each person. Some persons may find some moments more difficult than others do, some skip a step, some proceed through the continuum in matter of years, others may never find comfort in their sexual orientation, and some may reach a step and regress after a horrifying experience.

Many of these moments are challenging for even the strongest of persons. And, even though your gay and lesbian students may never inform you about these steps, knowing about them and how others before have struggled with them will help you better understand the youth should they ever come to you for advice, feedback, or support. The following moments are described as though youth were traversing through the steps into young adulthood.

Awareness of Stigma

At this step, youth have assumed that they are heterosexual and do not see homo- or bisexuality as personally relevant (McFarland, 1993). Sometime before puberty, they learn that there is a stigma associated with being gay or lesbian. Even though they may not fully understand what *gay* or other epithets mean, they quickly discover that to be referred to as "gay," "fag," "dyke," or "queer" is not good. They also learn that to be gay or lesbian is a sign of deviance and that such persons are likely to be punished. At schools and on playgrounds, it is common to witness that youth who do not conform to gender roles are laughed at, insulted, mocked, or attacked and called "gay" or "lesbian." Early on, youth hear the jokes, rumors, and myths about gay and lesbian persons, and any word even remotely associated with gay or lesbian is the best weapon in a battle of words. Essentially, what is discovered is that gay and lesbian persons and what they embody have no merit.

Realization That "I Am Different"

The youth at this step still hold themselves as heterosexual, but they perceive themselves as different from their same-gender peers. They have not entertained thoughts of being gay or lesbian because they do not fully understand what these concepts mean. In fact, any same-gender feelings and behavior the youth have at this step are likely to be gender focused rather than sexually based. Many gay and lesbian persons recall feeling "different" about themselves as early as four or five years of age (Rhode Island Task Force on Gay, Lesbian, Bisexual and Transgendered Youth, 1996). These persons often explain that they felt different from peers of their gender because they could not successfully fulfill the expectations typically assigned to their gender or because they did not enjoy the play, the games, and the behavior traditionally found in the activities of their gender. Consequently, some boys may feel different from the other boys because they are uninterested in sports or find comfort in being alone rather than playing with a team. For some girls, they may enjoy playing football rather than playing with dolls.

One gay adolescent reflected on why he felt different: "I really tried to force myself to do boy things. But my father never wanted to do anything with me, and no one ever taught me football or baseball or those kinds of things. And the boys just wanted to wrestle or roll around in the grass. I didn't like that. I don't want to be all sweaty, and I hate the way grass feels. I've never played football. I don't even know how to throw the ball. . . . And other boys would go to the ponds to catch frogs, and I would scream when they would show me" (Campos, 2003, p. 150). Keep in mind that feeling different is not a precursor to the development of a homo- or bisexual identity. Feeling different from same-gender peers or showing little or no interest in gender-appropriate play does not imply a likelihood of becoming gay or lesbian.

Sexualization of the Sense of Difference

At this next step, youth become consciously aware that they are sexually attracted to and aroused by members of their own gender. This self-awareness can occur as young as early childhood (Vare & Norton, 1998), but it often occurs during young adolescence (American Academy of Pediatrics, 2002; Herdt & Boxer, 1996; Savin-Williams, 1990; Remafedi, 1987). The research on the age at which most youth become aware of this same-gender attraction varies from 9 (Human Rights Watch, 2002) to 13 (McFarland, 1993; Sears, 1991) to 14 (Anderson, 1995) for boys, and from 10 (Human Rights Watch, 2002) to 14 to 26 (Vare & Norton, 1998) for girls. One study of 14- to 21-year-old gay and lesbian adolescents found that boys and girls had homosexual fantasies at an average age of 11.5 years old (Boxer, Cook, & Herdt, 1989).

At this step, youth can attribute feeling different to their having same-gender attractions, which directly contradicts social rules. They go through a lot of confusion at this step as they try to resolve (a) the fact that society simultaneously holds a negative value toward homosexual behavior and expects them to be heterosexual with (b) the genuine feelings that are difficult to subdue. Moreover, the very institution where they can derive support lacks accurate information about gay and lesbian persons, immediate role models, and opportunities for discussion regarding diverse sexual orientations. It is not surprising, then, that these youth commonly keep this awareness most secretive—even from the closest of friends—for fear of reprisals. Even though they may hide their attractions and never express their feelings, some youth will engage in same-gender sexual experimentation.

Denial and Resistance

In this step, youth engage in avoidance behaviors and resist answering the question, "Can I be homo- or bisexual?" They realize that it is easier to avoid the same-gender attractions than it is to act upon them, and they may go to great lengths to deny and resist their genuine feelings. Why should they accept these feelings so readily when they could be subjected to "verbal abuse, physical cruelty, condemnation by organized religion, overt discrimination, or outright rejection in response to suspicion or disclosure of their homosexuality" (Durby, 1994, p. 5). Instead, they may completely deny their feelings, rationalize that the feelings are temporary, and refuse to sexually explore (Troiden, 1989). They may attempt to change their feelings or to give the impression that they are heterosexual by imitating their peers and talking about heterosexual sex (e.g., even though a boy has homosexual feelings, he may talk about how "fine" a girl is), by engaging in heterosexual coitus (e.g., a girl may become pregnant to prove that she is heterosexual), or by exhibiting homophobic behaviors (e.g., accusing others of being "fags" or "dykes" and suggesting that homosexuals should be harassed). Unfortunately, other youth will escape their same-gender feelings and comfort themselves in illicit and addictive substances.

Some youth will immerse themselves in academics and extracurricular activities to create a sense of self-worth and to show how they excel in many ways (Gonsiorek, 1988). They may have high GPAs, perfect attendance, great sportsmanship, and hobbies that are favorably considered by peers and adults alike. They may have all the nonsexual events in their life under complete control and perfect order (Johnson, 1996). Whatever avoidance behaviors these youth choose, denying and resisting their same-gender attractions is sure to make them have a false sense of self and feel like a fraud.

Realization of Their Sexual Orientation

The next step for youth is at the heels of realizing they could be homosexual. For the first time, they apprehensively consider, "I am gay." As expected, the age for realizing that they are probably homosexual varies according to research, but it is likely to emerge by middle to late adolescence (McFarland, 1993). The Rhode Island Task Force on Gay, Lesbian, Bisexual and Transgendered Youth (1996) found that males first acknowledged their homosexuality between 14 and 16 years old, and females between 16 and 19 years old.

Youth still experience much confusion at this step, given that they probably do not see a commonality with other gay and lesbian persons (like those in the media) and given that they fail to see how they fit the stereotypes they have heard. They may still try to pass for straight because a disclosure of their homosexuality would be too risky. At this step, they painstakingly attempt to blend in, often studying and copying the straight kids—the way they walk, talk, dress, pose, and so forth. They constantly monitor their own gestures, body language, and fashion and are particular about the friends they have (Tharinger & Wells, 2000). Consider how emotionally draining this can be as they work toward keeping their true identity at bay, worrying, "What if others find out?" and promoting a false identity in all situations. Others avoid peer-group interactions because it easier to do so than to hide or lie about who they are, all of which drives them to feel alone with no one to talk to.

At this realization step, some may have their first sexual encounter. Research has found that same-gender sexual experiences occur at 13 years of age on average for boys and 15 years for girls (Herdt & Boxer, 1996). Those who turn to casual sex with strangers will surely meet further feelings of inferiority and worthlessness.

Acceptance of Their Sexual Orientation

Up until this point, youth may have had same-gender fantasies and engaged in same-gender sexual activity or coitus, but they might not necessarily have accepted the fact that they are homo- or bisexual. In fact, as Savin-Williams and Rodriguez (1993) found in a high school sample, less than 1% of the youth identified themselves as gay, lesbian, or bisexual, even though 6.4% reported having had homosexual attractions or behavior. Overall, less than 30% of those engaging in homosexual acts had identified themselves as homosexual.

At this step, youth come to accept that they are gay, lesbian, or bisexual, although they may not be fully comfortable with their sexual orientation. They may still engage in passing-for-straight behaviors, but they begin to inform others about their sexual orientation. The process of informing others is known as "coming out." (The phrase *coming out of the closet* represents the action of taking something that is hidden, in a closet per se, and showcasing to others; *closeted* refers to the idea of keeping one's sexual orientation hidden from others.)

Coming out is a stressful event because disclosing their sexual orientation places youth at risk for alienation, ostracism, rejection, and harassment. It is consequently no wonder that, although most youth may be self-identified at early ages, they are likely to remain closeted into late adolescence and adulthood (Taylor, 2000). In fact, some will come out years later, after having had same-gender romantic relationships.

The process of coming out varies from person to person and is contingent upon a host of factors such as the comfort level with the sexual orientation; the degree of support at home or from peers; the personality (e.g., someone with a brash personality would handle coming out differently than would someone with a shy personality); and so forth. Coming out is a life-long process that occurs every time a person discloses his or her sexual orientation. Presumably, some youth will feel comfortable enough to come out at school but not at work; others may feel inclined to come out to close friends but not to family members; and others may be closeted their whole lives. Research has found that most persons come out to others in the following order: gay, lesbian, and bisexual peers first; close heterosexual peers second; close family members next; and finally parents (American Counseling Association, 1999).

Most youth, however, do not come out, because they fear being thrown out of their homes and losing close friends. Research has found that one out of four gay or lesbian youth was forced to leave home when he or she came out to his or her family (Rhode Island Task Force on Gay, Lesbian, Bisexual and Transgendered Youth, 1996). Another study reported that 12% of mothers and 18% of fathers rejected their children upon learning of their sexual orientation (Hershberger & D'Augelli, 1995). As one government study noted, gay and lesbian youth may be "the only group of adolescents that face total rejection from their family unit with the prospect of no ongoing support" (Gibson, 1989, p. 112). Others remain in the closet to their closest of friends because they fear rejection. Many youth and adults have reported having lost a friend or two who could not tolerate the news.

You may ask why a youth would want to come out of the closet and, as the adage goes, "jump from the pan to the skillet." Openly gay youth are likely to encounter harassment and harsh criticism, no doubt, but quite frankly, youth who come out are tired of hav-

COMING OUT: THE NEVER-ENDING PROCESS

Why might gay and lesbian youth resist coming out? They fear the following:

- rejection from friends and family,
- losing close friends and loved ones,
- harassment and abuse,
- being thrown out of the family and/or house,
- being forced to undergo psychotherapy,
- being treated differently by teachers and peers,
- being judged and criticized,
- long lectures that plea for them to convert to heterosexuality,
- losing financial support,
- physical violence, and
- embarrassment or shame that family members may experience.

What are some other reasons that keep gay and lesbian youth from coming out? Why might gay and lesbian youth want to come out? They want to

- end the hiding game,
- live honestly,
- feel closer to family and friends,
- be able to feel "whole" around others,
- stop wasting energy by hiding all of the time,
- feel a sense of integrity, and
- make a statement that "gay is OK."

(Continued)

COMING OUT: THE NEVER-ENDING PROCESS (Continued)

What are some other reasons that gay and lesbian youth want to come out? How might a gay and lesbian youth feel after they've come out? They might feel

- scared, uncomfortable, vulnerable;
- shocked or disbelieving;
- uncertain about what happens next;
- relieved;
- disgusted;
- sad;
- supported; and
- angry.

Source: Adapted from Gill, K. J. (1998). Maintaining the dignity and rights of gay and lesbian students. *Reclaiming Children and Youth, 7*(1), 25–27; Saint Paul Public Schools. (n.d.). *Out for Equity/Out4Good Safe Schools Manual.* St. Paul, MN: Author.

ing to hide their genuine identity and live each day filled with lies. Other gay youth see the many outlets available to heterosexual youth and want to create their own outlets, establish support mechanisms, and join others like themselves. Others simply want to be like all the other adolescents and share the significant aspects of their lives, disclose deep thoughts and feelings, and receive validation for who they truly are. Below, two youths describe why it's easier to live life out of the closet:

PATRICK: For me being gay has not been an issue of just being gay, it's been more of an issue of being able to be myself. It's about being able to expose who I am and realize that if someone rejects me it doesn't mean I'm a bad person—not worth anything. It just means maybe they're an idiot; or they just don't like me. (Bass & Kaufman, 1996, p. 26)

MICHELLE: The rewarding aspect is being true to who I am, and being able to be a hundred percent of who I am to everybody I encounter, not just seventy-five percent of my personality. People didn't know all of me. They didn't know all of what I liked, and they had false perceptions of who I was. (Bass & Kaufman, 1996, p. 26)

Exploration of Gay, Lesbian, Bisexual, and Transgender Community

Youth at this step desire to connect with others like themselves. One openly gay man reflected on his exploration, "You think you're the only one until you know you're not. And then it's like, 'I have to go to where my people are.' I just remember feeling odd my whole life and then I found them. And it was like, 'Aha, my people; people who understand me and know what I'm about." Youth at this step seek out the gay and lesbian community in the following places: geographic locations in cities (e.g., Chelsea in New York City, Lakeview in Chicago, Castro in San Francisco); organizations that are committed to enhancing gay and lesbian spiritual and mental health (e.g., gay church support groups; community out-reaches); websites where people can meet online and establish pen pals; school clubs such as Gay–Straight Alliances; gay social events (gay-pride parades, benefits); and bars. They create a social network where they meet others, share emotional and physical intimacy, and enter into romantic relationships. Persons can be closeted at this step and still immerse themselves in the gay, lesbian, bisexual, and transgender community.

Opening up and Recognizing That Sexuality Is One Part of the Whole Person

At this final step, persons are openly gay or lesbian. They no longer see the benefits of passing for straight, and they are completely out of the closet. They are fully comfortable with their sexual orientation and do not fear the stigma or prejudice associated with being gay or lesbian. Chances are they will not introduce themselves with, "Hello, I'm gay," but neither will they deny being homo- or bisexual. At this step, being gay or lesbian is a way of life. They make reservations for a couple ("my partner and I"); they have commitment ceremonies; they adopt children (in states where it is legal); they have power of attorney for each other; and so forth. In short, they perceive themselves no differently than heterosexuals do. They also recognize that being homo- or bisexual is only one facet of a complex life, a facet that does not fully define a person. These individuals value their sexual orientation and what it represents (McFarland, 1993). In fact, when asked if they could take a magic pill to convert their sexual orientation to a heterosexual one, they emphatically answer, "No."

In sum, a gay or lesbian sexual identity develops over time, and it is an uphill battle for most gay or lesbian persons to produce a positive self-image of their sexual orientation. Youth may not go through all these steps under your watch, and some may never reach the final step. In fact, some persons may accept that they are gay and enter romantic relationships but never fully explore the gay and lesbian community. Others may say they never felt different or resisted being gay or lesbian. Some youth may even have same-gender sexual experiences, same-gender attractions, and contemplate whether they are gay, but later realize that they are heterosexual (American Academy of Child and Adolescent Psychiatry, 1999).

The common thread found in these steps is that, among gay and lesbian youth, many are bound to feel a range of untoward emotions, which are likely to hinder their ultimate development of self-worth and confidence (Tharinger & Wells, 2000):

- Anxiety, fear, and stress—because they worry that others will learn about their attractions and they do not want to contend with the repercussions the revelation may bring; because they are on guard at all times, protecting their sexual orientation (Tharinger & Wells, 2000).

- Self-loathing, shame, and depression—because of the perceptions they have regarding their membership in a stigmatized group; because of the realization that they will be unable to fulfill societal expectations, like getting married, having children, and so forth.
- Alone and isolated—because there is no one with whom to share their experiences; because it is easier to be alone than to pass for straight and dodge the questions raised by their heterosexual peers; because heterosexual youth want nothing to do with them.

Being gay or lesbian can certainly be a lonely place, as one 18 year old mentioned: "I felt as though I was the only gay person my age in the world. I felt as though I had nowhere to go to talk to anybody. Throughout eighth grade, I went to bed every night praying I would not be able to wake up in the morning, and every morning waking up and being disappointed. And so finally I decided that if I was going to die, it would have to be at my own hands" (Massachusetts Governor's Commission on Gay and Lesbian Youth, 1993, p. 12).

 Application

Consider when you have experienced despair in your life. Describe the emotions you felt. How might those feelings be similar to the untoward emotions gay and lesbian youth may have?

What Is the Kinsey Scale and What Should I Infer from It?

You may have heard expressions like, "1 out of 10 persons is gay" or "10% of America is gay or lesbian." This popular statistic, albeit inaccurate, is based on sexuality research conducted by Alfred Kinsey and his associates Pomeroy and Martin in the late 1940s and 1950s. Kinsey, Pomeroy, and Martin surveyed and interviewed over 10,000 adults about their conscious sexual behavior and interests. In their 1948 best-selling book regarding their findings from their white male sample, *Sexual Behavior in the Human Male*, the authors found, among other things, that

- 37% had had at least some overt homosexual experience since the onset of adolescence;
- 4% were exclusively homosexual throughout their lives;
- 8% were exclusively homosexual for at least three years between 16 and 65 years of age;
- 46% were neither exclusively heterosexual nor exclusively homosexual (Kinsey, Pomeroy, & Martin, 1948).

In their 1953 book, *Sexual Behavior in the Human Female*, the authors reported that

- 28% of the women reported erotic responses to other females;
- 28% of the women who reported homosexual activity had had an experience that extended for over three years;
- between 2% and 6% of unmarried females had been more-or-less exclusively homosexual in each of the years between 20 and 35 years old (Kinsey, Pomeroy, & Martin, 1953).

To help Kinsey and his associates fully comprehend the data collected, they developed a 0-to-6 sexuality scale, with 0 representing persons who were exclusively heterosexual and 6 representing persons who were exclusively homosexual. (See box 3.2.) For the first time in our history, human sexual behavior was no longer characterized as being either heterosexual or homosexual; Kinsey, Pomeroy, and Martin had postulated that human sexuality existed on a continuum. Needless to say, these findings caused a national sensation because homosexuality as it was known—pathological among a few—was now more widespread than previously assumed (Miller, 1995). Miller (1995) writes, "Kinsey put the whole notion that homosexuality was pathological into question. Could so many Americans—who were apparently having homosexual relations with regularity, at least at

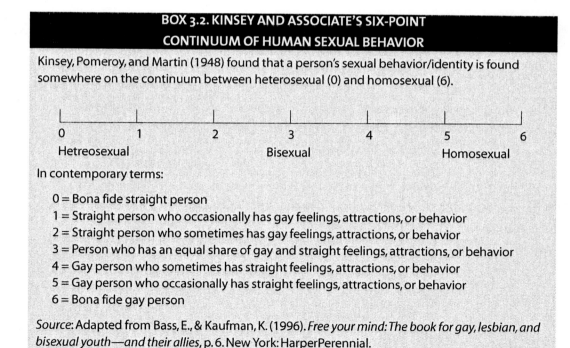

BOX 3.2. KINSEY AND ASSOCIATE'S SIX-POINT CONTINUUM OF HUMAN SEXUAL BEHAVIOR

Kinsey, Pomeroy, and Martin (1948) found that a person's sexual behavior/identity is found somewhere on the continuum between heterosexual (0) and homosexual (6).

0	1	2	3	4	5	6
Hetreosexual			Bisexual		Homosexual	

In contemporary terms:

0 = Bona fide straight person
1 = Straight person who occasionally has gay feelings, attractions, or behavior
2 = Straight person who sometimes has gay feelings, attractions, or behavior
3 = Person who has an equal share of gay and straight feelings, attractions, or behavior
4 = Gay person who sometimes has straight feelings, attractions, or behavior
5 = Gay person who occasionally has straight feelings, attractions, or behavior
6 = Bona fide gay person

Source: Adapted from Bass, E., & Kaufman, K. (1996). *Free your mind: The book for gay, lesbian, and bisexual youth—and their allies*, p. 6. New York: HarperPerennial.

some point in their lives—really be 'sick'?" (p. 252). Under public pressure, the Rockefeller Foundation even withdrew their financial support of Kinsey's research.

Times have certainly changed in the last 50 years since the releases of these books, yet despite the fact that other researchers have different estimates for the percentage of gay, lesbian, bisexual, and transgender persons living in the United States, the "10%" rule is still widely circulated. The most salient feature to infer from these reports and the Kinsey Scale is that some youth will have same-gender attractions, fantasies, dreams, and sexual experiences but may not be able to easily categorize their sexual orientation into one of the discrete categories imposed by society: gay, lesbian, bisexual, transgender, or heterosexual. In fact, many youth are likely to become confused with their same-gender feelings; experience stress over them; and contemplate, "Am I gay?" (American Academy of Child and Adolescent Psychiatry, 1999). In short, youth must be allowed to define who they are. You cannot assume that all youth will have a sexual orientation neatly compartmentalized into homo-, bi-, or heterosexual.

What Do I Do If a Student Tells Me He or She Is Gay or Lesbian?

Given that gay and lesbian youth experience intense internalized pain as they develop their sexual identity, you are now better able to understand the considerable courage a youth takes to come out. You should feel honored if a student has decided to come out to you. The student who comes out to you evidently respects, trusts, and likes you deeply enough to seek your support, advice, and help. Keep in mind that he or she has spent considerable time contemplating the risks of approaching you and has most likely rehearsed how to approach you. Even so, the student may be a bundle of nerves considering that he or she has no way of knowing what your actual response will be. The coming-out moment is sure to be a powerful one. Johnson (1996) writes, "The coming out experience is so powerful for the gay/lesbian person that it will be remembered in great detail by most for the rest of their lives. For the first time, the words about this core piece of identity have been spoken out loud to another human being" (p. 40).

If a student tells you that he or she is gay, lesbian, or bisexual, you should do the following:

Critical Thinking

Have you ever had students that you believed might be gay, lesbian, bisexual, or transgender? What made you believe that they might be?

Reflect and Write

What are your main concerns if a student were to come out to you? What would you do if a student told you that he or she was gay or lesbian?

- Listen to the student.
- Pause for a moment, allowing the student to fully finish what he or she has to say.
- If your personality is one to embrace, embrace the student. If not, offer a handshake or pat them on the shoulder. A student may cry upon coming out to you. If so, pause a moment to allow the student to regain his or her composure.
- Thank the student for sharing something so profound. Tell the student it means a lot to you that he or she has shared something so deep. You can say, "I'm honored you have come to me with this news" or "I appreciate that you considered me so important to tell me this."
- Acknowledge that it must have been very difficult for the student to share the information. You can say, "I know this must have been very hard for you."
- Tell the student you have no intention of sharing the news with any other faculty members, students, administrators, or parents unless he or she requests so. You can assure, "Your news is safe with me" or "You can bet that I won't tell a soul" or "I'll take this to my grave."
- Ask the student how he or she is coping with the issue. Ask, "Are you OK with this?" or "How are you handling this?"
- Listen.

At this point, you can handle the situation in two general ways. How you handle it is contingent upon your own personal convictions. In other words, your morals, your values, your religious and spiritual beliefs, and your comfort level should determine the course that best suits your character.

If your personal convictions are more conservative by nature and you hesitantly support persons with diverse sexual orientations, consider the following:

- If the student seems to want to talk some more about the topic, you can tell the student that as much as you would like to help them, there are persons on campus (or organizations) much better trained to handle these kinds of issues. Feel free to tell them that you are uncomfortable discussing the issue. You can respond, "I have some phone numbers of people who can help you much better than I can. I'm just an old lady (or man) deep down, and I get really uncomfortable with these kinds of issues." Or "Why don't you make an appointment with the counselor? He/she is much better about these kinds of things. I'm not very good at this." Or "Here are the names of some people that I think you should talk to. I'm just an old-fashioned math teacher who's not very good at stuff like this. I guess it's just the way I was raised."
- Give the student the names of people he or she can contact and ask if it is OK that you inform the counselor.

- Tell the student that you know he or she is going through a hard time and that it must be very difficult for them. You can say, "I know this must be very hard for you" or "You must have a lot on your mind" or "This must be so hard. I can't imagine what you're going through."
- Assure the student that many gay and lesbian persons turn out to be very successful despite the emotional setbacks. You can say, "I know that it's difficult now, and it may be difficult for a long time, but our society has many successful gay and lesbian people" or "Look at Rosie O'Donnell and Billy Bean. I'm sure they had it hard, too, and they seem to be getting along OK now" or "Everyone has tough times in their lives. Yours is probably tougher than most, but in the long run everything will work out OK for you."
- Encourage the student to contact others who can help and to let you know how things worked out. You can respond, "Please call this person. I know they can help you, and please let me know how things work out. I'm not telling them what it's about, but I'll ask them if you've paid them a visit."
- Assure the student that your opinion of him or her has not changed because of the disclosure and that you want them to always feel welcome in your classroom. You can say, "I still think you're a really neat kid. I appreciate you just as much as I did when you walked through that door" or "I'm glad you told me, and I promise you that my opinion of you has not changed whatsoever" or "In my eyes, you're still the same person."
- Ask if they feel safe in your classroom or school. You can say, "Do you feel threatened in any way by the students or faculty members?" or "What can I do so that you feel safe in my classroom?"
- Embrace the student, shake the student's hand, or pat the student on the shoulder and wish him or her well. You can finish with, "Thanks again for sharing with me. I'm sure everything will work out well for you. It may not be tonight or tomorrow, but one day it will." Or "I'm hoping for the best for you."

As tempted as you may be, please *do not* say any of the following:

- "You are going through a phase that you will outgrow";
- "You are going to hell because God says so";
- "You are an abomination according to the Bible";
- "You can change your sexual orientation if you just put your mind to it";
- "You are sick";
- "You should see a psychologist who can cure you";
- "You should not think too much about what you are going through";
- "You should just keep your mouth shut about such things";

- "You should make sure you are not breaking any laws";
- "You should date the opposite sex";
- "You should spend more time doing gender-appropriate activities";
- "You should never tell anyone else because it is bound to cause a lot of trouble";
- "You will never marry, have children, or be happy";
- "You are making a big deal out of nothing, and you will realize it the day you get married and have children";
- "You should not have come out to me";
- "I am disappointed in you";
- "So many people are going to be disappointed in you"; or
- "What's the matter with you?" or any comments of this nature.

You should *not* plan to or say that you will

- contact the student's parents and tell them about the news,
- contact a church leader and have him/her talk to the student,
- notify all administrators and some teachers about the situation,
- notify some students so they can help out with the situation, or
- notify the police that you have a child molester on your hands.

By all means, treat the student no differently than before you knew of his or her sexual orientation, and if the student permits you to discuss the matter with the counselor, do so.

If your personal convictions are liberal by nature and you fully support persons with diverse sexualities, consider the following:

- If the student seems to want to talk some more about the topic, you can tell him or her that your training in the topic is limited but that you are willing to talk about it as much as they want. You can also tell them you know of some people on campus or some organizations that can help them with their issues. Let the student do most of the talking, but you can ask questions like

  - How did you come to this awareness?
  - Have you come out to others? How did they respond?
  - What seems to be the hardest aspect of what you're going through?
  - Do you feel safe at school? In my classroom? At home?
  - Has anyone harassed you?
  - How are you handling the stress?
  - From where are you drawing strength? What resources are available to you now?
  - Are you dating anyone?

- Listen.
- Give the student the names of people or organizations they can contact. You can also provide them a reading list of material appropriate for gay and lesbian youth.
- Tell the student you know that he or she is going through a hard time and that it must be a very difficult time for them. You can say, "I know this must be very hard for you" or "You must have a lot on your mind" or "This must be so hard. I can't imagine what you're going through."
- Assure the student that he or she can come talk to you at any time. You can say, "My classroom is a safe zone. Feel free to come back and share" or "If you ever need someone to talk to, or if you find yourself in jam, please let me know" or "I'm in your corner, and I want these years to be as stable as possible."
- Ask what you can do to make life at school easier for them. You can ask, "Is there anything I can do for you?" or "What can I do to lessen some of the stress you're experiencing?"
- Assure them that many gay and lesbian persons turn out to be very successful people despite the emotional setbacks. You can say, "I know that it's difficult now, and it may be difficult for a long time, but our society has many successful gay and lesbian people" or "Look at Rosie O'Donnell and Billy Bean. I'm sure they had it hard, too, and they seem to be getting along OK now" or "Everyone has tough times in their lives. Yours is probably tougher than most, but in the long run I know that everything will work out OK for you."
- Name some notable gay and lesbian persons and their contributions to society.
- Encourage the student to contact others who can help and to let you know how things worked out. You can respond, "Please call this person. I know they can help you, and please let me know how things work out. I'm not telling them what it's about, but I'll ask them if you paid them a visit."
- Assure them that your opinion of them has not changed because of the disclosure and that you want them to always feel welcome in your classroom. You can say, "I still think you're a really neat kid. I appreciate you just as much as I did when you walked through that door" or "I'm glad you told me, and I promise you that my opinion of you has not changed whatsoever" or "In my eyes, you're still the same person."
- Embrace the student, shake the student's hand, or pat the student on the shoulder and wish him or her well. You can finish with, "Thanks again for sharing with me. I'm sure everything will work out well for you. It may not be tonight or tomorrow, but one day it will" or "I'm hoping for the best for you" or "You can always come back and talk."

As tempted as you may be, please *do not* do any of the following:

- Tell the student about other gay or lesbian students or about teachers you know or suspect are gay, lesbian, or bisexual.

- Encourage the student to come out to his or her parents.
- Encourage the student to come out at school and become a role model for other students.
- Encourage the student to start a gay support group.
- Encourage the student to explore the gay, lesbian, bisexual, and transgender community.
- Encourage the student to attend gay and lesbian pride parades or political and social events.
- Encourage the student to become a spokesperson for gay and lesbian youth.
- Set the student up on dates.

You are bound to feel overwhelmed if a student comes out to you, but consider yourself honored that you were chosen. Regardless of the direction you take with the student who comes out to you, you should listen to the student and thank him or her for sharing the information, safeguard the student's trust, provide the student with names of persons better suited to meet their needs, and ensure that you will treat the student no differently than before. Most importantly, ask for suggestions as to how you can make your classroom a safe place to learn. All teachers are morally obligated to create safe environments where students feel a mutual level of trust, respect, and acceptance for who they are.

Summary

A person's sexual identity develops over many years, and for some the development can take a lifetime. Every person comes to the sexual-orientation realization at different points in his or her life—some quicker than others—varying according to the person's unique circumstances. Youth who are experiencing same-gender attractions, sexual experiences, fantasies, and so forth are likely to feel a range of adverse emotions. The American Academy of Adolescent and Child Psychiatry (1999) writes, "Adolescence is an emotional minefield to begin with, filled with trepidation and insecurity and shaky self-esteem. Knowing that he is homosexually oriented compounds a teen's angst to a degree that's hard to imagine" (p. 164). For some youth, this internalized pain is so great that they feel the need to come out and risk themselves in the direct line of social

Put Yourself in the Picture

Some students approach you after school and tell you they heard that a student is a lesbian. Some argue there is nothing wrong with her sexual orientation; others argue that there is. Some pose, "Maybe there's something in this school that's turning students gay." Another student remarks, "My mom said that you turn gay if two boys hold hands or two girls hold hands." One student says, "It's easy to turn back straight. All she has to do is kiss a guy." How might you handle this situation? What would you say to the group?

rebuke, harassment, or violence. If a student comes out to you, make a concerted effort to assure them that your opinion of them is unchanged. Even if your personal convictions do not support a sexual orientation other than a heterosexual one, you can

- acknowledge the student's feelings;
- accept the student for who he or she is;
- maintain confidentiality; and
- direct the student to persons better suited to meet their individual needs.

Idea File

1. Identify a faculty member or administrator at your school who will be available for gay and lesbian youth. Ensure that the person receives additional training on the subject matter. Then refer students who are experiencing challenges associated with their sexual orientation to the designated person.
2. Contemplate how you might help a youth at each milestone. How might your advice or support statements differ from one level to the next?
3. Imagine that one of your students has come out to you. Practice how you would respond to the news.
4. Provide advice to a youth who has written Dear Abby. "Depressed" writes,

> Dear Abby:
> I'm beginning my senior year in high school and before the prior school year ended I "came out" to my soccer coach. I thought he was cool and would be understanding, but all he said was, "wait until you finish high school." Whenever I see him now he ignores me and doesn't even say hi to me or ask me how my practice is coming along, etc. Will all people I come out to be like this? Why would Mr. G be so mean about this? What should I do? I really thought he would be nice; now I'm just—
> Depressed and in the Closet in St. Cloud

References

American Academy of Child and Adolescent Psychiatry. (1999). *Your adolescent: Emotional, behavioral and cognitive development from early adolescence through the teen years.* New York: HarperCollins.

American Academy of Pediatrics. (2002). *Homosexuality and adolescence.* Retrieved July 18, 2002, from http://www.medem.com/search/a.../ZZZUHJP3KAC.html&soc+AAP&srch_typ+NAV_SERC.

American Counseling Association. (1999). *Just the facts about sexual orientation and youth: A primer for principals, educators, and school personnel.* Alexandria, VA: Author.

Anderson, D. A. (1995). Lesbian and gay adolescents: Social and developmental considerations. In G. Unks (Ed.), *The gay teen: Education practice and theory for lesbian, gay, and bisexual adolescents* (pp. 17–28). New York: Routledge.

Bass, E., & Kaufman, K. (1996). *Free your mind: The book for gay, lesbian, and bisexual youth—and their allies.* New York: HarperPerennial.

Boxer, A., Cook, J. A., & Herdt, G. (1989, August). *First homosexual and heterosexual experiences reported by gay and lesbian youth in an urban community.* Paper presented at the meeting of the American Sociological Association, San Francisco, CA.

Campos, D. (2003). *Diverse sexuality and schools: A reference handbook.* Santa Barbara: ABC-CLIO.

Cass, V. C. (1984). Homosexual identity formation: Testing a theoretical model. *Journal of Sex Research, 20*(2), 143–67.

Coleman, E. (1982). Developmental stages of the coming out process. In W. Paul, J. Weinrich, J. Gonsiorek, & M. Hotvedt (Eds.), *Homosexuality: Social, psychological, and biological issues* (pp. 149–58). Thousand Oaks, CA: Sage.

D'Augelli, A. R., & Patterson, C. J. (2001). *Lesbian, gay, and bisexual identities and youth.* New York: Oxford University Press.

Durby, D. D. (1994). Gay, lesbian, and bisexual youth. In T. DeCrescenzo (Ed.), *Helping gay and lesbian youth: New policies, new programs, new practices* (pp. 1–37). New York: Harrington Park Press.

Gibson, P. (1989). *Gay male and lesbian youth suicide: Report to the Secretary's Task Force on Youth Suicide, Volume 3: Preventions and interventions in youth suicide* (pp. 110–42) (DHHS Publication No. ADM. 89-1623). Washington, DC: U.S. Government Printing Office.

Gill, K. J. (1998). Maintaining the dignity and rights of gay and lesbian students. *Reclaiming Children and Youth, 7*(1), 25–27.

Gonsiorek, J. C. (1988). Mental health issues of gay and lesbian adolescents. *Journal of Adolescent Health Care, 9*(2), 114–22.

Herdt, G., & Boxer, A. (1996). *Children of horizons: How gay and lesbian teens are leading a new way out of the closet.* Boston: Beacon Press.

Hershberger, S. L., & D'Augelli, A. R. (1995). The impact of victimization on the mental health and suicidality of lesbian, gay, and bisexual youth. *Developmental Psychology, 31*(1), 65–74.

Human Rights Watch. (2002). *Hatred in the hallways: Violence and discrimination against lesbian, gay, bisexual, and transgender students in U.S. schools.* New York: Author.

Johnson, D. (1996). The developmental experience of gay/lesbian youth. *The Journal of College Admission, 151*, 38–41.

Kinsey, A. C., Pomeroy, W. B., & Martin, C. E. (1948). *Sexual behavior in the human male.* Philadelphia: W. B. Saunders.

Kinsey, A. C., Pomeroy, W. B., & Martin, C. E. (1953). *Sexual behavior in the human female.* Philadelphia: W. B. Saunders.

Lipkin, A. (1999). *Understanding homosexuality, changing schools.* Boulder, CO: Westview Press.

Massachusetts Governor's Commission on Gay and Lesbian Youth. (1993). *Making schools safe for gay and lesbian youth: Breaking the silence in schools and families.* Boston: Author.

McFarland, W. P. (1993). A developmental approach to gay and lesbian youth. *Journal of Humanistic Education and Development, 32*, 17–29.

Miller, N. (1995). *Out of the past: Gay and lesbian history from 1869 to the present.* New York: Vintage Books.

Remafedi, G. (1987). Male homosexuality: The adolescent's perspective. *Pediatrics, 79* (3), 326–30.

Rhode Island Task Force on Gay, Lesbian, Bisexual and Transgendered Youth. (1996). *School shouldn't hurt: Lifting the burden from gay, lesbian, bisexual, and transgendered youth.* Retrieved July 20, 2001, from http://members.tripod.com/~twood/safeschools.html.

Saint Paul Public Schools. (n.d.). *Out for equity/Out4good safe schools manual.* St. Paul, MN: Author.

Savin-Williams, R. C. (1990). Gay and lesbian adolescents. In F. W. Bozett & M. B. Sussman (Eds.), *Homosexuality and family relations* (pp. 197–216). New York: Harrington Park Press.

Savin-Williams, R. C., & Rodriguez, R. G. (1993). A developmental, clinical perspective on lesbian, gay male, and bisexual youths. In T. P. Gullotta, G. R. Adams, & R. Montemayor (Eds.), *Adolescent sexuality* (pp. 77–101). Newbury Park, CA: Sage.

Sears, J. T. (1991). *Growing up gay in the south.* New York: Harrington Park Press.

Taylor, H. E. (2000). Meeting the needs of lesbian and gay young adolescents. *Clearing House, 73*(4), 221–24.

Tharinger, D., & Wells, G. (2000). An attachment perspective on the developmental challenges of gay and lesbian adolescents: The need for continuity of caregiving from family and schools. *School Psychology Review, 29*(2), 158–72.

Troiden, R. R. (1989). The formation of homosexual identities. In G. Herdt (Ed.), *Gay and Lesbian Youth* (pp. 43–73). Binghamton, NY: Harrington Park Press.

Vare, J. W., & Norton, T. L. (1998). Understanding gay and lesbian youth: Sticks, stones, and silence. *Clearing House, 71*(6), 327–31.

Safe Schools and Legal Standards: These Youth Need to Be Protected

"HE LEFT THIS WORLD MUCH TOO SOON BECAUSE OF THOSE WHO FEAR AND HATE ANYONE WHO IS DIFFERENT."

I am Miss Pauline Mitchell. My son Fred C. Martinez Jr., F.C. as he was known by family and friends, left this world much too soon because of those who fear and hate anyone who is different. F.C. was my youngest child. He lived to the age of 16 years and was always ready to bring a laugh or smile to my heart when I needed it the most. He never saw another person as a stranger but as a fellow human being and was always ready to give a hug or compliment to anyone whom he believed to be hurting. F.C. loved life and to make others happy. He was my baby, my "tail" as I would call him. He was always ready to go with me on errands or trips I had to make. He cherished his friends and he had many. He would love to do make-up with his girlfriends, to share ideas. He was a free spirit and I loved him for his spirit and all of who he was.

F.C. had many difficult times in his short life. Much of this was related to the fact that he was Navajo living in a world that does not honor and respect different ways, and also that he was Nadleeh—two spirit—and he could comfortably walk the path of both male and female, that he would love differently from most. F.C. also felt the pain of what comes when your family is poor, but very proud. It is not easy to grow up Navajo, Nadleeh and poor. But these are facts of life. He was not ashamed of who he was and neither was I. I now tell you that I dearly loved my precious son and was proud of all that he was.

F.C. worked hard to overcome these hardships and he was beginning to find the path he would walk down for what should have been a long and fulfilling life, and to do so proudly. Why can't others allow our loved ones to express themselves freely? Those who speak of our children and loved ones with ignorance and hate are responsible for the pain I, and so many others, feel when our loved ones have been touched by hate violence.

F.C. was a member of the Native American Church, as am I and other family members. On a Sunday morning, a few weeks ago, I was leaving the teepee where a spiritual meeting and blessing ceremony had taken place throughout the entire night. Before me was a large eagle, sitting there so proudly. As I stood upright, the eagle took off and soared above me. I believe that the eagle held F.C.'s spirit and that he continues to guide me in my search for justice and to seek that no more children and loved ones will have to live in fear and leave this life in violence. F.C. would want us all to join together and work to the understanding that we can get along. He would want the schools to be a place where those who are different will find peace and joy in being at school instead of name calling, harassment and hate. That our homes and streets will also be free of this hate, and if it comes others will speak up and say, "No more!"

(Continued)

"HE LEFT THIS WORLD MUCH TOO SOON BECAUSE OF THOSE WHO FEAR AND HATE ANYONE WHO IS DIFFERENT." (Continued)

Source: Nationwide Press Release Statement by Mitchell, P. (2001, August 11). *Statement by Pauline Mitchell, mother of Fred C. Martinez Jr. for Cortez candlelight vigil.* Retrieved September 9, 2004, from http://www.tampabaycoalition.com/files/0814Fred.htm.

Overview

In mid-June 2001, an 18-year-old male chased 16-year-old Fred C. Martinez into a rocky, desolate area of New Mexico and bludgeoned him to death. The assailant later boasted he had "beat up a fag" (Quittner, 2001, p. 25). In Fred's short life, he had many challenges, some of which stemmed from being transgender. It was not uncommon for his peers to harass him at school because he wore makeup and fingernail polish and carried a purse. School administrators had even sent him home because his behavior did not conform to his gender. At the time of Fred's death, his mother emphasized, "Fred did not struggle with who he was but was hurt because of the people who had problems with my son expressing himself honestly" (Quittner, p. 26).

Indeed many youth and adults have a hard time understanding other gay, lesbian, bisexual, and transgender youth like Fred, let alone fully accepting their sexual orientation. Fred did not deserve to die simply because his sexual orientation was different from most. No one, for that matter, deserves to die or be harassed, intimidated, or bullied just because of his or her sexual orientation. Yet many gay and lesbian youth find themselves in learning environments where their mental and physical well-being is threatened and they fear for their safety.

Incidents like the shootings in Columbine have opened our metaphoric eyes, and as youth-serving professionals, you can no longer dismiss negative and cruel behaviors by just saying, "That's part of growing up." Teachers, counselors, and administrators have the responsibility to foster a learning climate that is completely safe and free of violence, including harassment, intimidation, bullying, and other threatening behaviors. It should not matter that a youth is gay or straight; all youth should feel safe walking in the hallways, studying in the school library, participating in class, and so forth. When we fail to provide them with a learning climate that values, respects, and treats them with dignity, they cannot and do not benefit from academic instruction and the social dynamics that are inherently found in the constructive relationships they make with one another. In this chapter, you will read about how gay and lesbian youth fit into the safe-schools paradigm, the legal aspects associated with protecting these youth, and what happens when school districts fail to protect them from harm. In particular, this chapter seeks to answer the following questions:

- How do gay and lesbian youth fit into the scheme of safe schools, bully-free zones, and so forth?

- Are there laws that mandate me to protect gay and lesbian youth?
- Have gay and lesbian youth legally challenged their school systems?

How Do Gay and Lesbian Youth Fit into the Scheme of Safe Schools, Bully-Free Zones, and So Forth?

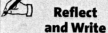

Reflect and Write

How would your students evaluate the safety of your school's learning climate? What would they say in terms of how safe they feel from harassment, intimidation, bullying, and other negative behaviors?

In the last few years, considerable attention has shifted to the safety of children in our schools. Much of this attention is in reaction to the tragic shootings in Littleton, Colorado; Jonesboro, Arkansas; West Paducah, Kentucky; and Springfield, Oregon. Over a dozen youth died in these shootings, and about two dozen were injured. The exact number of students traumatized by the event is surely in the thousands. These shootings have been a wake-up call for many, and for the first time in our educational history, people were asking, "How could this happen at school?"

The combined efforts to prevent further tragic incidents and to create safe schools nationwide are commonly referred to as the Safe Schools Initiative. The initiative serves as an umbrella for all the projects and curricula aimed at deterring hate- or bias-motivated behavior, bullying, and sexual harassment and at fostering a safe school environment. As a result of this initiative, which is heavily promoted by the Safe and Drug-Free Schools Program (U.S. Department of Education) and a number of state boards of education, many curricula and prevention/intervention projects have been created. (A bibliography of safe schools projects, *Great Ideas for Safe Schools: A Collection of Safe Schools Programs and Strategies from the Attorney General and State Superintendent of Public Instruction Safe Schools Task Force*, can be found on the California Department of Education website.) These efforts are critical in the times in which we live, considering that youth cannot learn if they fear for their safety while at school.

Hate- or bias-motivated behavior, bullying, and sexual harassment are independent constructs, and each has dedicated researchers investigating the dynamics of these among youth in schools. Their definitions, although they share some commonalities, are distinct. Consider their definitions:

- Hate- or bias-motivated behavior—"is intended to cause emotional suffering, physical injury, or property damage through intimidation, harassment, bigoted slurs or epithets, force or threat of force, or vandalism. Hateful or biased behavior is motivated in part or in whole by hostility toward a person's real or perceived race, nationality, religion, disability, gender, or sexual orientation" (California Department of Education, 2003, p. 4).

- Bullying—"is a conscious, willful, and deliberate hostile activity intended to harm, induce fear through threat of further aggression, and create terror" (Coloroso, 2003, p. 13). Coloroso emphasizes that bullying includes the elements of imbalance of power, intent to harm, and threat of further aggression, and when the behavior becomes escalated, terror is added.
- Sexual Harassment—"is undesired and offensive conduct that is sexually suggestive by means of taunts, gestures, or physical contact that is consistent and to a degree that makes a student uncomfortable and makes it difficult to participate in or enjoy the benefits of an education duly deserved" (Campos, 2002, p. 121).

Any student can engage in hate- or bias-motivated behavior or sexual harassment and not necessarily be a bully. A bully, for that matter, would not necessarily conduct a hate- or bias-motivated crime or sexually harass another student. And a student who sexually harasses another would not necessarily be a bully or engage in a hate- or bias-motivated crime. Most importantly, the common thread found among these constructs is that they all involve negative, destructive behavior whereupon one party intentionally harms another. In short, violence is exerted.

The Amherst H. Wilder Foundation released *The Little Book of Peace* (1997) to motivate the public to reflect upon and ultimately curb violence. In this guide, a synopsis of violence suggests that

- violence is words and actions that hurt people;
- violence is when a person uses pain, fear, or hurt to make you do something;
- violence is using words to scare, bully, embarrass, call names, or put someone down;
- violence is hurting a person's body or the things a person cares about; and
- violence is when someone touches you or asks you to touch them in a place or in a way that doesn't seem right to you. (p. 4)

This list may appear exhaustive, and you may question the reality of eliminating all of these behaviors (in schools, at least) given that it is commonly believed that teasing and taunting is an inherent part of growing up. Often it is the case, however, that "harmless" insults are a precursor to escalating harassment, intimidation, and bullying behavior (Washington State School Safety Center, 2003). It is strongly believed that Charles "Andy" Williams killed two of his Santee, California, classmates in retaliation for being intimidated and taunted as a "bitch" and a "wimp." Many others have come to the conclusion that the two students responsible for the Columbine massacre were lashing out for having been harassed by the "jocks."

As a whole, our schools are safe places (Dwyer, Osher, & Warger, 1998), and violent-crime rates in schools are down (National Center for Education Statistics, 2003; Bureau of Justice Statistics, 2000a, 2000b). In 1973, the Department of Justice (Bureau of Justice Statistics, 2000a) found that nearly 44 million incidents of violence in schools were reported compared to the 28.8 million similar crimes that were reported in 1999. Another study confirmed that violent crime rates in schools were down from 1992 to 2001—such crimes have declined from 48 victimizations per 1,000 students in 1992 to 28 per 1,000 in 2001 (National Center for Education Statistics, 2003). National Center for Education Statistics data suggest that between 1995 and 2001 the number of students who reported being a victim of a violent crime decreased from 3% to 2%.

Despite the declining trend in violence reported, however, many students still report that they feel unsafe in school (U.S. Department of Education, 2000). The Horatio Alger Association of Distinguished Americans (1999), for instance, found that the number of youth who felt safe in their school dropped from 44% in 1998 to 37% in 1999. The same study reported that the percentage of students who indicated they always felt safe in school dropped from 40% in 1998 to 33% in 1999. The *USA Weekend* (in conjunction with *Teen People*) 13th Annual Teen Survey (1999) found that only 71% of 129,593 6th through 12th graders said they felt safe from violence at school, and 60% said that a violent event similar to the one at Columbine could occur at their school. In a 2000 national survey of risk among youth, 4% reported they missed at least one day of school (in a 30-day period) because they felt unsafe at school. The Josephson Institute of Ethics (2001) most recently found that of 15,877 middle school and high school students, nearly 39% of middle school students and 36% of high school students said they didn't feel safe at school.

The fear that these students have regarding their safety is most likely due to the fact that violence, although its incidence has been in decline, is still prevalent in schools. Research strongly supports the contention that youth experience violence ranging from verbal insults to being pushed, shoved, grabbed, and threatened with physical harm. The following statistics provide a glimpse as to why some students may feel unsafe at school:

- Among Minnesota students in a 1998 study, 45% of freshman males and 46% of senior males indicated that they made fun of or threatened students of different races or backgrounds; 41% of freshman females and 44% of senior females reported the same behavior; 30% of freshman males and 20% of senior males mentioned that they had hit or beat up another person at least once or twice in the past 12 months; 20% of freshman females and 11% of senior females said they did the same (Kragthorpe & Jefferson, 1999).
- A *Journal of the American Medical Association* study (2001) found that 30% of 15,686 public school students mentioned that they were involved in bullying behavior as

a bully, target, or both on an occasional or frequent basis (Nansel, Overpeck, Pilla, Ruan, Simons-Morton, & Scheidt, 2001).

- One out of ten hate crimes occurs in schools and colleges (Southern Poverty Law Center, 1998).
- A San Francisco survey of 500 young adults found that as many as 50% of the males admitted to antigay aggression (Franklin, 2003).
- One University of Maine study found that about a third of 70,000 youth agreed with the statement, "students say things to hurt or insult me" (National Center for Student Aspirations, 2001).
- Among 14–17 year olds in one sample, over two-thirds indicated that there is a group of students at their school who sometimes or frequently intimidate others (The Empower Program, 2001).
- Seventy-five percent of children have been subject to bullying while at school (National Crime Prevention Council and ADT Services Inc., 1999).

These kinds of statistics speak volumes, and although the amount of violence in schools is in decline, bullying still appears to be a significant problem. The National Center for Education Statistics (2003) found that bullying behavior has increased in schools. In the 2001 school year, 8% of students reported being bullied in the last six months compared to 5% of students in 1999.

For most of our education history, it was generally understood that you (or a sibling or close friend) were likely to encounter a bully at school or in the playground. A school bully, in other words, was as fixed as a textbook or globe in the classroom. You may even remember a bully in your own childhood. The social attitude now toward bullies and bullying behavior has been significantly altered, and bullies are taken more seriously than ever before. The California Department of Education (2003) emphasizes, "The prevalence of bullying has come under scrutiny more recently because of the major role of bullying as a precursor to the notorious and avoidable incidents of school violence across the nation. It is now known that bullying behavior is common among children and that the harmful and lasting effects on children deserve special attention" (p. 3).

All of this discussion leads to the fact that we need programs, such as those spearheaded by the Safe Schools Initiative, to curb violence in schools because no youth who is a victim of a hate crime or who is intimidated, harassed, or bullied is in the frame of mind to learn. Which brings us back to the question, "How do gay and lesbian youth fit into the scheme of all this?" Because gay and lesbian youth often do not fit the "normal," heterosexist paradigm, they are frequent targets of hate crimes, bullies, sexual harassment, and other cruel and harmful behaviors. Moreover, youth seemingly do not tolerate others whose gender presentation does not conform to the traditional behaviors associated with their gender (e.g., a feminine boy or a masculine girl). Tonja Nansel of the National Institute of Child Health and Human Development explains,

> Considering our culture and its built-in prejudice [regarding] sexual orientation, it's likely to be quite common for kids to be targeted for being perceived as different or not within the cultural norm. . . . [Gay and lesbian youth] are the ones who are usually the most powerless to stop [the bullying]. They often don't get the support from other students or teachers. (Kirby, 2001, p. 33)

It is no surprise to learn, then, that gay and lesbian youth are more likely to feel vulnerable at school than are their heterosexual peers. One Massachusetts study reported that 19% of gay and lesbian youth skipped school because they felt unsafe at school, compared to 6% of their heterosexual peers who reported the same.

Violence has evident, untoward effects, leaving victims to develop academic problems and feel anxiety and stress as they avoid places where they become victims of hate- or bias-motivated behavior, bullying, sexual harassment, and so forth. This mother's letter to a magazine editor will give you an idea of what her son was going through at school:

> My 12-year-old son is being bullied. I was bullied. I remember the pain. But the new angle for the bully, especially if the victim is a boy, is to call the victim a fag, queer, or gay. I don't know or care whether my son is gay or not. . . . It doesn't matter to the bully whether it's true either. My son lives in a no-win situation. He is the one forced to change routines and routes to stay safe. His grades are the ones that go down every class in one semester. He is the one who skips lunch and won't use the restrooms (he had his head shoved in a urinal this year). (Readerforum, 2001, p. 4)

Society now recognizes the importance of safe schools, and throughout the country an increasing number of school districts are adopting policies to eliminate cruel and harmful behavior. All districts should have policies regarding a safe learning environment. More importantly, the policy should be taken to heart. School personnel can send students a powerful message when they observe physical, verbal, or psychological (e.g., manipulating social friendships) harm aimed at gay and lesbian youth, and they can intervene with comments such as, "None of that will be tolerated here," "That behavior is just not cool," or "Don't waste your energy; it's wrong to be like that." No physical, verbal, or psychological abuse should be dismissed or trivialized, regardless of the student's sexual orientation. If you act passively and ignore harmful, violent behavior, you are a definite medium of an unsafe school environment.

"I have no idea why students say they feel unsafe at school."

Are There Laws That Mandate Me to Protect Gay and Lesbian Youth?

As a youth-serving professional, you are morally and legally obligated to provide all your students a safe learning environment. The heart of this question seeks to determine whether federal or state laws exist that specifically mention that school districts and/or teachers have to protect gay and lesbian youth in schools. There is no federal law that specifically mandates the protection of gay and lesbian youth, but the education codes in Massachusetts, Connecticut, Wisconsin, and California specify that these youngsters are to be protected from harassment based on sexual orientation (Jennings, 2003). Other states impose similar codes that entitle protection through antidiscrimination laws (Minnesota and New Jersey) and antiharassment laws (Vermont and Washington) (Jennings, 2003). Box 4.1 outlines these mandates.

 BOX 4.1. STATES THAT MANDATE SAFE SCHOOL POLICIES

States (and the District of Columbia) that prohibit sexual orientation discrimination and harassment in school:

> California, Connecticut, Massachusetts, Minnesota, New Jersey, Vermont, Washington, and Wisconsin

States that have policies that can be interpreted to ban harassment and/or discrimination based on sexual orientation:

> Alaska, Florida, Hawaii, Pennsylvania, and Rhode Island

School districts throughout New Jersey, Washington, and Vermont are required to have antiharassment policies that include sexual orientation (and gender identity for New Jersey). Every school district in Wisconsin must have a nondiscrimination policy that includes sexual orientation.

Sources: American Civil Liberties Union. (2003). *States with Safe Schools Policies.* Retrieved October 15, 2003, from http://www.aclu.org/news/NewsPrint.cfm?ID=12902&c=106; Human Rights Campaign (2002). *State of the Family: Laws and Legislation Affecting Gay, Lesbian, Bisexual, and Transgender Families by Human Rights Campaign.* Retrieved October 15, 2003, from http://www.hrc.org/Template.cfm?Section=LGBT_Families.

California

Education Code Section 220–221.1

"No person shall be subjected to discrimination on the basis of sex, ethnic group identification, race, national origin, religion, color, mental or physical disability, or any basis that is contained

(Continued)

BOX 4.1. STATES THAT MANDATE SAFE SCHOOL POLICIES (Continued)

in the prohibition of hate crimes set forth in subdivision (a) of Section 422.6 of the Penal Code (person's race, color, religion, ancestry, national origin, disability, gender, or sexual orientation, or because he or she perceives that the other person has one or more of those characteristics) in any program or activity conducted by an educational institution that receives, or benefits from, state financial assistance or enrolls pupils who receive state student financial aid."

Connecticut

1997 Amendments to CGS Gen. Stat. Section 10–15c

"The public schools shall be open to all children five years of age and over . . . and each such child shall have, and shall be so advised by the appropriate school authorities, an equal opportunity to participate in the activities, programs and courses of study offered in such public schools . . . without discrimination on account of race, color, sex, religion, national origin or sexual orientation."

Massachusetts

Gen, Laws, chap. 76, sec.5

"No person shall be excluded from or discriminated against in admission to a public school of any town, or in obtaining the advantages, privileges and courses of study of such public school on account of race, color, sex, religion, national origin or sexual orientation."

Minnesota

Section 363.03 Subdivision 5

"Educational Institution. It is an unfair discriminatory practice: (1) To discriminate in any manner in the full utilization of or benefit from any educational institution, or the services rendered thereby to any person because of race, color, creed, religion, national origin, sex, age, marital status, status with regard to public assistance, sexual orientation, or disability, or to fail to ensure physical and program access for disabled persons."

Statutes 2002, 121A.03, Subdivision 2

"Sexual, religious, and racial harassment and violence policy. A school board must adopt a written sexual, religious, and racial harassment and sexual, religious, and racial violence policy that conforms with sections 363.01 to 363.15. The policy shall apply to pupils, teachers, administrators, and other school personnel, include reporting procedures, and set forth disciplinary actions that will be taken for violation of the policy."

(Continued)

🏛 BOX 4.1. STATES THAT MANDATE SAFE SCHOOL POLICIES (Continued)

Section 363.01, Subdivision 41a

"'Sexual orientation' means having or being perceived as having an emotional, physical, or sexual attachment to another person without regard to the sex of that person or having or being perceived as having an orientation for such attachment, or having or being perceived as having a self-image or identity not traditionally associated with one's biological maleness or femaleness. 'Sexual orientation' does not include a physical or sexual attachment to children by an adult."

New Jersey

NJAC 6A:7-1.4

"The proposed section 6A:7-1.4, Responsibilities of the District Board of Education, establishes the requirement for district boards of education to develop and implement policies and plans that recognize and value diversity within the society, establish and assure equality in educational programs, and prohibit all forms of discrimination and harassment in the public schools on the basis of race, creed, color, national origin, ancestry, age, marital status, affectional or sexual orientation, gender, religion, disability or socioeconomic status."

Vermont

State Board of Education 1250

"In order to provide equal educational and equal employment opportunities, no students and/or public school employee in the State of Vermont shall be excluded from participation in, be denied the benefits of, or be subject to discrimination under any educational program or activity receiving federal and/or state funds as the result of or based on sex, race, color, creed, national origin, sexual orientation, or solely by reason of handicap/disability."

Washington, DC

Section 2-1402.41

"It is unlawful discriminatory practice, subject to the exemptions in section 2-1401.03(b), for an educational institution:
(1) To deny, restrict, or to abridge or condition the use of, or access to, any of the facilities, services, programs, or benefits of any program or activity to any person otherwise qualified, wholly or partially, for a discriminatory reason, based upon the actual or perceived: race, color, religion, national origin, sex, age, marital status, personal appearance, sexual orientation, familial status, family responsibilities, political affiliation, source of income, or disability of any individual."

(Continued)

BOX 4.1. STATES THAT MANDATE SAFE SCHOOL POLICIES (Continued)

Washington State

New Section. Sec 2

"By August 1, 2003, each school district shall adopt or amend if necessary a policy, within the scope of its authority, that prohibits the harassment, intimidation, or bullying of any student. It is the responsibility of each school district to share this policy with parents or guardians, students, volunteers, and school employees.

(2) 'Harassment, intimidation, or bullying' means any intentional written, verbal, or physical act, including but not limited to one shown to be motivated by any characteristic in RCW 9A.36.080 (3) (race, color, religion, ancestry, national origin, gender, sexual orientation, or mental, physical, or sensory handicap), or other distinguishing characteristics, when the intentional written, verbal, or physical act:

(a) physically harms a student or damages the student's property; or
(b) had the effect of substantially interfering with a student's education; or
(c) is so severe, persistent, or pervasive that it creates an intimidating or threatening educational environment; or
(d) has the effect of substantially disrupting the orderly operation of the school.
Nothing in this section requires the affected student to actually possess a characteristic that is a basis for the harassment, intimidation, or bullying."

Wisconsin

Section 118.13

"No pupil may be excluded from a public school, or from any school activities or programs, or be denied any benefits or treated in a different manner because of: sex, race, religion, national origin (including a student whose primary language is not English), ancestry, creed, pregnancy, parental status, marital status, sexual orientation, physical disability, mental disability, emotional disability, and learning disability."

Despite the fact that your state or district may not incorporate policies of antidiscrimination or antiharassment based on a student's sexual orientation, be mindful that gay and lesbian youth are afforded some protection by other rightful means. Provided here are the federal laws that attorneys have used to legally determine whether a district or school official failed gay and lesbian youth. Buckel (2000) has designated these as "the array of tools available in the courts to challenge harassment and violence in schools" (p. 392).

Equal Protection Clause

The Equal Protection Clause of the 14th Amendment says it all: equal means equal. All public school students have to be equally protected from harassment and harm. In other words, a school official cannot arbitrarily choose who will be provided a safe learning environment. Just because you may believe that girls are more vulnerable than boys and that boys "can take care of themselves" does not give you the legal freedom to discount or deny the harassment of boys. Moreover, boys and girls cannot be treated differently when it comes to their claims of sexual harassment. Sexual harassment should be dealt with in a similar degree of seriousness regardless of whether a boy or a girl makes the claim. You are also mistaken if you think that because Hispanic and African-American students appear more street smart and savvy than the other students in your school they do not need a similar degree of protection from harassment.

Schools are similarly legally obligated to protect gay, lesbian, bisexual, and transgender youth from harassment as much as they do with all other students. In fact, school officials are violating the Equal Protection Clause when they dismiss a youth's plight with excuses such as, "The harassment is preparing that little lesbian for the real world" or "They're just boys. That rough play may just knock the gay right out of him." According to the Equal Protection Clause, school personnel are negligent of their duties when they fail to take action against antigay harassment for any of the following reasons:

- They believe gay and lesbian youth should be harassed—"That's what she gets for shoving her sexuality down everyone's throats."
- They believe gay and lesbian youth bring the harassment upon themselves because of the way they carry themselves—"None of this would happen if you would act more like a boy and play more sports."
- They are uncomfortable in dealing with sexual orientation issues—"Let's not deal with this. Let's just transfer her to another school."
- They are uneducated about such matters—"How do we handle this? Maybe it's best to ignore the situation." (GLSEN, 2002)

Under the Equal Protection Clause, a transgender student (a student whose biological gender is incongruent with his/her gender identity—e.g., a boy who considers himself girl) has the right to be treated according to the same standards applied to students of the same gender identity (GLSEN, 2002). In other words, if a transgender (female-to-male) student wants to dress as a boy, he is rightfully entitled to dress as the other boys. School districts cannot impose a dress code on female-to-male or male-to-female transgender students that is different from the code applied to biological boys and girls.

Title IX

Title IX of the Education Amendment Acts of 1972 (P.L. 92-318), like the Equal Protection Clause, mandates the equal treatment of youth. The act enforces that any education program that receives federal funding cannot discriminate against youth based on their gender—sexual discrimination is strictly prohibited. Under Title IX, school districts must ensure that boys and girls have equal opportunities in all aspects of academic and extracurricular programs, including admissions, recruitment, courses, athletics, and so forth, and that both groups of students have comparable locker rooms, bathrooms, and other facilities. It is through Title IX, for instance, that schools are not allowed to restrict girls from a calculus class or boys from a home-economics course. People often regard Title IX as the law that made high school athletic teams available to girls (Jones, 1999).

Title IX has a distinct feature, in that sexual harassment is subsumed under sexual discrimination, and therefore teachers, administrators, or school employees violate the law if they engage in, condone, or tolerate sexual harassment or allow it to continue (U.S. Department of Education, 2001). Under Title IX, sexual discrimination (harassing conduct) against gay or lesbian youth is unlawful; however, sexual-orientation discrimination is not. Some examples elucidate the difference:

- Prohibited by Title IX: sexual harassment against gay and lesbian youth

  - Boys mock raping an openly gay boy or one that is perceived to be gay
  - A boy grabbing a lesbian student, holding her tightly to suggest intercourse
  - Girls groping a gay boy and saying, "I know we can get you back on our team"

- Not prohibited by Title IX: sexual-orientation harassment against gay and lesbian youth

  - A group of students yelling out, "You're queer. We don't want you here. Get used to it."
  - A class laughing at a joke about gays
  - A student overhearing a teacher mentioning, "I wish all gays would move to San Francisco and die in a big earthquake."

In the first set of examples, the conduct directed toward the victims was of a sexual nature. Sexual advances were clearly made on all three students. If this type of harassment (severe enough that the victims and some of the bystanders were traumatized) was pervasive, a sexually hostile environment is in the making and Title IX would be defied. In the second set of examples, the conduct was offensive and certainly contributed to a hostile learning environment, but it was not sexually based and therefore does not constitute a violation of Title IX.

Lastly, Title IX also prohibits gender-based harassment—harassment by students and teachers toward youth who fail to conform to the traditional images and behavior associated with masculinity and femininity (GLSEN, 2002). This type of sexual discrimination, sexual stereotyping (Buckel, 2000), occurs when a principal or teacher dismisses a gay or lesbian youth's complaint of antigay harassment because the boy is overtly feminine or the girl is overtly masculine. Such school personnel are violating Title IX when they tell a boy, "Start acting more like a man," or the girl, "Just pretty yourself up like all the girls, and everyone will then leave you alone."

First Amendment

You will recall that the First Amendment of the U.S. Constitution guarantees our fundamental "right to free expression and free association." The First Amendment extends into schools and entitles students to freedom of speech, with school officials having limited rights in their censorship of students' speech or expression (GLSEN, 2002). This law protects students' right to exchange ideas freely and openly (provided the opinions do not "materially or substantially" disrupt classes or school activities) without fear of retribution (ACLU, 2003e). Under the First Amendment, school officials cannot suppress youth from expressing what they think in support of or in objection to gay, lesbian, bisexual, and transgender persons or issues. The ACLU (2003d), however, emphasizes, "Regardless of their point of view, . . . students do not have a right to express themselves if such an expression substantially interferes with the rights of a classmate. Students do not have the right to intimidate or attack other students because of their sexual orientation or gender identity."

Expression of sexual orientation, moreover, is a constitutional right, and school personnel therefore cannot stifle youth from being openly gay or lesbian. School districts violate students' rights if they, for instance, ask gay and lesbian students to "tone it down" or "quit being so gay," to remove their gay and lesbian symbol pins from their backpacks, or to dress more "like the other kids." One U.S. magistrate reprimanded a school district by saying, "education officials should have known that high school students have the right to speak out and express their sexual orientation in school settings" (Lambda Legal Defense and Education Fund, 2001, p. 1). In fact, the U.S. Department of Education (1999) document, *Protecting Students from Harassment and Hate Crimes: A Guide for Schools*, reminds schools to write their antiharassment policies in a style that recognizes the First Amendment rights of students.

The following news article appeared in the *Chicago Free Press* on July 31, 2002. As you read the article, consider the point of view held by the student, the assistant principal, the faculty, student's parents, other students, and other students' parents.

Principal Gives High Heels on Boys the Boot, by Gary Barlow, Staff Writer

A 15-year-old gay student at the Chicago High School for Agriculture Sciences expressed disbelief last week after the school's assistant principal allegedly told him he had to "dress as a boy" if he wanted to remain at the school.

"I had on some high heels for about 10 minutes," the student said. "She told me as long as I was at the school, I would dress as a boy, that I would not wear anything feminine."

The student also said CHSAS assistant principal Martha Hamilton told him his long hair was "offensive" when she reprimanded him in a hallway July 24.

Hamilton denied making the comment about the student's hair but acknowledged that she told him he couldn't wear high heels.

"We don't allow boys to wear high heels and earrings," Hamilton said. "Girls can wear earrings."

Asked whether girls at the school, part of the Chicago Public School system, are allowed to wear high heels, Hamilton said, "Girls are allowed to wear whatever shoes are appropriate for girls. How many boys do you know who wear high heel shoes?"

Hamilton said distinguishing what male and female students can wear is not discriminatory.

"It has nothing to do with his sexual orientation," she said. "Before (students) come here, we explain what our policies are. He's one of the ones who signs a contract to abide by them. If there's a problem with this, he can go somewhere else."

But the student said he feels the atmosphere at the school is not good for GLBT students, adding he's the only gay student he knows at CHSAS, 3857 W. 111th St.

"Everybody at the school, they look way down on it," he said.

He added that he's spoken about the atmosphere at the school with at least one teacher he knows is gay, but said the teacher told him if he spoke about it, "he would only be causing trouble."

"It's not right for them to tell you how to dress," the student said. "There's other guys, straight guys, who wear their hair long and in braids, and they haven't said anything to them."

The student said Hamilton's actions "were very traumatizing" and expressed additional concerns after Hamilton, following an interview with CFP, called his mother.

CPS chief legal counsel Marilyn Johnson said the school system has a strict policy barring discrimination based on sexual orientation.

"I can tell you this is an issue that arises from time to time," Johnson said. "We deal with these on a case-by-case basis. We do take these seriously."

Johnson said she would discuss the issues with Hamilton and CHSAS officials and take appropriate action.

(Continued)

PRINCIPAL GIVES HIGH HEELS ON BOYS THE BOOT (Continued)

Rick Garcia, political director for Equality Illinois, expressed outrage at Hamilton's actions.

"It certainly should not be the business of the school to tell this kid what to wear," Garcia said. "If there's no dress code and the child want to wear heels, then it's not appropriate for them to say he can't."

Each CPS school sets its own dress code. At CHSAS, that code is being revised, according to Hamilton. But Garcia and Johnson agreed that the code cannot be used to discriminate against GLBT students.

"It's entirely possible and necessary to accommodate (issues of) blanket discrimination," Johnson said.

The student, who returns to the school this fall as a sophomore, said he intends to continue dressing in a way that he feels is appropriate.

"I identify as whatever I put on in the morning," he said.

Source: Principal Gives High Heels on Boys the Boot. (2002, July 31). *Chicago Free Press.* Reprinted with permission.

Should the student be allowed to dress as a girl? What legal recourse might the student have if the school insists on him dressing like the other boys? Why would the principal and assistant principal be adamant about their position? How might the other students or their parents react to knowing that a boy attends school dressed as a girl?

State Tort and Criminal Law

State tort and criminal laws have also been applied in some cases that involved injury to gay and lesbian youth. Tort laws are the laws attorneys use when one party has caused injury or damage either willfully or negligently to another party (Buckel, 2000). It does not matter whether the person is homo-, bi-, or heterosexual, these laws provide legal recourse to any person who has endured a wrongful act and was injured as a result. So if a lesbian youth repeatedly complained to an assistant school principal that she was being harassed daily by fellow students, and if the assistant principal did nothing to intervene on her behalf, and if the girl was physically injured when a group of students assaulted her at school, the assistant principal (and the assailants, for that matter) would be liable for her sustained injuries. It would be because of his negligence—his failure to adequately address her concerns and the harassment—that she endured physical harm.

Criminal law, on the other hand, can be applied when one person has assaulted another. These laws, like the tort laws, do not necessarily specify sexual orientation or age. An assault is a criminal act, and any youth who assaults another is liable for the victim's sustained injuries. Therefore, if a gay youth is assaulted at school, his parents can file a complaint with police and have their local district attorney handle the case (Buckel, 2000).

Civil-Rights Protection

As we know it today, civil-rights legislation makes it illegal to discriminate against a person based on factors like race, gender, disability, age, and so forth. Because of our civil rights, for instance, a public restaurant cannot refuse service to an African American based solely on his race, and a major hotel chain cannot refuse to accommodate someone in a wheelchair. Currently, however, there is no federal measure that specifically prohibits discrimination based on sexual orientation, which is why gay and lesbian couples are not allowed to marry, and why employers in some states can fire an employee upon learning that he or she is gay or lesbian.

Some states, cities, and counties, however, have passed civil-rights or human-rights laws affording some protection to gay, lesbian, bisexual, or transgender persons against discrimination (see chapter 7). Voting districts that have such civil-rights laws make it illegal, for instance, to deny a lesbian couple from buying a home in a certain neighborhood or to refuse to sell a new car to an openly gay man. Eleven states have some civil-rights laws that prohibit this form of discrimination (Buckel, 2000), and 23 states include sexual orientation in their hate-crime laws. These are found in box 4.2. If a school district is within the jurisdic-

---

 BOX 4.2. GAY, LESBIAN, BISEXUAL, AND TRANSGENDER CIVIL RIGHTS LAWS IN THE UNITED STATES

Laws prohibiting discrimination based on sexual orientation and gender identity

California, Minnesota, New Mexico, and Rhode Island

Laws prohibiting discrimination based on sexual orientation

Connecticut, Hawaii, Maryland, Massachusetts, Nevada, New Hampshire, New Jersey, New York, Vermont, and Wisconsin

As of this writing:

- 119 cities and 23 counties have laws that prohibit sexual-orientation discrimination in private workplaces;
- nine states and the District of Columbia protect against sexual-orientation discrimination in public accommodations and housing; and
- 37 million Americans (14% of the American population) are only protected from sexual-orientation discrimination by their town, city, or county laws.

Sources: Compiled from National Gay and Lesbian Task Force. (2004). *National Gay and Lesbian Task Force GLBT Civil Rights Laws in the U.S.* Retrieved October 28, 2004, from http://www .thetaskforce.org/downloads/nondiscriminationmap.pdf; van der Meide, W. (2003). *Legislating Equality: A Review of Laws Affecting Gay, Lesbian, Bisexual, and Transgendered People Living in the United States.* Retrieved August 18, 2003, from http://www.thetaskforce.org/downloads/legeq99.pdf.

tion of such a law, gay and lesbian students are protected from antigay harassment and violence. A transgender youth who lives in Rhode Island, for instance, and is a target of consistent harassment at school would have recourse against a district for failing to intervene on his behalf.

Equal Access Act

Schools throughout the country generally offer students two types of clubs: (a) those that are directly related to the school curriculum—the marching band, the French club, the swim club, and the like—and (b) those that are noncurricular—the Bible club, the hikers club, the Young Republicans, and so forth. (Consult Lamdba Legal Defense and Education Fund, 1997, *The Equal Access Act: What Does it Mean?* for an in-depth discussion and outline of curricular and noncurricular clubs.) In other words, the curricular clubs are those that further enhance the skills or concepts taught in the school curriculum (e.g., the Spanish Club would be considered curricular if Spanish were a course taught on campus). Noncurricular clubs, whose content is not specifically taught in the curriculum, are often student initiated, social by nature, and are for the avocation of students. The Equal Access Act, passed in 1984 and best associated with allowing students to form Christian/religious clubs in the public schools and meet on campuses during noninstructional time, states,

> It shall be unlawful for any public secondary school which receives Federal financial assistance and which has limited open forum to deny equal access or a fair opportunity to, or discriminate against, any students who wish to conduct a meeting within that limited open forum on the basis of the religious, political, philosophical, or other content of the speech at such meetings. (Lambda Legal Defense and Education Fund, 1997)

Accordingly, if a district permits one noncurricular club to assemble on campus during noninstructional time, the district must allow all forms of noncurricular clubs to assemble (provided that the students are not engaged in lewd acts, harmful behavior, unbecoming conduct, disorderly conduct, etc.) (GLSEN, 2002).

If one noncurricular club exists on campus, then students who want to start a Gay–Straight Alliance (GSA) or other gay-and-lesbian-focused club have the right to equal access to school meeting rooms and resources (Buckel, 2000). Through the Equal Access Act, the courts have found that a district cannot refuse GSA assemblage on the grounds that the district believes that

- the GSA is morally objectionable;
- it might be perceived as "endorsing homosexuality";
- the GSA's discussions are inappropriate for high school students;

- the act does not apply in the district because there are no other noncurricular clubs (when in fact the community-service club, drama club, or class-officer organizations, for instance, exist on campus);
- the GSA will cause disruption among students, parents, and the community; or
- the GSA is under the control of an outside organization. (ACLU, 2003c)

Moreover, school officials cannot arbitrarily impose conditions that do not apply to all the other noncurricular clubs, and they are restricted from requiring that students change their club name from a sexual-orientation reference (e.g., gay, lesbian, diverse sexuality, straight, homosexual) to a more "suitable" one (ACLU, 2003c).

A school district can evade the Equal Access Act and deny access to students who want to start a Gay–Straight Alliance if *all* noncurricular clubs are eliminated. This seems like a drastic measure—to remove all the clubs on campus, from the dance quad to the drama club—simply to ensure that a GSA is not formed at school. And school officials that attempt to reinvent some noncurricular clubs into curricular ones are sure to find themselves in litigation. Lambda Legal Defense and Education has used the Equal Access Act over 20 times in helping students overturn their district's decision (Buckel, 1999).

Have Gay and Lesbian Youth Legally Challenged Their School Systems?

Up until the mid 1990s, virtually no lawsuits had been filed on behalf of gay and lesbian youth for the antigay harassment or discrimination they encountered at school (Buckel, 2000). In the course of gay and lesbian history, litigation for the community had been entirely focused on adult matters. In fact, only one case involving a gay youth had managed its way up to the U.S. district court. The case involved Aaron Fricke, who filed suit against his Cumberland, Rhode Island, high school because he was denied permission to take his love interest and male date, Paul Guilbert, to the senior prom. Fricke garnered much national attention when he won the lawsuit, took Paul to the prom, and went on to write about his experiences in "Reflections of a Rock Lobster." Not another lawsuit on behalf of gay and lesbian youth surfaced again until 1996. Since then, litigation encompassing these youth and their schools has been notable.

Gay and lesbian youth from all walks of life have summoned the courage to stand for what they believe is right and have challenged their school districts in courts of law. Despite the challenges and negative atmosphere associated with suing a district, these youth believed that the ultimate court decision would have a lasting impact on future generations of gay and lesbian youth. The following cases represent a snapshot of what some youth endured prior to the litigation and how their cases paved the way for youth who experience similar injustices.

Jamie Nabozny

Nabozny v. Podlesny was the first case of its kind and is certainly precedent setting (Logue, 1997). An Ashland, Wisconsin, youth, Jamie Nabozny, suffered from repeated harassment and assault throughout his years in middle school and high school because he was gay. He was shoved in a urinal, urinated on, assaulted, mock raped, and even kicked in the stomach so badly he required surgery to stop internal bleeding (Jones, 1999). Despite for his pleas to his principals for help, they did nothing to intervene and responded with comments such as, "boys will be boys" and "[if] you are going to be so openly gay, you have to learn to expect this" (Logue, 1997). His parents' complaints to the principals were also ignored. The harassment became unbearable, and Jamie eventually dropped out of school to pursue his GED.

In 1995, Jamie filed suit against the Ashland Independent School District for failure to protect him from antigay harassment and discrimination. The case was initially dismissed, but after an appeal, a judge ruled that Jamie's case could go to trial. Jamie's attorneys were able to convince a jury that his middle school and high school principals had violated the Equal Protection Clause and had in fact discriminated against him by failing to protect him because of his gender and sexual orientation. The jury found that Jamie deserved recourse, but before damages were awarded, the district settled with Jamie's attorneys for $900,000. In an article summarizing the case, Logue (1997) stated, "For schools that receive reports of anti-gay abuse, Lambda's advice is really quite basic: treat it as seriously as any other type of student abuse. What happened to Jamie is not unusual, and no school should lose sight of the fact that the harassers, not the gay students, are the problem. If classes are to be missed, bus routes changed, schedules altered—it should be those of the perpetrators."

Mark Iversen

The Kent School District (Washington) had antiharassment policies in effect when Mark Iversen was attending their schools. The policies did not stop the students, however, from continuously harassing, assaulting, and discriminating against him. And school officials did little to nothing to enforce the policies or disciplinary actions against the perpetrators.

Mark was in seventh grade when the rumors began that he was gay. As these spread throughout school, the students were relentless in their harassment. Pushing, shoving, taunting him with slurs, and threatening him with physical violence were a daily occurrence. In the course of five years Mark experienced the following:

- A P.E. teacher told him, "I already have 20 girls in my class. I don't need another."
- Students shoved him into a locker with a broomstick and told him to "fuck it."
- His nipples were violently rubbed by a boy who had lifted Mark's shirt and had made harassing comments.

- Another student slapped a death-threat letter to Mark's chest. The note read, "You [*sic*] dead fag."
- Students harassed him after a teacher told students that gay men put gerbils in their rectums for sexual pleasure (an urban myth).
- A student tried to poison Mark by dipping his pencil in chemicals; the student admitted to wanting to kill Mark, but school officials dismissed the student's concession.
- A teacher commented, "Are you sure they would want your blood?" when Mark was about to donate blood. (Iversen, 1998)

Mark's mother, Alice, appealed to school officials (14 times) in vain, often hearing comments such as "What did Mark do to start this?" "What can Mark do to stop it?" and "Mark should expect this" (Iversen, 1998).

In October 1996, shortly after having left a letter with his principal, again asking for help, some students went looking for Mark. As he sat on a stool, working on the school yearbook, some eight students surrounded him, shoved him to the floor, and proceeded to kick him. Nearly 30 students witnessed and encouraged the beating. Some spit on him, and others yelled, "kill the faggot." This incident was the last straw for the Iversens, and they decided to file suit against the Kent School District. Nearly a year later, Mark reached an out-of-court settlement that required the district to compensate Mark $40,000, enforce antiharassment policies protecting all students from persecution, and provide professional development to school personnel on antigay harassment and discrimination matters (ACLU, 1998b). Alice Iversen reflected on her son's ordeal and mentioned, "My husband and I were raised as Christians, and we have raised our children in a Christian home. The religious extremist attitudes of intolerance, hatred, judgment and condemnation are not what Christianity is about. God doesn't want hatred and violence. He wants people to be more tolerant, compassionate, understanding and to help others. God loves everyone" (Iversen, 1998).

Alma McGowen

That students perceived Alma McGowen to be a lesbian was reason enough for some to launch harassment toward her, ranging from taunts to the sexually explicit. The Kentucky student experienced harassment throughout her middle school years, and despite her complaints to Spencer County Public School District school officials, the harassment continued, allegedly because school officials did nothing to curb the harassment other than talk to or suspend the perpetrators. An assistant principal even told her that she should take the boys' flirtations with stride and "be friendly" with them because the flirts were their way of showing they thought she was cute. One student stabbed Alma's hand with a pen and later told her he was not punished for the incident because he was the son of a board member; another youth, the principal's nephew, demanded in front of other students that Alma confirm whether she was "gay" (Associated Press, 2000a).

As early as her second day in sixth grade, some students yelled, "Oh, there's that German gay girl, that new girl that just moved here" (Russell, 2000). During her middle school years, the harassment she experienced grew severe:

- a male student asked her to describe oral sex;
- students shoved her against walls;
- students grabbed her personal belongings and destroyed them;
- students propositioned her for sex in nearly every class;
- books were thrown at her;
- a male student told her the KKK would burn down her house;
- a male student called her a "whore" and a "motherfucker," hit her, snapped her bra, and grabbed her buttocks; and
- a male student touched her chest and buttocks and asked for her for sex. (Russell, 2000)

Alma, taunted as the "lezzie," was even once held by a group of students while they pulled off her blouse, and a boy, who had pulled down his pants, proceeded to threaten her with rape (Associated Press, 2000a). In response to the incident, a teacher brought the group of boys together, sat Alma among them, and asked her to tell them what they had done wrong. When Alma complained about one particular boy, school officials talked to him, but the boy later recounted to her that he did not "give a damn about it and he would do whatever he wanted to" (Russell, 2000).

No matter the degree of her complaints, the harassment never subsided and grew too much for Alma to handle. She withdrew from school on August 31, 1995, and later filed suit against the Spencer County School District. Alma's lawyers were able to prove that even though the school officials had known she could be harmed in the hostile environment, they had failed to act effectively to stop the harassment. Alma won her case and was awarded $220,000. A spokesperson for Equal Rights Advocates, a public-interest law firm for women and girls, emphasized, "The court really makes it clear that if you do something and it doesn't work, you need to do something else. . . . That's where the school system failed—they didn't take stronger measures to try to make it stop" (We Are Michigan, 2000).

Bradley Putman

In southeastern Kentucky, Bradley Putman was a student at Somerset High School for the 1997–1998 school year, where he was victim to "hostile, offensive, threatening and unwelcome verbal, visual, and physical conduct of a sexual nature," all because fellow classmates perceived that Brad was gay (Williams, 2000). Brad complained to school officials, but nothing was done to stop the harassment, as the perpetrators were never punished or suspended.

In addition to being ridiculed on a nearly daily basis, two incidents magnified the degree of hostility directed toward him. During Christmastime, a group of students, motivated to embarrass and humiliate Brad, created a card that was to be from Brad to another male student also suspected of being gay. Sexually explicit comments were written on the Christmas card and then circulated among the student body. The students then yelled derisive comments at Brad as he walked through the hallway. In another incident, unidentified students spray painted on the parking lot surface two male stick figures engaged in sex. Below the painting was the caption, "This is for you Brad Butman [sic]" (Williams, 2000). Even though Brad's father complained to the principal about the lewd drawing, the painting was not removed for four days.

Brad endured many forms of harassment, including receiving three death threats, being grabbed in the groin to test how he would respond, and being verbally abused and asked if he was gay. His complaints and those of his parents seemed to matter to no one. School officials told the Putmans that Brad should "hold his head high" and "not pay attention to these students" (Williams, 2000). One school official responded that she did not know what to do; another said, "boys will boys"; and the school board chairman never responded to the Putman's letter of complaint. The Putmans, who complained to six district officials, filed suit against the Somerset Independent School District because the district "discriminated against him by deliberately and intentionally failing to take prompt and effective steps to end the hostile and offensive sexual-harassment campaign" (Famularo, 2000). The district later settled with the Putmans, agreeing to pay Brad $135,000. The district also adopted a stringent policy forbidding harassment and discrimination based on real or perceived sexual orientation.

Timothy Dahle

Even though the Titusville Area School District denies any wrongdoing, they settled to pay their former student Timothy Dahle $312,000 because of his claims that school officials failed to protect him from the verbal and physical harassment he experienced in their schools. Timothy (and his classmates) came to realize he was gay/bisexual when he was in sixth grade, and shortly thereafter he became victim to name-calling, obscene jokes, and taunting. He was punched in the neck, sent threatening notes, and was even pushed down a flight of stairs (Associated Press, 2000b). Timothy complained about the harassment to school officials, and they responded by removing him from the classes where his tormentors were. The harassment, however, continued. According to Timothy, school officials seemed indifferent to his pleas for help. During one complaint, the principal responded that it was Timothy's own fault that he was being harassed (Sherman, 2002). And when the harassment became very bad for him during gym class and he walked to the principal's office to complain, he was reprimanded for leaving a class in the middle of a period.

Timothy started to skip school to avoid the harassment, he became depressed, and he even ended up in the hospital from an overdose on drugs days before he was to be a sophomore. His mother testified, "It was a struggle to get him to go to school because he was afraid. . . . He'd get up in the morning and start getting ready for school. He would start throwing up, literally shaking, almost like a panic attack" (Palattella, 2001). Timothy eventually dropped out of high school and filed suit against the district, to which the district replied, "Our fundamental position is that if what he says was happening, he wasn't telling the administrators about it" (Palattella, 2001). District officials also asserted that his aggressiveness was to blame for his problems with the students. A settlement was reached before the case was set for trial.

George Loomis

Golden West High School student George Loomis was an active student council member before his classmates singled him out as gay, whereupon his troubles began (McIntosh, 2001). In fact, he dropped out of school in the remaining months of his senior year because the hostility directed toward him was overwhelming. George was spit on and subjected to many antigay epithets. One of George's teachers even said to him, "There are only two types of guys who wear earrings—pirates and faggots—and there isn't any water around here" (Heredia, 2002).

George complained to his administrators, and the most they could do for him was transfer him to a tutoring program. George explained why he filed suit against the Visalia Unified School District: "I couldn't stand silent while they violated my civil rights or the civil rights of other students. It's an injustice if I stay quiet about it, because we're at a perfect time to speak out and create change. And I know how hard it is to be harassed at school because you're gay or perceived to be gay. I wasn't out at school, and that made it worse, because at that time I was only perceived as being gay" (McIntosh, 2001, p. 37). The district settled with George for $130,000, and as part of a consent decree agreed to

- institute harassment and discrimination policies and procedures;
- provide professional development for K–12 teachers that leads to the prevention of harassment and discrimination based on a student's sexual orientation;
- provide training for all freshmen that leads to the prevention of sexual-orientation harassment or discrimination; and

• designate compliance coordinators to monitor sexual-orientation harassment and discrimination reports at each school. (Ashoka.org, 2002)

Derek Henkle

Derek Henkle was attending Galena High School in Reno, Nevada, when he experienced a living nightmare. A group of boys surrounded him in a parking lot, took out a lasso, and said, "Let's lasso the fag and tie him to the back of the truck and drag him down the highway" (Shenitz, 2002, p. 99). Derek literally ran for his life and managed to escape the lasso that was tied around his neck three times. Derek ran to a classroom and called the vice principal, who showed up two hours later. Derek was hysterical, but instead of understanding the seriousness of the incident, the vice principal laughed over the fact that Derek couldn't speak coherently. She then put Derek on the same school bus that the perpetrators rode. Luckily the bus driver honored Derek's request to drop off all the students first (Shenitz, 2002).

Derek came out to his mother at the young age of 12, after she asked him if he was gay. Because there were no support programs for gay and lesbian youth in his community, he began to hang out with the college students at the gay, lesbian, and bisexual student association at the University of Nevada at Reno (Shenitz, 2002). At school he had been the target of some verbal abuse, but it was not until after he appeared on a public-access TV show about gay high school students that the severity of the harassment intensified. He appeared on the show because he did not think anyone would watch it, given its small viewership. A student recognized Derek on the segment and later asked him if he had been on a show with a "bunch of fags" and if he was gay. Derek answered honestly, and that's when the hatred and intolerance poured on.

Students assaulted him; teased him with epithets such "fag," "butt muncher," and "butt pirate"; shoved him in lockers; threw things at him; pushed him in the hallways; and spit food on him. His school officials seemed to do nothing to help him out of the hostile environment, sometimes ignoring his plight. He filled out one incident report after another to no avail. In fact, school administrators told him that he was the problem and accused him of visiting the administrative office (where he filled out the reports) to avoid class. His school administrators finally decided to transfer him, "the problem," to an alternative high school, but he was instructed not to talk about being gay. There, he was told to take the political pins off of his backpack, and the principal told him, "I will not have you acting like a fag in my school" (Shenitz, 2002, p. 103). Derek eventually transferred to a third school to take college prep courses, whereupon he was beaten in the schoolyard while two security officers did nothing to intervene.

Derek dropped out of school and filed a lawsuit against the Washoe County School District. Derek and school officials signed a settlement agreement that awarded him

$451,000. The district also agreed to create and implement policies protecting gay and lesbian youth and to train faculty and staff in how to respond to antigay harassment and intimidation (Lamba Legal Defense and Education Fund, 2002).

Flores v. Morgan Hill Unified School District

Six students in Santa Clara, California, filed suit against the Morgan Hill Unified School District because of their school administrators' (at Live Oak High School and Murphy Middle School) failure to protect them from the antigay harassment they endured at school. At the time of the harassment, which occurred from 1991 to 1998, all of the students were or were perceived to be gay, lesbian, or bisexual. The students allege that each suffered repeated antigay harassment in one form or another and that school administrators refused to take the action needed to protect them from harm.

One student, Alana Flores, had a note and a pornographic photo taped to her locker that read, "Die, die, dyke bitch. Fuck off. We'll kill you" (PFLAG, 2003). When she went to complain, the principal reportedly said, "You need to go back to class. Don't bring me this trash anymore. This is disgusting" (PFLAG, 2003). Alana asked to change lockers, but her request was denied, even though the administrators had before allowed students to change lockers to be closer to their friends (ACLU, 1998a). Alana claims that her school administrators did very little to remedy her learning environment, which included bullying behavior and harassment. The middle school student, referred to as F.F., was hospitalized with severe bruising of his ribs when a group of six boys shouted, "Faggot, you don't belong here," and began to hit and kick him on the school bus. The bus driver had full view of the incident but took no action (ACLU, 1998a). F.F.'s mother complained to the police and to school administrators, but the only disciplinary action taken was against one of the perpetrators. School administrators later transferred F.F. to another school. In another case, two female high school students who were dating each other during their senior year had students yell antigay comments and make sexual gestures at them. Once, a group of boys shouted slurs at them and threw a plastic cup at them. When the two females complained to the assistant principal, she advised them to report the incident to the campus police officer, but she never followed up on the matter.

In 1998, the students filed suit against their school administrators. School officials denied treating the antigay harassment any differently than other harassment complaints and pled that they should be immune from the law because, at the time, it was unclear as to how schools should handle antigay harassment (Worrall, 2003). The ninth circuit court of appeals decided that it was the duty and responsibility of school officials to protect students from antigay harassment and abuse and returned the case to the federal district court for trial (National Center for Lesbian Rights, 2003). The district settled out of court for

$1.1 million in 2004 and agreed to hold training sessions for students and teachers (until 2008) to deter future antigay harassment (Associated Press, 2004). The Lesbian and Gay Rights Project of the ACLU (representing the students) asserted, "The court made it clear that going through the motions is not enough. Schools have to really deal with the problem of antigay harassment" (Worrall, 2003).

Thomas McLaughlin

In 2003, a lawsuit was filed on behalf of 14-year-old Thomas McLaughlin against the Pulaski County Special School District (Little Rock, Arkansas) when school officials at Jacksonville Junior High repeatedly punished Thomas for being openly gay. According to Thomas's attorneys at the ACLU (2003b), the school officials were out of line in the following actions:

- A school official phoned Thomas's mother to inform her that her son was gay; Thomas was not inclined or prepared to come out to his parents.
- A teacher had a conference with Thomas's mother and principal to complain that she opposed Thomas's being so openly gay, to which the principal replied that she found it equally objectionable that Thomas was walking around school and talking about being gay.
- A teacher told Thomas and his mother that she was "sickened" by his sexual orientation.
- A school official preached the Bible to him and asked him to read aloud verses from it as punishment for disagreeing with a teacher for calling him "abnormal" and "unnatural."
- A school official suspended him for telling his friends that he was forced to read from the Bible.
- Thomas was disciplined for talking with a female friend about a boy they both considered "cute"; his friend was not disciplined.

Thomas settled with the school district for $25,000, a letter of apology from school officials, and clearance of his disciplinary record. In accordance with the settlement, the district was barred from disclosing a student's sexual orientation to others, punishing students for discussing their sexual orientation outside the classroom, discriminating against students based on their sexual orientation, and preaching to students or making them read from the Bible. An ACLU (2003a) attorney emphasized, "What happened to Thomas McLaughlin probably happens more often than you might suspect, and his bravery in coming forward is amazing."

East High Gay–Straight Alliance v. Board of Education of Salt Lake City School District and *Colin v. Orange Unified School District*

The students at East High School in Utah and the students in Orange County, California, shared similar discrimination by school officials when the students decided to start Gay–Straight Alliances in their high schools. In October 1995, the students at East High were eager to start a club to increase diversity awareness and to provide a forum to discuss and discourage homophobia, prejudice, antigay violence, and so forth (Lambda Legal Defense and Education Fund, 1998). Soon after the students formed the GSA, however, the school board banned all noncurricular clubs so that the GSA could not be honored as an official club and allowed to meet on campus. By doing so, the district was in compliance with the Equal Access Act. In all, 46 noncurricular student clubs were eliminated. Members of the GSA, however, noted that some former noncurricular clubs were being reclassified as curricular and that other noncurricular clubs were still allowed to meet. In 1998, the students filed suit against the board for violation of the Equal Access Act. The board then announced a policy indicating "that there was no prohibition on expression of gay-positive viewpoints in curricular settings" (Lambda Legal Defense and Education Fund, 2000b).

In 1999, students submitted an application to start a curricular club focusing on government, history, and sociology matters that affect gay and lesbian persons. The club was to be called PRISM, which stood for People Respecting Important Social Movements (Lambda Legal Defense and Education Fund, 2000a). The district denied them the recognition of a student club, and the students filed suit. A preliminary injunction allowed the club to meet while the students' case was tied up in the courts. The school board eventually lifted the ban, and both lawsuits were dropped in 2000. David Buckel, senior staff attorney for Lambda Legal Defense and Education Fund (representing the students), ended, "The trend in schools is to recognize that gay-supportive student groups promote better and safer schools. The lesson from Salt Lake City is in big block letters on the chalkboard: do not harm your students to block a gay-supportive club and do not spend hundreds of thousands in education dollars defending that harm. Do the right thing from the beginning" (Lambda Legal Defense and Education Fund, 2000b).

About the same time the Utah students were having their legal woes, some students in Orange County were having theirs. Even though the school board had a nondiscrimination policy that read, "The board shall not discriminate or deny access to any student initiated group on the basis of religious, political, philosophical or any other content to be addressed at such meetings," the school board stalled in giving the students permission to meet as an official club (Lamda Legal Defense and Education Fund, 1999). About 50 students at El Modena High School expressed interest in starting and joining a Gay–Straight Alliance in fall 1999, but the delay left them unable to meet for a whole semester. When the students again asked for approval and recognition to meet as a club, the district asked for more time and then asked how the GSA would be categorized. During this whole time, the students were banned from meeting, and their principal denied them permission to set up a table or hang a banner, like other school clubs did, during a school fair. The students filed suit against the district, and a U.S. district court judge issued a preliminary injunction allowing the students to meet on campus while the case proceeded. The district settled that they would recognize the GSA as an official school club.

In short, a pattern exists among these cases. All of these students were harassed in ways unimaginable for most, and when they summoned the courage to complain, the school administrators seemed indifferent and ignored or trivialized the complaints. In some instances, perhaps, an administrator or two tried to intervene, but the fact of the matter is that not enough was done, because the harassment continued. Simply put, if a student complains about antigay harassment to you, do something about it. It is not enough to dismiss the matter with, "I did the best I could." The harassment, bullying behavior, antigay discrimination, or whatever you name it has to be eliminated. Even if you disapprove of or remain uncomfortable around gay and lesbian persons, it is your duty as a youth-serving professional to shield all students from verbal and physical harm and to promote a hostility-free learning environment. Neglecting this duty is sure to leave some students robbed of their adolescence and scarred for life.

 HOW WOULD YOU DECIDE?

The following are actual cases where students or their parents filed legal complaints against their educational organization. How would you decide the outcomes?

1. School administrators expel 18-year-old student Jeffrey Woodard from the Jupiter Christian School after they find out that he is gay. A Bible-class teacher pulled Jeffrey Woodard aside and in confidence asked him if he was gay. Jeffrey said yes, and the teacher then told Jeffrey's mother. The school told Jeffery he had three choices: get therapy for his "problem," voluntarily leave school, or be expelled. Private schools in Florida have the right to discriminate because of sexual orientation.

2. Students of a Department of Defense high school in Okinawa, Japan, have their gay-and-lesbian-youth support club officially terminated, in part because of the "Don't Ask, Don't Tell" military rule. The students want their club reinstated.

3. A father of a 12-year-old boy files a claim for over $100,000 in damages against the Pacifica School District, alleging that school administrators did nothing to prevent the physical abuse and taunts his son endured. The father met with school principals and had documented 120 incidents of harassment directed toward his son, including the following:

   • boys telling him in the bathroom, "You don't belong in this one";
   • boys calling him a "gay fashion model";

(Continued)

HOW WOULD YOU DECIDE? (Continued)

- boys singing loudly that he "is gay";
- having gum thrown in his hair;
- having his backpack ripped from him; and
- being almost kicked to the ground.

The school claims that it took the necessary steps to respond to the harassment by suspending one boy, disciplining others, sending letters to the parents of the perpetrators, and so forth.

4. A lesbian student at Encinas High School in Sacramento wanted to run for prom king, but she alleges that she was discriminated against because her school officials would not allow her name to be on the ballot. Administrators assert that only boys can run for prom king, and girls can run for prom queen. Was the student discriminated against?

5. Josh Rivers was a 15-year-old student attending a Texas high school when he told a close friend that he was gay. Some students found out about his sexual orientation, and then they started to spread rumors about him. When one student alleged that Josh had fondled him and had then threatened to burn down the school, a local sheriff jailed Josh for two weeks in a juvenile detention center. The charges were eventually dropped, but Josh was told he could only return to the district's alternative-education program for students with emotional disturbances. Josh was the only student in the program without prior emotional problems.

6. Students at Westside High School in Nebraska wanted to place an advertisement in their high school newspaper for Proud Horizons, a support group for gay, lesbian, bisexual, and transgender youth. The newspaper refused to run the ad even though they had run other politically charged ads before.

Sources: (1) Ortega, F. (2003). *Student sues after school expels him for being gay.* Retrieved on October 28, 2003, from http://www.easyboyfriend.com/news-66.htm; (2) Lambda. (1997). *Gay youth support group v. Department of Defense.* Retrieved on October 28, 2003, from http://www.lambdalegal.org/cgi-bin/iowa/cases/record?record=58; (3) Wong, N. (2003). *Father sues school; alleges district allowed antigay slurs against son.* Retrieved on October 2, 2003, from http://www.glsen.org/templates/news/record.htm?section=12&record=1637; (4) Associated Press. (2002). *Lesbian not allowed to run for prom king.* Retrieved on July 23, 2003, from http://www.glsen.org/templates/news/record.html?section=12&record=1317; (5) and (6) ACLU. (2001). *Schools and youth highlights.* Retrieved on October 28, 2003, from http://www.aclu.org/safeschools/Update.html.

Summary

In his years as an elementary school teacher in rural Alabama and Harlem, New York, Ron Clark (2003) created a series of rules to help his students acquire proper social skills and manners. All of these rules were consolidated into his book titled *The Essential 55: An Award-*

Winning Educator's Rules for Discovering the Successful Student in Every Child. Among the 55
rules, one captures the sentiment of this chapter best. Rule #48 reads,

> If any child in this school is bothering you, let me know. I am your teacher, and I am here
> to look after you and protect you. I am not going to let anyone in this school bully you
> or make you feel uncomfortable. In return, I ask that you do not take matters into your
> own hands; let me deal with the students.

All students, regardless of their sexual orientation, should know that their teachers care
enough to protect them as much as they can from all forms of harm. All students should
feel safe from physical and emotional harm in your classroom and school regardless of their
gender, academic and physical ability, socioeconomic status, race or ethic background, sexual orientation, or anything else. No harassment, intimidation, or bullying in school should
be tolerated or trivialized, period. How in the world can we expect youth to reach their academic, emotional, and social potential if they feel unsafe in school?

Although no federal law exists clearly defining that school districts must specifically
protect gay and lesbian students from violent behaviors, the Office of Civil Rights has provided school districts with guidelines on how to protect all students from harassment and
hate crimes. Needless to say, gay and lesbian youth are addressed throughout the U.S.
Department of Education document *Protecting Students from Harassment and Hate Crimes:
A Guide for School.* Any school employee that fails to protect gay and lesbian youth from
any maltreatment (or antigay violence) is likely to land themselves in a losing court battle.

None of the youth who legally challenged their school district ever set out to sue their
school officials. These youth wanted a normal adolescence without the fear of going to or
being at school. They all believed and expected that their teachers and staff were looking
out for their best interest and were going to support them in their time of need. They were
unfortunately mistaken. Their ordeals could have been averted had school personnel taken
the time to plan for and demand a respectful, tolerant, and safe learning environment.

Idea File

1. Read the cases outlined in box 4.2 and contemplate how you would handle the
   matters.
2. Devise a survey to evaluate how safe your students feel in school. Administer the
   survey to some students and then use their responses to spark a discussion on
   respect, tolerance, and safety in school. Design a safe-schools initiative of your own;
   perhaps have students sign contractual agreements pledging to facilitate a safer
   learning environment. Review *Great Ideas for Safe Schools: A Collection of Safe*

Schools Programs and Strategies from the Attorney General and State Superintendent of Public Instruction Safe Schools Task Force (found on the California Department of Education website) for additional suggestions.

References

American Civil Liberties Union. (1998a). *Federal court upholds students' right to sue school district over harassment.* Retrieved October 26, 2003, from http://archive.aclu.org/news/n110598a.html.

American Civil Liberties Union. (1998b). *Settlement reached with school district in lawsuit over gay student harassment.* Retrieved October 18, 2003, from http://archive.aclu.org/news/n111398a.html.

American Civil Liberties Union. (2003a). *ACLU secures sweeping changes in Arkansas school district.* Retrieved October 18, 2003, from www.glsenscw.org/aclu_in_ark.pdf.

American Civil Liberties Union. (2003b). *ACLU warns Arkansas school to stop persecuting gay student.* Retrieved October 18, 2003, from http://www.aclu.org/news/NewsPrint.cfm?ID=12082&c=106.

American Civil Liberties Union. (2003c). *Letter to school officials regarding gay/straight alliances.* Retrieved October 15, 2003, from http://www.aclu.org/news/NewsPrint.cfm?ID=9180&c=106.

American Civil Liberties Union. (2003d). *Preventing harassment and protecting free speech in school.* Retrieved October 15, 2003, from http://aclu.org/news/NewsPrint.cfm?ID=12901&c=106.

American Civil Liberties Union. (2003e). *Your right to free expression.* Retrieved October 15, 2003, from http://www.aclu.org/news/NewsPrint.cfm?ID=13149&c=159.

Amherst H. Wilder Foundation. (1997). *The little book of peace.* St. Paul, MN: Author.

Ashoka.org. (2002). *GSA network and Visalia Unified School District reach historic settlement in anti-discrimination case.* Retrieved October 24, 2003, from http://www.ashoka.org/us-canada/about/us_090302.cmf.

Associated Press. (2000a). Harassment case in Ky. puts schools on notice: Ky. girl's lawsuit, damages are upheld. *The Enquirer.* Retrieved October 22, 2003, from http://www.enquirer.com/editions/2000/11/11/loc_harassment_case_in.html.

Associated Press. (2000b). Teen sues school district over anti-gay harassment. *Pittsburgh Post-Gazette.* Retrieved October 24, 2003, from http://www.post-gazette.com/regionstate/20000626gay8.asp.

Associated Press. (2004). *California school district settles gay harassment suit.* Retrieved January 29, 2004, from http://cnnfyi.printhis.clickability.com/pt/cpt?action=cpt&title=CNN.com+-+California+sc.

Buckel, D. S. (1999). *Youth bring gay rights movement to school.* Retrieved October 2, 2003, from http://www.lambdalegal.org/cgi-bin/iowa/documents/record?record=494.

Buckel, D. S. (2000). Legal perspective on ensuring a safe and nondiscriminatory school environment for lesbian, gay, bisexual, and transgendered students. *Education and Urban Society, 32*(3), 390–98.

Bureau of Justice Statistics. (2000a). *Criminal victimization 1999—Changes 1998–99 with trends 1993–99.* Washington, DC: U.S. Department of Justice.

Bureau of Justice Statistics. (2000b). *Indicators of school crime and safety 2000.* Washington, DC: U.S. Department of Justice.

California Department of Education. (2003). *Bullying at school.* Sacramento: Counseling and Student Support Office, California Department of Education.

Campos, D. (2002). *Sex, youth, and sex education: A reference handbook.* Santa Barbara: ABC-CLIO.

Clark, R. (2003). *The Essential 55: An Award-Winning Educator's Rules for Discovering the Successful Student in Every Child.* New York: Hyperion Press.

Coloroso, B. (2003). *The bully, the bullied, and the bystander: From preschool to high school—how parents and teachers can help break the cycle of violence.* New York: HarperCollins.

Dwyer, K., Osher, D., & Warger, C. (1998). *Early warning, timely response: A guide to safe schools.* Washington, DC: U.S. Department of Education.

Empower Program. (2001). *Knowledge network survey.* New York: Liz Claiborne Inc., Author.

Famularo, J. L. (2000). *United States' Memorandum as amicus curiae in opposition to defendants' motion to dismiss introduction and interest of the United States.* Retrieved on October 22, 2003, from http://www.usdoj.gov/crt/edo/documents/utmanbr1.htm.

Franklin, K. (2003). *Psychosocial Motivations of Hate Crime Perpetrators: Implications for Prevention and Policy.* Retrieved November 25, 2003, from http://www.apa.org/ppo/issues/pfranklin.html.

Gay, Lesbian and Straight Education Network. (2002). *Laws and policies impacting LGBT youth in schools.* Retrieved October 1, 2003, from http://glsen.com.

Heredia, C. (2002). *Gay tolerance program to be implemented.* Retrieved August 23, 2002, from http://www.glsen.org/templates/news/record.html?section=12&record=1394.

Horatio Alger Association of Distinguished Americans. (1999). *State of our nation's youth 1999.* Alexandria, VA: Author.

Iversen, A. (1998). *Alice Iversen speaks out on child abuse against gay kids.* Retrieved October 18, 2003, from http://www.aclu-wa.org/issues/lesbiangay/AliceIversen.html.

Jennings, K. (2003). *Always my child: A parent's guide to understanding your gay, lesbian, bisexual, transgendered or questioning son or daughter.* New York: Simon & Schuster.

Jones, R. (1999). "I don't feel safe here anymore": Your legal duty to protect gay kids from harassment. *American School Board Journal, 186*(11), 27–31.

Josephson Institute of Ethics. (2001). *Report card on the ethics of American youth 2000, report #1: Violence, guns and alcohol.* Los Angeles: Author.

Kirby, D. (2001, July 3). What makes a bully? *The Advocate,* pp. 31–34.

Kragthorpe, C, & Jefferson, K. (1999). *Kids killing kids: A thoughtful response.* St. Paul, MN: Minnesota Department of Human Services.

Lambda Legal Defense and Education Fund. (1997). *The Equal Access Act: What does it mean?* Retrieved October 15, 2003, from http://www.lambdalegal.org/cgi-bin/pages/documents/record?record=78.

Lambda Legal Defense and Education Fund. (1998). *High school students sue Salt Lake City school board.* Retrieved October 26, 2003, from http://www.lambdalegal.org/cgi-bin/pages/documents/record?record=222.

Lambda Legal Defense and Education Fund. (1999). *Gay/straight alliance students sue Orange County high school.* Retrieved October 26, 2003, from http://www.lambdalegal.org/cgi-bin/pages/documents/record?record=529.

Lambda Legal Defense and Education Fund. (2000a). *Judge orders school to make room for student club with gay perspective.* Retrieved October 26, 2003, from http://www.lambdalegal.org/cgi-bin/pages/documents/record?record=630.

Lambda Legal Defense and Education Fund. (2000b). *Students and Salt Lake City school board end feud over gay-supportive clubs.* Retrieved October 26, 2003, from http://www.lambdalegal.org/cgi-bin/pages/documents/record?record=721.

Lambda Legal Defense and Education Fund. (2001). Henkle v. Gregory: *Preliminary victory!* Retrieved October 12, 2003, from http://www.lambdalegal.org/cgi-bin/pages/cases/record?record=128.

Lambda Legal Defense and Education Fund. (2002). *Groundbreaking legal settlement is first to recognize constitutional right of gay and lesbian students to be out at school & protected from harassment.* Retrieved October 2, 2003, from http://www.lambdalegal.org/cgi-bin/iowa/documents/record?record=119.

Logue, P. M. (1997). *Near $1 million settlement raises standard for protection of gay youth.* Retrieved October 12, 2003, from http://lambdalegal.org/cgi-bin/iowa/documents/record?record=56.

McIntosh, S. (2001, April 10). The new gay youth revolution. *The Advocate,* pp. 34–37.

Nansel, T., Overpeck, M., Pilla, R., Ruan, W., Simons-Morton, B., & Scheidt, P. (2001). Bullying behaviors among U.S. youth: Prevalence and association with psychosocial adjustment. *Journal of the American Medical Association, 285*(16), 2094–2100.

National Center for Education Statistics. (2003). *Indicators of school crime and safety: 2003.* Washington, DC: U.S. Department of Education & U.S. Department of Justice.

National Center for Lesbian Rights. (2003). Flores v. Morgan Hill Unified School District. Retrieved on October 26, 2003, from http://nclr.org/cases/flores.htm.

National Center for Student Aspirations. (2001). *The students speak survey.* Orono, MN: University of Maine.

National Crime Prevention Council and ADT Security Services Inc. (1999). *Are we safe? The 1999 national crime prevention survey.* Washington,m DC: Author.

Palattella, E. (2001). *Gay teenager pushes claims that school didn't stop harassment.* Retrieved October 24, 2003, from http://www.youth.org/loco/PERSONProject/Alerts/States/Pennsylvania/lawsuit3.html.

PFLAG. (2003). *PFLAG applauds groundbreaking decision proclaiming that schools must protect gay students from harassment.* Retrieved October 26, 2003, from http://www.pflag.org/press/030410.html.

Quittner, J. (2001, August 28). Death of a two spirit: A Colorado town searches for answers in the senseless death of a transgendered Navajo teenager. *The Advocate,* pp. 24–26.

Readerforum. (2001, August 28). Bully pulpit. *The Advocate, 845,* 4-6.

Russell, T. B. (2000). *Appeal from the United States district court for the western district of Kentucky at Louisville.* Retrieved October 22, 2003, from http://laws.lpfindlaw.com/6th/00a0385p.html.

Shenitz, B. (2002, March). Fighting back. *Out,* pp. 99–103, 118–20.

Sherman, J. (2002). *District settles suit.* Retrieved October 24, 2003, from http://www.kidithart.com/titusville.htm.

Southern Poverty Law Center. (1998). *Ten ways to fight hate: A community response guide to hate crime and hate groups*. Retrieved November 26, 2003, from http://www.tolerance.org/10_ways/index/html.

USA Weekend. (2000). *A special report on teens & safety: Our kids are afraid*. Retrieved November 22, 2003, from http://www.usaweekend.com/00_issues/000416/000416teen.html.

U.S. Department of Education. (2000). *2000 annual report on school safety*. Washington, DC: Author.

U.S. Department of Education. (2001). *Sexual discrimination: Overview of the law*. Washington, DC: U.S. Department of Education.

Washington State School Safety Center. (2003). *Model harassment, intimidation and bullying training*. Retrieved October 17, 2003, from http://www.k12.wa.us/safetycenter/bullying.asp.

We Are Michigan. (2000). *Verdict upheld in harassment of student thought to be lesbian*. Retrieved October 22, 2003, from http://www.wearemichigan.com/safeschools/articles/art33.html.

Williams, D. (2000). *Kentucky student sues school officials over anti-gay harassment: high school teen forced to change schools after 3 death threats*. Retrieved October 22, 2003, from http://gaytoday.badpuppy.com/garchive/events/040500ev.htm.

Worrall, M. (2003). *Gay students win major court battle*. Retrieved October 26, 2003, from http://www.tampabaycoalition.com/files/409GayStudentsWinMajorCourtBattle.html.

2

Rainbow Flags, Stonewall Inn, and GLBT Persons: A Primer about the Gay and Lesbian Community

Terms and Symbols Defined

MATCHING QUIZ

How well do you know the terms associated with the gay, lesbian, bisexual, and transgender community? Take a moment to test your knowledge on the following terms:

1. Bi _____
2. Breeder(s) _____
3. Butch _____
4. Coming out _____
5. Closeted _____
6. Drag _____
7. FTM _____
8. Gender identity _____
9. Heterosexism _____
10. Intersexual _____
11. Lambda _____
12. Gay pride _____
13. Questioning _____
14. Sexual orientation _____
15. Transgender _____

a. phrase that describes acknowledging or revealing a sexual identity

b. to dress in clothes traditionally assigned to the opposite sex, often in an exaggerated or stereotypical manner

c. describes female-to-male transgender persons

d. a Greek alphabet letter that represents the community

e. celebration of the gay, lesbian, bisexual, and transgender community

f. persons born with genitals of both genders

g. the assumption that everyone is or should be heterosexual

h. slang term for bisexual persons

i. concealing or hiding a sexual identity or sexual orientation

j. self-perception of being male, female, both, or neither

k. a person's core romantic and erotic attractions for the opposite, same, or both genders

l. an umbrella term used to describe persons whose gender identity and expression is opposite of their biological gender

m. slang term for heterosexual persons

n. persons exploring their sexual and/or gender identity

o. slang term for males or females with masculine qualities

Overview

This next sequence of chapters discusses aspects of the gay and lesbian community. Use these as an introduction to this unique community and as a reference guide to unfamiliar matters in the text. You may be inclined to skip over the chapters, but doing so deprives you of the opportunity to learn about an interesting, historically significant, and eminent group of persons. Reading these chapters not only broadens your horizons, but it provides a foundation for the impromptu moments when students, faculty, staff, or parents seek clarification (e.g., "Mrs. R, is it OK to refer to someone as queer?"), or for lessons that demystify students' notions about gay and lesbian persons (e.g., "Mr. K, I heard that sexual orientation is a choice. Is that true?"). Moreover, you model respect when you use accurate and inclusive language and references.

The matching quiz provided here introduces some of the terms and symbols commonly associated with the gay and lesbian community. The definitions to these terms in this chapter are basic and are likely debatable because they are labels that carry cultural, economic, generational, geographic, and political influences (Saint Paul Public Schools, n.d.).

Nonetheless, they are a starting point. Keep in mind that just because you will be familiar with these terms, many gay, lesbian, bisexual, and transgender youth will not be (e.g., Leslie may tell you she's gay, but she may be insulted or offended if you call her a lesbian or a dyke). As such, use the labels or terms carefully and avoid the slang. This chapter addresses the following questions:

- What are the definitions to common terms and phrases associated with the gay and lesbian community?
- What is the significance of the symbols associated with the gay and lesbian community?
- What is gay pride or Pride?

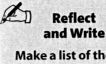

Reflect and Write

Make a list of the terminology you know associated with the gay and lesbian community and compare them to the definitions below. Why do you suppose it is important to know the proper terminology?

What Are the Definitions to Common Terms and Phrases Associated with the Gay and Lesbian Community?

You have certainly heard or read some of the terms that describe gay, lesbian, bisexual, and transgender persons. But how well do you know the meanings of these terms? Throughout this text, you will be exposed to terms that you will recognize and others that will be new to you. The terms and their definitions have been clustered in this section so that you can use them accurately in your discussions with or about gay and lesbian youth. In your discussions, you will not only teach students that some terms describe the community appropriately but that other terms are politically incorrect, offensive, and better not used.

Alternative lifestyle—is a peculiar phrase. Generally, it is inappropriately used to describe being and living as a gay, lesbian, bisexual, or transgender person. However, the term *lifestyle* largely suggests how one leads one's life, such as living on a ranch or living in Manhattan. Being gay or lesbian is not any more a lifestyle than being heterosexual is a lifestyle (Wilson, 1999). The lifestyles of gay and lesbian persons are diverse and unique and are not distinctly categorized into the one rubric, "alternative lifestyle." Usage of the phrase has also been criticized because *alternative* connotes significantly different, which perpetuates the idea that the state of being heterosexual is superior to the state of being "alternatively" homo- or bisexual (Gay, Lesbian and Straight Education Network of Colorado, 2002). Rather than using *alternative lifestyle* (e.g., "He leads an alternative lifestyle"), simply refer to the person's sexual identity (e.g., Mark is gay) or use *gay* and *lesbian* directly (e.g., "gay and lesbian persons in society . . ." instead of "the alternative lifestyle in society . . .").

Antigay—is used to modify terms such as *bias, harassment,* and *violence* to denote that they are against gay, lesbian, bisexual, and transgender persons.

Bi—is slang for bisexual persons, as is *AC/DC,* and "sways both ways."

Bisexuality—describes the sexual orientation, behavior, and identity of persons inclined to be physically, sexually/erotically, and emotionally attracted to, committed to, or romantically interested in persons of both genders. Westheimer (2000) adds, "Some persons have sexual relationships with men and women at the same time, while others alternate with male and female partners, one after the other. Some persons engage in bisexual behavior for relatively short periods of their lives, while for others it is a more stable behavior pattern" (p. 53). Such persons are referred to as bisexual.

Breeder—a slang term often used to refer to heterosexual persons. Gay and lesbian youth commonly use the term to describe the sexual orientation of their heterosexual peers.

Butch—a slang term used by the gay and lesbian community to describe masculine qualities observed among gay, lesbian, bisexual, or transgender persons. A butch lesbian, for instance, would be a lesbian who has masculine qualities.

Coming out (of the closet)—a popular phrase that describes the ongoing process of unveiling one's sexual identity. The closet is a metaphor for hiding or keeping a secret, such as one's sexual orientation. In coming out, a person first self-recognizes, acknowledges, or affirms his or her nonheterosexual status and then can decide to reveal the sexual orientation to others. Every time a person shares this information, he or she comes out of the closet. Coming-out events are unique to each person (just as are the reasons for coming out), and some persons choose to not come out at all.

Coparent—has several meanings. Often, *coparents* refers to the members of a same-gender couple raising a child (or children) together. Sometimes *coparent* identifies the companion of the parent of a biological child, and other times *coparent* refers to the parent in a same-gender couple who has no biological relationship to or adoptive rights of the couple's child or children.

Cross-dressers—hetero-, homo-, or bisexual persons who enjoy wearing clothes traditionally assigned to the opposite gender and do so publicly or privately. "Cross dressers generally want to relate as, and be accepted as, a person of the gender they are presenting" (Saint Paul Public Schools, n.d., p. 3-1).

Drag—describes dressing up as the opposite gender, often in an exaggerated, stereotypical style. Drag queens, men who dress up as women, and drag kings, women who dress up as men, often impersonate celebrities (e.g., Barbra Streisand, Judy Garland, Elvis Presley) and perform a comedy routine. The impersonators generally have clever stage names such as Hedda Lettuce, Carlota Tendent, and Bang Bang Ladesh. Perhaps the most notorious drag queen in pop culture is actor/performer RuPaul.

Dyke—is slang for lesbian. The term was initially used in the pejorative to describe masculine lesbians. Despite its negative inception, many lesbians now use the term to symbolize their pride. Dykes-on-Bikes, for instance, is a national organization of lesbian motorcycle enthusiasts that marches at yearly gay-pride parades. *Dyke* is used as a slur in many contexts, and its usage is prohibited in many schools nationwide. For the most part, use the term *lesbian* instead of *dyke*.

Fag, faggot, fagala—are slang, derogatory terms used to describe men who are gay, feminine, and/or weak. There are many speculations regarding the term's history, but the most widely circulated is that in medieval times the execution of homosexuals was usually carried out by burning them. The bundle of twigs used as kindling was called a "faggot." Fag is used as a slur, and its usage is prohibited in many schools nationwide.

Fag hag—is slang for a girl or woman whose friends are predominantly gay.

Female-to-male (FTM)—describes biological women who feel like and/or identify themselves as a male and take on the male persona of dress, behavior, and mannerisms, often electing for hormones or surgery to modify their body into a male one (Jennings, 2003). Use this label to refer to such a person if he/she is self-identified as an FTM. Such persons often like to be referred to by male pronouns.

Femme—is used by the gay and lesbian community to suggest feminine qualities, characteristics, and behavior and originates from the term effeminate.

Gay—has several meanings. *Gay* is synonymous with *homosexual* and most commonly refers to a homosexual male (e.g., "he's gay"), although it is often used to describe a lesbian (e.g., "she's gay"). *Gay* is also used as an umbrella term for the gay, lesbian, bisexual, and transgender community (e.g., the gay community, a gay organization) or elements thereof (e.g., gay culture, gay studies, gay marriage). The *American Heritage College Dictionary* (2002) adds, "Gay may be regarded as offensive when used as a noun to refer to particular individuals, as in, "There were two gays on the panel"; here a phrase such as *gay people* should be used instead. But there is no objection to the use of the noun in the plural to refer to the general gay community" (p. 565). As a rule of thumb, use *gay* to refer to homosexual men (e.g., "the gay man" or "the gay men's magazine"), and *lesbian* for homosexual women (e.g., "the lesbian" or "the lesbian march").

Gaydar—the supposed telepathic ability to perceive, without any evident signs, that a person is gay, lesbian, or bisexual. Gaydar is like a metaphoric radar that can track a person's sexual orientation. Someone, for instance, might intuit, "He may seem straight, but my gaydar tells me he's gay" or "My gaydar doesn't pick up that she's lesbian."

Gay bashing—refers to physical violence (like attacks, which are sometimes fatal) directed toward persons who are or are perceived to be gay, lesbian, bisexual, or transgender. Perpetrators of gay bashing are homophobic and intentionally seek to destroy and demoralize persons who are nonheterosexual.

Gender identity—is a person's self-perception or self-acceptance of being male, female, both, or neither (androgynous). A person's gender identity is not necessarily congruent with his or her biological gender. Some biological males, for instance, may identify as a woman, while some biological females may identify as a man.

Gender roles—are behaviors, appearances, and mannerisms socially imposed and expected of men and women. By osmosis, girls in our society become increasingly feminine, and boys masculine. At an early age, girls are expected to play with dolls, tea sets, and dishes and to dress in pink clothing, while boys are given toy cars, trucks, and footballs and are expected to play roughly. Youth who express interest in roles traditionally assigned to the opposite gender (e.g., a boy who wants to become a baton twirler, or a girl who wants to wear a tuxedo to the prom) are likely to receive social censure and rebuke.

GLBT—is shorthand for gay, lesbian, bisexual, and transgender. The letters are often rearranged so that *L* (for *lesbian*) is the initial letter, as in *LGBT*. At times, *Q*, which represents the word *questioning*, appears as the final letter to emphasize the inclusion of persons who are questioning their sexual orientation (GLBTQ).

Heterosexism or heterosexist (bias)—has several important meanings. First, *heterosexism* refers to the general assumption that everyone is heterosexual. As such, heterosexuality is reinforced as the natural, normal, universal, and preferred sexual orientation that is superior to diverse sexual orientations. Under this false conceptualization, everyone should be heterosexual, and those who are not are abnormal and unnatural. *Heterosexism* also describes the institutional discrimination in laws and policies against nonheterosexuals. Blumenfeld (1992, cited in Project 10 East, 2002) adds, "Heterosexism excludes the needs, concerns, and life experiences of lesbian, gay, and bisexual people while it gives advantages to heterosexual people. It is often a subtle form of oppression which reinforces realities of silence and invisibility for gay and lesbian youth."

Heterosexuality—describes the sexual orientation, behavior, and/or identity of persons inclined to be physically, sexually/erotically, and emotionally attracted to, committed to, or interested in persons of the opposite gender. Such persons are referred to as heterosexual.

Homophobia—literally suggests an irrational fear of homosexuals and homosexuality. In the last century, however, the term has evolved to describe personal and institutional hatred, dislike, and intolerance against persons who are or appear to be gay, lesbian, bisexual, or transgender. Homophobia is based on false notions, stereotypes, and the fear of being homosexual, which propels a prejudice that often leads to avoidance of, discomfort around, harassment toward, discrimination against, and violence toward persons with diverse sexualities. Persons with same-gender attractions can also develop an internalized form of homophobia. Due to the pervasiveness of antigay sentiment in society, these persons develop a self-hatred toward authentic same-gender feelings, attractions, and fantasies and will often go to great lengths to prove their heterosexual status (e.g., by engaging in gay bashing or by engaging in heterosexual relationships and coitus).

Homosexuality—describes the sexual orientation, behavior, and/or identity of persons inclined to be physically, sexually/erotically, and emotionally attracted, committed to, or interested in persons of the same gender. The term has a clinical basis and connotation and can be used to describe behavior (as in homosexual behavior), but use the term *gay* for homosexual men, and *lesbian* for homosexual women.

In the closet, closeted—refers to a person hiding or concealing his or her sexual identity or orientation. The phrase stems from keeping secrets, like a nonheterosexual orientation hidden in a metaphoric closet. Statements such as "She's in the closet" or "She's closeted" suggest that a woman is a lesbian but has not disclosed the news to some friends, family members, or coworkers. People stay in the closet for various reasons, including fear of losing friends and loved ones, protection from prejudice and discrimination, and uncertainty of the direction to progress. A person can be in the closet with some persons, out of the closet with others, or in the closet his or her whole life. Often you will hear that a couple is closeted, which implies that a same-gender couple is not open about their union.

Intersexual—describes persons born with the combined anatomy of a male and a female. Parents often elect to alter their intersexual infant's body (through surgery and hormone therapy) into a male or a female, which later leads to psychological adversity. *Hermaphrodite* defined these persons in the past, but the term is now considered offensive.

Lesbian—is the common term for homosexual women and associations thereof (e.g., lesbian magazine, lesbian organization). This female-specific term originated from Lesbos, the Aegean island home of Sappho (ca. 400 BCE), a teacher, poet, and lover of women.

Male-to-Female (MTF)—biological men who feel like and/or identify themselves as a female and take on the female persona of dress, behavior, and mannerisms, often electing for hormones or surgery to modify their body into a female one (Jennings, 2003). Use this label to refer to such a person if she/he is self-identified as an MTF. Such persons often like to be referred to by female pronouns.

Metrosexual—refers to heterosexual men who are often mistaken for being gay because of their seemingly impeccable appearance. These men are generally urban dwellers who maintain impressive and state-of-the-art wardrobes, hairstyles, and body-maintenance procedures (i.e., facials, manicures, and body-hair removal) (Whittall, 2003).

Out, Out of the closet—persons who have disclosed their sexual orientation. You might hear, "Pablo is out of the closet to everyone at work," indicating that Pablo is openly gay at work. *Out* commonly refers to persons who are comfortable with their sexual orientation and are publicly open about their sexuality, as in "Rosie O'Donnell is out."

Outing, outed—the process of exposing a person's sexual orientation to others without the person's knowledge and/or consent. If someone were to comment, "Two years ago Margaret told me she was lesbian, but she told me not to tell anyone," that person would be outing Margaret. As a rule, usage of the term suggests that the person was unwillingly outed (of the closet), such as when a student confides in a teacher who then informs the student's parents that their child is gay.

Queer—has been used as offensive slang since the 1930s and 1940s to describe the nature of gay, lesbian, bisexual, and transgender persons. But in the 1980s, the political activist group known as Queer Nation transformed the term with their mantra, "We're here! We're queer! Get used to it!" Now queer is an umbrella term symbolizing the community's strength and pride. "Albeit offensive to some and at times politically charged, queer has become a term of empowerment and is more socially acceptable. Many universities now have Queer Studies programs, and some academic discourse is appropriately assigned under Queer Literature" (Campos, 2003, p. 7). *Queer* is still used as a slur in many contexts, and its usage is prohibited in many schools nationwide.

Queen—slang term for a gay, flamboyant, and/or effeminate man. Banter such as "Michael is a big queen" can suggest that Michael is gay or stereotypically flamboyant. Usage of the term to describe a student who is gay or who is perceived to be gay is offensive, especially if he has not identified with the label.

Questioning—applies to persons who are exploring their sexual and gender identity and who have not identified, accepted, or committed to any of the labels associated with a nonheterosexual status—gay, lesbian, bisexual, or transgender. If a student explained,

"I'm questioning," this would suggest that she has not fully identified with a sexual orientation. Her sexual identity and sexual orientation could be in transition between hetero-, homo-, or bisexuality, or she might later discover that she is in fact heterosexual.

Sexual identity—describes the recognition, definition, and label a person assigns to his or her sexuality. The term refers to how a person regards his or her gender identity, sexual orientation, and sexual behavior. A person's sexual identity is generally congruent with his or her sexual behavior, such as a woman who regards herself as a lesbian and has a long-term, committed relationship with a woman. But often the sexual identity does not correspond to the sexual behavior. For example, Frank has been married for seven years and has two children. He considers his sexual identity to be a heterosexual one. That is, he recognizes, defines, and labels himself as a heterosexual because he identifies himself as a heterosexual. Despite his sexual identity, though, Frank has consistent extramarital affairs with men. Even though many might label him "gay" or "bisexual," his sexual identity is heterosexual. Once, a high school student insisted that he was a heterosexual girl. He had the mannerisms and the appearance of a girl, asked to be addressed by female pronouns, and had had a series of boyfriends. Even though many would label this young man a transgender, he clearly recognized, defined, and labeled himself with a heterosexual sexual identity.

Sexual minority—refers to persons who identify as gay, lesbian, bisexual, or transgender (transvestite or transsexual). A person who is a sexual minority is not necessarily gay. For instance, someone's statement, "Elizabeth is a sexual minority," suggests that Elizabeth could be a lesbian or transgender.

Sexual orientation—is a person's emotional, physical, and sexual attractions to members of the opposite gender (heterosexual), same gender (gay or lesbian), or both (bisexual). It is a person's core romantic and erotic inclination and does not refer to sexual experience or activity. For instance, a gay man can sexually desire men yet have a one-night stand with a woman, and a heterosexual woman can sexually desire men yet have a sexual affair with a woman.

Sexual preference—has been used interchangeably with sexual orientation. However, the term implies that persons have a choice in the matter of their sexuality, when in fact they do not. Because growing evidence indicates that sexual orientation is an innate trait and not a random choice, use the term sexual orientation instead of sexual preference.

Significant other—a term that gay, lesbian, bisexual, and transgender persons use to describe the person they are romantically involved with and committed to. The term generally implies a serious, stable, and long-term relationship, often equated to marriage. Other synonymous terms include *longtime companion*, *life* or *domestic partner*, *lover*, and *spouse*.

Stonewall—refers to the Stonewall Inn, a small gay bar in Greenwich Village that the New York City police raided on June 27, 1969, to "moralize" the area and "rid" the gay patrons.

Such raids were common at the time, and on that evening (early morning, June 28) the gay patrons had had enough. On that evening (and the next day) the patrons fought back into what became known as the first gay riot. The event spearheaded the modern gay-rights movement and has since united the gay and lesbian community to demand for equal rights.

Straight—a commonly used term for heterosexual.

Transgender—describes persons whose gender identity and/or expression is opposite their biological gender and who consequently do not follow traditional gender roles and social expectations. For example, a girl who says she is a boy, dresses as a boy, has changed her name to Bill, and wants to have the anatomy of a boy is a transgender youth, an FTM. The term includes persons who are intersexed; are inclined to cross-dress; are surgically modified (called gender-reassignment surgery) so that their anatomy complements their gender identity; or are seeking such measures. (Some transgender persons have no desire to alter their anatomy through surgery or hormonal therapy.) Transgender persons can be heterosexual, gay, lesbian, or bisexual.

Transsexual—is a transgender person. Such persons often explain that they were born with a body they do not resonate with, and they seek to present/express themselves as the opposite gender. The term includes persons who elect for gender-reassignment surgery (and are preoperative or postoperative) and those who do not. See MTF and FTM.

Transvestite—is synonymous with cross-dresser. Such persons enjoy presenting themselves as the opposite gender but do not necessarily want to alter their anatomy through surgery or hormonal therapy.

What Is the Significance of the Symbols Associated with the Gay and Lesbian Community?

Companies and organizations regularly adopt a symbol, emblem, or logo to represent their products, services, or history. The gay, lesbian, bisexual, and transgender community is no different, and in the last few decades it has adopted several symbols to make a statement about the community and what it embodies. Many of these are known as symbols of pride, some of which include the inverted pink triangle, the rainbow flag, the lambda, and the yellow equal signs in a blue square.

Critical Thinking

Make a list of all the symbols you know associated with the gay, lesbian, bisexual, and transgender community. Why do you suppose symbols are needed to represent their community?

Pink Triangle

One of the most widely recognized symbols for the gay and lesbian community is the inverted, equilateral pink triangle, which has historical roots that date back to the Hitler regime and the Holocaust. Prior to Hitler's rise in power, a law, Paragraph 175, had been passed in Germany in 1871. The law made it illegal for men to have sex with men, and violators were punished with a prison sentence ranging from three to seven years (Hogan & Hudson, 1998). During Hitler's regime, Paragraph 175 was strengthened. In fact, a kiss or an embrace between men was a felony, and persons with convictions or records of such were sent to labor-intensive concentration camps (Lautmann, 1980).

The Nazis created a classification system that could easily identify Jews and other "undesirables" in the concentration and extermination camps. Each group, including gay men, was forced to wear a colored symbol on a band that wrapped around the upper arm. The Jews wore a yellow Star of David, and gay men (among the pedophiles and incest felons) wore an inverted pink triangle. The pink color represented effeminacy. In total, there were 18 prisoner markings of assorted triangles and colors, including the following:

- red triangles for political prisoners;
- violet triangles for Jehovah's Witnesses;
- blue triangles for émigrés;
- green triangles for criminals;
- black triangles for asocials or labor disciplinary prisoners; and
- brown triangles for gypsies. (Lautmann, 1980)

Lesbians were sometimes forced to wear the Star of David or red (if considered a socialist), black (if considered an antisocial, pervert, and/or prostitute), or pink triangles. About 50,000 persons were convicted under Paragraph 175, and about 5,000 to 15,000 were sentenced to concentration (labor-intensive) camps, where they died (Adam, 1987, cited in Jennings, 1994). The camp conditions were brutal, and thousands were tortured, assaulted, and abused. In the Nazi campaign to eradicate homosexuals, about half a million were executed between 1934 and 1945 (Feig, 1978, cited in Saint Paul Public Schools, n.d.).

In the 1970s, members of the gay, lesbian, bisexual, and transgender community began to wear the pink triangle as a symbol of pride and to raise social consciousness of their horrific past. The pink triangles became more visible in the late eighties when the AIDS activist group ACT UP adopted the symbol and slogan "Silence = Death." St. Paul Public Schools (n.d.) emphasizes, "Not only is the symbol easily recognized, but it draws attention to oppression and persecution. Today, for many the pink triangle represents pride, solidarity, and a reminder of what can happen when fanatics gain control and launch social 'hate wars' against minorities" (p. 3–9). Oftentimes the word *ally* is printed on or beneath the pink triangle to indicate an area friendly to or safe for gay, lesbian, bisexual, and transgender patrons.

Rainbow Flag

Another widely recognized symbol is the rainbow flag, which features the colors (from top to bottom) red, orange, yellow, green, blue, and violet. Well-known organizations such as Jesse Jackson's Rainbow Coalition have used the rainbow as a campaign or movement logo to represent their work on behalf of diverse groups. But when artist Gilbert Baker wanted a symbol to celebrate the community in an upcoming gay-pride parade in San Francisco on June 25, 1978, he designed the multiple-colored flag to capture the essence of the community. He used hot pink for sex, red for life, orange for healing, yellow for the sun, green for serenity, turquoise for art, indigo for harmony, and violet for spirit (Hogan & Hudson, 1998). The colors were later adapted because of manufacturing problems, which resulted in the combined six colors that now serve as the international symbol of gay and lesbian community pride. Many people interpret the colors to celebrate the diversity in the community, since persons from all walks of life—regardless of race, ethnicity, origin, financial background, or faith—can be gay, lesbian, bisexual, or transgender.

The Lambda

Another popular symbol for the community is the 11th lowercase letter of the Greek alphabet, lambda. The lambda has been used for centuries to symbolize balance and wavelength in chemistry and physics. But in 1970, when the organization known as the Gay Activists Alliance (GAA) was searching for an emblem that fitted their mission, artist Tom Doerr suggested the lambda because it represented their drive and potential for social change. According to early GAA literature (cited in Hogan & Hudson, 1998), lambda, as "a complete exchange of energy," would come to represent "a commitment among men and women to achieve and defend their human rights as homosexual citizens" (p. 341). The lambda gained prominence and was dispersed on posters, buttons, T-shirts, and so forth, and in 1974, the first International Gay Rights Congress adopted it as the official international symbol of the movement (Hogan & Hudson, 1998).

Yellow Equal Sign in the Blue Box

The Human Rights Campaign (HRC) contributed another popular symbol for the gay and lesbian community, the yellow equal sign in the blue box. The HRC is the largest political organization that lobbies state and federal officials on behalf of gay, lesbian, bisexual, and transgender persons. HRC officials emphasize, "Equality is the heart of everything HRC stands for—an equal opportunity to share in the rights and responsibilities of our society . . . [and] an equal hope of living free from the threat of discrimination" (HRC, 2004). The emblem, which was designed by Stone and Yamashita of San Francisco in 1995, has come to represent this equality.

What Is Gay Pride or Pride?

Gay pride and Pride generally refer to the international celebration of the gay, lesbian, bisexual, and transgender community. Many cities each year hold themed parades, marches, lectures, festivals, concerts, and street fairs for and about the gay and lesbian community and their allies. Past event themes include the following: Alive with Pride in '85 (1985), Look to the Future (1990), Pride—From Silence to Celebration (1995), Take Pride, Take Joy, Take Action (2000), and Peace to Pride (2003).

Reflect and Write

Do you have pride in your sexual orientation? Why or why not? Why would some persons have and show pride in their sexual orientation?

Most events are held in June to commemorate the Stonewall Inn riots that occurred on June 27, 1969. While some cities elect for Pride events in other months, the celebrations nonetheless mark the community's "visibility, unity, and progress toward equal rights" (Hogan & Hudson, 1998, p. 450). Some of the larger elaborate celebrations in the nation occur in New York City, San Francisco, Chicago, Los Angeles, and Atlanta. San Francisco Pride is one of the world's largest, and it attracts well over one million people (San Francisco Pride, 2004). The events can be costly, over half a million dollars for the 2003 Atlanta budget alone, but corporate sponsors such as Anheuser-Busch Bud Light, Wells Fargo, Bank of America, and Whole Foods Market help alleviate some of the costs (Neff, 2003).

 WHAT PRIDE MEANS TO ME: CONFESSIONS OF A LESBIAN

I never had pride in anything until now. I guess a lot of it had to do with the fact that my father let all the kids in my family know that we were stupid, lazy, and would never amount to much. It just seems like we couldn't get things right.

At an early age, I immersed myself in books and athletics. I wanted to prove that I wasn't stupid and lazy and that I would amount to something. In the process I became an overachiever. I'm the first in my family to be at a university, the first to get an academic and athletic scholarship, and the first to have a 4.0. But I was never proud of these accomplishments. Things changed, though, when I met Andrea.

I knew I was lesbian since I was four. While I was in elementary school, I was in love with Daphne, the cartoon character in *Scooby-Doo*, Julia Roberts in *Pretty Woman*, and Mary Stuart
(Continued)

WHAT PRIDE MEANS TO ME: CONFESSIONS OF A LESBIAN (Continued)

Masterson in *Fried Green Tomatoes*. But when I met Andrea, I could not hold back the romantic emotions that engulfed me. I had fallen in love with a real person who offered me so much. We've been together for two years now, and I love her tremendously; she gives me the support that had been missing in my life.

We've been pretty closeted until now. Most people thought that we were just best friends. I had been pretty hesitant and resistant to doing lesbian things, like going to the lesbian bars. So you can imagine how I felt about going to Pride. But when Andrea said she wanted to go, I gave it [a] shot. When I saw the thousands of gay and lesbian people, I was so inspired. I was so happy to see so many out there just like me, saying, "This is who I am. I'm nothing to fear. I'm not that different than you." And the more events we went to, the more strengthened I became. I thought, "Yes, this is where I am supposed to be. This is the way it is supposed to be." Andrea and I held hands in public, we met other young lesbians, and we even signed up to join a lesbian club.

For the first time in my life I was proud. I was proud to be a lesbian. I was proud of my relationship. And I was proud that there were others out there like me. Many straight people, especially conservative ones, don't understand what we are proud of; after all, they don't have heterosexual pride. But they don't understand that their sexual identity is accepted and validated every day, and when you're gay, you don't have that. Gay and lesbian people can go years without hearing one positive comment about their sexual identity or meeting another gay person. So when you see a sea of people basically saying, "Yeah, you're okay; you're one of us," you become overwhelmed with happiness. Eventually you grow to accept your sexual orientation; you begin to meet others like you. You learn about the community's history, and you know that you can help its future. Through all this, you can't help but develop Pride. I know I sure have.

Pride events can be very liberating for some gay and lesbian persons. Former NFL defensive lineman Esera Tuaolo, grand marshal for the 2004 Chicago parade, shares, "I was carrying this pain and, running onto the field, instead of feeling the excitement I was feeling the fear. Pride is about not hiding in the shadows anymore, about the freedom to be who we truly are" (Neff, 2004, p. 78). At the events, there are same-gender couples embracing; drag queens and drag kings in stage gear; out celebrities; members of PFLAG (Parents, Family and Friends of Lesbians and Gays) chapters; and people holding signs that read, "Proud to be gay," "I love my gay son," and "Gay Gals Rock." Heterosexual allies also attend the events to show their support. The grand marshal for the 2002 Pride Parade in Austin, Texas, was a suburban mother of five and grandmother of three. She explains why she participated in Pride: "Being in the parade is a way to tell the world it is OK to love and embrace, because there are

 Put Yourself in the Picture

One of your students says to another, "I have no idea what gay pride is all about. Gays and lesbians have nothing to be proud of. If anything they should have gay shame and Shame events." How would you respond to the student's comments?

people out there who aren't loved because of their sexual orientation. . . . If we can persuade one parent to say to their child, 'Come home. We love you the way you are,' that will really be worth it, really something" (Neff, 2004, p. 74).

Summary

This chapter began with a matching quiz on terms and symbols commonly associated with the gay and lesbian community. While there certainly is no test at the end of the text, you should make an effort to know the meanings of these terms and use them properly, especially in contexts where youth are present. When you do so, you model that you respect the community enough to know and use the terms accurately. Moreover, you are better able to explain why it is important for youth to use the terms that are not offensive or insulting but politically correct and validating. And for your students who are out or closeted, making this effort conveys that you do not judge them for who they are or how they behave.

Idea File

1. Pick up the national gay and lesbian newsmagazine *The Advocate* and look for some terms and slang that are not defined in the chapter, such as *transphobia*. Research their definitions and add them to the list found on page 105–11.
2. Use the Internet to research the theme of next year's Pride events. Go to www.InterPride.com for starters. Find what your city (or the closest one) will do in celebration and make plans to attend an event.
3. June is considered the month for gay and lesbian pride. Find out what local television stations (including PBS) will air (e.g., movies or documentaries) pertinent to gay and lesbian issues. Make plans to watch a program.
4. Make a list of things a teacher, counselor, or principal could do at school in support of gay pride.

References

Adam, B. (1987). *The rise of gay and lesbian movement.* Boston: Alyson Publications.

American heritage college dictionary (4th ed.). (2002). Boston: Houghton Mifflin.

Blumenfeld, W. J. (Ed.). (1992). *Homophobia: How we all pay the price.* Boston: Beacon Press.

Campos, D. (2003). *Diverse sexuality in schools: A reference handbook.* Santa Barbara: ABC-CLIO.

Feig, K. (1978). *Hitler's death camps.* New York: Holmes & Meier Publishing.

Gay, Lesbian and Straight Education Network of Colorado. (2002). *Definitions.* Retrieved September 19, 2002, from http://www.glsenco.org/General%20resources.htm.

Heger, H. (1980). *The men with the pink triangle.* Boston: Alyson Publications.

Hogan, S., & Hudson, L. (1998). *Completely queer: The gay and lesbian encyclopedia.* New York: Henry Holt and Company.

Human Rights Campaign. (2004). *Corner store: Our symbol, equality.* Retrieved July 20, 2004, from http://hrccornerstore.myimagefirst.com/store.

Jennings, K. (1994). *Becoming visible: A reader in gay and lesbian history for high school and college students.* Los Angeles: Alyson Publications.

Jennings, K. (2003). *Always my child: A parent's guide to understanding your gay, lesbian, bisexual, transgendered or questioning son or daughter.* New York: Fireside.

Lautmann, R. (1980). The pink triangle: The persecution of homosexual males in concentration camps in Nazi Germany. In S. J. Licata & R. P. Petersen (Eds.), *Historical perspectives on homosexuality* (pp. 141–60). New York: The Haworth Press.

Neff, L. (2003, June 24). Who pays for pride? *The Advocate, 892,* 64–71.

Neff, L. (2004, June 22). Leading the parade. *The Advocate, 917,* 74–79.

Project 10 East. (2002). *The Project 10 East GSA handbook: Some definitions.* Retrieved July 18, 2002, from http://www.project10east.org/handbook.html.

San Francisco Pride. (2004). *Forms and information.* Retrieved July 20, 2004, from http://www.sfpride.org.

St. Paul Public Schools. (n.d.). *Out for equity/Out4good safe schools manual.* St. Paul, MN: Author.

Westheimer, R. K. (2000). *Encyclopedia of sex.* New York: Continuum.

Whittall, J. (2003). *Metrosexmania: Or how to tell mister from myth.* Retrieved July 17, 2004, from http://www.menessentials.com/tips/metrosexual.html.

Wilson, P. M. (1999). *Our whole lives: Sexuality education for grades 7–9.* Boston: Unitarian Universalist Association.

CHAPTER 6

Refuting the Myths

How well can you discern stereotypes from reality? Take a moment to test your knowledge about some myths circulating about gay and lesbian persons.

1. Heterosexual men account for most cases of child sexual abuse.	True	False
2. Gay and lesbian persons can be happy individuals who are proud to be gay.	True	False
3. Gay men generally become florists, hair stylists, and interior decorators.	True	False
4. Scientists do not know exactly what causes someone to become gay or lesbian.	True	False
5. Lesbians want to be men.	True	False
6. Persons choose to become gay or lesbian.	True	False
7. Adolescents who have same-gender sexual experiences do not necessarily grow up to be gay or lesbian.	True	False
8. Heterosexuals can get AIDS too.	True	False
9. Bisexuals are confused individuals.	True	False
10. Gay and lesbian persons live in cities, suburbs, and rural areas.	True	False
11. In the Bible, Jesus specifically addressed homosexuality.	True	False
12. Gay and lesbian persons can serve in the military only if they do not disclose their sexual orientation to other service personnel.	True	False
13. Gay and lesbian couples living in certain states are banned from jointly adopting children.	True	False
14. Homosexuality is recognized by the American Psychiatric Association as a mental disorder.	True	False
15. You can always tell when someone is gay or lesbian simply by their mannerisms.	True	False

Overview

Quite often in our society individuals are evaluated solely on their race or ethnicity, their cognitive or physical prowess, or their perceived or known sexual orientation. Unfortunately, such evaluations are based largely on inaccurate assumptions that have been transmitted by others and the media. It is not by chance that you have heard that African Americans enjoy eating fried chicken and watermelon, that Mexican Americans are lazy, that Jews are frugal, or that all people with disabilities are slow and simple minded. Many people believe these myths, and others find them humorous and innocent, but those who continue to think of these groups in the paradigm of myths never grow to understand and appreciate the unique contributions that each member has in society. In addition, people who believe such myths are less likely to approach these groups of people, less likely to feel compassion for them, and more likely to dismiss whatever predicament they may be in.

To enhance your understanding of gay and lesbian persons, some of the most common stereotypes about the collective group are presented in this chapter. The second half of the chapter addresses questions frequently asked about the community. The discussion that follows the stereotypes and the questions will help you think of gay and lesbian persons in ways other than the myths you have become accustomed to. As a rule of thumb, though, just remember that gay and lesbian persons are no different than heterosexuals—they have needs, desires, ambitions, and so forth, similar to the ones that you have. The questions answered in this chapter are as follows:

- What are common stereotypes about gay and lesbian persons?
- What are the answers to general questions about the gay and lesbian community?

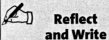 **Reflect and Write**

Complete the following statements with words that describe the first images that come to your mind:

Gay men are:
Lesbians are:
Bisexuals are:
Transgender persons are:

What do you believe is the source of these images? Which of these images do you believe are stereotypes?

What Are Common Stereotypes about Gay and Lesbian Persons?

Stereotypes exist about all groups of people. Some of the stereotypes are neutral (e.g., "Many Indians chant Hare Krishna") or positive (e.g., "Asian students excel in math and science"), but generally they are negative (e.g.,"Hispanics prefer jobs in the service industry"). According to Cushner, McClelland, and Safford (1996, pp. 72–73), a stereotype is a "summary generalization that obscures the differences within a group," and stereotyping occurs when all persons from a group are depicted as having the same attributes (Hernandez, 2001). Essentially, stereotypes simplify the way we perceive individual persons, because rather than appreciating the complexity of individuals, many people find it easier to project socially learned (and culturally transmitted) characteristics and rigid roles onto them (Gollnick & Chinn, 1998). Stereotypes also affect how members regard and evaluate their own status in a group (Hernandez, 1989). Members of the Hispanic culture who have no accents and who refrain from eating tortillas, rice, and beans, for instance, might judge themselves as better than (or different from) those whom they believe stereotypically do.

Stereotypes can be egregiously incorrect and damaging. Shiman (1994) underscores that stereotypes prevent us from thinking and feeling about members of certain groups in new and different ways and that stereotypes deter us from enhancing our ability to perceive others as unique persons. Accordingly, if you believe the stereotype that gay and lesbian persons recruit heterosexual persons into becoming homosexual, you are less likely to (1) befriend a person with a diverse sexual orientation for fear of being recruited, (2) perceive the person as more than a recruiter for the gay and lesbian community, and (3) perceive the person as a unique contributory member of society. In short, you inevitably reduce the opportunities to acquaint with another person simply because of a false, negative notion. Shiman elaborates that stereotypes often have an element of truth, which enables some persons to use them to justify or rationalize their own discriminatory behavior. For example, a foreman might observe that a number of gay men are feminine. The foreman might then use this observation to support his assumption that all gay men are effeminate, inherently weak, and only capable of "woman's work," and then he might refuse to hire them for labor-intensive jobs. Shiman also indicates that stereotypes are often used to rationalize treating certain groups unfairly. Essentially stereotypes deny certain groups of people a place in society (Gollnick & Chinn, 1998). Indeed, members of the gay and lesbian community are often treated poorly because stereotypes lead many people to believe that they are deviants and degenerates. You can understand why someone would hate gay and lesbian persons if he or she believed the stereotypes that they molest children and that they lead dark, mysterious lives.

Unfortunately for the group of gay, lesbian, bisexual, and transgender persons, the stereotypes attributed to them are often of a sinister nature, which causes many people to distrust, fear, and hate them collectively. Some gay and lesbian persons, especially those unsure or insecure about their sexual identity, will even go to great lengths to disassociate themselves from the community simply because of the stereotypes they know. While the times are changing and some stereotypes are becoming dismissed as the number of openly gay and lesbian persons increases, many of the stereotypes still exist, especially among youngsters. Below are some of the stereotypes associated with gay and lesbian persons, followed by an explanation that sets the record straight.

Stereotype: Gay and Lesbian Persons Molest Children

One of the most circulated stereotypes about gay and lesbian persons is that they sexually molest children. Such a stereotype can have devastating effects, including the following: (1) distrusting adults see to it that children are nowhere near gay and lesbian persons, which limits children's exposure to gay and lesbian role models; (2) children become fearful of gay and lesbian persons, which can linger with them into adulthood; and (3) youth with homosexual inclinations distress over the idea that they could grow up to be child molesters. Gay and lesbian persons do not molest children or take advantage of them sexually, and they are less likely a threat to them than are heterosexuals (Sanford, 1999). Research finds that heterosexual men account for over 90% of child molestations and that child sexual abuse is usually perpetrated by someone the child knows and trusts, like a family member or friend (Wilson, 1999).

One 1994 American Academy of Pediatrics study (cited in PERSON Project, 2002) found that of 249 cases of child sexual abuse, only two offenders were identified as gay or lesbian. The PERSON Project underscored, "In this sample, a child's risk of being molested by the heterosexual partner of a relative is more than 100 times greater than by somebody who might be identifiable as being homosexual, lesbian or bisexual." One other study conducted by the U.S. Department of Health (cited in Kozik-Rosabal, 2000) indicated that 95% of child-molestation cases are by heterosexual men against female children, and heterosexual men were found to be the perpetrators in most cases involving the molestation of boys.

Stereotype: Gay and Lesbian Persons are Sad and Lonely

Many persons believe this stereotype because they cannot understand how someone who is gay or lesbian could be happy, considering the difficulties they face in society. Others believe that because gay and lesbian persons are not valued in or validated by society, they have a tough time sustaining relationships, employment, and a social life, which lends itself to a life of gloom and doom. On the contrary, gay and lesbian persons are no more sad or lonely than heterosexuals. While some may find challenges in their lives that cause emotional setbacks, many gay and lesbian persons are happy, productive members of our society who find pride in their sexual orientation and support in the community. Many gay and lesbian persons report that they find strength in the courage of other gay and lesbian persons.

Stereotype: Gay and Lesbian Persons Want to Be the Opposite Gender; or Gay and Lesbian Persons Hate or Are Scared of the Opposite Gender

People often perpetuate these stereotypes because they cannot fathom how someone can be comfortable with and desire members of their gender for romance, affection, and sex. Gay and lesbian persons, however, are comfortable and satisfied with their gender and sexual orientation and have attractions and sexual needs that can be met by members of the same gender. Most gay and lesbian persons are happy the way they are and do not hate, are not scared of, and do not want to be the opposite gender. Persons who want to be the opposite gender are considered transgender, and those persons who hate or are scared of the opposite gender have emotional issues that have nothing (or very little) to do with their sexual orientation.

Stereotype: Gay and Lesbian Persons Are Destined for Careers in Designated Fields; or Gay Men Are Destined to Become Florists, Hair Stylists, and Interior Decorators, and Lesbians Can Only Become Coaches, Athletes, and Auto Mechanics

Gay and lesbian persons are not limited in their choices of occupations. They enter all fields and are found in every profession. They, like heterosexual persons, pursue their interests and enter occupations that they are best skilled for and interested in. While there may be gay men who are hair stylists and interior decorators, and while there may be lesbians who are construction workers and professional athletes, there are gay and lesbian accountants, attorneys, teachers, doctors, nurses, real-estate agents, managers, engineers, stock brokers, professors, plumbers, carpenters, and so forth. Often, a gay or lesbian person will be denied the opportunity for a job (e.g., an openly gay man denied a promotion to manager because others find his sexual orientation offensive), but this refers to discrimination (often on an individual basis) and does not suggest that gay and lesbian persons are better suited for or should enter specific occupations and professions.

Stereotype: You Can Identify Gay and Lesbian Persons by Their Mannerisms; or Gay Men Are Feminine—"Sissies" (Have High-Pitched Voices, Limp Wrists, and Wear Tight Clothes), and Lesbians Are Masculine—"Tomboys" (Have Short Hairstyles and Wear Loose-Fitting Menswear)

People often form stereotypes based on patterns they observe. So, when they see particular mannerisms among gay men and women, they make generalizations about all gay and lesbian persons. Because gay and lesbian persons are often portrayed in the media as having certain mannerisms, many people believe that feminine men are likely to be gay or that gay men are feminine and that masculine women are likely to be lesbian or that lesbians are masculine. In reality, a person's mannerisms do not suggest his or her sexual orientation. While some gay and lesbian persons fit the stereotype, there are also masculine gay men (and feminine heterosexual men), and there are feminine lesbians (and masculine heterosexual women). Lambda 10 Project (n.d.) elaborates,

> While some persons who are lesbian, gay, or bisexual do exhibit stereotypic "gay" behavior . . . they are not representative of all lesbians, gays, and bisexuals. In fact, we all probably know a number of persons who are lesbian, gay, or bisexual, but we may not be aware of it because these persons look and act like everyone else. In addition, many heterosexuals exhibit a variety of behaviors commonly stereotyped as "gay." (p. 89)

Never assume a student's sexual orientation based on his or her mannerisms.

Stereotype: Gay and Lesbian Persons Can Be Cured of Their Homosexuality; or Gay and Lesbian Persons Just Need to Have Sex with the Opposite Gender to Change Back to Heterosexuality.

Contrary to this stereotype, there is no "cure" for homosexuality, nor does there seem to be a rush or need to find one, because homosexuality is not a sickness and is not recognized by the American Psychiatric Association as a mental disorder. Many gay and lesbian persons report that they are happy with their sexual orientation and would not become heterosexual if they could. Indeed, many gay and lesbian persons enter into heterosexual relationships, often out of denial or obligation to social and familial expectations, and they get married and have children, but these circumstances do not change the fact that these persons have a deep-rooted homosexual inclination. As an example, in August of 2004, the governor of New Jersey announced that he was gay. Even though he was married (for the second time) and had fathered two children, he had led a double life and had had a homosexual affair. (See box 6.1 for excerpts from his resignation speech.) Many gay and lesbian students will experiment with the opposite sex despite their attractions to members of their own gender. A person's sexual behavior might change, but his or her sexual orientation does not.

Stereotype: People Choose to Be Gay or Lesbian

A person's sexuality is not a preference or a choice. Gay and lesbian persons do not choose their sexual orientation any more than heterosexuals do. Instead, everyone acts on authentic attractions. Many gay and lesbian persons report that they had romantic attractions for members of their own gender at very young ages even though they had never had same-gender sexual experiences. Many even tried to change those attractions, but the feelings

**BOX 6.1. EXCERPTS FROM
THE NEW JERSEY GOVERNOR'S RESIGNATION SPEECH**

New Jersey Governor James McGreevey resigned from his post, effective November 15, 2004. Here is an excerpt from the speech he gave on August 13, 2004:

Throughout my life, I have grappled with my own identity, who I am. As a young child, I often felt ambivalent about myself, in fact, confused. By virtue of my traditions, and my community, I worked hard to ensure that I was accepted as part of the traditional family of America. . . .

Yet, from my early days in school, until the present day, I acknowledged some feelings, a certain sense that separated me from others. . . .

At a point in every person's life, one has to look deeply into the mirror of one's soul and decide one's unique truth in the world, not as we may want to see it or hope to see it, but as it is. And so my truth is that I am a gay American. And I am blessed to live in the greatest nation with the tradition of civil liberties in the world, in a country which provides so much to its people.

Source: Associated Press. (2004, August 13). Excerpts from his resignation speech. *USA Today*, p. 3A. Reprinted with permission.

remained. Scientists do not fully know the specific causes of hetero-, homo-, and bisexuality, although theories of causation exist ranging from the biologically based (heredity, genetics, hormonal, and hypothalamus size) to the environmentally based (psychological).

Stereotype: AIDS Is a Gay and Lesbian Person's Disease

AIDS affects all groups of people, from infants to senior citizens. At the disease's advent, the community of gay and bisexual men (especially those in urban areas such as San Francisco, New York City, and Los Angeles) was hit especially hard by AIDS, which is how this stereotype came to be. But now cases of AIDS can be found across cultures and continents, and it afflicts hetero-, homo-, and bisexual persons alike. It is critical that youth understand that there is still a high risk of contracting AIDS when they engage in unprotected sex or use drugs that involve the sharing of needles.

Stereotype: In a Homosexual Relationship,
One Person Plays the Woman, and the Other Plays the Man

This stereotype evolved to rationalize what happens in a same-gender relationship, considering that in some people's minds gender-role stereotypes have to be fulfilled—someone has to tend to the yard (generally the husband), someone has to cook and clean (generally the wife), someone has to tend to the cars (generally the husband), and someone has to take care of the children (generally the wife)—and what happens when there is no husband-wife partnership but a husband-husband or wife-wife partnership instead? While some people believe that in a heterosexual relationship one person can be more dominant than the other, presumably the man, this is certainly not the case for every heterosexual couple. In many families, husbands and wives do not fulfill stereotypic roles but discuss the matter and assume the household jobs that each is best suited for (husbands do cook, and wives certainly do mow lawns) and share those that neither wants. This principle holds true for gay and lesbian couples, in which neither partner figuratively or sexually plays the role of the man or the woman. They collaborate to accomplish all tasks.

Stereotype: You Will Grow Up to Be Gay or Lesbian If You Have a Homosexual Experience during Youth or Adolescence

Many youngsters commonly have same-gender experiences including hugging, kissing, petting, oral sex, and coitus. While some do grow up to become gay or lesbian, most do not. Clearly sexual activity alone does not predict one's future sexual orientation. The American Academy of Child & Adolescent Psychiatry (1999) explains,

> It isn't unusual for adolescents—particularly young adolescents—to find themselves attracted to a friend or a teacher of the same sex. Pleasurable erotic contact with someone of the same sex is almost as common. Typically teens are dismayed by their reactions and wonder Am I gay? Such thoughts don't mean the youngster is gay or lesbian, but merely that the teen's sexual orientation is crystallizing. (p. 163)

Stereotype: Gay and Lesbian Persons Like to Flaunt Their Sexual Orientation

Society is accustomed to seeing heterosexual couples publicly displaying their affection, and rarely would anyone object to a heterosexual couple holding hands at the mall or to a man kissing his wife at the airport as she prepares to depart on a flight. But because homosexuality is fairly unacceptable in society, many heterosexuals express that gay and lesbian persons like to flaunt their sexuality when they see them being affectionate in public. It may seem like gay and lesbian persons are engaging in such conduct for shock value or to make a political statement, but they are merely showing sincere affection for people they love. In fact, most gay and lesbian persons are socially compelled to keep their sexuality in the closet and refrain from publicly sharing any affection with their partner or same-gender friend. You may believe that gay and lesbian students flaunt their sexual orientation when they wear Pride jewelry or merchandise or when they make gay and lesbian references, but they are simply sharing their lives with others.

Stereotype: Gay and Lesbian Persons Do Not Have Stable Relationships; or Gay and Lesbian Persons Are Promiscuous

Gay and lesbian couples are no different than heterosexual ones. Some relationships last a long time, and others do not. Some stay together as long as some marriages, and others fall apart after a few months. Some gay men and lesbians, like heterosexuals, are monogamous, and others are promiscuous. Many people believe in these stereotypes because they assume that gay men, for example, want and can have sex with all the available gay men. But, just because they find men attractive does not mean they find them all attractive, nor does it imply that they want and can have sex with all of them. Surely no one expects heterosexuals to find all members of the opposite gender sexually attractive. Why would anyone expect gay and lesbian persons to sexually desire all members of their gender?

Stereotype: Gay and Lesbian Persons Are Horrible Role Models Who Contribute Nothing to Society

There are gay and lesbians persons in every field, from the arts to the sciences, who offer incredible contributions to society. Some entertain us with their acting and musical talents; others lead us politically or as organizational heads; while others serve us as accountants, attorneys, medical professionals, and so on. Gay and lesbian persons are productive, tax-paying citizens whose sexual orientation has not changed the fact that they were raised to be spiritual, helpful, kind, ambitious, goal-oriented, charitable, hardworking, and the like. Many gay and lesbian persons exhibit qualities that are valued in society, and they are excellent role models for adults and youth alike. (See chapter 8 for a list of gay and lesbian persons and their contributions to society.)

Stereotype: Bisexual Persons Have Sex with Both Genders because They Cannot Make up Their Minds

Bisexuality is a legitimate sexual orientation (Wilson, 1999). Bisexuals are not confused, exploring their sexuality, or in a transition phase toward being gay or lesbian. While many bisexuals go through a period of confusion about their sexual orientation, just like gay and lesbian persons do, many come to realize that they are sexually and emotionally satisfied with and fulfilled by members of both genders (Wilson, 1999). Bisexuals do not change their sexual attractions and feelings from one day to the next in a random or flippant manner.

What Are the Answers to General Questions about the Gay and Lesbian Community?

Topics that are foreign evoke a number of questions, and issues regarding gay and lesbian persons are certainly no different. While many of the answers are embedded throughout this text, this section is a FAQ about the gay and lesbian community. Some of the most common questions that teachers, counselors, and administrators have about gay and lesbian persons are discussed below.

 Reflect and Write

If you had the opportunity, what are some questions that you would ask a gay, lesbian, bisexual, or transgender person?

What Causes Someone to Become Gay or Lesbian?

Medical researchers and scientists do not know exactly what causes diverse sexual orientations. According to the Lesbian & Gay Rights Project of the American Civil Liberties Union (2002), there are four theories of causation, however. One suggests that homosexuality has to do with heredity or genes. Although the research in this area has been inconsistent, some have suggested that homosexuality runs in families. A 1991 study found that for 161 gay men with twin or adoptive brothers, 52% of the identical twins, 22% of the fraternal twins, and 11% of the adoptive brothers were homosexual as well (Bailey & Pillard, 1991, cited in Saint Paul Public Schools, n.d.) The second theory has to do with the hormonal levels during a woman's pregnancy. Supposedly the fetus is denied enough hormones to make him or her heterosexual. Many consider the third theory a myth. This psychologically based theory explains that a male becomes gay because he has a domineering mother and a submissive father, and females become lesbian because of a deeper relationship with the mother and an inadequate one with the father. The fourth theory is based on the size of the hypothalamus (in the brain) and was proposed after a study found that gay men have a smaller hypothalamus than do nongay men. The study, however, was criticized for a number of design flaws. Most psychiatric professionals agree that sexual orientation develops as a result of a complex interaction of biological, psychological, and social factors (National Education Association, 2001).

Is Homosexuality a Mental Illness or Disorder?

For much of our history, homosexuality was considered a mental illness that could be treated. In fact, the American Psychiatric Association listed homosexuality as a sociopathic personality disturbance in their first edition of the Diagnostic Statistical Manual (DSM), and it remained in the DSM until 1973, when it was removed (Hogan & Hudson, 1998). Since then, medical and mental health professionals do not regard homosexuality as a mental illness or disorder.

Can Therapy Help Turn a Gay Man or Lesbian Heterosexual?

Medical and mental health professionals emphatically agree that no form of counseling or therapy can change a person's sexual orientation. The American Psychological Association has even stated that "orientation reparative therapy" or "conversion therapy" is not a valid form of therapy (Gay and Lesbian Educators of BC, 2000). Many professional organizations, including the National Association of School Psychologists, the National Association of Social Workers, and the American Academy of Pediatrics, recognize that gay and lesbian persons deserve respect and equitable opportunities in life and should not be approached with the notion that therapy can convert them to heterosexuality.

How Does Someone Know That They Are Gay?

Most gay and lesbian persons report that they felt different at an early age and that later those feelings grew into attractions for members of the same gender. Contrary to popular belief, people do not wake up one day and decide to turn gay. Instead, a gay sexual identity develops over time and is an introspective process that begins as genuine attractions and fantasies for members of the same gender. Most gay and lesbian youth become aware of same-gender attractions between the ages of 10 to 12 (D'Augelli & Dark, 1995, cited in Tharinger & Wells, 2000); begin to label those feelings as gay, lesbian, or bisexual around 15; and then come out to someone around the age of 16 (Tharinger & Wells, 2000).

Do Gay and Lesbian Persons Recruit Heterosexuals to Become Homosexual?

Gay and lesbian persons do not recruit heterosexual adults or children into becoming homosexual. Many people have grown to believe this myth because of the faulty assumption that people choose to become gay and that everyone is therefore vulnerable and readily influenced into "the lifestyle." Many heterosexuals further believe that gay and lesbian couples cannot have biological children of their own and will therefore do what they can to get them, which includes recruiting them. The fact is that many gay and lesbian couples have children—through previous relationships with heterosexuals, sperm donations for lesbian couples, females (lesbian or heterosexual) who bear children for gay couples, and adoption—and many do not want children. In recent years, the gay and lesbian community has made light of this myth by asserting that a person who successfully converts a heterosexual receives a toaster.

How Do Gay, Lesbian, and Bisexual Persons Compare Cognitively and/or Biologically with Heterosexuals?

There are no apparent cognitive and biological differences between heterosexuals, homosexuals, and bisexual persons. Everyone is unique, and a person's sexual orientation certainly does not prescribe specific physical, intellectual, or emotional qualities. Just as heterosexuals vary in their emotional and physical characteristics, gay, lesbian, and bisexual persons do too. Malyon (1981, cited in McFarland, 1993) emphasizes, "there is no evidence that homosexual and heterosexual adolescents are different in their progress through biological and cognitive changes, but a social environment characterized by hostile fear of homosexuality does affect their emotional and social development" (p. 20).

About How Many People Are There Who Are Gay or Lesbian?

It is difficult to ascertain the exact number of people who are gay or lesbian because many of them are not open about their sexual orientation and because many people are not exclusively homo-, bi-, or heterosexual. In the late 1940s, Alfred Kinsey and his associates estimated that about 10% of the population was gay or lesbian. The 10% statistic has remained popular in society, although researchers estimate lower numbers (Hogan & Hudson, 1998). Accordingly, if 6% to 10% of the American population is gay or lesbian, that means that their community has a population between 7 and 15 million (Tharinger & Wells, 2000), and if the 10% statistic is applied to households in America, then one of every five families has a gay or lesbian child (Dahlheimer & Feigal, 1991, cited in Fontaine & Hammond, 1996). Ginsberg (1998) estimates that about 1 in 20 adolescents in the nation's public schools today is likely to be gay or lesbian, which is about two million.

Are People of Color Gay and Lesbian Too?

A diverse sexual orientation is not exclusive to Caucasian Americans. Gay and lesbian persons are found in every culture and ethnicity. There are gay and lesbian African Americans, Asian American, Latino Americans, Native Americans, Pacific Islanders, and so on. Many people of color who are gay or lesbian experience discrimination from the dominant culture based on their culture/ethnicity and their sexual orientation, and they experience additional prejudice from people of their own culture/ethnic group who do not understand or accept their sexuality. Many people of color also indicate that many Caucasian gay and lesbian persons do not fully accept them in the community. The 2001 GLSEN National School Climate Survey (Kosciw & Cullen, 2001) found that 48% of gay, lesbian, bisexual, and transgender youth of color encountered verbal harassment that had a sexual-orientation or race/ethnicity nature. It is easy to understand why gay and lesbian youth of color would have additional challenges. Jennings (2003) writes,

> Not only must LGBTQ teens of color confront pervasive antigay bias in the broader culture, but they also face an LGBTQ culture dominated by Whites who can be ignorant or even hostile toward people of color. Add to this the fact that communities of color have many traditions that impact LGBTQ issues in different ways, and you can see how a young LGBTQ person of color faces multiple "identity" issues that teens from the dominant culture do not. (p. 215)

Why Would Someone Want to Come out of the Closet?

Gay and lesbian persons come out of the closet for various reasons. Some persons are tired of hiding or passing for straight; others want their closest friends and family members to know who they really are; and others want the freedom to openly discuss who they are dating, the events in their social lives, and gay and lesbian political issues. For many gay and lesbian persons, coming out enhances their mental health and builds a positive self-esteem (National Education Association, 2001).

Why Is It So Hard for Someone to Come out of the Closet?

Coming out of the closet can be especially difficult for some gay and lesbian persons because of the uncertainty of people's reactions. They never know if they will be rejected or accepted by those hearing the news. Indeed, many gay and lesbian persons have lost close friends and have been disowned by families, and others have been violently beaten, cursed and yelled at, and thrown out of their homes. Some indicate that coming out is upsetting because they are disclosing a secret that has been kept hidden for so long, and they are finally admitting that they have a sexual orientation that is a stigma in society. Coming out can be frightening for gay and lesbian youth because they fear the hostility that homophobic students (and faculty) will have if they find out the news.

Are There Schools Specifically for
Gay, Lesbian, Bisexual, and Transgender Students?

There are three publicized schools specifically for gay, lesbian, bisexual, and transgender students. Two are part of a public school system, and one is private. The first school, Harvey Milk School, was founded in 1985 and is located in New York City. The New York City Board of Education and the Hetrick-Martin Institute collaborate to serve the students. The name of the second school is OASIS, which stands for Out Adolescents Staying In School, and its branches are located throughout Los Angeles. The private school, located in Dallas, Texas, is called Walt Whitman Community School. While the first two schools serve students in their districts alone, Walt Whitman admits gay, lesbian, bisexual, and transgender students from across the country.

How Do Gay and Lesbian Persons Meet Each Other?

Gay and lesbian persons have varied methods for finding dates and making friends. Some live in heavily populated gay and lesbian communities like Castro in San Francisco, Lake View in Chicago, or Montrose in Houston, making it easy to socialize at community-sponsored events or to meet others in local stores or restaurants. Many frequent bars specifically for gay and lesbian clientele. Gay bars can be found in major cities and offer patrons a chance to dance (a dance club), hear others sing (a piano bar), or relax and socialize with other patrons. Many gay and lesbian persons also join national organizations as a way to meet new friends. Some join political groups like the Gay and Lesbian Alliance Against Defamation or clubs of specific interests like the running club Frontrunners. Gay and lesbian persons also use dating services and the Internet to meet potential partners.

Where Do Gay and Lesbian Persons Live?

Gay and lesbian persons live in cities, suburbs, and rural areas throughout the country. Large urban cities like Los Angeles, Atlanta, Chicago, New York City, and so forth have distinct communities of gay and lesbian persons. Even though it may seem that there are no gay and lesbian persons in your neighborhood, some of your neighbors may very well be gay, lesbian, bisexual, or transgender.

What Does the Bible Say about Homosexuality?

Scanzoni and Mollenkott (1978) assert that the Bible hardly refers to homosexual behavior, and the term *homosexuality* is never used in the original language. (Karoly Maria Kertbeny first coined the term in 1868 [Hogan & Hudson, 1998].) In all, there are about 12 brief references to homosexual behavior (Hays, 1994). The most widely known reference is the story of Sodom and Gomorrah in Genesis 19:1–25. According to this story, two men disguised as angels visited Lot. Upon hearing this news, the "men of Sodom" demanded to "know" the two visitors. They shouted, "Bring them out unto us, that we may know them" (Genesis 19:5, King James Version, 2000, p. 12). Lot begged for the men to leave and offered his daughters instead. Eventually the angels blinded the angry, violent men and God destroyed Sodom after Lot and his daughters had reached safety in Zoar.

Many biblical scholars agree that this story was not about homosexual behavior but about one of the greatest sins of the time, inhospitality. Bishop Herbert W. Chilstrom (cited in Tideman, n.d.) writes,

> We find no suggestion that homosexual acts were the essence of their sin. Instead, it is clear that the lack of hospitality is seen as the basic issue. Neither Ezekiel nor Jesus (Ezekiel 16:48–50; Matthew 10:14–15; Luke 10:10–12) mentions homosexuality in referring to Sodom and Gomorrah. Both cite inhospitality—a cardinal sin in that culture—as the primary allegation." (p. 3)

Scanzoni and Mollenkott (1978) add,

> It should be noted that some Bible scholars do not believe that the intent of the men of Sodom was sexual. They have pointed out that the Hebrew word translated "know". . . can mean simply communication—in this case, a desire to examine the strangers' credentials. Whether the intent was sexual or not, however, the strangers were treated abominably and the sin of inhospitality was committed—one more instance of the city's wickedness that called forth God's righteous judgment. (p. 55)

Homosexual behavior is also listed among the offenses prohibited in Israel's Holiness Codes found in Leviticus 18:23 and 20:13 (Hays, 1994). Many people certainly use these to denounce homosexuality because the Bible spells it out clearly: it is an abomination for persons of the same gender to have sex with one another as they would with persons of the opposite gender. The scriptures read, "If a man also lie with mankind, as he lieth with a woman, both of them have committed an abomination: they shall surely be put to death, their blood shall be upon them" (Levitcus 20:13, King James Version, 2000, p. 85).

However, many biblical scholars assert that the codes were imposed to maintain purity—to keep clean and whole in a literal sense—and does not refer to moral defilement (Furnish, 1994). In fact, the codes prohibit sowing fields with two kinds of seeds and wearing a garment comprised of two different materials. Hays adds,

> The Old Testament contains many prohibitions and commandments that have, ever since the first century, generally been disregarded or deemed obsolete by the church, most notably rules concerning circumcision and dietary practices. Some ethicists have argued that the prohibition of homosexuality is similarly superseded for Christians: it is merely part of the Old Testament's ritual "purity rules" and therefore morally irrelevant today. (p. 6)

Another scripture that mentions homosexual behavior can be found in Romans 1:24–27:

> Therefore God gave them up in the lusts of their hearts to impurity, to the degrading of
> their bodies among themselves, because they exchanged the truth about God for a lie
> and worshipped and served the creature rather than the Creator. . . . For this reason God
> gave them up to degrading passions. Their women exchanged natural intercourse for
> unnatural, and the same way also the men, giving up natural intercourse with women,
> were consumed with passion for one another. Men committed shameless acts with men
> and received in their own persons the due penalty for their own error. (Romans 1:24–27)

Here, biblical scholars maintain that the heart of the matter is idolatry (Tideman, n.d.).
Scanzoni and Mollenkott (1978) write, "The passage in Romans says nothing about homosexual love. The emphasis is entirely on sexual activity in a context of lust and idolatry" (p.
63). Tideman notes, "Clearly, we have here a proper condemnation of perverted, violent relationships in which there is no love and no care for one another" (p. 3), to which many gay
and lesbian persons would argue that they certainly impart love and care in their relationships. Further, Hays (1994) reasons that the scriptures lead to a discussion of the sin of passing judgment in Romans 2:1: "Therefore you have no excuse, whoever you are, when you
judge others; for in passing judgment on another you condemn yourself, because you, the
judge are doing the very same things." Hays concludes,

> We all stand without excuse under God's judgment. Self-righteous judgment of homo-
> sexuality is just as sinful as the homosexual behavior itself. That does not mean that Paul
> is disingenuous in his rejection of homosexual acts and all the other sinful activities
> mentioned in Romans 1; all the evils listed there remain evils. But no one should pre-
> sume to be above God's judgment; all of us stand in radical need of God's mercy. (p. 9)

Consult your Bible for other references on homosexuality found in Genesis 1:27–28,
2:18–25, I Timothy 1:10, and I Corinthians 6:9–10, and read some of the books found in box
6.2 to further your understanding about homosexuality in the biblical context.

Have There Always Been Gay and Lesbian Persons?

Many documents and artifacts strongly suggest that homosexual behavior existed in early
civilizations. One artifact found in Mesopotamia circa 3000 BCE depicts men having sex
with men, and records reveal that in 1866, in St. Augustine, Florida, the Spanish executed a
Frenchman for homosexuality (Witt, Thomas, & Marcus, 1995). While the terms gay, lesbian,
bisexual, homosexual, bisexual, and so forth are relatively new terms that developed during the last two centuries or so, homosexual behavior is not. Clearly some prominent figures in early history have exhibited homosexual behavior, including Alexander the Great
(356–323 BCE), Julius Caesar (100–44 BCE), Leonardo da Vinci (1452–1519), and Plato
(427?–347 BCE) (Fiorello, 1999).

BOX 6.2. ADDITIONAL READINGS ON THE BIBLE AND HOMOSEXUALITY

England, M. E. (1998). *The Bible and homosexuality* (5th ed.). Gaithersburg, MD: Chi Rho Press.

Gagnon, R. A. J. (2002). *The Bible and homosexual practice: Texts and hermeneutics.* Nashville, TN: Abingdon Press.

Helminiak, D. (2000). *What the Bible really says about homosexuality.* San Francisco: Alamo Square Press.

Jones, S. L., & Yarhouse, M. A. (2000). *Homosexuality: The use of scientific research in the church's moral debate.* Downers Grove, IL: InterVarsity Press.

McNeill, J. J. (1993). *The church and the homosexual.* Boston: Beacon Press.

Miner, J., & Connoley, T. (2002). *The children are free: Reexamining the biblical evidence on same-sex relationships.* Indianapolis, IN: Jesus Metropolitan Community Church.

Scanzoni, L. D. (1994). *Is the homosexual my neighbor? Revised and updated: A positive Christian response.* San Francisco: HarperSanFrancisco.

Seow, C. L. (Ed.). (1996). *Homosexuality and Christian community.* Louisville, KY: Westminster John Knox Press.

Siker, J. S. (Ed.). (1994). *Homosexuality in the church: Both sides of the debate.* Louisville, KY: Westminster John Knox Press.

Thelos, P. (2004). *God is not a homophobe: An unbiased look at homosexuality in the Bible.* Victoria, BC, Canada: Trafford Publishing.

Via, D. O., & Gagnon, R. A. J. (2003). *Homosexuality and the Bible: Two views.* Minneapolis, MN: Fortress Press.

White, J. R., & Niell, J. D. (2002). *The same-sex controversy: Defending and clarifying the Bible's message about homosexuality.* Bloomington, MN: Bethany House Publishers.

White, M. (1995). *Stranger at the gate: To be gay and Christian in America.* New York: Plume.

Wink, W. (Ed.). (1999). *Homosexuality and Christian faith: Questions of conscience for the churches.* Minneapolis, MN: Fortress Press.

Wink, W. (2003). *Jesus and nonviolence: A third way.* Minneapolis, MN: Fortress Press.

Can Gay and Lesbian Persons Serve in the Military?

Yes. However, they cannot serve as an openly gay or lesbian enlistee. In 1943, the federal government imposed a ban on homosexual personnel in the military, and during a 50-year span, over 80,000 enlistees were discharged on the basis of homosexual conduct (Bull, 1993). In 1993, President Bill Clinton lifted the ban and introduced the current "Don't Ask, Don't Tell" policy, which allows gay and lesbian persons to serve in the military, although they risk a discharge if the military discovers their homo- or bisexual orientation. Silence is a way of life for gay and lesbian enlistees, and they will go to great lengths to protect their military careers (Gross, 2003). Often they fabricate a heterosexual relationship, mask their letters to partners with encoded messages, and limit the number of people who know about their sexual orientation or partners (Gross, 2003). To complicate matters, enlistees who seek mental-health counseling (by military personnel) are not promised confidentiality. Gross explains, "In the field, military personnel have no assurance of safe havens in which to discuss the difficulties of being separated from civilian partners. Gay service members cannot be assured of discretion when they confide in military chaplains, and a soldier's disclosure of sexual orientation to a mental health professional is not protected by physician-patient privilege" (p. 46).

Can Gay and Lesbian Couples Get Married?

As of the writing of this text, there is no federal law that sanctions gay and lesbian couples to marry. In fact, 39 states impose the Defense of Marriage Act, which defines marriage as the union between a man and a woman and allows states to ignore same-gender unions performed in other states (Lindell, 2003). In November 2003, however, the Massachusetts Supreme Court ruled that same-gender couples could legally marry, and on May 17, 2004, Massachusetts became the first state to grant marriage licenses to same-gender couples. Officials in San Francisco, New York, New Mexico, and Oregon issued marriage licenses to same-gender couples as well. Four thousand were issued in San Francisco in February and March of 2004 alone but were voided on August 12, 2004, when the California Supreme Court found that the San Francisco mayor did not have the authority to issue them (Kravets, 2004). President George W. Bush endorses a federal constitutional amendment to ban gay marriage but allows for civil unions like those in Vermont. (A constitutional amendment is found in box 6.3.) The topic has become quite contentious indeed, and polls are finding that Americans are split about their support for gay marriages—half in the United States support a gay-marriage ban (Seelye & Elder, 2003). In the meantime, same-gender couples (living outside of Massachusetts) are deprived of a legal matrimony.

 BOX 6.3. MARRIAGE AMENDMENT

President George W. Bush and many other elected officials support the Marriage Amendment:

> Marriage in the United States shall consist only of the union of a man and a woman. Neither this Constitution, nor the constitution of any state, nor state or federal law, shall be construed to require that marital status or the legal incidents thereof be conferred upon unmarried couples or groups.

House, HJ Res. 56; Senate, SJ Res. 26

Source: Lindell, C. (2003, December 21). Gays, marriage and the constitution: Legal decisions renew call for amendment to ban same-sex unions. *Austin American-Statesman*, pp. A1, A12–13. Reprinted with permission.

Can Gay and Lesbian Couples Adopt Children?

Because adoption and foster-care rights are largely controlled by state governments, some gay and lesbian persons and couples can adopt children, depending on the state in which they live. Gay and lesbian couples living in the District of Columbia, California, Connecticut, Massachusetts, New Jersey, New York, and Vermont can jointly adopt children. In Florida, however, single gay and lesbian persons and gay and lesbian couples are barred from adopting children (Caldwell, 2003). In addition, Mississippi and Utah deny same-gender couples from adopting (National Gay and Lesbian Task Force, 2003; Caldwell, 2003), Oklahoma does not recognize adoptions by gay and lesbian couples (The Advocate Report, 2004b), and Virginia bans adoptions by unmarried couples, which includes gay and lesbian couples (The Advocate Report, 2004a). Arkansas, Nebraska, and Utah have laws that ban gay and lesbian persons from becoming foster parents (The Advocate Report, 2004a; National Gay and Lesbian Task Force, 2003).

Summary

Few groups of people are fortunate enough that stereotypes are not circulated about them, but the group of gay and lesbian persons is not one of them. You now know that stereotypes do nothing for the ultimate acceptance of gay and lesbian persons. After all, how can you trust, befriend, or admire persons of this group when you have heard only of stereotypes that depict the members as evil at worse and confused at best, or if the questions that you have about them remain unanswered or are answered by people (generally straight) who believe the same myths? At one time, you could ignore gay and lesbian persons because it seemed that the nearest one was a galaxy away. But times are changing, and you no longer have that option. The likelihood of having gay or lesbian youth (or a student with a gay or lesbian family member or close friend) in your class is high. Assigning myths to who they are is simply unfair to them.

Idea File

1. Make a list of other stereotypes you have heard about gay and lesbian persons and then search for explanations that dispel them.
2. Have your colleagues (or students) take the true-false quiz at the beginning of this chapter and then discuss the correct answers and where these myths may have originated.
3. Find instances in the media (magazines, newspapers, or television) where some myths about gay and lesbian persons are perpetuated.

References

The Advocate Report. (2004a, March 16). A family fight: Will the battle for adoption rights get more difficult as same-sex marriage advances? *The Advocate, 910*, 13.

The Advocate Report. (2004b, June 8). Orphaned in Oklahoma. *The Advocate, 916*, 14.

American Academy of Child & Adolescent Psychiatry. (1999). *Your adolescent: Emotional, behavioral and cognitive development from early adolescence through the teen years*. New York: HarperCollins.

American Civil Liberties Union. (2002). *Making schools safe*. New York: Anti-Harassment Training Program.

Bailey, J., & Pillard, R. (1991). A genetic study of male sexual orientation. *Archives of General Psychology, 48*, 1089–96.

Bull, C. (1993, March 9). And the ban played on: Behind the scene with Bill Clinton, gay activists, and the pentagon. *The Advocate, 625*, 37–42.

Caldwell, J. (2003, June 10). Little victories for gay adoption: A Mississippi ruling in favor of two lesbian moms shows that states may be forced to allow gay parents even as they reject gay couples. *The Advocate, 891*, 38–39.

Cushner, K., McClelland, A., & Safford, P. (1996). *Human diversity in education: An integrative approach*. New York: McGraw-Hill.

Dahlheimer, D., & Feigal, J. (1991, January/February). Gays and lesbians in therapy: Bridging the gap. *The Family Therapy Networker*, pp. 44–53.

D'Augelli, A. R., & Dark, L. (1995). Lesbian, gay, and bisexual youths. In L. Eron, J. Gentry, & P. Schlegel (Eds.), *Reason to hope: A psychosocial perspective on violence and youth* (pp. 177–196). Washington, DC: American Psychological Association.

Fiorello, M. (1999). Naming names: A list of prominent figures who have been identified as lesbian, gay, bisexual or transgendered. In L. Mitchell (Ed.), *Tackling gay issues in school: A resource module* (pp. 99–104). Watertown, CT: GLSEN Connecticut and Planned Parenthood of Connecticut.

Fontaine, J. H., & Hammond, N. L. (1996). Counseling issues with gay and lesbian adolescents. *Adolescence, 31*(124), 817–30.

Furnish, V. P. (1994). The Bible and homosexuality: Reading the texts in context. In J. S. Siker (Ed.), *Homosexuality in the church: Both sides of the debate* (pp. 18–35). Louisville, KY: Westminster John Knox Press.

Gay and Lesbian Educators of BC. (2000). *Challenging homophobia in schools: A K to 12 resource for educators, counsellors and administrators to aid in the support of, and education about lesbian, gay, bisexual, and transgender youth and families*. Vancouver, BC: Author.

Ginsberg, R. W. (1998). Silenced voices inside our schools. *Initiatives, 58*(3), 1–15.

Gollnick, D. M., & Chinn, P. G. (1998). *Multicultural education in a pluralistic society*. Upper Saddle River, NJ: Merrill Prentice Hall.

Gross, M. J. (2003, April 29). Family life during wartime: "Don't ask, don't tell" is keeping America's gay soldiers in the closet as they fight overseas—but what is it doing to the loved ones they've left behind? *The Advocate, 888*, 42–48.

Hays, R. B. (1994). Awaiting the redemption of our bodies: The witness of scripture concerning homo-sexuality. In J. S. Siker (Ed.), *Homosexuality in the church: Both sides of the debate* (pp. 3–17). Louisville, KY: Westminster John Knox Press.

Hernandez, H. (1989). *Multicultural education: A teacher's guide to content and process.* New York: Merrill.

Hernandez, H. (2001). *Multicultural education: A teacher's guide to linking context, process, and content.* Upper Saddle River, NJ: Merrill.

Hogan, S., & Hudson, L. (1998). *Completely queer: The gay and lesbian encyclopedia.* New York: Henry Holt and Company.

Jennings, K. (2003). *Always my child: A parent's guide to understanding your gay, lesbian, bisexual, trans-gendered or questioning son of daughter.* New York: Fireside.

King James Version Bible. (2000). *The Holy Bible containing the old and new testaments: Translated out of the original tongues: And with the former translations diligently compared and revised, by his majesty's special command.* Salt Lake City, UT: The Church of Jesus Christ of Latter-Day Saints.

Kosciw, J., & Cullen, M. (2001). *The 2001 National school climate survey: The school related experiences of our nation's lesbian, gay, bisexual, and transgender youth.* Washington, DC: Gay, Lesbian and Straight Education Network.

Kozik-Rosabal, G. (2000). "Well, we haven't noticed anything bad going on," said the principal: Parents speak about their gay families and schools. *Education and Urban Society, 32*(3), 368–89.

Kravets, D. (2004, May 26). California justices hear gay marriage case: Court seems skeptical about legality of San Francisco licenses. *Austin American-Statesman,* p. A10.

Lambda 10 Project. (n.d.). *Fraternity and sorority anti-homophobia train the trainer manual.* Bloomington, IN: National Clearinghouse for Gay, Lesbian, Bisexual, Fraternity & Sorority Issues.

Lindell, C. (2003, December 21). Gays, marriage and the constitution: Legal decisions renew call for amendment to ban same-sex unions. *Austin American-Statesman,* pp. A1, A12–13.

Malyon, A. (1981). The homosexual adolescent: Developmental issues and social bias. *Child Welfare, 60,* 321–30.

McFarland, W. R. (1993). A developmental approach to gay and lesbian youth. *Journal of Humanistic Education and Development, 32,* 17–29.

National Education Association. (2001). *NEA's human and civil rights: Focus on gays, lesbians, & bisexu-als.* Washington, DC: Author.

National Gay and Lesbian Task Force. (2003, January 22). *Family policy: Issues affecting gay, lesbian, bisexual and transgender families.* Washington, DC: Author.

PERSON Project. (2002). *The P.E.R.S.O.N. Project organizing handbook.* Retrieved July 29, 2002, from http://www.youth.org/loco/PERSONProject/Handbook/contents.html.

Saint Paul Public Schools. (n.d.). *Out for equity/out4good safe schools manual.* St. Paul, MN: Author.

Sanford, G. (1999). Breaking the silence: Supporting gay, lesbian, bisexual, transgender, and ques-tioning youth. *New Designs for Youth Development, 15*(2), 19–24.

Scanzoni, L., & Mollenkott, V. R. (1978). *Is the homosexual my neighbor? Another Christian view.* San Francisco: Harper & Row.

Seelye, K. Q., & Elder, J. (2003, December 23). Poll: Half in U.S. support gay marriage ban. *Austin American-Statesman,* p. A13.

Shiman, D. A. (1994). *The prejudice book: Activities for the classroom.* New York: Anti-Defamation League.

Tharinger, D., & Wells, G. (2000). An attachment perspective on the developmental challenges of gay and lesbian adolescents: The need for continuity of caregiving from family and schools. *School Psychology Review, 29*(2), 158–72.

Tideman, P. (n.d.). *Homosexuality and the Bible.* St. Paul, MN: Wingspan: A Ministry With and On Behalf of Gay and Lesbian People of St. Paul-Reformation Lutheran Church.

Wilson, P. M. (1999). *Our whole lives: Sexuality education for grades 7–9.* Boston: Unitarian Universalist Association.

Witt, L., Thomas, S., & Marcus, E. (Eds.). (1995). *Out in all directions: The almanac of gay and lesbian America.* New York: Warner Books.

CHAPTER 7

History of the Gay and Lesbian Community

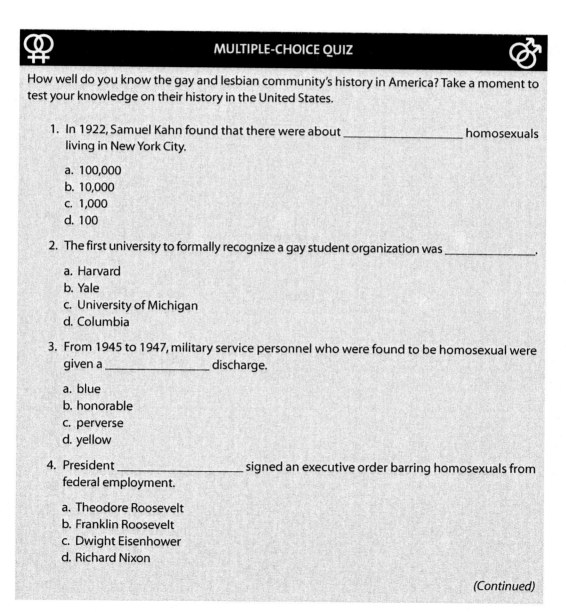

MULTIPLE-CHOICE QUIZ

How well do you know the gay and lesbian community's history in America? Take a moment to test your knowledge on their history in the United States.

1. In 1922, Samuel Kahn found that there were about _____ homosexuals living in New York City.

   a. 100,000
   b. 10,000
   c. 1,000
   d. 100

2. The first university to formally recognize a gay student organization was _____.

   a. Harvard
   b. Yale
   c. University of Michigan
   d. Columbia

3. From 1945 to 1947, military service personnel who were found to be homosexual were given a _____ discharge.

   a. blue
   b. honorable
   c. perverse
   d. yellow

4. President _____ signed an executive order barring homosexuals from federal employment.

   a. Theodore Roosevelt
   b. Franklin Roosevelt
   c. Dwight Eisenhower
   d. Richard Nixon

(Continued)

5. President _____ replaced the ban of gay and lesbian persons in the military with the "Don't Ask, Don't Tell" policy.

    a. Ronald Reagan
    b. George W. Bush
    c. Bill Clinton
    d. Gerald Ford

6. The church founded in 1968 for the gay and lesbian community is known as _____.

    a. The Apostles
    b. Christians for All
    c. The Adventists
    d. The Metropolitan Community Church

7. The first lesbian couple to have a baby in TV sitcom history was _____.

    a. Carol and Susan from *Friends*
    b. Blair and Jo from *Facts of Life*
    c. Nancy and Marla from *Roseanne*
    d. Lavern and Shirley from *Laverne and Shirley*

8. The "rare cancer" (which would become known as AIDS) found among 41 gay men was first reported in the *New York Times* in _____.

    a. 1980
    b. 1981
    c. 1982
    d. 1983

9. The first cities to pass laws prohibiting antigay discrimination in employment, housing, and public accommodations were _____.

    a. Ann Arbor and East Lansing, Michigan
    b. Los Angeles and San Francisco, California
    c. Washington, D.C., and Baltimore, Maryland
    d. Austin and Round Rock, Texas

10. The Stonewall Riots that launched the gay-rights movement occurred one early morning in June _____.

    a. 1968
    b. 1969
    c. 1970
    d. 1971

Overview

No group in America lives in a vacuum. Cultural diversity is a fact of life in our society, and each group has shaped our historical, cultural, and political landscape. Students today learn about the ideals that our country was founded upon—freedom, justice, equality, and human dignity—and about groups in our American history that have been denied these rights (Grant, 1994). Students are taught about the setbacks by way of the racism, prejudice, and discrimination that Native Americans, African Americans, people with disabilities, Latino Americans, Jews, women, and so forth have encountered in the past and today. More importantly, students learn how these groups have battled apparent social injustices to ensure that future generations live in a genuinely equitable democracy. As they learn about these groups, students begin to better understand their ancestry, background, and self, and they become empowered to use "courage, knowledge, and wisdom to control their life circumstances and transform society" (Grant, p. 5).

Gay and lesbian persons are among the cultural groups that have had an especially difficult time in our society, and rarely is their history discussed in classrooms, even though statistics strongly suggest that there are gay and lesbian youth in schools. A synopsis of the gay and lesbian community's history is presented here to enhance your own understanding of gay and lesbian persons. You can use this information (and the timelines) to initiate discussions with your students (especially those who are gay or lesbian) when opportunities become available. Such discussions are likely to help gay and lesbian youth feel less isolated and better about themselves when they learn about the group's history. Moreover, gay and lesbian students can develop the courage, knowledge, and wisdom about who they are when they learn about the group's challenges and achievements. This chapter answers the following questions:

- How have gay and lesbian persons been treated in this country?
- When and how did things change for the gay and lesbian community?
- What events have unfolded for the gay and lesbian community in the millennium?

How Have Gay and Lesbian Persons Been Treated in This Country?

At the beginning of the last century, society believed that gay and lesbian persons were "deviants" and "perverts" and deserved to be arrested, tortured, or committed to psychiatric hospitals. They were believed to have no dignity and were consequently denied the status of contributing mem-

 Reflect and Write

List the three events in American history that have impacted the gay and lesbian community.

bers of society. Many early reports on homosexuality focused on the apparent gay man—calling him queer, pansy, and fairy—and warned parents to watch out for him because he was likely to harm children. After World War II, homosexuality was accepted as an illness that could be cured. The military began to conduct psychiatric interviews on recruits and servicemen, and those who were found to be homosexual were discharged. It did not matter if they only had homosexual feelings and had never acted on them; they were deemed unfit, unstable for military service, and discharged. In the 1950s, the government began to fire known homosexuals from federal jobs because they were considered a security threat to the government. President Eisenhower even signed an executive order banning homosexuals from employment within the Federal government. No advocacy group or person publicly protested.

By the 1960s, things were beginning to change for gay and lesbian persons. They formed advocacy organizations, held demonstrations to protest inequities, filed lawsuits challenging unfair or inhumane treatment, published magazines, and started religious worship services for their community. Despite these advances, gay and lesbian persons, or "known homosexuals," could be denied services at local bars and could be asked if they were homosexual on employment application forms, according to New York City ordinances. They were accustomed to police harassment, entrapment, and arrests, but on the eve of June 28, 1969, things changed for the community. When police came to raid a bar in Greenwich Village, the Stonewall Inn, the clientele felt they had had enough, and they fought back with force. A full riot erupted that lasted for four hours, but the event sparked a momentum that would last for decades. Many now believe the Stonewall Inn riot launched the gay-rights movement. The timeline from 1900 to 1969 below shows how gay and lesbian persons have been treated in this county and introduces the image of who they are today.

1900–1910s

1906

Homosexuality and homophobia are the subjects of the first homosexual novel in America, *Imre*, written by Edward Prime Stevenson. In the story, one Hungarian man falls in love with a Hungarian military officer, and the two have an affair when one confesses his love for the other (Fone, 2000).

1908

Edward Prime Stevenson publishes *The Intersexes: A History of Similisexualism as a Problem in Social Life*. He describes the lives of homosexual men and women and lists the cities where homosexual activity occurs (Licata, 1981).

1911

The Chicago Vice Commission reports that homosexuals have a sexual cult and engage in "practices which are nauseous and repulsive" (cited in Fone, 2000, p. 372).

William Lee Howard writes a book titled *Confidential Chats with Boys* and warns readers, "Never trust yourself in bed with a boy or a man. . . . Be suspicious of any man in trousers who avoids real men, who never takes interest in manly sports, who tries to see you alone and prefers to go bathing with boys instead of men." (Fone, 2000, p. 372).

1912

Dozens of men, including attorneys and businessmen, in Portland, Oregon, are arrested for their participation in a YMCA homosexual sex ring (Loughery, 1998).

1918

Police raid a club in San Francisco and arrest over thirty patrons; plans for investigations are dropped when high-powered citizens are mentioned in court proceedings (Loughery, 1998).

1919

The U.S. Navy, under suspicions that there were sailors engaging in homosexual behavior, plans to rid the "fairies" and "trades" (masculine men who did not consider themselves "queer") from the naval training station in Newport, Rhode Island (Loughery, 1998). A team of Navy investigators solicits the help of young enlistees (over 40 in all) to gather as much information as they can about the "degenerates," which includes engaging in sexual activities with the alleged homosexuals. Several sailors are arrested, and by May 1, 15 servicemen are court-martialed.

1920S

1922

For his master's thesis, Samuel Kahn studies male and female homosexuality among prison inmates and discovers that about 100,000 New Yorkers are homosexual.

1924

German immigrant Henry Gerber starts an advocacy organization for homosexuals, which he calls the Society for Human Rights (SHR). Part of the SHR objectives read, "to promote and to protect the interests of people who by reason of mental or physical abnormalities are abused and hindered in the legal pursuit of happiness which is guaranteed them by the Declaration of Independence" (cited in Licata, 1981, p. 164; Loughery, 1998, p. 54). The Chicago-based organization composed of 10 members begins their work to reform the Illinois sodomy law but soon disbands after police search Gerber's apartment (without a warrant) and jail the organization's officers. Apparently, the estranged wife of the SHR's vice president had given some of their literature to a social worker who then notified the police (Licata, 1981).

1926

Joseph Collins publishes *The Doctor Looks at Life and Love*. He emphasizes that homosexuals have existed throughout history and can be found throughout society. Collins insists that homosexuals are healthy and productive citizens (Loughery, 1998).

1927

The Captive, a New York City play about a lesbian who wins over a married woman, is forced to close, and the entire cast is arrested (Loughery, 1998).

1930s

1930

The John Huston film *The Maltese Falcon*, starring Humphrey Bogart, includes a homosexual villain played by Peter Lorre (Loughery, 1998).

1931

Doctor William Sadler writes *Piloting Modern Youth*. He advises fathers to warn their sons about homosexuality. He writes, "Young men should be told frankly that they will come into contact with men who are a bit queer sexually . . . who want to fondle [them], who seek to make social contacts" (cited in Loughery, 1998, p. 35). The author does not mention what fathers should say to their sons who are homosexual.

1933

Dr. La Forest Potter writes a book, *Strange Love: A Study in Sexual Abnormalities*, and advises parents to closely monitor their boys who are interested in playing with paper dolls or in embroidering their initials on handkerchiefs. He also discusses the physical features of male homosexuals—the men apparently have feminine facial features, their skin is more delicate (and white), and they are gracefully round—and contends that marriage can cure the common homosexual (Fone, 2000).

1937

George S. Thompson, a doctor in Atlanta, Georgia, begins to treat homosexual men with convulsive shock therapy because he is concerned with the rapid growth in the number of the "degenerates." He reports that six of his homosexual patients who received ten shocks were cured and were able to live life normally. No other doctors are able to replicate his successful treatment, and years later a doctor confirms that Thompson's treatment did not alter his patients' homosexual orientation (Spencer, 1995).

1940s

1942

The American Psychiatric Association classifies homosexuality as an illness, which influences psychiatrists and society to assume that homosexuality can be cured (Higgins, 1993).

The military begins to employ psychiatrists to interview recruits and servicemen for signs of homosexual feelings, behavior, and characteristics (Miller, 1995). Those deemed homosexual (or who admit to being homosexual) are given a blue discharge (the document is printed on blue paper). Prior to this time period, soldiers were discharged for homosexual behavior (e.g., caught in the act of sodomy), but now they can be kicked out for having homosexual feelings (Miller, 1995).

1945

The Veterans Administration rules that "blue discharges" (homosexual veterans) are ineligible for GI Bill benefits (Loughery, 1998).

1946

The married homosexual is the premise of two novels, *The Dazzling Crystal* by Janet Shame and *The Fall of Valor* by Charles Jackson (Loughery, 1998).

1947

Californian Lisa Ben (anagram for *lesbian*) publishes nine editions of her periodical, *Vice-Versa: America's Gayest Magazine* (Licata, 1981).

The Army replaces the "blue discharge" form with a general discharge for unsuitability (Loughery, 1998).

1948

A group of doctors, lawyers, and clergy establish the George W. Henry Foundation to "cure homosexuals" (Licata, 1981).

Gore Vidal publishes a story about a man in love with another man in the book *The City and the Pillar* (Kaiser, 1997).

Alfred Kinsey publishes *Sexual Behavior in the Human Male*. The Kinsey Report, as it becomes known, is considered an important event in the history of gay men (Higgins, 1993). In the study sample, Kinsey indicates that 37% had experienced some homosexual activity and that 10% were exclusively homosexual.

1950s

1950

The U.S. Senate believes that the "sexual deviants" (homosexuals) working for the federal government pose a security risk and launches a full-scale investigation to find and fire them (Loughery, 1998). The Senate committee reports, "The lack of emotional stability which is found in most sex perverts and the weakness of their moral fiber makes them susceptible to the blandishments of foreign espionage agents [and] easy prey to blackmailers" (cited in Fone, 2000, p. 391). One of the Senators who spearheads the investigation tells a *New York Post* reporter "Mind you . . . I don't say every homosexual is a subversive, and I don't say every subversive is a homosexual. But a man of low morality is a menace in the government, whatever he is, and they are all tied together" (cited in Loughery, 1998, p. 202). Police estimate that the government employs as many as 3,700 homosexuals (Loughery, 1998).

A group of homosexual men meet regularly to discuss some of the problems that homosexuals are experiencing, and they begin to call themselves the Mattachine Foundation (Licata, 1981). Other groups form to expose injustices against homosexuals nationwide.

1951

Donald Webster Cory (pseudonym for Edward Sagarin) publishes *The Homosexual in America*. Sagarin introduces the concept of homosexuals as a persecuted minority group and reveals postwar gay culture (Hogan & Hudson, 1998). He writes that homosexuality is an involuntary and innate characteristic and that homosexuals are a minority group without a spokesman, leader, publication, organization, or philosophy of life (Kaiser, 1997). Even though Sagarin was married and had a son, his family knew nothing of his secret life as a gay author (Kaiser, 1997).

About 60 civil federal-service employees are fired each month, and 2,000 servicemen are discharged after investigations uncover their homosexual pasts (Miller, 1995).

1953

President Dwight D. Eisenhower signs Executive Order 10450 denying employment with the federal government to any person considered sexually perverse, including homosexuals. Homosexuals could be denied or fired from a federal job. Loughery (1998) notes, "For the first time, the federal government had addressed itself to the place of the homosexual in American society and concurred with those who argued that gay men and lesbians were not like other people and should not be trusted" (p. 208). No political organization protests the order (Licata, 1981).

A group from the Mattachine Foundation publishes *ONE Magazine: The Homosexual Viewpoint*, which acts as the unofficial voice of the homosexual-rights movement (Licata, 1981).

Thus far, 381 civil-service employees have been fired from their federal-government jobs because investigations find they are homosexual; about 150 personnel have been dismissed for other security risks (e.g., being communist) (Kaiser, 1997).

In their article "The Problem of Homosexuality," two doctors recommend that the medical community investigate the results of castration on homosexuals (Spencer, 1995).

1954

The Mattachine Society (formerly Mattachine Foundation) organizes to support its members and inform and educate society about homosexual matters (Licata, 1981). The Los Angeles postmaster seizes the October issue of *ONE* magazine and bans its delivery because he considers it obscene. The Supreme Court lifts the ban on the issue four years later (Licata, 1981).

1955

Four lesbian couples in San Francisco form the first lesbian organization in the nation, the Daughters of the Bilitis. The founders propose that they function as a personal- and social-support network, but the group later expands to advocate for social change (Hogan & Hudson, 1998). They publish a magazine, *Ladder*, and initiate chapters in major cities.

In their publication *The Model Penal Code*, the American Law Institute proposes that all private, consensual relations between adults be decriminalized. Members of the institute assert that "no harm to sexual interests of the community is involved in atypical sex practice(s)" (cited in Licata, 1981, p. 171), and they therefore question whether states have the right to interfere in the private affairs of American citizens.

ONE magazine has a circulation of nearly 2,000 (Loughery, 1998).

1956

James Baldwin publishes *Giovanni's Room*. The novel is about a homosexual affair between an Italian sculptor and an American man (Hogan & Hudson, 1998). According to Baldwin, the book is a milestone in his life because his sexuality "tormented and frightened" him (Kaiser, 1997).

After securing a grant from the National Institute of Mental Health to study homosexual men, psychologist Dr. Evelyn Hooker presents her findings to the American Psychological Association in the paper "The Adjustment of the Male Overt Homosexual." She finds that homosexual men are as well-adjusted as heterosexual men (Witt, Thomas, & Marcus, 1995), which contradicts the modern assumption that homosexuality is a mental illness.

1957

The Daughters of the Bilitis have 54 members (Licata, 1981).

Franklin Kameny graduates from Harvard with a PhD in astronomy and is hired by the U.S. Army Map Services. Five months later, he is fired when the government discovers that he had been arrested before for "lewd conduct." He legally challenges the federal government's exclusionary statute banning homosexuals from employment, but the Supreme Court refuses to hear his case years later (Kaiser, 1997). Kameny cannot get a security clearance for work and becomes destitute. His unfortunate circumstances, however, compel him to promote that homosexuality is not a sickness or immoral, and he becomes an influential advocate for the homosexual-rights movement (Hogan & Hudson, 1998).

1959

The Mattachine Society has 250 members (Licata, 1981).

ONE magazine sells 3,600 issues a month (Licata, 1981).

1960s

1960

The Daughters of the Bilitis sponsor the first national lesbian convention (Hogan & Hudson, 1998).

1961

A Tampa, Florida, police chief vows to "run every homosexual out of the city" (Loughery, 1998, p. 255).

1963

The December 17 *New York Times* features the front-page headline "Growth of Homosexuality in City Provokes Wide Concern." The 5,000-word report discusses the "homosexual problem" in the city and goes on to discuss that homosexuality can be prevented and cured (Kaiser, 1997).

1964

The Society for Individual Rights (SIR) forms. The organization provides social activities for its members, advocates for social reform, files lawsuits against police raids and entrapment, and sponsors demonstrations (Licata, 1981). Within two years, SIR boasts a membership of over a thousand, and their monthly magazine, *Vector*, is their communication link.

The June 26 issue of *Life* magazine runs a 14-page article on homosexuality in America, complete with a spread of photographs. The article describes a "sad" and "sordid" society that homosexuals have created and warns that they are increasingly "discarding their furtive ways" and becoming "opener and bolder" (Loughery, 1998, p. 258).

1966

Various homophile organizations write the Homosexual Bill of Rights demanding five basic rights (Licata, 1981). (See box 7.1.)

**BOX 7.1. THE FIVE BASIC RIGHTS FROM
THE HOMOSEXUAL BILL OF RIGHTS (CA. 1968)**

1. Private consensual sex acts between persons over the age of consent shall not be an offense.
2. Solicitation for a sexual act shall not be an offense except upon the filing of a complaint by the aggrieved part, not a police officer or agent.
3. A person's sexual orientation or practice shall not be a factor in the granting or renewal of federal security clearance, visas, and the granting of citizenship.
4. Service in and discharge from the armed forces and eligibility shall be without reference to homosexuality.
5. A person's sexual orientation or practice shall not affect his eligibility for employment with federal, state, or local governments.

Source: Licata, S. J. (1981). The homosexual rights movement in the United States: A traditional overlooked area of American history. In S. J. Licata & R. P. Petersen (Eds.), *Historical perspectives on homosexuality* (pp. 177). New York: The Haworth Press.

Three gay men engage in a sit-in demonstration at a Manhattan bar to protest the New York State law prohibiting service to "known homosexuals" (Loughery, 1998).

New York City police declare they will no longer use undercover cops to entrap homosexuals.

1967

The Mattachine Society of New York disavows the City of New York policy that asks employment applicants if they are homosexual (Licata, 1981).

The monthly magazine *The Los Angeles Advocate* originates. The magazine, which later becomes *The Advocate*, features news about the gay and lesbian community that is unreported in other periodicals (Loughery, 1998).

Ninety Episcopalian priests convene a conference in New York and declare that homosexuality is not wrong (Kaiser, 1997). In his speech, a reverend mentions, "A homosexual relationship between two consenting adults should be judged by the same criteria as a heterosexual marriage. That is, whether it is intended to foster a permanent relationship of love" (cited in Kaiser, p. 143).

The New Jersey Supreme Court invalidates the state policy that any bar where "apparent homosexual congregate" can be closed (Kaiser, 1997, p. 146).

Columbia University is the first college to formally recognize a homosexual students organization, the Student Homophile League (Kaiser, 1997).

Illinois is the only state that has legalized homosexual behavior between consenting adults (Kaiser, 1997).

1968

Ordained minister Troy Perry founds a church for the homosexual community in Los Angeles (Licata, 1981). Perry began the Metropolitan Community Church in his home with 11 men and one woman (Witt, Thomas, & Marcus, 1995), and by the end of the year, the number grew to 300 (Licata, 1981; Hogan & Hudson, 1998).

1969

On June 27 (early morning, June 28), police raid the Stonewall Inn, a gay bar in Greenwich Village. At the time, New York City police had been regularly harassing gay-bar owners and clientele, but the early morning of June 28, when the police were preparing for routine arrests, the customers fight back, and a riot erupts. Although the event does not initially draw considerable public attention, it does start the gay-rights movement.

The Gay Liberation Front (GLF) and the Gay Activist Alliance (GAA) form in response to the Stonewall Riot. The GLF supports various liberation initiatives and publishes a paper for the community called *Come Out* (Hogan & Hudson, 1998), and the GAA works on specific issues such as the struggle to end police entrapment (Licata, 1981).

The Metropolitan Community Church buys property in Los Angeles and has a thousand worshippers attend services each week (Loughery, 1998).

When and How Did Things Change for the Gay and Lesbian Community?

The gay and lesbian community began to see marked changes in the seventies, eighties, and nineties. One of the greatest events to impact the community was the paradigm shift in the mental health profession. In 1952, the American Psychiatric Association (APA) categorized homosexuality as a "sociopathic personality disturbance" and later reclassified it as a "non-psychotic mental disorder" (Hogan & Hudson, 1998). For decades, the medical profession accepted and promoted that homosexuality was a mental illness, which influenced society into assuming that gay and lesbian persons were sick and could be cured. But in 1973, the APA voted to permanently remove homosexuality from the Diagnostic and Statistical Manual. At long last, gay and lesbian persons were unshackled from the medical-profession-supported notion that they were deranged.

In the 1970s, the gay and lesbian community's voice grew stronger than ever. It began to hold marches and celebrate gay pride, drawing record numbers of supporters at media-covered events. A march commemorating the first anniversary of the Stonewall Riot (in 1970) laid the groundwork for the tradition of annual gay-pride celebrations. The community was featured in mainstream magazines, professional journals, newspapers, and talk shows. In 1972, ABC aired a TV movie with a positive spin on homosexuality. One reviewer called it the "most tasteful, sensitive, accurate, and compelling story on homosexuality to reach the screens thus far" (Fairbanks, 1972, p. 26). The movie, *That Certain Summer,* featured Hal Holbrook's character coming to terms with his homosexuality and entering a relationship with Martin Sheen's character. PBS also broadcast a 12-hour documentary titled "An American Family" that portrayed a typical American family, the Louds. In the series' second episode, ten million viewers witnessed the 20-year-old son Lance come out of the closet.

Polls during this period suggest that society was slowly beginning to support gay and lesbian persons. In fact, two cities, Ann Arbor and East Lansing, passed city ordinances prohibiting discrimination based on sexual orientation. Despite this progress, the community encountered a flow of opposition. Policies were passed in some school districts that banned the employment of gay or lesbian teachers; a California legislator proposed a statewide initiative that would fire any teacher who supported homosexuality; and Anita Bryant led a powerful crusade against gay rights in Florida.

The eighties was a trying decade for the community. While an increasing number of cities were passing legislation protecting gay and lesbian persons from sexual-orientation discrimination, the community suffered a dreadful setback, AIDS. Thousands of gay men died from AIDS in the eighties, and society immediately identified it as a gay man's disease (Hogan & Hudson, 1998). Members of the community strongly believed that the federal government was responding too slowly to the increasing number of AIDS cases, and they mobilized themselves to pressure the president and his administration to do something about it. A number of activists organized themselves into groups such as Gay Men's Health Crisis, AIDS Coalition to Unleash Power (ACT UP), Gay and Lesbian Alliance Against Defamation (GLAAD), and the Human Rights Campaign in 1980, and by 1987, 200,000 members of the community rallied in Washington, D.C., for the second time in history. The gay and lesbian community was more visible than ever before.

In the nineties, the community entered social consciousness. Gay and lesbian persons were the topic of widespread debates and conversations: the federal government had to respond to the issue of gays in the military; celebrities (e.g., K. D. Lang, Melissa Etheridge, Chastity Bono, Dan Butler, Patrick Bristow) were coming out of the closet; states were deciding on the issue of adoption by gay and lesbian persons; the main character in Ellen DeGeneres's sitcom *Ellen* came out to millions of TV viewers; studies were validating that gay and lesbian youth (and those perceived to be gay and lesbian) were routinely harassed in schools; a number of TV shows were featuring gay and lesbian characters and themes; gay youth began to sue their school districts because their administrators failed to protect them from harassment; and so forth.

The gay and lesbian community made significant strides in the last three decades of the 20th century. The timeline below captures some of the events and issues that impacted the community during this critical period.

1970s

1970

On June 28, between 5,000 to 10,000 gay and lesbian persons march in Central Park to celebrate the Stonewall Inn Riot (Licata, 1981; Spencer, 1995). Nearly 1,200 people march down Hollywood Boulevard in Los Angeles to commemorate the event (Spencer, 1995).

The Advocate has more than 20,000 subscribers (Loughery, 1998).

In its article "The Homosexual in America," *Time* reports that there are 4 million gay and lesbian persons living in the United States (Jackson, 1970).

Two gay men petition the State of Minnesota for a license to marry (Cole, 1970).

Psychologist Martin Hoffman encourages school personnel to accept homosexual adolescents in his *Today's Education* article. He emphasizes, "I believe that what the student really needs is acceptance from the family, and in many cases this is only possible if the parents are told (by someone they will listen to) that they cannot change their child's sexual preference. The only choice they have at this stage is how much guilt they will burden the child with" (Hoffman, 1970, p. 48).

1971

A school counselor in Hartford, Connecticut, is suspended without pay after appearing on TV to describe his advocacy work for the gay and lesbian community (*The Advocate*, 1971a).

Five members of the Gay Activist Alliance are arrested for protesting against the New York City Board of Education for its policies denying teaching positions to known homosexuals (Hunter, 1971).

An Iowa City, Iowa, high school teacher is fired because he invites member of the University of Iowa Gay Liberation Front to speak to his eighth-grade sex-education class. The students had requested a discussion on homosexuality from a relevant viewpoint. The teacher is rehired a few months later (*The Advocate*, 1971b).

1972

The United Church of Christ ordains the first openly gay man, Reverend Bill Johnson (Witt, Thomas, & Marcus, 1995).

A Minneapolis poll finds that adults between the ages of 18 and 24 support gay and lesbian persons. Seventy-four percent of the respondents agree that no one should be denied a job because of their sexual orientation; 62% believe that the law should allow for any sexual acts between consenting adults; and nearly half indicate that gay and lesbian persons should be allowed to marry (*The Advocate*, 1972d).

Gay, lesbian, and heterosexual youth from a California YMCA and the Metropolitan Community Church gather for a meeting about homosexuality. Early parent protests do not stop the youngsters from learning about homosexual marriage, love affairs, and so forth. One students remarks "[we are] going home to tell [our] parents that homosexuals are 'no different' than we are" (*The Advocate*, 1972c, p. 7).

A teacher in Salem, Oregon, is fired from her job when it is rumored that she is lesbian (*The Advocate*, 1972b).

The District of Columbia Board of Education resolves to end their policies denying the employment of gay and lesbian persons. The board emphasizes, "[The board] hereby recognizes the right of each individual to freely choose a lifestyle, as guaranteed under the

Constitution and the Bill of Rights. The board further recognizes that sexual orientation, in and of itself, does not relate to ability in job performance or service" (*The Advocate*, 1972a, p. 3).

Ann Arbor and East Lansing, Michigan, are the first cities in the country to have laws that prohibit discrimination based on sexual orientation in employment, housing, and public accommodations (The Advocate Report, 1999b).

1973

The TV show *Marcus Welby, M.D.* features an episode about a patient with a "homosexual problem." Welby tells the character that his homosexual urges are not legitimate and are "insurmountable obstacles to happiness and self-respect" (Loughery, 1998, p. 342).

The Metropolitan Community Church building in Los Angeles is firebombed twice within six months.

PBS airs a 12-hour documentary, *An American Family*. Millions of viewers nationwide learn that the couple's "flamboyant" son, Lance, is gay. The film captures Lance living in New York and discussing his sexuality with his mother.

Members of the American Psychiatric Association Committee on Nomenclature discuss the removal of homosexuality as a mental disorder from their Diagnostic and Statistical Manual (Wicker, 1973).

1974

American Psychiatric Association removes homosexuality as a sickness from their Diagnostic and Statistical Manual and supports legislation for homosexual civil rights (Licata, 1981).

Lambda Legal Defense and Education Fund, a gay-rights activist group, is formed.

A large-scale study of public attitudes toward homosexuality is published in the first issue of *Journal of Homosexuality*. Some of the findings are presented in box 7.2.

1975

A Washington State judge rules that an openly gay high school sophomore cannot be placed in a "gay" foster home. Earlier, the boy's father, who had a difficult time accepting his son's sexual orientation, deemed him "incorrigible" and handed him over to the foster-care system. Social workers initially had the youth live with his biological mother, but she abandoned him. He was then placed in a group home, but he was rejected because of his sexual orientation. Finally, he was placed in the home of a gay couple where he was well cared for. The news of the placement horrified the county judge who claimed, "No boy from Clark

BOX 7.2. PUBLIC ATTITUDES TOWARD HOMOSEXUALITY: 1970 NATIONAL SURVEY

In a survey of 30,018 Americans:

- 70.2% believed that sex between persons of the same gender is always wrong;
- 67.4% or more believed that homosexual men should not be allowed to work as a teacher, judge, minister, doctor, or similar professionals;
- 71.7% or more believed that homosexual men should be allowed to work as a beautician, artist, musician, or florist;
- 73.5% agreed that homosexuals are dangerous and try to become sexually involved with children;
- 48.8% agreed that homosexuality can cause the downfall of civilization;
- 83.8% agreed that homosexuality is obscene and vulgar;
- 72.9% disagreed that homosexuals should be allowed to display affection for one another in public;
- 43.1% disagreed that there should be bars serving homosexuals;
- 78.4% believed that homosexuals should be allowed in churches or synagogues;
- 68% believed that what happens between homosexuals in their own privacy is no one else's business;
- 80.9% said they would prefer not to associate with homosexuals; and
- 64.6% thought that most homosexuals are OK, but still do not like them.

Source: Adapted from Levitt, E. E., & Klassen, A. D. (1974). Public attitudes toward homosexuality: Part of the 1970 national survey by the Institute for Sex Research. *Journal of Homosexuality, 1*(1), 29–43.

County will be placed in a gay foster home. If need be, I'll take this matter all the way to the Supreme Court" (Shilts, 1975, p. 12).

1976

In his interview with *Playboy*, presidential candidate Jimmy Carter mentions that homosexuality makes him nervous because of two factors: his Baptist faith and lack of knowledge on the subject. He explains that homosexuality is "strange territory" for him (Scanzoni & Mollenkott, 1978, p. 46).

1977

Forty American cities agree on new ordinances forbidding discrimination against gay and lesbian persons in housing and employment (Spencer, 1995). In response, Florida Orange Juice spokesperson and former beauty queen Anita Bryant starts an antigay campaign,

"Save Our Children," in Dade County. Bryant and her associates promote that homosexuals are pedophiles and do not deserve rights (Loughery, 1998). They use the slogan "What right is there to corrupt our Children? Vote for Human Rights. Vote for Religious Freedom" (Loughery, p. 376). She remarks, "If homosexuality were the normal way, God would have made Adam and Bruce" (Hogan & Hudson, 1998, p. 291). The Dade County voters repeal the gay-rights law (Spencer, 1995).

Gallup poll finds that 56% of a sample believes that homosexuals deserve equal rights in employment, and 65% disprove of homosexuals teaching in elementary schools (Licata, 1981).

Openly gay politician Harvey Milk is elected to the San Francisco Board of Supervisors and vows, "I understand the responsibility of being gay. . . . I was elected by the people of this district, but I also have a responsibility to gays—not just in this city, but elsewhere" (cited in Witt, Thomas, & Marcus, 1995, p. 10). Milk works to eradicate antigay discrimination in employment, housing, and public accommodations.

The June 1 issue of *The Advocate* features a report entitled "Gay Youth: The Lonely Young." Shilts (1977) reports that the lives of an estimated two million gay and lesbian youth are difficult and that very few social-service agencies exist for them.

1978

Nearly 250,000 people attend the Gay Pride Parade in San Francisco (Loughery, 1998).

Former San Francisco city supervisor Dan White assassinates Harvey Milk and city mayor George Moscone (Witt, Thomas, & Marcus, 1995; Hogan & Hudson, 1998).

California voters reject Proposition 6 (the Briggs Initiative), which would have banned gay and lesbian persons (or anyone advocating on their behalf) from teaching in the public schools (Witt, Thomas, & Marcus, 1995; Hogan & Hudson, 1998). Briggs, the California legislator, insists, "There are many teachers who have a lot of abnormalities that they keep inside and don't project to their students. But I'm talking about a public homosexual . . . one who will advertise to the world, 'I am a homosexual and I am proud of it.' That's when they should be removed. . . . I think it's a bunch of garbage when homosexuals maintain they have a right to be teachers" (Oddone, 1977, p. 15).

An Alaskan school district passes a resolution banning the employment of anyone openly gay or lesbian, anyone who engages in sodomy, and any unmarried person living with his or her partner. The district insists that homosexuality and cohabitation are "'inconsistent with decency, good order and propriety of personal conduct,' and constitute 'unfitness to teach' in the district" (*The Advocate*, 1978, p. 12).

1979

Assassin Dan White is found guilty of manslaughter and sentenced to seven years and eight months for the murders of Harvey Milk and George Moscone (Witt, Thomas, & Marcus, 1995).

17-year-old gay student Randy Rohl takes a male date to his senior prom in Sioux Falls, South Dakota (Kaiser, 1997).

Nearly 100 youth attend a high school prom for gay and lesbian youth in Boston (Shister, 1979).

Emery Hetrick and A. Damien Martin found the Institute for the Protection of Lesbian and Gay Youth (IPLGY) in New York City. The Institute would become world famous for offering the first school for gay and lesbian youth, Harvey Milk School.

1980s

1980

School administrators try to stop Aaron Fricke of Rockport, Rhode Island, from bringing a same-gender date to the senior prom. Aaron Fricke files suit against the school, and the court rules in his favor (Witt, Thomas, & Marcus, 1995).

By this time, 120 of the largest American corporations adopted policies protecting gay and lesbian personnel from discrimination. Forty towns and cities have passed similar measures (Kaiser, 1997).

Presidential candidate George H. W. Bush tells the *Los Angeles Times*, "I don't think American society should be asked to accept that homosexuality is a standard which should be held up for acceptance. . . . I just don't believe that, and I'm not going to push for it" (*The Advocate*, 1980a, p. 7). His contender, who would win the nomination bid and become the U.S. president, Ronald Reagan, shares, "My criticism of the gay rights movement is that it isn't asking for civil rights; it is asking for a recognition and acceptance of an alternative lifestyle which I do not believe society can condone, nor can I. . . . In the Bible it says that in the eyes of the Lord, this homosexuality is an abomination" (*The Advocate*, 1980b, p. 7).

1981

Billie Jean King is forced out of the closet (Kaiser, 1997).

Nineteen-year-old Eagle Scout, Timothy Curran, sues the Boy Scouts of America for expelling him for being homosexual (Clendinen & Nagourney, 2001; Schroeder, 1994).

On July-4th weekend, senior *Times* medical writer Lawrence K. Altman writes about a rare, "rapidly fatal" cancer found in 41 homosexuals (Kaiser, 1997). No one knows anything about the disease, how it is transmitted, or if there is cure. The "cancer" would become known as AIDS.

1982

Wisconsin is the first state to pass gay-civil-rights law. An aide to a state representative tells *The Advocate*, "The line we took was, 'This is not a moral issue. This is about bigotry. You can not debate a person's human rights'" (*The Advocate*, 1982a, p. 9).

A Michigan State University fraternity expels a member because he is gay. The University's Anti-Discrimination Judicial Board orders the Delta Sigma Phi fraternity to reinstate him (*The Advocate*, 1982a).

The Illinois Gay and Lesbian Task Force sends packets of information on gay and lesbian students to Chicago-area high school counselors (*The Advocate*, 1982b).

1984

Berkeley, California, becomes the first city in the nation to offer spousal benefits to same-gender couples who live together (Witt, Thomas, & Marcus, 1995).

The federal government declares that it has found the virus that causes AIDS (Kaiser, 1997).

Los Angeles high school teacher and activist Dr. Virginia Uribe starts Project 10, the first school-based program in the nation to support gay, lesbian, and bisexual youth (Uribe & Harbeck, 1992). Uribe and Harbeck elaborate on Project 10: "(It) was originally envisioned as an in-school counseling program providing emotional support, information, resources, and referrals to young people who identified themselves as lesbian, gay, or bisexual or who wanted accurate information on the subject of sexual orientation. A second goal of the program was to heighten the school community's acceptance of and sensitivity to gay, lesbian, and bisexual issues. Subsequently, Project 10 has become a districtwide and nationwide forum for the articulation of the needs of lesbian, gay, and bisexual teenagers" (p. 11).

1985

A test becomes available to determine exposure to the virus that causes AIDS (Kaiser, 1997). There are still no effective treatments.

Virginia Supreme Court rules in *Roe v. Roe* that a father does not have parental rights to his biological daughter because he is gay. The Court rules, "continuous exposure of the child to his immoral and illicit relationship [with his lover] renders him an unfit and improper custodian" (Schroeder, 1994, p. 30).

The first school in the nation for gay, lesbian, and bisexual youth opens in New York City. The school is named after slain politician and gay activist, Harvey Milk. Early reports suggest that the school is making great strides in the lives of the students (Woog, 1996). Woog writes, "Virtually every student leaves Harvey Milk with heightened confidence and self-esteem. For perhaps the first time in their lives they have met men and women who care about their progress, both as students and as human beings; men and women who discuss with them math, science, English, history, sex, and AIDS—men and women who, like them, are gay" (Woog, p. 237).

A Lutheran-based social-service agency in Philadelphia plans for a foster care system for gay and lesbian youth. The program provides them a safe home where they are loved and protected. Gay and lesbian couples are encouraged to apply as foster parents (Freiberg, 1985).

A Dallas school superintendent rejects the idea of the Dallas Gay Alliance proposal to adopt an elementary school through the Adopt-A-School program. He says, "(The idea) was just too controversial . . . just out of the question" (Baker, 1985, p. 21).

1986

The Supreme Court finds in *Bowers v. Hardwick* that states have the right to regulate same-gender relations (Nava & Dawidoff, 1994; Hogan & Hudson, 1998). Hardwick challenged the Georgia State sodomy law after police entered his home to serve him with a traffic warrant and then arrested him when they found him in bed with a man. Hardwick claimed that the law violated his right to privacy; the Supreme Court ruled otherwise (Nava & Dawidoff, 1994). Twenty-five states impose sodomy statutes (Bull, 2002).

An array of Minnesota-based medical and social agencies sponsor the first national conference on adolescent homosexuality.

1987

The Advocate features the article "Sex Education and the Gay Issue: What Are They Teaching about Us in the Schools?" The author underscores that schools nationwide fail to address homosexuality in sex-education classes. One social-services director explains, "Homosexuality, bisexuality, heterosexuality are all part of the human spectrum . . . but the problem is when they teach it in school, they discuss only . . . heterosexuality. Homosexuality is always seen as this special piece out there that's kept separate and apart from the rest of the course. That's a major problem for a lot of kids, especially if they're concerned about their sexual orientation" (Freiberg, 1987, p. 42).

The New Hampshire Supreme Court rules that the state can bar gay and lesbian persons from adopting children, becoming foster parents, or directing child-care centers (Schroeder, 1994).

An estimated 200,000 persons gather for the gay and lesbian community march and rally in Washington, D.C. One participant later remarked, "That day I discovered that my queer sisters and brothers represented every color, class, and creed; that they—were not a menace to this country but a powerful, loving, gifted, creative presence, a rainbow of promise and productivity" (White, 2002, p. 64).

1988

National Coming Out Day is first celebrated. Artist Keith Haring paints the official logo that depicts a human figure coming out of closet (Witt, Thomas, & Marcus, 1995).

Gay and lesbian adolescents are the topic of an entire issue of the *Journal of Adolescent Health Care*, published by the Society of Adolescent Medicine.

1989

The federal document *The Report of the Secretary's Task Force on Youth Suicide, Volume 3: Prevention and Interventions in Youth Suicide*, reveals that gay and lesbian youth are two to three times more likely to attempt suicide.

Alyson Publications releases Leslea Newman's children's book, *Heather Has Two Mommies*.

1990s

1990

The Cracker Barrel restaurants impose a policy that employees could be fired for being gay (Witt, Thomas, & Marcus, 1995).

Michael Willhoite publishes his children's book on a gay male couple, *Daddy's Roommate*.

The Boy Scouts of America expel Eagle Scout James Dale after learning that he is gay.

1991

There is a 31% increase in harassment and violence directed at gay and lesbian persons living in New York City, San Francisco, Chicago, Boston, and Minneapolis-St. Paul (Nava & Dawidoff, 1994).

The Battelle Human Affairs Research Center in Seattle conducts 3,321 interviews with men between the ages of 20 to 39 and finds that 1% identify themselves as gay (Witt, Thomas, & Marcus, 1995).

Martina Navratilova comes out of the closet in a national TV interview (Gallagher, 1999).

1992

Fifty-three percent of Colorado voters amend their state constitution to prohibit government agencies from enacting statutes or policies protecting gay and lesbian citizens from discrimination (Nava & Dawidoff, 1994; Kaiser, 1997).

MTV introduces *Real World*, a reality-format soap opera featuring housemates from diverse backgrounds living and working together for several months. One of the housemates is gay.

President Bush mentions that same-gender couples make poor parents, and Vice President Dan Quayle describes homosexuality as a wrong "lifestyle choice" (Kaiser, 1997, p. 331).

Researcher Simon LeVay finds that the hypothalamus of gay men is smaller than that of heterosexual men. His studies on lab animals reveal that those with modified hypothalamuses do not respond sexually to the opposite gender.

A police officer in El Cajon, California, is forced out of the Boys Scouts of America because he is openly gay and therefore not a "morally straight" role model.

Musician K. D. Lang comes out of the closet in an exclusive story with *The Advocate* (Gallagher, 1999).

1993

The Christian Life Commission of the Southern Baptist Convention responds to gay and lesbian rights with this statement in their newsletter:

> The CLC opposes homosexuality, because it is clear in the Bible, God condemns it as a sinful lifestyle harmful to the individual and society. Therefore, the CLC opposes the granting of civil rights normally reserved for immutable characteristics, such as race, to a group based on its members' sexual behavior. . . . The CLC proclaims the gospel because the Scriptures declare the Lord Jesus can change homosexuals. To accept homosexuality as an appropriate, alternative lifestyle would betray the life-changing sacrifice of Christ and leave homosexuals without hope for a new and eternal life (cited in Nava & Dawidoff, 1994, p. 98).

A contentious debate continues in New York City schools after the public school chancellor, Joseph Fernandez, urges school boards to adopt a curriculum on diversity and multiculturalism entitled *Children of the Rainbow*. Three pages of the curriculum receive considerable criticism because they introduce and discuss families headed by gay and lesbian parents. An attorney for an opposing school board mentions, "I continue to be of the opinion that introducing the subject of lesbianism and homosexuality to first graders is highly inappropriate" (Osborne, 1993, p. 23). The school board elects not to renew Fernandez's contract.

President Bill Clinton lifts the military's ban of gay and lesbian service personnel after 50 years. During the ban's tenure, over 80,000 persons had been discharged. He later announces the "Don't Ask, Don't Tell" plan that will replace the ban.

About 300,000 gay, lesbian, bisexual, and transgender persons and their allies march in Washington, D.C. The march makes demands, calling for legislation against antigay discrimination and for increased funding for AIDS research, education, and service programs.

In the comic strip *For Better or For Worse*, cartoonist Lynn Johnston creates a storyline about an adolescent coming to terms with his homosexuality. In the four-week story, Lawrence comes out to his friend Michael and then to his parents. Despite the fact that the syndicate office and newspapers around the country receive a flood of letters, threats, obscenities, and subscription cancellations, nearly 70% of the responses are favorable (Walling, 1996).

Carlos Vizcarra, the president of the Gay and Lesbian Association at California State University, Los Angeles, becomes the first openly gay homecoming king.

The Hawaii Supreme Court rules in support of marriage rights for same-gender couples. A reporter later reflects, "[The decision] put the issue of 'gay marriage' on the table and caused many Americans to recognize for the first time that gay and lesbian relationships are as loving and as worthy of legal recognition as the straight ones they grew up with" (Barrett, 2002, p. 77).

1994

There are more than 150 gay and lesbian persons holding political office through appointment or election (Witt, Thomas, & Marcus, 1995).

Two gay men buying a dining-room table are featured in an IKEA furniture store commercial (Kaiser, 1997).

MTV's *Real World* features a gay housemate who is HIV positive, Pedro Zamora.

Outspoken Surgeon General Joycelyn Elders emphasizes that gay youth are at high risk for HIV infection because they do not know how to protect themselves from sexually transmitted diseases, and she insists that the federal government has the duty to educate all Americans about sex and AIDS. She asserts, "Society wants to keep all sexuality in the closet. We have to be more open about sex, and we need to speak out to tell people that sex is good, sex is wonderful. It's a normal part and healthy part of our being, whether it is homosexual or heterosexual" (Bull, 1994, p. 35). Elders is a strong advocate for gay rights, and after she does an interview with *The Advocate*, a Catholic archbishop writes President Clinton: "It is one thing to defend the human rights of homosexual men and women; it is quite another to encourage, as she does, a lifestyle which puts so-called homosexual unions on a par with marriage and family and condones homosexual behavior among young people" (Bull & Gallagher, 1994, p. 26).

Olympic gold-medal winner Greg Louganis comes out of the closet (Gallagher, 1999).

1995

Reverend Fred Phelps declares that "homosexuals" should be given the death penalty (Fone, 2000).

The Supreme Court rules that sponsors of the Boston St. Patrick's Day Parade can rightfully ban gay and lesbian marchers.

In New York City, a gay Irish organization is excluded from marching in the St. Patrick's Day Parade; 300 people react with a protest, and 88 are arrested (Simmons, 1995).

The Illinois State court of appeals rules that gay and lesbian couples have the right to adopt children.

Carol and Susan, a lesbian couple with a baby, are featured on the popular TV show *Friends*. They are the first lesbian parents in sitcom history (Frutkin, 1995).

New Hampshire high school teacher Penny Culliton risks losing her job after administrators discover that she uses gay-themed books in her senior English class (Gallagher, 1995).

Kelli Peterson of Salt Lake City, Utah, starts a Gay–Straight Alliance (GSA) in her high school to "end the misery and isolation of being gay in high school" (Snow, 1996, p. 24). The district's school board elects to ban all noncurricular clubs rather than let the GSA organize on campus.

1996

The Metropolitan Community Church has 40,000 members and about 300 churches in 16 countries (Hogan & Hudson, 1998, p. 387).

President Bill Clinton signs the Defense of Marriage Act, which means that federal and state governments do not recognize same-gender marriages (Kaiser, 1997). Marriage is strictly known as the union between a man and a woman (Fone, 2000).

The U.S. Supreme Court rules in *Romer v. Evans* that the Colorado State Constitution cannot be amended to ban a protection for gay and lesbian persons against sexual-orientation discrimination (Kaiser, 1997).

A study finds that gay and bisexual males are 14 times more likely to attempt suicide than are heterosexual males. Gay and heterosexual young men who are celibate are more likely to harm or kill themselves (King, 1996).

1997

Within a few months after adding sexual-orientation protection policies for students and staff, a suburban school board of Detroit, Michigan, votes for a repeal of the policies.

The American Journal of Public Health publishes a study in which gay and bisexual males between the ages of 13 to 18 are found to be seven times more likely to attempt suicide than are their heterosexual counterparts (The Advocate Report, 1997b).

After a meeting of Catholic bishops, a pastoral letter is distributed to American Catholics titled "Always Our Children." The bishops ask priests to accept gay and lesbian persons in their congregations and emphasize, "God loves every person as a unique individual. . . . God does not love someone any less simply because he or she is homosexual. . . . Do everything possible to continue demonstrating love for your child" (The Advocate Report, 1997a, p. 13).

Ellen DeGeneres's character, Ellen Morgan, comes out of the closet in her sitcom, *Ellen*.

The Southern Baptist Convention elects to boycott The Walt Disney Corporation because it promotes homosexuality by way of its movies and corporate employee policies.

Three Vermont gay couples file suit against the state because they believe the state constitution allows them to marry.

The FBI reports that there were over 1,000 antigay crimes in 1996.

1998

The Metropolitan Community Church has branches in 48 states, with nearly 48,000 members (Loughery, 1998).

The appellate division of the New Jersey superior court rules in favor of expelled Eagle Scout Master James Dale. (Dale had been forced out of the Boy Scouts when his local council found out he was gay.) The court emphasized, "There is absolutely no evidence before us, empirical or otherwise, supporting a conclusion that a gay scoutmaster, solely because he is a homosexual, does not possess the strength of character necessary to properly care for, or to impart BSA humanitarian ideals to, the young boys in his charge" (The Advocate Report, 1998, p. 14).

Will & Grace premieres on NBC.

Christian-based ex-gay ministries that claim they can "cure" homosexuality are found in 39 states.

An "ex-gay" couple, John Paulk (former drag queen) and his wife Anne (former lesbian), appears on the cover of *Newsweek* for a story documenting the ex-gay movement (The Advocate Report, 2001c).

Two men murder Matthew Shepard in Laramie, Wyoming.

Twenty-six homosexual characters are featured in the season's TV lineup, including Carter Heywood of *Spin City*, Dennis Hancock of *Chicago Hope*, Maggie Doyle of *ER*, Gil Chesterton of *Frasier*, Tim Bayliss of *Homicide: Life on the Street*, and Stanford Blatch of *Sex and the City* (Frutkin, 1998).

About 150 Gay–Straight Alliances are in schools nationwide.

1999

On January 19, President Bill Clinton becomes the first U.S. president to mention sexual orientation in a state of the union address. He states, "Discrimination or violence because of race or religion, ancestry or gender, disability or sexual orientation, is wrong and ought to be illegal. Therefore I call upon Congress to make the Employment Non-Discrimination Act and the Hate Crimes Prevention Act the law of the land" (The Advocate Report, 1999a, p. 15).

Nearly 100 students at Notre Dame go on a hunger strike to protest a university decision to not prohibit discrimination based on sexual orientation (The Advocate Report, 1999c, p. 14).

Dawson's Creek, the WB network youth drama, features a main character exploring his sexuality. Even though Michael is taunted and teased by his homophobic schoolmates, the show's central characters remain supportive of him (Epstein, 1999).

The Human Rights Campaign finds that 42 states have some form of hate-crimes laws, while 21 states specifically mention sexual orientation as a protected class (Lemon, 1999).

An article in the *Archives of Pediatric & Adolescent Medicine* reports that in a sample of 4,167 high school students, those who indicated they were gay, lesbian, bisexual, or uncertain of their sexual orientation were 3.4 times more likely to have attempted suicide within the previous year (Savage, 1999).

Pfc. Barry Winchell is bludgeoned to death inside his 101st Airborne infantry barracks at Fort Campbell, Kentucky. Winchell was romantically involved with a transgender entertainer, which overwhelmed a homophobic enlistee into killing him.

What Events Have Unfolded for the Gay and Lesbian Community in the Millennium?

If the gay and lesbian community is a pendulum, its members have witnessed some highs and some lows in the millennium thus far. One of the most significant events to impact the community was the Supreme Court landmark decision in the case of *Lawrence and Garner vs. Texas*. Up until June 26, 2003, it was illegal to engage in gay sex in Alabama, Florida, Idaho, Kansas, Louisiana, Mississippi, Missouri, North Carolina, Oklahoma, South Carolina, Texas, Utah, and Virginia, and violators of the law could be fined and imprisoned (Neff, 2003a). The court decision, however, now enforces that states can no longer ban consensual sodomy. Justice Anthony M. Kennedy ruled, "Adults may choose to enter upon this relationship in the confines of their homes and their own private lives and still retain their dignity as free persons. When sexuality finds overt expression in intimate conduct with another person, the conduct can be but one element in a personal bond that is more enduring. The liberty protected by the Constitution allows homosexual persons the right to make this choice" (cited in Neff, p. 12). The ruling is significant because gay and lesbian persons are no longer ascribed as criminals, which was often the perspective taken in a variety of concerning matters. Neff explains, "The decision dismantles a tool used in legal and political venues to justify discrimination against gays and lesbians seeking to become parents or retain custody of their children, to work for the government or in certain private sector jobs, to obtain housing or secure partnership benefits and recognition" (p. 14).

The issue of same-gender marriages has also drawn widespread debate ever since civil unions became legal in Vermont in 2000. The *New York Times* even published a gay couple's civil union in Vermont in 2002. The focus of gay marriages quickly shifted from civil unions, however, when seven gay and lesbian couples were denied marriage licenses in Massachusetts in 2001. The couples challenged the state's ban on gay marriage in Suffolk Superior Court in Boston, but the judge ruled against them. The case eventually reached the Massachusetts Supreme Judicial Court, which ruled that it is unconstitutional to ban same-gender couples from marriage (Peter, 2004). As a result, same-gender couples were allowed to wed (in Massachusetts) for the first time in our nation's history. In the interim, San Francisco Mayor Gavin Newsom ordered the city clerk to issue marriage licenses to nearly 4,000 same-gender couples even though California state law prohibits same-gender marriages. (The California Supreme Court later voided the marriages.) Same-gender couples have since been applying for marriage licenses in New Mexico (67 couples), Oregon (3,000 couples), and New York (24 couples). The issue of gay marriages has caused quite a nuptial stir that is sure to be a lasting one, and as of this writing, hetero- and homosexual persons alike wait for what happens next: full marriage rights for same-gender couples, a constitutional amendment banning same-gender marriages, or civil unions to be decided upon and recognized by individual states.

The adoption of children by gay and lesbian persons is also a concerning issue in the millennium, which was brought to light when advocate, actor, and former talk-show host Rosie O'Donnell came out of the closet in an interview with Diane Sawyer on ABC's *Primetime Live* in 2002. O'Donnell shared how she and her partner Kelli Carpenter are kind, loving, warm, and embracing mothers (of adopted children) who just happen to be lesbians. She also recognized Steve Lofton and Roger Croteau, the Florida gay couple who want to adopt their foster children but cannot because the state strictly prohibits gay and lesbian persons from adopting children. Because O'Donnell is lesbian, she was also unable to adopt the daughter that she fostered in Florida (Wieder, 2003). In the interview, O'Donnell revealed that emotionally healthy and stable gay and lesbian persons and couples, like heterosexual ones, can adopt children and raise them in nurturing and supportive homes. By her own example, she confirmed that adopted children of same-gender parents grow up to be just as healthy and stable as other children.

This adoption issue has weighed heavily on gay and lesbian persons because many of them believe that some children would be better off living in a loving, stable home of same-gender parents than being shuffled from one temporary home of heterosexual parents to another. And many believe that a sizable number of gay and lesbian persons are able to successfully raise children because they have the wherewithal (i.e., nurturing personalities, education, financial means, etc.) to do so. Many gay and lesbian persons and couples are genuinely interested in adopting children, but only three states rightfully enable them to do so: California, Connecticut, and Vermont. Unfortunately for these gay and lesbian persons, Mississippi and Utah, like Florida, ban same-gender couples from adopting children (Caldwell, 2003), and other states allow judges to prevent a placement with gay and lesbian parents even though they can technically adopt them (Cahill, Ellen, & Tobias, 2003). Child welfare experts agree that gay and lesbian couples make good parents (Delgado, 2004), but until more states believe this, gay and lesbian persons and their advocates will continue to fight for their right to adopt children.

Indeed, society has witnessed the gay and lesbian community make some advances in this millennium alone. There are more gay and lesbian persons elected to political offices, featured in TV programs, discussed in the media, honored for their contributions, and so forth. But the community has also suffered some disappointments. Hundreds of military personnel are still discharged under the "Don't Ask, Don't Tell" policy, antigay hate crimes increase whenever initiatives are passed that favor the community, and persons are still killed because of their sexual orientation. The timeline of events below uncovers some of the ups and downs that the gay and lesbian community has witnessed since the beginning of this millennium.

The Millennium

2000

The U.S. Supreme Court rules that the Boy Scouts of America (BSA) can bar gay members. In response to the judgment, a number of school districts and United Way agencies sever their alliances with BSA.

The National Coalition of Anti-Violence Programs reports that antigay hate crimes increase 8% from 1999.

Hundreds of thousands of gay-rights supporters attend the Millennium March.

Under the "Don't Ask, Don't Tell" plan, 1,231 military service personnel are discharged.

Vermont recognizes civil unions after a same-gender couple have an official ceremony (Lisotta, 2003).

2001

CBS airs a contemporary version of *The Odd Couple*, except one roommate is straight and the other one is gay. Jason Bateman and Danny Nucci star in the sitcom *Some of My Best Friends*.

Maryland becomes the 12th state of the union to pass a bill banning antigay discrimination (The Advocate Report, 2001d).

Chicago Cubs pitcher Julian Tavarez makes a public apology for calling San Francisco fans "faggots" (The Advocate Report, 2001a).

The Alliance for Marriage proposes that the U.S. Constitution be amended to ban gay marriages (The Advocate Report, 2001b).

And Baby, a magazine for gay and lesbian parents, joins the ranks of *Proud Parenting*, a magazine for families headed by gay and lesbian persons (The Advocate Report, 2001d).

Brigham Young University (BYU) in Salt Lake City, Utah, asks premed student Matthew Grierson to withdraw for violating its honor code prohibiting "homosexual conduct." A student had spotted Grierson holding hands with his boyfriend at a local mall and reported the incident to the authorities. The university also asks another student, Ricky Escoto, to leave the university because others allege that he had kissed men, received flowers from them, and visited gay Internet chat rooms. Escoto, who claims that 13 other students had been expelled from the university for watching the Showtime drama *Queer As Folk*, discovers that BYU's actions are legal because it is a private institution and there are no antigay laws in Utah. In order for the two to return to school, they must convince counselors that they are no longer gay (Mardesich, 2001).

A Florida judge rules that a 1977 law barring gay and lesbian persons from adopting children is constitutional. The judge declares that the plaintiffs had "not asserted that they can demonstrate that homosexual families are equivalently stable, are able to provide proper gender identification, [and] are no more socially stigmatizing than married heterosexual families." He then follows with, "[a] child's best interest is to be raised in a home stabilized by a mother and a father" (The Advocate Report, 2001f, p. 15).

A study commissioned by the Gay, Lesbian and Straight Education Network surveys 1,000 parents and finds that over 80% favor programs and policies that reduce antigay harassment and discrimination in schools. Moreover, 63% of the parents indicated that they want middle school and high school health-education classes to discuss gay and lesbian issues (Brune, 2001).

2002

A Georgia appeals court rules that Vermont civil unions are not legally equivalent to a marriage.

Cable networks *Showtime* and *MTV* begin plans to offer viewers a 24-hour cable channel devoted to gay and lesbian programming (Meers, 2002b).

In an interview with Diane Sawyer for *Primetime*, actor/comedienne/talk-show host Rosie O'Donnell comes out of the closet. O'Donnell, who has adopted children with her partner Kelli Carpenter, speaks out against Florida's ban of adoptions by gay and lesbian persons (DuLong, 2002).

The Servicemembers Legal Defense Network reports that 1,250 military personnel were discharged in 2001 for breaking the "Don't Ask, Don't Tell" policy (The Advocate Report, 2002a).

Elementary school principal Mark French of Maple Grove, Minnesota, appears on a Nickelodeon special, *Nick News Special Edition: My Family Is Different.* The well-respected, openly gay educator emphasizes that gay teachers can be good role models for children. One parent reacts to the news with, "This isn't about homophobia. It's about a child's innocence; childhood is supposed to be about fireflies and laughter, and you lose that when you have to deal with something like this" (Blotcher, 2002, p. 18).

Kansas, Missouri, Oklahoma, and Texas have laws against same-gender sodomy; Alabama, Florida, Idaho, Louisiana, Massachusetts, Michigan, Mississippi, North Carolina, South Carolina, Utah, and Virginia have bans on same-gender and opposite-gender sodomy. Lambda Legal Defense and Education Fund appeals the Texas court ruling that the state's same-gender sodomy law is constitutional (Bull, 2002, p. 51), which makes it illegal for consenting adults to engage in same-gender sex. The case is filed on behalf of two men who were having sex in the home of one of the men when they were arrested in 1998 (The Advocate Report, 2002c).

The Pennsylvania Supreme Court rules that gay and lesbian persons are entitled to adopting their partner's children. A spokesperson for FamilyNet, a Human Rights Campaign project, asserts, "There's been incredible progress made this year. People are realizing that what the judge [in the Pennsylvania case] said is true—it's absurd to deny kids a loving home because both parents happen to be of the same sex" (The Advocate Report, 2002b, p. 13).

The civil union in Vermont between Daniel Andrew Gross and Steven Goldstein is the first same-gender nuptial announcement in the *New York Times* (Gay Marriage: A History, 2004).

Two transgender teenagers are murdered in Washington, D.C. One of the girls' mother insists that they were victims of a hate crime because each girl was riddled with 10 bullets (Meers, 2002a).

Twenty-two gay and lesbian persons survive their partners' deaths in the September 11 attacks on the World Trade Center. Two have applied to the Victim Compensation Fund, although there are no guarantees that gay and lesbian survivors will receive financial assistance.

Voters in Miami-Dade uphold an ordinance protecting gay and lesbian persons from sexual-orientation discrimination in housing, employment, and public accommodations (The Advocate Report, 2002d).

Former NFL football player Esera Tuaolo comes out of the closet.

Student-body president Brad Clark of Central College (Iowa) comes out of the closet. Soon after his public disclosure, he is asked to step down from a leadership position with the InterVarsity Christian Fellowship.

Students at a suburban Chicago high school elect two girls for the title "cutest couple." One student claims, "I think it's a good thing. They can express themselves openly, and we don't have a problem with that" (Trice & Rubin, 2002, p. 3). The girls' parents did not know the girls were dating until the district contacted them for permission to run their photograph in the school's yearbook.

Voters of Providence, Rhode Island, elect the first openly gay mayor in the United States, David Cicilline (Dahir, 2002).

2003

Openly gay 19-year-old Jim Verraros is among the top ten finalists on *American Idol*. In an interview with *The Advocate*, he describes his life in junior high school: "I was pinpointed as gay the minute I set foot in junior high. My voice wasn't as low as the other guys'. I loved choir. I loved theatre. I was a lot more effeminate than most of the guys were, and of course guys pick up on that right away. And it got really, really bad. I was called 'faggot' every day for a long time. I would literally run from class to class" (Steele, 2003, p. 76).

After losing her partner of 18 years to the September 11 attacks on the Pentagon, Peggy Neff receives $557,390 from the Victim Compensation Fund. A spokesperson for the Lambda Legal Defense and Education Fund emphasizes, "It's the first time the federal government has provided economic relief to a gay or lesbian partner that approaches that of a married spouse" (Dahir, 2003a, p. 15).

Charles R. Middleton becomes the first openly gay president of a major university, Roosevelt University in Chicago (Neff, 2003b).

Two years after a Colorado youth was a victim of an antigay hate crime—he was severely beaten with a baseball bat and a two-by-four—he is awarded $1.22 million in damages after the court finds that his civil rights were violated. He reflects on his experiences, "When I got beat up, it kicked me out of the closet. I thought my family would hate that I was gay. But they hated that I was beaten because of it. They fought for me. They went to court for me" (Neff, 2003c, p. 27).

After participating in the National Day of Silence and being verbally abused by a student, 16-year-old Caitlin Meuse suffers severe facial injuries when she is attacked with a blunt object. Meuse believes that she is a victim of gay bashing (Dahir, 2003b).

After spending the evening in New York City with four of her friends, 16-year-old Sakia Gunn is stabbed and killed after the girls let the assailants know that they were lesbian (The Advocate Report, 2003e).

The Bravo network premiers *Queer Eye for the Straight Guy*.

In *Lawrence v. Texas*, the U.S. Supreme Court rules against the state's law banning same-gender sodomy. Same-gender intercourse between consenting adults is now legal in all 50 states. Justice Anthony Kennedy stated that such a law "demeans the lives of homosexual persons. . . . [The petitioners] are entitled to respect for their private lives. It is a promise of the Constitution that there is a realm of personal liberty which the government may not enter" (Bull, 2003, p. 35). Justice Sandra Day O'Connor declares, "A law branding one class of persons as criminal solely based on the state's moral disapproval of that class and the conduct associated with that class runs contrary to the values of the Constitution" (Bull, p. 35).

At a White House press conference, President George W. Bush affirms, "I believe a marriage is between a man and a woman, and I think we ought to codify that one way or the other, and we've got lawyers looking at the best way to do that" (The Advocate Report, 2003b).

The Walt Disney Company awards openly gay kindergarten teacher Randy Heite "Outstanding Teacher of the Year." The Evanston, Illinois, teacher explains, "I think I have proven that it doesn't matter if you're gay. . . . I was accepted in my community for who I am. Every year parents request me to teach their child" (The Advocate Report, 2003d, p. 14).

The Episcopal Church confirms Reverend V. Gene Robinson as bishop. He is the first openly gay bishop in a large denomination (Freiberg, 2003).

In Washington, D.C., two transgender persons, Bella Evangelista and Emonie Kiera, are shot to death, and another is injured with a bullet wound (The Advocate Report, 2003c).

A gay couple wins $1 million in CBS's reality contest, *The Amazing Race*. Throughout the 13-week season, CBS promotes the couple, Riechen Lehmkul and Chip Arndt, as married (The Advocate Report, 2003a).

Arkansas, Indiana, South Carolina, and Wyoming have no hate-crime laws. Alabama, Alaska, Colorado, Georgia, Idaho, Maryland, Michigan, Mississippi, Montana, North Carolina, North Dakota, Oklahoma, Ohio, South Dakota, Utah, Virginia, and West Virginia have hate-crime laws that do not cover sexual orientation. The remaining states include hate-crime laws based on sexual orientation (Where We Stand, 2003).

California passes the domestic-partnership law, which recognizes same-gender couples that have registered with the secretary of state. The law entitles same-gender couples' rights in areas such as "child custody, legal claims, housing protections, bereavement leave, and state government benefits" (Lisotta, 2003, p. 18).

The ABC season lineup includes a sitcom about a gay couple with a 23-year-old daughter. The show, *It's All Relative*, stars Christopher Sieber and John Benjamin Hickey (Goodridge, 2003). Sieber, who also played Mary-Kate and Ashley Olsen's father in the sitcom *Two of a Kind*, comes out of the closet.

A Louisiana second-grade classroom teacher punishes a student because he explains to another child that his mother is lesbian—"Gay is when a girl likes another girl" (The Advocate Report, 2004b, p. 16). The student was scolded, given a behavior contract, instructed to contemplate and resolve his "problem," and was ordered to repeatedly write "I will never use the word 'gay' in school again."

In a 4 to 3 vote, the Massachusetts Supreme Judicial Court rules that same-gender couples can marry (Seelye & Elder, 2003). In response, Governor Mitt Romney immediately endorses a constitutional amendment to ban gay marriages.

2004

New Jersey joins the ranks of Vermont, Hawaii, California, and Massachusetts in legally recognizing same-gender couples. The New Jersey law affords registered domestic partners "hospital visitation rights, the ability to make medical decisions for their partners, an exemption from state inheritance taxes, and equal access to spousal benefits from insurance companies" (Dahir, 2004, p. 13).

A Virginia judge rules that the adopted children of three couples from New York, Pennsylvania, and Maryland cannot assume their adoptive parents' names. The adoptions are legal in the three states; however, the children were born in Virginia, which outlaws unmarried couples from adopting children (Delgado, 2004).

Gay and lesbian persons are barred from legally adopting children in Florida, Mississippi, Utah, and Virginia. Additionally, Nebraska and Arkansas ban gay and lesbian persons from becoming foster-care parents.

Although the State of California bars same-gender nuptials, San Francisco mayor Gavin Newsom orders the county clerk's office to issue marriage licenses to same-gender couples (Kher, Mustafa, Novack, & Taseer, 2004). In one week, 3,200 same-gender couples were married (Breslau & Stone, 2004), including Rosie O'Donnell and Kelli Carpenter (Quittner, 2004b). A few months later, the California Supreme Court rules that the approximate 4,000 same-gender marriages are void.

The National Coalition of Anti-Violence Programs reports that following the Supreme Court's 2003 ruling there was a 24% increase in antigay hate crimes (Healy, 2004).

Jazz saxophone player, Dave Koz, publicly comes out of the closet (Vary, 2004).

Twenty-eight states and the District of Columbia have some form of hate-crime laws that include sexual orientation. (See box 7.3.)

Three Westminster School District trustees (in Orange County, California) refuse to obey a law to protect transgender students, which puts the district at risk of losing nearly $40 million in federal funding. One trustee believes that the government is forcing (by way of blackmail) an agenda on the district (The Advocate Report, 2004c).

BOX 7.3. HATE CRIME LAWS IN THE UNITED STATES

Hate-crime laws that include crimes based on sexual orientation and gender identity:

California, New Mexico, Missouri, Minnesota, Pennsylvania, Vermont, and the District of Columbia

Hate-crime laws that include crimes based on sexual orientation:

Arizona, Connecticut, Delaware, Florida, Illinois, Iowa, Kansas, Kentucky, Louisiana, Maine, Massachusetts, Nebraska, New Hampshire, New Jersey, New York, Nevada, Oregon, Rhode Island, Tennessee, Texas, Washington, and Wisconsin

Source: National Gay and Lesbian Task Force. (2004). *Hate crime laws in the U.S.* Retrieved October 28, 2004, from http://www.thetaskforce.org/downloads/hatecrimesmap.pdf.

Parents of students at a Nebraska high school refuse permission for their children to attend a band trip to Orlando, Florida, because it will coincide with the city's Gay Days (The Advocate Report, 2004a).

On May 17, Massachusetts becomes the first state in the nation's history to allow gay and lesbian couples to marry.

New Jersey governor, James McGreevey, announces that he had an extramarital affair with a man and will resign from his political office.

The number of military discharges in 2003 under the "Don't Ask, Don't Tell" policy totals 787 (Quittner, 2004b).

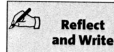

Reflect and Write

Which of the events in the timelines did you find most surprising? Why? Which of the events in the timelines are you most likely to introduce to or discuss with students? Why?

Summary

The timelines in this chapter are a snapshot of how gay and lesbian persons have been treated in the United States. For much of their history, they have been persecuted because society believed they were deviant and sick, and very few people protested against the unjust treatment they endured. Things changed for the community when the patrons of the Stonewall Inn, tired of the intimidation and social laws against them, fought back. Little did they know it at the time, but the spark of that early-morning riot would ignite a movement that would make the gay and lesbian community more visible and vocal. Gay and lesbian persons have advocated for the rights they believe they are entitled to, and while they are certainly making advances in the millennium, they are still victims of unfair and unsettling circumstances. The community is likely to witness ups and downs in the future as long as others refuse to believe that gay and lesbian persons are entitled to the rights that heterosexual have.

Idea File

1. Watch a documentary covering events or issues that have impacted the gay and lesbian community, such as *The Celluloid Closet, Paragraph 175, Licensed to Kill, Out of the Past, The Times of Harvey Milk, Common Threads, Stories from the Quilt, Trembling before G-D.*, and *Frontline: Assault on Gay America.*

2. Outline arguments for and against a critical issue for the gay and lesbian community, such as same-gender marriages, adoption by gay and lesbian persons and couples, and antigay hate-crime legislation.

References

The Advocate. (1971a, January 20). School suspends counselor after appearance on TV. *The Advocate*, p. 1.

The Advocate. (1971b, May 26). Teacher appeals firing. *The Advocate*, p. 4.

The Advocate. (1972a, June 21). D.C. school board bans gay bias. *The Advocate*, p. 3.

The Advocate. (1972b, June 21). Fired because of rumor, rural teacher fights back. *The Advocate*, p. 1.

The Advocate. (1972c, March 28). Gay, straight kids groove at "Y" meet. *The Advocate*, p. 7.

The Advocate. (1972d, February 16). Poll says young adults back gays. *The Advocate*, p. 4.

The Advocate. (1978, March 8). Alaskan school board bans gay teachers. *The Advocate*, p. 12.

The Advocate. (1980a, March 6). Bush comes out hard against gay rights. *The Advocate*, p. 7.

The Advocate. (1980b, April 17). Reagan won't "condone" gays, will take funds from fundamentalists. *The Advocate*, p. 7.

The Advocate. (1982a, April 1). Wisconsin first state to pass gay rights law. *The Advocate*, p. 9.

The Advocate. (1982b, June 24). MSU frat must retain gay member, board says. *The Advocate*, p. 15.

The Advocate. (1982c, October 14). Illinois high schoolers get gay info packet. *The Advocate*, pp. 18–19.

The Advocate Report. (1997a, November 11). Children before church: Catholic bishops say parents must love their children—even the gay ones. *The Advocate, 746*, 13.

The Advocate Report. (1997b, October 14). Youth at risk: Are gay youth suicide risks? New research may settle the debate. *The Advocate, 744*, 15.

The Advocate Report. (1998, March 31). New Jersey court salutes gay scouts. *The Advocate, 754*, 14.

The Advocate Report. (1999a, March 2). He said it first. *The Advocate, 780*, 15.

The Advocate Report. (1999b, October 26). In good company. *The Advocate, 795*, 14.

The Advocate Report. (1999c, March 16). Notre Dame students are hungry for equality. *The Advocate, 781*, 14.

The Advocate Report. (2001a, June 5). Confused cub. *The Advocate, 839*, 16.

The Advocate Report. (2001b, August 28). The Constitution and gay marriage: Antigay activists propose a constitutional amendment to keep gay people from going down the aisle. *The Advocate, 845*, 13.

The Advocate Report. (2001c, May 8). Exodus forgives John Paulk. *The Advocate, 837,* 20.

The Advocate Report. (2001d, September 25). Focusing on the family. *The Advocate, 847,* 18.

The Advocate Report. (2001e, May 8). Maryland we roll along. It took nearly a quarter century, but the "Free State" has become the 12th in the nation with a gay rights law. *The Advocate, 837,* 15.

The Advocate Report. (2001f, October 9). Preventing parenting: A federal judge upholds Florida's ban on adoption by gays. *The Advocate, 848,* 15.

The Advocate Report. (2002a, April 16). "Don't ask" discharges at an all-time high. *The Advocate, 861,* 18.

The Advocate Report. (2002b, October 1). Gay families go mainstream: Reaction to a ruling in favor of gay adoption suggests that same-gender parents are winning hearts and minds. But is it too soon to declare victory? *The Advocate, 873,* 13.

The Advocate Report. (2002c, September 3). Sodomy takes the stand. *The Advocate, 871,* 16.

The Advocate Report. (2002d, October 15). Victory in Miami-Dade. *The Advocate, 874,* 16.

The Advocate Report. (2003a, September 30). A million reasons to stay married. *The Advocate, 899,* 20.

The Advocate Report. (2003b, September 2). Backlash fever: Is the mainstream push for gay marriage actually setting the movement back? *The Advocate, 897,* 13.

The Advocate Report. (2003c, September 30). D.C. nightmare. *The Advocate, 899,* 14.

The Advocate Report. (2003d, September 2). Gay teacher gets Disney distinction. *The Advocate, 897,* 14.

The Advocate Report. (2003e, June 24). Young and in danger in New Jersey. *The Advocate, 892,* 26.

The Advocate Report. (2004a, May 25). Across the nation. *The Advocate, 915,* 18.

The Advocate Report. (2004b, February 4). "Bad wurds" in Louisiana: A lesbian mom faces a defiant school board after her young son is punished for telling his classmates that she is gay. *The Advocate, 907,* 16.

The Advocate Report. (2004c, May 11). Heaven trumps gender equality. *The Advocate, 914,* 23.

Baker, J. (1985, October 1). Dallas gays won't "adopt" school. *The Advocate,* p. 21.

Barrett, J. (2002, November 12). Marriage in Hawaii: When Hawaii's Supreme Court rules in favor of marriage rights for same-sex couples, the debate quickly goes nationwide. *The Advocate, 876,* 77.

Blotcher, J. (2002, July 23). Teaching by example: Fresh from an appearance on Nickelodeon, a Minnesota educator wants parents to know that gay teachers are nothing to be afraid of. *The Advocate, 868,* 18.

Breslau, K., & Stone, B. (2004, March 1). Outlaw vows: A brash young mayor issues marriage licenses to same-sex couples and opens a new front in America's culture wars. *Newsweek, 143*(9), 40–44.

Brune, A. (2001, December 25). Power to the parents. *The Advocate, 853,* 16.

Bull, C. (1994, March 22). The condom queen reigns: Surgeon General Elders speaks out where the president fears to tread. *The Advocate, 651,* 31–38.

Bull, C. (2002, August 20). Full assault on sodomy laws: The repeal of Arkansas's sodomy law and the arrest of six men at a Missouri video store are just the latest examples of turmoil over these archaic antigay laws. *The Advocate, 689/670,* 51–53.

Bull, C. (2003, August 19). Justice served: As the Supreme Court closed the door on sodomy laws, it may have opened a door for other causes—including gay marriage and the ensuing antigay backlash. *The Advocate, 895/896,* 35–38.

Bull, C., & Gallagher, J. (1994). The surgeon general's cardinal sin: Elders's kind words for gays and lesbians in an *Advocate* interview have a Catholic cardinal seeing red. *The Advocate, 653,* 26.

Cahill, S., Ellen, M., & Tobias, S. (2003). *Family policy: Issues affecting gay, lesbian, bisexual, and transgender families.* New York: National Gay and Lesbian Task Force.

Caldwell, J. (2003, June 10). Little victories for gay adoption: A Mississippi ruling in favor of two lesbian moms shows that states may be forced to allow gay parents even as they reject gay couples. *The Advocate, 891,* 38–39.

Clendinen, D., & Nagourney, A. (2001). *Out for good: The struggle to build a gay rights movement in America.* New York: Simon and Schuster.

Cole, R. (1970, June 10–23). Two men ask Minnesota license for first legal U.S. gay marriage. *The Advocate, 4,* 1.

Dahir, M. (2002, December 24). Leading providence: David Cicilline becomes the first openly gay mayor of a U.S. state capital. *The Advocate, 879,* 26–27.

Dahir, M. (2003a, March 4). A federal nod to gay partners: Will Peggy Neff's award from the federal Victim Compensation Fund help all same-sex couples win more legal recognition? *The Advocate, 884,* 15.

Dahir, M. (2003b, May 27). Silence, then violence: One day after taking part in the national Day of Silence, a 16-year-old is herself a victim of an apparent antigay attack. *The Advocate, 890,* 26.

Dahir, M. (2004, February 17). Garden state of bliss: While awaiting a decision on same-sex marriage from its highest court, New Jersey passes a landmark statewide domestic-partnership law. *The Advocate, 908,* 13.

Delgado, R. (2004, March 16). A family fight: Will the battle for adoption rights get more difficult as same-sex marriage advances? *The Advocate, 910,* 13.

DuLong, J. (2002, April 16). Rosie's crusade: Could the "queen of nice" turn the tide for gay adoption rights? *The Advocate, 861,* 15.

Epstein, J. (1999, March 16). Outings on the creek: What inspired *Dawson's Creek* to tackle a gay teen story line? Credit series creator Kevin Williams. *The Advocate, 781,* 46–49.

Fairbanks, H. (1972, November 8). ABC to air sensitive story on real-life gays. *The Advocate, 98,* 26.

Fone, B. (2000). *Homophobia: A history.* New York: Metropolitan Books.

Freiberg, P. (1985). Lutherans plan foster-care system for gay youths in Philadelphia. *The Advocate,* p. 10.

Freiberg, P. (1987). Sex education and the gay issue: What are they teaching about us in the schools? *The Advocate,* pp. 42–49.

Freiberg, P. (2003, September 16). Gay man of God. The Reverend V. Gene Robinson recounts the scandal-ridden process that led to his confirmation as the first openly gay Episcopal bishop. *The Advocate, 898,* 28.

Frutkin, A. (1995). Family outings: The arrival of a bouncing baby boy on *Friends* makes headway for lesbian sitcom families. *The Advocate, 679,* 30–31.

Frutkin, A. (1998, September 15). TV's 26 gay characters. *The Advocate,* pp. 34–35.

Gallagher, J. (1995, October 17). Indirect assault: Assaults on gay-related school curricula are providing religious conservatives with a powerful organizing tool for the 1996 presidential campaign. *The Advocate, 692,* 18–19.

Gallagher, J. (1999, August 17). Take a Wilde ride: From Oscar Wilde to the Rev. Jimmy Creech, a selective history of gay and lesbian activism. *The Advocate, 791,* 9–16.

Gay Marriage: A History. (2004, February 16). *Time, 163*(7), 58–59.

Goodridge, M. (2003, October 14). Relatively revolutionary: A sitcom featuring a gay couple with a daughter—shocking, or just good business sense? Both, say producers. *The Advocate, 900,* 52–54.

Grant, C. A. (1994). Challenging the myths about multicultural education. *Multicultural Education, 2,* 4–9.

Healy, C. (2004, April 27). Marriage's bloody backlash: Legal victories and the movement to legalize gay marriage have meant an increase in gay bashing. *The Advocate, 913,* 38–40.

Higgins, P. (Ed.). (1993). *A queer reader: 2500 years of male homosexuality.* New York: The New Press.

Hoffman, M. (1970). Homosexuality. *Today's Education, 59*(8), 46–49.

Hogan, S., & Hudson, L. (1998). *Completely queer: The gay and lesbian encyclopedia.* New York: Henry Holt and Company.

Hunter, J. F. (1971, May 12). Gays busted at N.Y. school board sit-in. *The Advocate,* pp. 3–14.

Jackson, E. (1970, April). Gaydom is largest city in America. *The Advocate, 4,* 10.

Kaiser, C. (1997). *The gay metropolis: 1940–1996.* New York: Houghton Mifflin Company.

Kher, U., Mustafa, N., Novack, K., & Taseer, A. (2004, February 23). Married. Hundreds of Gay and Lesbian Couples. *Time, 163*(3, Notebook: Milestones), 16.

King, M. (1996, November 12). Suicide watch: A new study suggests that young gay men are at even higher risk for attempting to kill themselves than previously thought. *The Advocate, 713/714,* 41–44.

Lemon, B. (1999, April 13). The state of hate. *The Advocate, 783,* 24–31.

Licata, S. J. (1981). The homosexual rights movement in the United States: A traditional overlooked area of American history. In S. J. Licata, & R. P. Petersen (Eds.), *Historical perspectives on homosexuality* (pp. 161–89). New York: The Haworth Press.

Lisotta, C. (2003, October 14). Toward perfect unions: California's new domestic partnership law is second only to Vermont's. *The Advocate, 900,* 17.

Loughery, J. (1998). *The other side of silence: Men's lives and gay identities: A twentieth-century history.* New York: Henry Holt and Company.

Mardesich, J. (2001, September 25). Pass or fail: Students at religious schools often have to give up their safety for their sanity when they come out of the closet. *The Advocate, 847,* 26–31.

Meers, E. (2002a). Capital murders: Two transgendered teenagers are gunned down in Washington, D.C., leaving their families reeling and police searching for clues. *The Advocate, 872,* 22.

Meers, E. (2002b). We want our gay TV: Showtime and MTV partner to create a gay cable channel—but will they be first across the finish line? *The Advocate, 858,* 56–57.

Miller, N. (1995). *Out of the past: Gay and lesbian history from 1869 to the present.* New York: Vintage Books.

Nava, M., & Dawidoff, R. (1994). *Created equal: Why gay rights matter to America.* New York: St. Martin's Press.

Neff, L. (2003a, July 2). Court ruling marks new era in gay rights. *Chicago Free Press, 4*(46), 1, 12–14.

Neff, L. (2003b, April 1). History-making professor: As the nation's first out university president, Charles R. Middleton is determined to make Chicago's Roosevelt U. "a welcoming place." *The Advocate, 886,* 18.

Neff, L. (2003c, April 29). The wounds money can't heal: A Colorado teen wins a million dollars in damages after an alleged attack—but local police still doubt his story. *The Advocate, 888,* 26–27.

Oddone, M. (1977, December 14). Of all, the most vulnerable: Homophobia hits the classroom. *The Advocate,* pp. 15–17.

Osborne, D. (1993, March 9). N.Y. changes curriculum, but the fight goes on. *The Advocate,* p. 23.

Peter, J. (2004, May 17). Gays camp out to be the first to wed. *Houston Chronicle,* pp. 3A.

Quittner, J. (2004a, March 30). Gavin's gay gamble: Mayor Gavin Newsom makes San Francisco a mecca for gay marriage. What was this straight guy thinking? *The Advocate, 911,* 28–31.

Quittner, J. (2004b, September 28). The truth about "unit cohesion": The excuse for barring out soldiers is the reverse of the truth, according to a new survey released exclusively to *The Advocate*. *The Advocate, 923*, 28–29.

Savage, T. (1999, June 22). Gay teens face high suicide risk. *The Advocate, 787*, 24.

Scanzoni, L., & Mollenkott, V. R. (1978). *Is the homosexual my neighbor? Another Christian view*. San Francisco: Harper & Row.

Schroeder, J. (1994, August 23). Twenty-five years of courtroom trauma. *The Advocate, 659*, 26–31.

Seelye, K. Q, & Elder, J. (2003, December 21). Poll: Half in U.S. support gay marriage ban. *Austin American-Statesman*, p. A13.

Shilts, R. (1975, December 17). Foster homes for gay children—Justice or prejudice. *The Advocate*, pp. 11–12.

Shilts, R. (1977, June 1). Gay youth: The lonely young. *The Advocate*, pp. 31–44.

Shister, G. (1979, August 9). Guilbert gets his "prom." *The Advocate*, pp. 12.

Simmons, J. (1995, April 18). St. Patrick's Day massacre: A big protest in New York City puts the "ire" back in Ireland. *The Advocate, 679*, 25.

Snow, K. (1996, April 2). Utah high school students have galvanized the state's gay movement—and set the stage for a national debate. *The Advocate, 704*, 24.

Spencer, C. (1995). *Homosexuality in history*. New York: Harcourt Brace & Company.

Steele, B. (2003, January 21). A teen Idol's dream: Jim Verraros, the 19-year-old American Idol finalist, talks for the first time about overcoming antigay abuse in school and finding the strength to come out and take on Hollywood. *The Advocate, 880/881*, 74–77.

Trice, D. T., & Rubin, B. M. (2002, November 20). Students stage walkout to back "cutest couple." *Chicago Tribune*, sec. 2, p. 3.

Uribe, V., & Harbeck, K. M. (1992). Addressing the needs of lesbian, gay, and bisexual youth: The origins of Project 10 and school-based intervention. In K. M. Harbeck (Ed.), *Coming out of the classroom closet: Gay and lesbian students, teachers and curricula* (pp. 9–28). New York: Harrington Park Press.

Vary, A. B. (2004). Just Koz: Smooth-jazz golden boy Dave Koz comes out—fresh off his adventurous new album, Saxophonic. *The Advocate, 913*, 44–49.

Walling, D. R. (1996). Coming out in the comics: A look at Lynn Johnston's "For Better or For Worse." In D. R. Walling (Ed.), *Open lives: Safe schools* (pp. 145–171). Bloomington, IN: Phi Delta Kappa.

Where we stand. (2003, September 30). *The Advocate, 899*, 35.

White, M. (2002, November 12). Safety in numbers: The 1987 march on Washington. *The Advocate, 876*, 64.

Wicker, R. (1973, March 28). Psychiatrists consider reclassifying homosexuality. *The Advocate*, p. 3.

Wieder, J. (2003, January 21). The real Rosie: 365 days of amazing challenges and feisty decisions turned America's sweetheart into the fighter she's always been—and *The Advocate*'s leading lady for 2002. *The Advocate, 880/881*, 52–69.

Witt, L., Thomas, S., & Marcus, E. (1995). *Out in all directions: The almanac of gay and lesbian America*. New York: Warner Books.

Woog, D. (1996). *School's out: The impact of gay and lesbian issues on American's schools*. New York: Alyson Books.

CHAPTER 8

Famous Gay and Lesbian Persons and Resourceful Organizations

<table>
<tr><td colspan="2">♀️   *JEOPARDY* QUIZ   ♂️</td></tr>
</table>

JEOPARDY QUIZ

How well do you know prominent gay and lesbian persons? The answers to the following statements are people who are either gay or lesbian. Take a moment to answer these with a question, like the game show *Jeopardy*.

1. Baseball pitcher for the Detroit Tigers, the Dodgers, and the San Diego Padres

2. Founded Hull House, which started a nationwide settlement movement

3. Author of *Breakfast at Tiffany's*

4. Author of *My Antonia*

5. Advocate of women's suffrage and cofounder of the National Woman Suffrage Association

6. Starred as the father in the sitcom *The Brady Bunch*

7. Wrote *The Picture of Dorian Gray*

8. First openly gay U.S. representative

9. Author and advocate who is the daughter of Sonny and Cher

10. Mathematician whose life was portrayed in *A Beautiful Mind*

11. Lead singer of R.E.M.

12. Christmas ornament designer

Overview

A number of people were shocked when in 2003 they first heard the news about one of America's heartthrobs of the '60s, '70s, and '80s, Richard Chamberlain. Famed for his roles in *Dr. Kildare*, *The Thorn Birds*, and *Shogun*, Chamberlain disclosed in his autobiography and various interviews that he is gay. The 69-year-old kept his sexuality secret his whole life and hid his 27-year relationship with a man from the public. You may be surprised to learn that a famous person, like Chamberlain, is gay because you have assumed that he or she was heterosexual. Consequently, you are left reconciling the image of the person you thought was heterosexual with the perception you have of gay and lesbian persons. It is important to know about prominent gay and lesbian persons because it furthers your understanding that the group of gay and lesbian persons is heterogeneous and that its members are capable of accomplishing great feats.

The *Jeopardy*-like quiz provided here is to get you thinking about some notable gay and lesbian persons. Some of these historic and contemporary gay and lesbian figures are introduced in the first half of the chapter. As you review the biographies, contemplate how they could be applied in your classroom by way of a lesson plan or discussion to help students learn more about gay and lesbian persons. The latter half of the chapter outlines national organizations that serve the gay and lesbian community through a variety of means. These should be helpful in times when you or your students are seeking emotional- or spiritual-support services or general information about the community. This chapter answers the following questions:

- Who are some famous gay and lesbian persons?
- What organizations will provide me with additional information to help me better understand gay and lesbian youth?

Reflect and Write

Who are famous gay and lesbians persons that you know of in society?

Who Are Some Famous Gay and Lesbian Persons?

For the National Coming Out Day on October 11, 1988, OutFront Minnesota created and distributed a poster that read, "Unfortunately, history has set the record a little too straight" (Casagrande, 1989). Under the caption were the faces of James Baldwin, Willa Cather, Errol Flynn, Michelangelo, Edna St. Vincent, Cole Porter, Eleanor Roosevelt, Bessie Smith, Walt Whitman, and Virginia Woolf. Beneath their faces the poster read, "Sexual orientation has nothing to do with the ability to make a mark, let alone make history" (Casagrande, 1989). OutFront organizers created this slogan because they knew how textbooks and historians rarely mention a prominent figure's sexual orientation and that people often assume that great figures in society are heterosexual. The organizers used the poster to raise the awareness that hetero-, homo-, and bisexual persons alike contribute to society.

Knowing about famous gay and lesbian persons, such as those mentioned in the OutFront poster, helps demystify who they (as a collective group) are and helps you understand that all persons, regardless of sexual orientation, are capable of great accomplishments. By learning about them, you and your students begin to understand that gay and lesbian persons are not the monsters or freaks that many envision them to be. Below are the names of some prominent persons who were or are open about their sexuality or who were or are presumed to be gay or lesbian. The list is not an exhaustive one, but it is certainly a basis for lesson plans or group discussion.

Historical Figures

Jane Addams (1860–1935)—This 1931 Nobel Peace Prize winner was a devoted activist, social reformer, and writer in the late 19th century who founded Hull House, a Chicago settlement (Miller, 2003). Davis (1973) and Cook (1979) (cited in Hogan & Hudson, 1998) assert that Addams had romantic relationships with two women, Ellen Gates Starr and Mary Rozet Smith.

Alexander the Great (356–323 B.C.)—This Ancient Greek ruler conquered empires from Greece to India. Although he was married and had children, historians believe that his confidante, Hephaestion, was also his lover.

Susan B. Anthony (1820–1906)—This well-known suffragette and abolitionist is believed to have had a 50-year relationship with Elizabeth Cady Stanton.

James Baldwin (1924–1987)—This American was an author of novels (including *Go Tell It on the Mountain*), essays, and poetry relative to the African-American experience. His work also included homosexual themes, as in *Giovanni's Room* and *Another Country* (Russell, 2002). He had a male lover named Lucien Happersberger.

Truman Capote (1924–1984)—This American author and playwright, famous for his novel *Breakfast at Tiffany's*, was openly gay. Miller (1995) writes, "In 1948, Truman Capote virtually announced his homosexuality with a suggestive photograph on the dust jacket of his first novel, *Other Voices, Other Rooms*. The picture attracted almost as much attention as the book itself" (p. 309).

Willa Cather (1873–1947)—This American journalist-turned-author often wrote about pioneer life, as in her novel *My Antonia*. Cather was considered masculine, often went by the name William, and wore men's clothing. In her letters to a Louise Pound, she indicated she had an "'unnatural' attraction and love for" her (Hogan & Hudson, 1998, p. 124).

Julius Caesar (100–44 B.C.)—This Roman general and conqueror is the man who said, "I came, I saw, I conquered." Despite his reputation as seducer of women, he had an affair with Nicomedes, the king of Bithynia (Spencer, 1995).

Leonardo da Vinci (1452–1519)—This Italian artist, scientist, inventor, and architect painted *Mona Lisa*, *Madonna on the Rocks*, and *The Last Supper*. At 24, da Vinci and two of his peers were accused and later reprimanded for having committed "godless" acts with a male model, and many speculate that he had homosexual inclinations because his string of assistants were all male, including one young lad that da Vinci painted for over a 20-year period (Russell, 2002).

Emily Dickinson (1830–1886)—This American poet had intimate relationships with men and women. Patterson (1951) believes that Dickinson had a love affair with Kate Scott Turner, and the two spent a "crucial night" together in late February or early March 1860 (cited in Katz, 1992).

Michelangelo (1475–1564)—This Italian artist painted the ceiling of the Sistine Chapel, sculpted the statue *David* and the *Pieta*, and designed the dome of Saint Peter's Basilica. Historians note that Michelangelo never had sex with anyone but had romantic friendships with Tommaso de'Cavalieri and Vittoria Colonna (Hogan & Hudson, 1998). Russell (2002), moreover, asserts that Michelangelo wrote over three hundred sonnets to young men.

Eleanor Roosevelt (1884–1962)—This humanitarian and diplomat was wife to the 32nd president of the United States, Franklin Delano Roosevelt. Many speculate that love letters between Roosevelt and Lorena "Hick" Hickock reveal that the two had a lesbian affair for years. In a letter to "Hick," Roosevelt wrote, "Hick darling, All day I've thought of you & another birthday I will be with you & yet tonite you sounded so far away & formal. Oh! I want to put my arms around you. I ache to hold you close. Your ring is a great comfort. I look at it and think she does love me, or I wouldn't be wearing it" (*Times* Literary Supplement, 1980, cited in Katz, 1983, p. 479). Roosevelt's closest friends were two lesbian couples (Miller, 1995).

Gertrude Stein (1874–1946)—This American poet and author lived in France. Her longtime companion was Alice B. Toklas. Stein wittily titled her autobiography *The Autobiography of Alice B. Toklas*.

Pyotr (Peter) Ilich Tchaikovsky (1840–1893)—This Russian composer wrote *Romeo and Juliet*, *The Nutcracker*, *Swan Lake*, and *Sleeping Beauty*. Despite relationships with women, including a short marriage to one, he had several relationships with men (Hogan & Hudson, 1998).

Walt Whitman (1819–1892)—This American poet wrote *Leaves of Grass* and other celebrated poems. Historians believe that Whitman was fond of young, uneducated workmen and had romantic relationships with Peter Doyle (Spencer, 1995) and Harry Stafford (Russell, 2002).

Oscar Wilde (1854–1900)—This Irish-born writer spent much of his adult life in England and was author of *The Importance of Being Earnest* and *The Picture of Dorian Gray*. He was married and had two sons. However, Wilde had a young lover, Lord Alfred Douglas. When Douglas's father referred to Wilde as a sodomite, Wilde sued him for criminal libel. Wilde lost the court battle and was convicted of homosexual activity and sentenced to prison (Fone, 2000).

Tennessee (Thomas Lanier) Williams (1911–1983)—This American playwright is notorious for his plays *A Streetcar Named Desire* and *Cat on a Hot Tin Roof* in which female characters ironically desire homosexual men because they are unobtainable (Fone, 2000).

Williams had a significant relationship with Fran Merlo for 14 years and later said, "I've never hidden my homosexuality, I don't think. I haven't meant to. But then, I haven't tried to flaunt it, as some have said. In many ways it has been such as an integral part of my creativity, however" (Miller, 1995, p. 312).

Virginia Woolf (1882–1941)—This English writer was author of *Mrs. Dalloway*, *The Waves*, and *Between the Acts* (Hogan & Hudson, 1998). Although Woolf was married, she had a long affair with Vita Sackville-West (Russell, 2002).

Contemporary Figures

Kevyn Aucoin—This late makeup artist to celebrities and runway models died in 2002 and is survived by his partner, Jeremy Antunes.

Billy Bean—This baseball player for the Detroit Tigers, Dodgers, and San Diego Padres wrote *Going the Other Way*, which chronicled his experiences as a closeted sports figure. He and his partner, Efrain Veiga, live in Miami Beach, Florida (Gross, 2003).

Sandra Bernhard—This comedienne and actor played lover to Morgan Fairchild's character in the sitcom *Roseanne*.

Chastity Bono—This author and activist is the daughter of Sonny and Cher. She reflected on being lesbian in her memoirs *Family Outing* and *The End of Innocence*.

Rita Mae Brown—This American author, activist, and screenplay writer has been involved in many political groups, including the National Organization for Women, Radicalesbians, and Redstockings (Hogan & Hudson, 1998). She has written critically acclaimed novels (*Rubyfruit Jungle* and *Sudden Death*), poems (*The Hand that Rocks the Cradles* and *A Plain Brown Rapper*), and has received Emmy nominations. Russell (2002) affirms, "Rita Mae Brown is still going strong, a prolific writer whose *Rubyfruit Jungle* remains one of the most popular accounts—and celebrations—of lesbian experience ever written" (p. 280). She had a lesbian relationship with tennis star Martina Navritilova (Miller, 1995).

Richard Chamberlain—This actor is best known for his roles in the drama *Dr. Kildare* and in the miniseries *The Thorn Birds*. He came out of the closet in 2003.

Margaret Cho—This Korean-American comedienne, actor, and writer is known for her *I'm the One That I Want* and *The Notorious C.H.O.*, both of which have been major hits (O'Brien, 2002). Her work often includes references to her bisexuality.

James Dean—This cultural icon and actor made three films, *East of Eden*, *Rebel without a Cause*, and *Giant*. While there is no certainty of his actual sexual orientation, Dean visited gay bars in the 1950s (Hogan & Hudson, 1998).

Ellen DeGeneres—This actress and comedienne used her character on her sitcom *Ellen* to come out. Despite losing *Ellen* and a subsequent show, *The Ellen Show*, DeGeneres now hosts a talk show appropriately titled *Ellen*. Her relationship with actress Anne Heche ended in 2001.

Melissa Etheridge—This musician is famous for albums such as *Skin and Lucky*. Etheridge publicly came out at President Bill Clinton's inauguration in 1993. She has had relationships with women including one when she was 17, another 12-year relationship with filmmaker Julie Cypher (Hensley, 2001), and now a relationship with actress Tammy Lynn Michaels (of the WB's *Popular*) (Steele, 2004). In fact, Etheridge and Michaels had a wedding on September 20, 2003 (Steele, 2004).

Rupert Everett—This British-born stage and film actor is known for his roles in such films as *My Best Friend's Wedding* and *Shakespeare in Love*. Everett publicly declared his homosexuality in 1989 (Internet Movie Database, 2004a).

Barney Frank—This was the first U.S. representative to come out of the closet. In 1987, Frank decided it to stop living in the closet. He recounted, "I noted that trying to live a closeted life while being publicly prominent proved to be emotionally, physically, and in every other way more difficult than I had anticipated, resulting in extreme emotional stupidity ("U.S. Representative," 2002, p. 55).

Rock Hudson—This actor is best known for his work in films with Doris Day. Hudson was working on the TV drama *Dynasty* when he announced in July 1985 that he had AIDS ("Liz Smith on," 2002). He died on October 2 of that year.

Sir Elton John—This famed British-born pop-music star and composer is best known for songs like "Philadelphia," "Don't Let the Sun Go Down on Me," "Tiny Dancer," "Don't Go Breaking My Heart," and a host of other hits. He announced in 1976 that he was bisexual and later married Renate Blauel. After a divorce and years later, he accepted that he is gay. His long-time partner is filmmaker David Furnish (Internet Movie Database, 2004b).

Billie Jean King—This world-class tennis player beat tennis player Bobby Riggs in the "battle-of-the-sexes" match in 1973. Schwartz (2004) writes, "Unlike most athletes, King's sexual preference became a matter of public record. Two decades ago, having a lover of the same sex was viewed quite unkindly, and was sensational news. In 1981, King admitted her bisexuality amid a palimony suit brought by a former woman lover." The suit was dismissed, but she lost lucrative endorsements over the scandal (Hogan & Hudson, 1998).

K. D. Lang—This famed Canadian-born rock star came out as a lesbian in 1992. Many believe that her coming out was encouragement for the wave of entertainers who came out during the 1990s (Romesburg, 2001).

Liberace—This famed piano player and singer was widely known for the lavish costumes he wore while performing in his Las Vegas shows. He sued two publications for libel—both insinuated that he was gay, but Liberace won both suits. In the early eighties, his chauffeur, Scott Thorson, claimed that he was Liberace's lover and demanded for palimony. Liberace settled out of court before his death in 1987 (Russell, 2002).

Greg Louganis—This U.S. Olympic diver won incredible diving accolades, including a silver medal at the 1976 Olympics and two gold medals, one for the 1984 and the other for the

1988 Olympics. He is considered the greatest diver of all time (Wulfe, 1995). On February 22, 1995, he announced that he had AIDS.

Frank McGreevey—This former governor of New Jersey resigned from his post after the man he had an affair with, Golan Cipel, threatened to disclose their relationship to the media. In his resignation speech, McGreevey, who is married, publicly announced that he is gay.

Sir Ian McKellen—This gay activist and British actor played the wizard Gandalf in *The Lord of the Rings* (Steele, 2001). McKellen, who starred in a number of accolade-receiving plays, has had relationships with men including actor/director Sean Mathias. He came out publicly in 1988 when he debated a British law banning discussion of homosexuality in schools (Steele, 2001).

Megan Mullally—This actress is best known for her role as the feisty-tongued Karen Walker on the hit sitcom *Will & Grace*. Although she has been married and is engaged to actor Nick Offerman, she has publicly admitted that she is bisexual. She elaborates, "I had always been attracted to both men and women, even when I was a little girl. . . . And I liked boys too. Later, I had crushes but never a full-on relationship with a woman because all the women I liked were straight and were, like, 'What is happening?'" (Musto, 2003, p. 35).

John Nash—This brilliant mathematician's biography was made into the movie *A Beautiful Mind*. Despite the fact that Nash married (and divorced and remarried the same woman decades later) and fathered a son, he was attracted to men. Giltz (2002) writes, "According to the Nasar's National Book Critics Circle Award–winning biography, Nash developed intense emotional attachments to men, was sexually attracted to them, and was belittled as a 'homo' during his undergraduate career (when he did his first important mathematical work)" (p. 40).

Martina Navratilova—This woman is regarded as the greatest women's tennis player of all time (Hogan & Hudson, 1998). Navratilova has had relationships with women, and in 1981, she spoke candidly about the relationship she had with American writer Rita Mae Brown (Russell, 2002).

Rosie O'Donnell—She is an actress, a comedienne, a journalist, and a talk show host. The multitalented O'Donnell and her partner Kelli Carpenter have four children, and the two women were among the 4,000 same-gender couples in San Francisco who were married between February and March 2004. California's high court, however, voided all marriages on August 12, 2004 (Willing, 2004).

Christopher Radko—This renowned holiday-ornament designer is openly gay but admits, "Being gay for me is not what I consider a driving force in my life (Lyon, 2003, p. 34).

Robert Reed—This actor starred as the father, Michael Brady, in the 1970s sitcom *The Brady Bunch*. Reed died of AIDS in 1995.

RuPaul (Andre Charles)—This drag queen, musician, and actor began his stage performance in New York, and his popularity grew nationwide in the 1990s. He has a wide
range of credits, including starring in *To Wong Foo, Thanks for Everything! Julie Newmar*,
Crooklyn, and *The Brady Bunch Movie*. RuPaul is openly gay and has written his memoirs,
entitled *Letting It All Hang Out*. He has been honored by The Most Beautiful Transsexuals
In The World Association for his work on behalf of the gay and lesbian community
(Internet Movie Database, 2004c).

Christopher Sieber—This Broadway and Hollywood actor starred as the father of Mary-Kate
and Ashley Olsen in the sitcom *Two of a Kind* (Stockwell, 2003). Sieber currently plays Simon
in the sitcom *It's All Relative*, which revolves around a same-gender couple, Simon and Philip,
and their daughter (Goodridge, 2003). Sieber's long-time partner is Kevin Burrows.

Michael Stipe—This lead singer for the famed rock group R.E.M. came out in 1999.

Esera Tuaolo—NFL football player for the Atlanta Falcons, Carolina Panthers, and Minnesota
Vikings. He and his partner, Mitchell Wherley, have twins, a boy and a girl, Mitchell and
Michelle (Steele, 2002).

What Organizations Will Provide Me with Additional Information to Help Me Better Understand Gay and Lesbian Youth?

 **Application**

What local organizations do you know that can provide you information to help better understand and meet the needs of gay and lesbian youth?

There are many organizations that cater to the gay and lesbian community. Some organizations are political and lobby
on behalf of gay and lesbian persons; others offer school
personnel ideas and resources that promote safe school
environments; and others impart lifestyle, cultural, and current news events relative to the gay and lesbian community.
Visit the websites below to learn how the respective organizations serve gay and lesbian persons, and retrieve
resources to help you improve how members of your learning community behave toward
gay and lesbian youth. The reviews below highlight the resources and their utility in
schools. Because websites are updated and restructured frequently, it is likely that the information supplied in the review may not reflect what is currently available on the website.

AIDS Action
1906 Sunderland Place NW
Washington, DC 20036
(202) 530-8030
www.aidsaction.org

AIDS Action is a warehouse of detailed information about HIV/AIDS and other sexually transmitted diseases. While much of this information may be best suited for health professionals, one of the buttons will educate readers about safe sex and the prevention of HIV.

American Civil Liberties Union (ACLU)
Lesbian and Gay Rights Project
125 Broad Street, 18th Floor
New York, NY 10004
(212) 549-2627
www.aclu.org

The ACLU is best known for litigating on behalf of persons whose rights and liberties have been violated. A button titled "Lesbian and Gay Rights" allows school personnel to access information about gay and lesbian youth in schools. This button will provide readers with current news on the topic, a PDF file of the publication *Making School Safe*, and other resourceful documents.

Gender Education and Advocacy
American Educational Gender Information Service (AEGIS)
PO Box 33724
Decatur, GA 30033
(404) 939-0244
www.gender.org
www.gender.org/aegis

AEGIS collaborates with Gender Education and Advocacy to provide a clearinghouse of credible information about transgender issues. While much of the information may not be applicable in the classroom, buttons allow visitors to access the organization's publications and gain insight into the needs of transgender persons.

American Federation of Teachers (AFT)
555 New Jersey Avenue NW
Washington, DC 20001
(202) 879-4400
www.aft.org

As a strong advocate for the education community, AFT offers its constituents a range of resources on their website. The "Departments" button has an added link to "Issues in

Education," allowing school personnel to review the material on "Discipline and School Safety," which offers material to enhance a safe school environment.

American Library Association (ALA)
Gay, Lesbian, Bisexual, and Transgender Roundtable
50 East Heron Street
Chicago, IL 60611
(800) 545-2433
www.ala.org/ala/glbtrt/welcomeglbtround.htm

Each year the Roundtable awards the Stonewall Book Award to a literature piece and a non-fiction text. Members also meet throughout the year to work on various initiatives, including augmenting gay- and lesbian-themed books for children and mainstreaming gay publishing. Their website features buttons to access previous Stonewall Book Award winners, newsletters, a listserv, and a bibliography of books for youth by genre.

American Psychological Association (APA)
Lesbian, Gay, and Bisexual Concerns
750 First Street NE
Washington, DC 20002-4242
(800) 374-2721
www.apa.org/pi/lgbc

The Lesbian, Gay, and Bisexual Concerns home page of the APA website offers visitors various buttons to access information on gay and lesbian youth. The "Publications and Other Resources" button allows you to retrieve current and past APA-sponsored publications, including *Just the Facts About Sexual Orientation and Youth: A Primer for Principals, Educators, & School Personnel*, online brochures such as *"What Does Gay Mean?" How to Talk with Kids about Sexual Orientation and Prejudice*, and assorted news articles related to the topic. The "Healthy LGB" link, http://www.apa.org/ed/hlgb/, allows readers to search the site's database.

Association of Supervision and Curriculum Development (ASCD)
1703 N Beauregard Street
Alexandria, VA 22311
(800) 933-2723
www.ascd.org

ASCD members, composed of education professionals, work toward ensuring success for all learners. While much of the ASCD website is restricted to current members, visitors can use the search button to retrieve past articles on gay and lesbian youth from the professional journal *Educational Leadership*. The "Network Directory" button will direct you to contact information on the Gay, Lesbian, Bisexual, Transgender, and Allied Issues in Education group.

Children of Lesbians and Gays Everywhere (COLAGE)
2300 Market Street, Box 165
San Francisco, CA 94114
(415) 861-5437
www.colage.org

While most of the information on the COLAGE website is primarily for the children of gay and lesbian parents, the "Resources" button will give visitors access to their publications, *Books for Children and Young Adults, Media for Children and Young Adults,* and *Tips for Making Classrooms Safer for Students with LGBT Parents.*

Family Diversity Projects Inc.
PO Box 1246
Amherst, MA 01004
(413) 256-0502
www.lovemakesafamily.org

The Family Diversity Projects is a traveling photo exhibit of different families in the United States. Visitors of the website can find information on the curriculum guides that accompany the exhibits and help school personnel convey that diversity (among families) is to be expected, respected, and appreciated. *Love Makes a Family* is the book of portraits of gay, lesbian, bisexual, and transgender persons and their families.

Gay and Lesbian Alliance Against Defamation (GLAAD)
5455 Wilshire Blvd., #1500
Los Angeles, CA 90036
(323) 933-2240
www.glaad.org

The GLAAD website slogan says it all: "Fair, Accurate and Inclusive Representation." The members of this organization work to eliminate homophobia and discrimination in the media. Much of the information on the GLAAD website appears inapplicable in the classroom, but current news articles on gay and lesbian persons (including youth) are available through the "Headlines" button. Teachers can also plan lessons around TV programs with the help of a button that outlines the shows for the week that will feature gay and lesbian characters or persons. The "Publications and Resources" button will access the publication *How the Media Can Help Combat Homophobia Among American Teenagers*.

Gay, Lesbian and Straight Education Network (GLSEN)
121 W 27th Street, Suite 804
New York, NY 10001
(212) 727-0135
www.glsen.org

GLSEN is a consortium of committed youth-serving professionals all working toward the common goal of educating students to respect one another regardless of a person's sexual orientation or gender identity/expression. This website should be the first stop for any teacher, counselor, or principal who wants to effectively meet the needs of gay and lesbian youth and teach others about respect, tolerance, and acceptance. The website is abundantly rich with resources for students, teachers, and local chapters and includes a bookstore of recommended teaching tools, lesson plans for immediate implementation, current events, and so forth.

Hetrick-Martin Institute (HMI)
2 Astor Place
New York, NY 10003
(212) 674-2400
www.hmi.org

This New York City–based agency serves gay, lesbian, bisexual, transgender, and questioning youth through a drop-in center, counseling, the Harvey Milk School (a high school devoted entirely to this population), and a variety of other programs. Visitors to the website will find, among other interesting aspects, statistics on the population, a list of resources for youth and adults, and a bibliography of books and videos for and about gay and lesbian youth.

Human Rights Campaign (HRC)
1640 Rhode Island Avenue NW
Washington, DC 20036-3278
(800) 777-4723
www.hrc.org

Most persons recognize HRC when they see the yellow equal sign inside the blue box. The logo is symbolic of their work, which is fighting for the equal rights of the gay, lesbian, bisexual, and transgender community. While school personnel may not be interested in becoming involved in the fight for equality, website visitors will find a range of news articles that deal with current political issues. The website has a "Youth/Schools" button that will direct you to information that can be used in the classroom. Additional information is shared in a Q & A format through the "Ask the Experts" button.

The Institute for Gay and Lesbian Strategic Studies (IGLSS)
PO Box 2603
Amherst, MA 01004
(413) 577-0145
www.iglss.org

Considered "an independent think tank answering questions that affect the lesbian, gay, bisexual, and transgender communities, IGLSS confronts tough issues—using credible methodology to assure reliable answers." Much of the research is presented on the site along with highlights on the latest news about the gay and lesbian community. School personnel who access the "Angles" (the organization's professional journal), "Publications," and "Resources" buttons can download informative reports.

International Foundation for Gender Education (IFGE)
PO Box 540229
Waltham, MA 02454
(781) 899-2212
www.ifge.org

The IFGE website is for and about the transgender community. This can be a first stop for any school personnel looking to understand transgender youth and what they experience. Website visitors have access to *Transgender Tapestry* (the IFGE magazine), a "FAQ" button, a bookstore of recommended texts on the community, and current news about the transgender community.

Lambda Legal Defense and Education Fund (Lambda Legal)
120 Wall Street, Suite 1500
New York, NY 10005
(212) 809-8585
www.lambdalegal.org

Lambda Legal is "committed to achieving full recognition of the civil rights of lesbians, gay men, bisexuals, the transgendered, and people with HIV or AIDS through impact litigation, education, and public policy work." Consequently, many of the resources found on their website are about cases that are in litigation or the outcomes of closed cases. School personnel who visit the site will find an array of articles and other resources under the "Library" button, and the "Search" (type in *gay and lesbian youth*) and "Publications" buttons will retrieve additional information on gay and lesbian youth.

National Association of School Psychologists (NASP)
Work Group on Gay, Lesbian, and Bisexual Issues
4340 E West Highway, Suite 402
Bethesda, MD 20814
www.nasponline.org/advocacy/glb.html

This work group's website is accessed through NASP's home page under the "NASP Advocacy Programs" button. While much of the information on the site outlines the work group's objectives, links will provide visitors with *Safe and Affirmative Schools for Sexual Minority Youth, Just the Facts about Sexual Orientation*, the NASP/APA resolution statement on gay, lesbian, and bisexual youth in school, and a host of other resources.

National Center for Lesbian Rights (NCLR)
Youth Project
870 Market Street, Suite 570
San Francisco, CA 94102
(415) 392-6257
www.nclrights.org

Although NCLR is primarily committed to advancing lesbians' rights, the organization represents gay, bisexual, and transgender persons as well. Their home page has current news, summaries of current litigation, legal briefs, and so forth. The "Youth" button, listed under "Projects," offers publications on harassment, discrimination, school policies, school safety, and so forth.

National Education Association (NEA)
Gay and Lesbian Caucus
1201 16th Street NW
Washington, DC 20036
(202) 833-4000
www.nea.org

The NEA search button will retrieve essays, press releases, and publications on gay and lesbian youth. Visitors can also access valuable tools on how to contend with bullying behavior through the "School Safety" button located on the "NEA on the Issues" button on the home page sidebar.

National Gay and Lesbian Task Force (NGLTF)
1325 Massachusetts Avenue NW, Suite 600
Washington, DC 20005
(202) 393-5177
www.thetaskforce.org

The NGLTF is committed to "training state and local activists and leaders and organizing broad-based campaigns to defeat anti-LGBT referenda and advance pro-LGBT legislation." Their home page offers headline news associated with the community and rich resources through the "Library and Publications" and "Policy Institute" buttons. The "Youth" button, located under "Issues," will direct visitors to a description of their youth-based projects and current publications associated with gay and lesbian youth.

National Latina/o Gay, Lesbian, Bisexual, and Transgender Organization (LLEGO)
1612 K Street NW, Suite 500
Washington, DC 20006
(202) 466-8240
www.llego.org

LLEGO is targeted to the Latina/o gay, lesbian, bisexual, and transgender community. Their home page describes their current projects, but the "Resources" button will prove most useful to school personnel. The button has various topics significant to the community (spirituality, coming out, etc.), and the "Youth" button provides visitors with a bibliography of readings, phone services for youth, and information about online organizations.

National Youth Advocacy Coalition (NYAC)
1638 R Street NW, Suite 300
Washington, DC 20009
(800) 541-6922
www.nyacyouth.org

NYAC prides itself on being the "only national organization focused solely on improving the lives of lesbian, gay, bisexual, transgender and questioning (LGBTQ) youth through advocacy, education, and information." If GLSEN is your first stop for resources, then NYAC should be your second, and it should certainly be a website you recommend to your students (if the need presents itself). Their website is resourceful. A number of buttons allow youth to access forums and connect with local groups, read current newsletters and headlines, and even lobby political officials. The "Youth Connections" button has an extensive resource list that is categorized for ease. The "Get Materials and Training?" button will provide school personnel with online monographs, access to a resource database, and so forth.

OutProud
The National Coalition for Gay, Lesbian, Bisexual & Transgender Youth
369 Third Street, Suite B-362
San Rafael, CA 94901
www.outproud.org

OutProud is committed to helping gay, lesbian, bisexual, and transgender youth "become happy, successful, confident and vital gay, lesbian and bisexual adults." Their website offers many resources, including a search button to find gay and lesbian role models in history; an online library (of fact sheets, articles, reports, and brochures); a system to find local sources of support; an online magazine; headline news; and a forum to connect with youth.

Parents, Family and Friends of Lesbians and Gays (PFLAG)
1726 M Street NW, Suite 400
Washington, DC 20036
(202) 467-8180
www.pflag.org

PFLAG is an excellent resource for people, especially parents, who seek to learn about supporting the community of gay and lesbian persons. Their vision statement reads, "We, the parents, families and friends of lesbian, gay, bisexual and transgendered persons, celebrate diversity and envision a society that embraces everyone, including those of diverse sexual orientations and gender identities." Visitors to the website have access to PFLAG's current initiatives; explanations on how to be supportive; and issues, publications, and resources central to education. The "Education" button provides visitors with fact sheets about these youth, resources for and about youth, and access to the publication *From Our House to the Schoolhouse.*

The PERSON (Public Education Regarding Sexual Orientation Nationally) Project
586 62nd Street
Oakland, CA 95609-1245
www.personproject.org

The PERSON Project seeks to provide fair, accurate, unbiased information about the community of gay and lesbian persons and share this information with K–12 school personnel. Although their website is updated infrequently and is more archival, visitors can still access the PERSON Project Handbook, which provides useful and beneficial information to help organize students and faculty on campus. The handbook also has a state-by-state listing of resources, and website buttons provide visitors with access to legal resources, hotline numbers, organizing tactics, research studies, curricular resources, and online brochures.

> Project 10
> Los Angeles Unified School District
> 355 S Grand Avenue, KPMG, 10th Floor
> Los Angeles, CA 90071
> (213) 633-7826
> www.Project10.org

Project 10 provides educational support to gay, lesbian, bisexual, and transgender youth who attend public schools. While the organization's history is in Los Angeles and it serves students and personnel of the LA Unified School District, it collaborates with many other national organizations, including the ACLU, Lamdba Legal, HRW, and the Anti-Defamation League. Their website offers recommendations and resources for students, administrators, policy makers, and teachers.

> Project 10 East Inc.
> 402A Highland Avenue, Suite K
> Somerville, MA 02144
> (617) 864-GLBT
> www.project10east.org

Project 10 East works "to create and sustain safe space in schools and communities where young people can experience mutual respect with a focus on personal excellence, regardless of gender identity or sexual orientation or the perception thereof." Their website provides visitors with additional information about their initiatives and services for gay and lesbian youth on the East Coast. School personnel interested in starting and sustaining a GSA on their campus should print a copy of *The Project 10 East GSA Handbook*, which offers many ideas and recommendations. Other website buttons provide access to community organizing tips, links to other sites, and a bibliography of books and videos.

Rethinking Schools
1001 E Keefe Avenue
Milwaukee, WI 53212
(800) 669-4192
www.rethinkingschools.org

The Rethinking Schools website has many tools that school personnel can use to teach about a variety of topics related to equity. Rethinking Schools is committed "to the vision that public education is central to the creation of a humane, caring, multiracial democracy," and their publications often address the problems that urban schools encounter. Their search button will retrieve articles, essays, and so forth on gay and lesbian youth issues.

Safe Schools Coalition
2124 Fourth Avenue
Seattle, WA 98121
(206) 632-0662 x49
(866) HF-ZONE-1 (crisis hotline)
www.safeschoolscoalition.org

The Safe Schools Coalition was initially created to serve the gay, lesbian, bisexual, and transgender youth of Washington State. Now the Coalition supports youth worldwide by helping school personnel better understand these youth and meet their needs. Their website offers wonderful resources that are categorized by topic and type and gives visitors access to reports, handouts, posters, and hotlines. The "Youth" button offers visitors an array of links to issues pertinent to the gay and lesbian population.

Sex Information and Education Council of the United States (SIECUS)
130 W 42nd Street, Suite 350
New York, NY 10036
(212) 819-9770
www.siecus.org

The SIECUS website is an excellent stop for sex and health educators seeking information on school health topics, including the prevention of HIV transmission. School personnel who visit the website should use the search button to retrieve a thorough bibliography on gay, lesbian, bisexual, and transgender issues and other critical resources.

YouthResource
Advocates for Youth
200 M Street NW, Suite 750
Washington, DC 20036
(202) 419-3420
www.youthresource.com

YouthResource is an Advocates for Youth project and is a website created for and by gay, lesbian, bisexual, transgender, and questioning (GLBTQ) youth. YouthResource "takes a holistic approach to sexual health by offering support, community, resources, and peer-to-peer education about issues of concern to GLBTQ young people." The website offers information in four broad areas: health, advocacy, community, and contemporary issues. Website visitors can e-mail a peer educator a question or find local community groups that meet regularly.

Southern Poverty Law Center
Teaching Tolerance Project
400 Washington Avenue
Montgomery, AL 36104
(334) 956-8200
www.tolerance.org/teach

The Teaching Tolerance Project helps school personnel "promote respect for differences and an appreciation of diversity." The website has many teaching tools (curricula, videos, posters, books on themes) that can be used in the classroom, many of which are free. A sidebar allows visitors to access information related to "Responding to Problems," "Expanding Resources," "Examining Your Roles," and so forth. A search button will locate specific information on gay and lesbian youth.

Summary

The few prominent gay and lesbian persons in history and contemporary society presented in this chapter are the tip of the iceberg. There are many other successful and extraordinary persons, like slain politician Harvey Milk; British author and actor Quentin Crisp; activist, author, and playwright Larry Kramer; politician Barbara Jordan; activist Chrissy Gephardt; and jazz musician Dave Koz, who happen to be gay or lesbian. Emphasizing who these people are augments the ordinary and anonymous and demonstrates that all gay and lesbian persons contribute considerably to society. Contrarily, failing to spotlight such persons perpetuates the myth that gay and lesbian persons are rare, hideous, and a danger to society.

This chapter also focused on national organizations that serve the gay and lesbian community. Some of these are politically based, some offer databases of information, and others offer a variety of support services. These can prove resourceful in the event that you or your students need additional information for research or support.

Idea File

1. Make a list of organizations nearest your community that offer services to support gay and lesbian youth and their families.
2. Cluster some pictures of current and historic gay and lesbian figures and post them with a clever slogan showing support or tolerance. For example, you could post "Who says all athletes are straight?" under pictures of Billy Bean, Martina Navratilova, Billie Jean King, and Esera Tuaolo.
3. Read *Out of the Past* (1995) by Neil Miller and *The Gay 100* (2002) by Paul Russell and write down the names of the persons you were most surprised to learn were gay or lesbian. Then contemplate why their sexual orientation was not widely publicized.
4. To motivate students for a lesson on diverse sexuality, write the names of prominent gay and lesbian persons on "Hello My Name Is . . ." self-adhesive labels. Post these on students' backs and have their peers give them hints to figure out who they are.

References

Casagrande, L. (1989). *Unfortunately, history has set the record a little too straight.* Minneapolis, MN: OutFront Minnesota.

Cook, B. W. (1979). *Women and support networks.* Brooklyn, New York: Out & Out Books.

Davis, A. F. (1973). *American heroine: The life and legend of Jane Addams.* New York: Oxford University Press.

Fone, B. (2000). *Homophobia: A history.* New York: Metropolitan Books.

Giltz, M. (2002). A beautiful mind: The makers of *A Beautiful Mind* chose to ignore John Nash's love of men. What were they thinking? *The Advocate, 860,* 38–47.

Goodridge, M. (2003, October 14). Relatively revolutionary: A sitcom featuring a gay couple with a daughter—shocking, or just good business? Both, say producers. *The Advocate, 900,* 52–54.

Gross, M. J. (2003, June 24). Billy Bean's pitch: Four years after coming out the ex-major leaguer faces a quandary: Should he now push other pro athletes to do the same? *The Advocate, 892,* 76–84.

Hensley, D. (2001, May 8). Shedding her skin: As Melissa Etheridge prepares her new CD, Skin, for its summer release, she talks for the first time about her split with Julie Cypher, the revelations in her upcoming book, and how she makes no apologies for turning her life into art. *The Advocate, 837,* 30–36.

Hogan, L., & Hudson, S. (1998). *Completely queer: The gay and lesbian encyclopedia*. New York: Henry Holt and Company.

Internet Movie Database. (2004a). *Rupert Everett*. Retrieved September 15, 2004, from http://us .imdb.com/name/nm0000391.

Internet Movie Database. (2004b). *Elton John*. Retrieved September 15, 2004, from http://us .imdb.com/name/nm0005056/bio.

Internet Movie Database. (2004c). *RuPaul*. Retrieved September 15, 2004, from http://us .imdb.com/name/nm0750412.

Katz, J. N. (1983). *Gay/lesbian almanac: A new documentary*. New York: Harper & Row.

Katz, J. N. (1992). *Gay American history: Lesbians & gay men in the U.S.A.* New York: Meridian.

Liz Smith on her friend Rock, who by acknowledging his illness put a face on the AIDS crises for his fans all over the world. (2002, November 12). *The Advocate, 876*, 72–73.

Lyon, C. (2003, December). The man who made Christmas: Christopher Radko, who helped enhance the holiday ornament industry, comes out just in time for Yule season. *Out*, pp. 32–34.

Miller, D. L. (2003). *City of the century: The epic of Chicago and the making of America*. New York: Simon & Schuster.

Miller, N. (1995). *Out of the past: Gay and lesbian history from 1869 to the present*. New York: Vintage Books.

Musto, M. (2003, January). Plush life. Michael Musto gets acquainted with the serious side of Karen Walker's alter ego, Megan Mullally, who talks about the still-top-rated *Will & Grace*, her successful recent album, and what her fiancé really thinks about her bisexuality. *Out*, pp. 30–37.

O'Brien, J. (2002, December). The Out 100: 2002. *Out*, p. 69.

Patterson, R. (1951). *The riddle of Emily Dickinson*. Boston: Houghton Mifflin.

Romesburg, D. (2001, August 9). Innovation through the ages: Events taken for granted today were once part of a cutting-edge journey to a new frontier. *The Advocate, 843–44*, 9–14.

Russell, P. (2002). *The gay 100: A ranking of the most influential gay men and lesbians, past and present*. New York: Kensington Books.

Schwartz, L. (2004). *Billie Jean won for all women*. Retrieved September 15, 2004, from http://espn .go.com/sportscentury/features/00016060.html.

Spencer, C. (1995). *Homosexuality in history*. New York: Harcourt Brace & Company.

Steele, B. C. (2001, December 25). The knight's crusade: Playing the wizard Gandalf in *The Lord of the Rings* may make Sir Ian McKellen the world's best-known gay man. And he's armed and ready to carry the fight for equality with him. *The Advocate, 853*, 36–45.

Steele, B. C. (2002, November 26). Tackling football's closet: In his first gay-press interview, former Minnesota Viking Esera Tuaolo gives an insider's view of sports homophobia from the locker room to the Super Bowl and talks for the first time about his partner and their children. *The Advocate, 877*, 30–39.

Steele, B. C. (2004, January 20). Melissa & Tammy: A love story. *The Advocate, 906*, 50–64.

Stockwell, A. (2003, October 14). New stage for an out actor: Christopher Sieber comes to it's all relative from a long career in Broadway musicals. Now he's singing a new tune: That of an openly gay TV star. *The Advocate, 900*, 58–67.

Times Literary Supplement. (1980, July 11). New York: *The New York Times*.

U.S. representative Barney Frank remembers when he became the first congressman to come out on his own. (2002, November 12). *The Advocate, 876*, 55.

Willing, R. (2004, August 13). Court voids about 4,000 gay marriages in California. *USA Today*, p. 15A.

♀♀ **3**

New Territory: Becoming an Ally to Gay and Lesbian Students

Developing Support in Your Learning Community

Overview

Emily in the vignette above is fortunate. She may be struggling to debunk the notion of a "traditional" lesbian youth, but judging from her narrative, it appears that her learning community has accepted her. She may be perceived as the token lesbian on campus and as the authority on gay and lesbian issues, but at least she has wielded that status to start a Day of Silence and to teach others that gay and lesbian youth are unique individuals. Many gay and lesbian youth are not as lucky as Amy. In fact, they risk experiencing a number of mental, social, and cognitive challenges because they attend schools that are not accepting of them. To lessen those experiences, this chapter discusses methods to establish a learning climate that is safe, friendly, and nonthreatening for gay and lesbian students.

Indeed, all students need and want learning communities where they do not fear discrimination, judgment, intimidation, harassment, or bullying, but gay and lesbian students especially need communities that value who they are. August Scornaienchi, superintendent of schools for Alameda County, California, explains, "That [gay and lesbian youth] are a minority does not in any way lessen their right to an educational experience that values who they are, that acknowledges their strengths and resources, and that holds up mirrors that help them to develop powerful self-identities" (Todd, 2002, p. 5). To help you promote such a learning community, the questions addressed in this chapter are as follows:

- What can I do so that gay and lesbian students feel accepted and supported in my classroom and school?
- What lessons could I implement in my classroom?
- What is a Gay–Straight Alliance, and should I sponsor one?

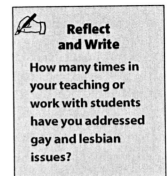

Reflect and Write

How many times in your teaching or work with students have you addressed gay and lesbian issues?

What Can I Do So That Gay and Lesbian Students Feel Accepted and Supported in My Classroom and School?

As an education professional, society expects you to nurture and support the growth of all youth. You have an obligation to create a learning community that tolerates all groups of students. It certainly does not matter that some students have a different color of skin; that some are in special education; that some speak a different language at home; or that some excel in music or sports, and others do not. By this token, it should not matter that some are gay or lesbian, or that some students' gender presentation does not complement their behavior or mannerisms. So that gay and lesbian students feel accepted and supported in your classroom, you must be willing to do the following:

1. Speak out against (in hallways, classrooms, club meetings, playgrounds, extracurricular activities, and so forth) any disparaging language about or harmful behavior toward gay or lesbian persons (or students) or the behaviors they stereotypically embody.
2. Outwardly present a neutral (i.e., nonjudgmental) to positive attitude toward gay and lesbian persons.

3. Work toward enhancing the understanding of gay and lesbian persons to the best of your ability.

Speak out against Disparaging Language about Gay and Lesbian Persons

Very few teachers tolerate any racial, ethnic, gender, or special-needs slur. One student calling another "chink," "skank," or "retard" is sure to receive a stern look and lecture. Quite often, however, teachers do not reprimand students who use antigay language to insult one another. In the GLSEN (2001b) survey, for instance, less that a quarter of the students indicated that faculty and staff intervened always or most of the time when homophobic remarks were made in their presence. Make a concerted effort to challenge all forms of antigay language in your classroom, and react as quickly and as seriously to any antigay name-calling or insults as you would a racial, ethnic, or gender slur.

Let's look at the following events that occurred in classrooms when teachers failed to intervene. As you read these descriptions, ponder the impact the comments and/or behavior have when they remain unchallenged.

- When Jaime sees Jason, who happens to have feminine mannerisms, he sings, to the tune of "Here Comes the Bride," "Here comes the fag; here comes the fag; he'll die of AIDS, and we'll all be so glad." Everyone in the classroom begins to laugh.
- Tony teases Jeannie, "You lesbo, you don't wear make up, you prefer jeans and sneakers over dresses and heels, and you wear your hair short. You know you want to be a man."
- Mark yells across the classroom, "Look at the way you're holding your book, Rob. You're so gay." Rob snaps back, "No I'm not. You're the one with the higher voice."
- Janice tells Christina, "All the girls on the basketball team are nothing but a bunch of dykes."
- Raymond grabs James around the neck and puts his fist up against his face (students often call this "mushing") and says, "You probably like this, you little fag."

The teachers in these cases did very little to intervene. One teacher told the students to settle down, another encouraged the students to go to their next class, and another turned her attention to the lesson. They chose to ignore the comments and behaviors for good reasons:

- "Talking about it would have detracted time away from my instruction";
- "I didn't want to give the perpetrators the attention they were already seeking";
- "I didn't have the time or energy to engage in a debate with them"; and
- "To be honest, I didn't see a need for addressing their situation."

One teacher summed up their sentiment, "It was just easier than making a big thing out of it." While you can understand that it is easier to ignore or trivialize these types of comments and behavior, by dismissing them you essentially forgive the students for their actions and validate the beliefs they have about gay and lesbian persons. Essentially students learn that there is nothing wrong with degrading others with gay and lesbian epithets and that such persons have no value in the classroom, school, or society.

This message scores deeply in the spirit of openly or closeted gay and lesbian students. Some are already vulnerable, feel awful for having same-gender feelings and attractions, and are conscientious about the way they are perceived. Others are stressed in ways unimaginable, and they behold what to them is a person they respect and admire denouncing the core of their being. Whatever feelings of hopelessness they have are compounded by the impression that you have made clear that you are not a source of support. You have inadvertently abandoned them.

When you remain silent, you are part of a vicious cycle for the gay and lesbian student that begins when other students use antigay language to humiliate one another. When students witness that the teacher intentionally ignores or dismisses the comments, everyone within earshot begins to believe that this type of language is socially acceptable. The students also begin to believe that whatever images they have about gay and lesbian persons, stereotypic as they may be, are accurate. Gay and lesbian students feel further devalued, causing them to feel worse about who they are. Many of them begin to think that they deserve this type of reproach. Many begin to feel anxiety, fear, stress, isolation, depression, and worthlessness (as discussed in chapter 2), which makes it difficult for them to learn. Some will engage in future antigay language; others will deny their sexual orientation; and many will isolate themselves, furthering their distress. Other antigay comments will be made, perhaps by students who have learned that antigay language is permissible, and the cycle continues. (See box 9.1.) Once your students begin to believe that antigay language is permissible, some begin to believe that it is equally acceptable to physically harm students who are gay and lesbian or are perceived to be.

 BOX 9.1. SILENCE = VICIOUS CYCLE FOR GAY AND LESBIAN STUDENTS

Students use gay and lesbian epithets to humiliate one another.
Teacher does not intervene.
Students believe that such comments are acceptable.
Some gay and lesbian students feel devalued and alienated.
Some gay and lesbian students close up and become distressed.
Again, students use gay and lesbian epithets to humiliate one another.

When Jason's teacher failed to intervene on his behalf, a couple of aspects from Jaime's song, "Here Comes the Fag," were inadvertently reinforced. Students who witnessed the event quite possibly learned that feminine men are gay, they die of AIDS, and society is better off without them. Jason, whether he is gay or not, was humiliated in front of his peers. He learned that his mannerisms (and perhaps his sexual orientation) are socially unacceptable and that if he is a "fag" he is destined (and deserves) to die of a tragic disease. Jaime continued to believe that it is permissible to degrade feminine or gay men and that it is good that "fags" die of AIDS.

Tony and Jeannie's teacher may very well have believed that their conversation was harmless banter, but their teacher's dismissal of the comments reinforced the belief that lesbians are stereotypically masculine and desire to be men. Jeannie, whether she is a lesbian or not, learned that her style of dress is gender inappropriate and that others will judge her (and others like her) as a "lesbo" for not conforming. Tony continued to believe that women who wear looser clothing and shorter hairstyles can be classified as "lesbos."

When Mark and Rob's teacher ignored their exchange, she reinforced the belief that gay men have a stereotypic way of behaving. The students also learned that one sure way of upsetting a boy is to draw attention to his mannerisms and equate them with homosexuality. Everyone learned that nothing good can come out of these gay associations. The boys learned the importance of demonstrating masculinity.

Janice and Christina's teacher thought they were envious of the girls on the basketball team. When the teacher trivialized Janice's comment, she reinforced that girls who excel in sports are most likely lesbian. This may affect some girls to the point that they do not participate in sports because they do not want to be perceived as a lesbian. And girls who are in sports may take offense to being perceived as lesbian. Janice and Christina learned that they can denounce any girl by referring to her as a "dyke."

That James's teacher did nothing to intervene on his behalf is unfortunate. His teacher could not see the harm in Raymond's horseplay, but James was beyond verbal humiliation; he was physically harmed and threatened. When the teacher turned her attention from the event, the students learned that "fags" and feminine or gay men deserve to be physically harassed. Raymond learned that he could continue to bully students he considered "fags."

Teachers often believe that if they intervene when antigay language, negative judgments, and insults are spoken, they begin treading in unfamiliar territory, which makes them nervous and uncomfortable. Consequently, it is easier for them to pretend that antigay language and behavior do not occur. You do not have to enter a diatribe about gay and lesbian issues, begin a lengthy discussion on tolerance, or administer punishment when you witness such behavior. If you find that the opportunity lends itself well to an impromptu lesson on respect for gay and lesbian persons, then proceed with your impulse and discuss how the students have engaged in a form of bigotry, slander, or stereotypic language, for example. At the bare minimum, the teachers in these scenarios could have challenged the students with the following comments:

- "Jaime, as creative as you are, there is nothing humorous about your song. Hetero- and homosexual persons die from AIDS each year. They are mothers, fathers, aunts, uncles, cousins, and children. I thought I made it clear when I said I won't have any derogatory comments in this classroom, and 'fag' is one of them. You owe Jason, the class, and me an apology."
- "Tony, I know that you and Jeannie are friends and that you are teasing her with that comment. But the way people dress is not indicative of their sexual orientation; it's more an expression of who they are. I and millions of other Americans would prefer that you not refer to lesbians as 'lesbos.'"
- "Mark and Rob, settle down. I know that you're just horsing around, but just to make one thing perfectly clear, you cannot tell whether a person is gay or lesbian based on the way he or she acts. The two of you need to apologize to each other and the class."
- "Hey girls, that is not true. Just because a girl excels in sports does not mean that she is lesbian. You shouldn't spread rumors like that."
- "Raymond, stop. You've invaded James' personal space, and that's grounds for the office. If you were out on the street and you did this to James, he could file assault charges against you. What you did was wrong. No one wants to be physically assaulted. You owe everyone in this room an apology, especially James."

If you witness any antigay language, insults, or harassment on school grounds, respond in a similar fashion immediately. If you should see verbal or physical assaults, loudly (enough for other students to hear) demand that the harassers stop their comments or behavior. Then mention that their comments or behaviors are uncalled for and are not tolerated in the school. If you fail to do this, students might believe that it is permissible to harass students outside of your classroom. You can say, "Comments and behavior that are hateful, harmful, and hurtful violate our school policy. We do not tolerate harassment of any kind" or "No one should harass or be harassed in this school."

If the harassers have violated school rules, policy, or codes of behavior, follow through with the appropriate consequences, but stress that the students need to change their behavior and that no good can come out of harassing someone. You can say, "James, change your behavior and language. Your name-calling is simply unappreciated. If you're having a bad day, come talk to me or the counselor, but don't take it out on someone that you think deserves it." You can also add, "If I see this happen again, I'm sending you to the office, and I'm going to recommend that the principal call your parents and suspend you."

If the harasser yells out, "You must be gay yourself" or a comment to that effect, you can respond with something like the following:

- "It doesn't matter what my sexual orientation is. I take a stand against harassment."
- "You shouldn't care what my sexual orientation is. What you did was mean, wrong, and violated the school rules. I protect all of my students."
- "No, I'm not. I'm just doing my job to keep this school safe."

You should then ask the harassers to apologize to everyone around, especially the victim. Then turn your attention to the victim and emphasize the need for him or her (and others listening) to report this type of behavior. To give all students the impression that faculty and staff are serious about fostering a safe school climate, loudly mention, "If this happens again, I want someone to tell me so that I can take care of this. If you see harassment of any kind, let me know. We have to do what we can to have a safe school." You can then take the victim aside and ask if he or she is OK or if he or she needs someone to talk to.

Outwardly Present a Neutral-to-Positive Attitude toward Gay and Lesbian Persons

You are certainly entitled to harbor whatever feelings you have about gay and lesbian persons, but if you choose to be repulsed by them (e.g., finding them sick, sinful, demonic, and in need of reparation), take pity on them (e.g., "Those poor souls—it's so sad that they're not straight"), or belittle them (e.g., believing they exist, but as a trivial class with no credible qualities) for whatever religious or personal reasons, you should refrain from deliberately expressing these beliefs in front of your students. As a youth-serving professional, you are bound to impose some of your own convictions, especially those associated with civility and other proprieties. But when you convey a negative attitude toward or express disparaging comments about gay and lesbian persons, their community, or the things they embody, you are demoralizing gay and lesbian students and those who have gay and lesbian persons in their lives. Consequently, whenever you interact with students, you should outwardly present a neutral-to-positive attitude toward gay and lesbian persons, which means you unfailingly quash all antigay behavior.

Whether you hold a neutral or positive attitude, always ask the students to stop their antigay behavior. You can use any number of phrases, like the following:

- "Stop. Cut it out."
- "Halt. Not in my room."
- "Stop. Don't even go there."

- "You're out of line."
- "Whoa. Knock it off."

Then ask the students to refrain from using any disparaging language (jokes, too) in your classroom, including any that denounces gay and lesbian persons—*fag, faggot, queer, homo, dyke, transy, lesbo, lezzie, light on the loafers, several feet off the ground, tinkerbell, butch, limp wrist, flamer, Ben Tover, Phil McCrevice, pie* or *carpet muncher, fudge packer, doughnut rubber,* and so forth. You can then proceed with one of the following:

- "You know the rule. That kind of language is not permitted in my classroom."
- "No need for that type of talk in here or the school."
- "I thought I made it clear: no dissing at all."
- "That type of language is unacceptable."
- "There's nothing amusing about that kind of talk."
- "I don't talk like that; you shouldn't either."

Add that an apology is warranted to the student who was insulted (and to everyone within earshot). Despite the fact that there is an excellent opportunity for discussion, a teacher with a neutral attitude will end the matter and redirect the students' attention elsewhere (such as to a preplanned lesson or activity).

A teacher with a positive attitude toward gay and lesbian persons, however, will continue to

1. convey disappointment in the students' behavior;
2. explain why their behavior is offensive;
3. teach a microlesson on the impact their behavior has on gay or lesbian persons;
4. ask the students to never engage in the behavior again; and then
5. redirect their attention to your agenda item.

The following cases demonstrate your options.

Case 1—The Homophobic Joke

A teacher overhears the beginning of Melissa's joke: "What do you call three dykes at a hardware store?"

Teacher A has a conservative nature and chooses to take the neutral route: "Melissa, you need to stop. I know I won't find that one funny, and I don't think others will either. I don't like to hear homophobic jokes in my classroom." The teacher then proceeds with her lesson, "Everyone, take out your books and turn to page . . ."

Teacher B chooses to take the positive route: "Hey, I don't want to hear it. You know better than to tell a homophobic joke. I'm disappointed that you would use that kind of language in my classroom. Gay and lesbian persons wouldn't appreciate that kind of joke because it gives people a false impression about their community. I know that some of you have notions about gay and lesbian persons that are untrue. What are some stereotypes that you have?" The teacher continues in this vein for 10 minutes, dispelling the myths and explaining how the stereotypes have harmed the image of gay and lesbian persons. She proceeds to elaborate on some of the contributions of gay or lesbian persons and closes the lesson by insisting that students not tell homophobic jokes. She then transitions into her planned lesson, "Everyone, take out your books and turn to page . . ."

Case 2—The Speculation

Ryan asks the teacher, "They say that Mr. Salazar is a big fag. Do you think he is?"

Teacher A: "Don't use that word to refer to someone's sexual orientation. It doesn't matter whether he is or isn't. When people want you to know their sexual orientation, they will tell you. Get out your notes and let's review chapter . . ."

Teacher B: "Hey, I meant it when I said no demeaning words in this classroom. I'm disappointed in you. Don't use words like that again; it shows that you're narrow-minded. And what difference does it make whether he's gay or not? I've heard he's a good teacher and an excellent coach, and that's all that seems to matter. That's all that matters in a person—that they are hardworking, good at what they do, and nice to others. Let's think about the qualities of a good and bad person." The teacher has the students elicit various qualities and rate their importance in terms of how valuable they are in a person's character. The teacher underscores that one's sexual orientation is not of great importance when it comes to respecting the person as whole. He then concludes, "So to answer your question, I don't know, and I don't care. I respect Mr. Salazar as a person and as a teacher. You should do the same. Get out your notes and let's review chapter . . ."

Case 3—Satisfaction of an Attack

Malik remarks to Mario, "I'm glad they kicked that little fag's ass. He's so gay."

Teacher A: "You know not to use words like that because they do nothing for our learning community. Also, no one deserves to be assaulted. I don't care if he is gay or if you take offense to the way he acts or dresses; he doesn't deserve to be assaulted. That's why there are laws against assault. Let's get back to the assignment . . ."

Teacher B: "Malik, I'm so disappointed that you would use that word and that you would support someone being attacked. Nobody deserves to be hurt or harmed in any way. If you don't like him for whatever reason, then don't associate with him. But don't go around saying you're happy that he was attacked. I'm sure you wouldn't like it if others were saying they were glad that you were attacked because of the way you carry yourself. What happened to that student is an example of a hate crime. Hate crimes are . . ." The teacher proceeds with a minilesson on hate crimes and has the students imagine what it would feel like for them if they were hated and attacked because of their race, ethnicity, gender, age, and so forth. She emphasizes that all groups of people across the country, including gay and lesbian persons, have something valuable to offer to our society. She closes, "I don't want to hear these types of comments from any of you. Let's get back to the assignment . . ."

Work toward Enhancing the Understanding of Gay and Lesbian Persons

As difficult as it may be for you to digest, at one time or another you will have to contend with a gay and lesbian issue. You should prepare for the inevitable. Perhaps one of the following might occur: an openly gay student attends the school, a same-gender couple wants to attend the prom or a social event, there is a suicide attempt by a lesbian student, students want answers to questions about gay and lesbian persons, a student has same-gender parents, or students want to start a Gay–Straight Alliance. You may find yourself uncomfortable with such a situation, but try as you may to resist, you will have to respond to the situation. To help you better cope with the inevitable, you should take into account that what gay and lesbian students endure heavily outweighs your own discomfort with the matter. Granted, schools are places where knowledge is imparted, so it stands to reason that your students deserve to receive accurate information about gay and lesbian persons.

To help you work toward enhancing your understanding of gay and lesbian persons, consider the reading below, which is based on the work of Sivertsen and Thames (1995) and Martin Rochlin (found in Mitchell, 1999). Think for a moment about what life would be like if you awoke one day and found yourself in a world where everyone is homosexual and you are a heterosexual youth. Read "Breeder" below and then contemplate the questions that follow.

 "BREEDER"

You awaken to a radio alarm and hear a song about men loving men and another about a woman who cannot seem to find the right woman. As you get ready for school, you hear callers on a radio program wishing to dedicate songs to their transgender sweethearts. A few minutes later, the female radio host begins a conversation about not knowing what to buy her wife for her birthday. On your way to school, you see three lesbian couples holding hands and four billboards for and about gay couples. You see a friend who asks you to list the top five same-gender students at school that you would make out with. You hesitantly answer because you want to pass for homosexual.

(Continued)

In the school parking lot, you observe a same-gender couple holding hands and kissing. A student yells at you in disgust, "Breeder!" You know that a faculty member has heard the comment but says nothing. You enter class, and your homeroom teacher has just been asked what she and her wife did over the weekend. Other students start discussing what they did. Some went to see movies, many of which involved love stories about same-gender couples and all of which involved characters that were gay, lesbian, bisexual, or transgender. On your way to your first class, you hear students insulting one another: "Don't wear that, it makes you look straight"; "Shut up, you hetero"; "Here comes the nut-n-screw."

You open up your books in your classes and see pictures of gay and lesbian couples, discussions about gay and lesbian issues, and problems involving gay and lesbian persons. Not one time so far has someone referred to heterosexuals positively. Later, you go to your school library and ask if there are books about heterosexuals, to which the librarian sternly replies, "Only one, and you have to get your parents' permission to check it out." You enter your favorite class, and you become excited because the teacher is going to talk about heterosexual rights. You are soon disappointed because you hear the students talking.

"I don't think straight people should have children. Look at all the problems they have raising them."

"Heteros shouldn't be allowed to marry. That's just sick."

"It's because of breeders that we have sexually transmitted diseases."

"I get so nauseous whenever I see heterosexual persons. I don't think they should be out in public."

"Heterosexuals shouldn't be allowed to serve in the military because they would want to turn all the gays and lesbians heterosexual."

There are posters up about school social events, and they all depict gay and lesbian students having a fun time. All of your social discussions involve same-gender dating and couples. A student asks if you want to be set up on a date with a same-gender student. You reply no, and she negatively responds, "What's the matter with you? You must be a sick breeder." After a while, some students ask you to look through a gay and lesbian fashion magazine and rate the same-gender persons you find most attractive. You later get a ride home with your best friend's same-gender parents. They ask if you have a "same-genderfriend." You reply no, and they assure you not worry. After all, Mr. and Mr. Witt met and dated in college, not high school.

After watching television shows, reading news and popular magazines, and having discussions with friends, all of which involved same-gender issues, you become tired of passing for homosexual. You summon the courage to come out as a heterosexual. You approach your favorite teacher, but he brushes you off. "You can become gay," he says. "You just have to set your mind to it. Why don't you talk to your pastor? Maybe he can suggest what to pray so that you can stay gay." You go see your school counselor, and she talks to you for a few minutes but concludes, "Don't worry about it. It's a phase you're going through. You'll turn homosexual again in no time." When you tell your best friend that you are heterosexual, she refuses to talk to you and ignores you completely. She cannot risk others believing that she is heterosexual too.

(Continued)

"BREEDER" (Continued)

You go see your principal because you want to start a club for heterosexuals, and he says, "You don't want to start a club like that. Why don't you just join the multicultural club? I think they talk about things like that." Students are afraid to associate with you because you are a "breeder," and the faculty and staff perceive you as a nuisance because they believe you feel entitled to special support because you are heterosexual. You are shoved in the hallways; rumors are spread about you wanting to rape the gay and lesbian students; others yell that you are going to die of the "straight person" disease. Some threaten you with bodily harm, and you receive a death threat: "Die, breeder, die. I'm going to kill you if you don't leave this school, you damn breeder."

Finally, a few teachers gather with you to show their support. You disappointedly try to answer some of their questions:

- What makes you think that you're straight? Maybe you just haven't met the right same-gender person. Maybe you're just scared to have a same-gender relationship. Have you at least tried a same-gender relationship? Maybe you think you're heterosexual because you see some on TV.
- Heterosexuals aren't happy. They don't stay married long. You know their divorce rate is 50%? Heterosexuals are always having affairs. Just think about that movie *Fatal Attraction* and *First Wives Club*. Are you sure you want to be a heterosexual?
- Are you going to start dressing funny like all those other heterosexuals? Are you going to start acting straight now? We hope you don't want to take a heterosexual to the prom. We don't think the students or their parents would like that.
- How long have you had heterosexual tendencies? Did a heterosexual molest you? We hope you don't hang around with children, because statistics show that heterosexuals like to molest children.
- Why do you heterosexuals have to flaunt your sexuality? Why do you all want so much attention? Why do you all want all those special rights? It would be better if you just accepted that we live in a world that doesn't appreciate heterosexuals.
- Why do you heterosexuals like to talk so much about sex? Whenever we see movies about heterosexuals, they're always in love or having sex. Why is that? And why do they like to do drugs? Heterosexuals do drugs in bars, and that's why we have so many problems in society. It's always straight people that are caught in marijuana, cocaine, or heroine busts.
- Why do you want to start a heterosexual club? Do you want to recruit some of our gay and lesbian students so that you can talk about heterosexual sex?

This passage is a microexample of the types of feelings that some gay and lesbian youth experience in their lifetime. If you became frustrated or anxious while reading this short passage, you can begin to understand how much relief and appreciation a gay or lesbian youth would feel knowing that you are a teacher who is trying to understand them.

You can develop a finer understanding and ultimate acceptance of gay and lesbian youth in your school by examining some of your own biases. You can use the Gay and

Lesbian Bias Thermometer (GLBT) below to assist in your personal examination. The thermometer is not scientifically based (nor was it meant to be) with validity or reliability measures. Instead, the results highlight the areas where some of your biases may exist. If you strongly disagree with some items, challenge some of your notions with these three questions:

1. What are my biases based on?
2. What factual information and multiple examples do I have that support my beliefs?
3. What is the worst that would happen if I adjusted my values, attitudes, or behaviors so that they were more favorable toward gay and lesbian students?

 THE GAY AND LESBIAN BIAS THERMOMETER

This survey is designed to measure your own bias and behavior toward gay and lesbian youth. There are no right or wrong answers. Rate each statement as carefully and as accurately as you can by writing a number beside each statement.

1 = Strongly disagree
2 = Disagree
3 = Neither agree nor disagree
4 = Agree
5 = Strongly agree

To the best of my knowledge I find that . . .
in terms of my beliefs . . .

1. Gay and lesbian students should be accepted just as they are. _____
2. Gay and lesbian students should attend our school openly with no threat of harm whatsoever. _____
3. Gay and lesbian students should receive information (in our curriculum, textbooks, and in our library) about gay and lesbian issues. _____
4. Gay and lesbian students enhance the diversity in our school. _____
5. Gay and lesbian students can lead happy, fulfilled lives. _____
6. Gay and lesbian students should attend our school prom with same-gender dates. _____
7. Gay and lesbian students should have a "safe person" to talk to in our school. _____
8. Gay and lesbian students should be able to show affection (holding hands, embracing) to one another just as the heterosexual students do. _____
9. There is nothing wrong, immoral, or sick about our gay and lesbian students. _____
10. No group of students is superior to another. _____

(Continued)

in terms of my attitude . . .

11. I would welcome gay and lesbian students in our school. _____
12. I would work closely with gay and lesbian students. _____
13. I would inform all of my students that they can privately approach me if they are questioning their sexual orientation. _____
14. I would speak to a group of gay and lesbian students about gay and lesbian issues. _____
15. I would collaborate with school administrators and board members to develop policies supporting gay and lesbian students. _____
16. I would work with my colleagues to develop supplementary materials about gay and lesbian persons (e.g., lesson plans, bibliographies, factual information sheets, and posters) to be used in appropriate classrooms. _____
17. I would be the designated "safe person" at my school. _____
18. I would volunteer my classroom as the designated "safe zone" at my school. _____

in terms of my behavior at school . . .

19. I challenge all antigay behaviors (actions and comments) made by students and faculty alike. _____
20. I avoid all stereotypes about gay and lesbian persons. _____
21. I teach student to avoid stereotypes about all groups of people, including gay and lesbian persons. _____
22. I teach students to become informed about an issue or a person before making a judgment. _____
23. I make an effort to show students that I believe that gay and lesbian persons are a viable group that makes contributions to our society. _____
24. I would sponsor a gay-and-lesbian-person-awareness week or an event (e.g., a writing contest) for gay and lesbian pride in June. _____
25. I would sponsor a Gay–Straight Alliance at my school. _____
26. I would attend a Gay–Straight Alliance meeting or sponsored event. _____
27. I would invite a gay or lesbian person to speak to my class about gay and lesbian issues. _____
28. I would show a documentary or video about gay and lesbian persons in class (if appropriate to my content area). _____
29. I would hold discussions with my students that include accurate information about and portrayals of gay and lesbian persons. _____
30. I would include gay and lesbian persons in my discussion of equity, social justice, multicultural education, tolerance, and oppression issues. _____

(Continued)

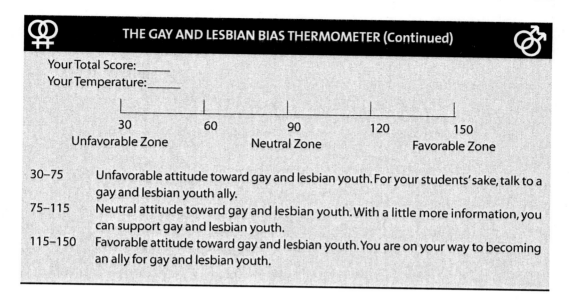

THE GAY AND LESBIAN BIAS THERMOMETER (Continued)

Your Total Score: _____
Your Temperature: _____

30	60	90	120	150
Unfavorable Zone		Neutral Zone		Favorable Zone

30–75   Unfavorable attitude toward gay and lesbian youth. For your students' sake, talk to a gay and lesbian youth ally.

75–115   Neutral attitude toward gay and lesbian youth. With a little more information, you can support gay and lesbian youth.

115–150   Favorable attitude toward gay and lesbian youth. You are on your way to becoming an ally for gay and lesbian youth.

For instance, if you strongly disagreed with item 5, "Gay and lesbian students can lead happy, fulfilled lives," you should contemplate, "Where did I learn that gay and lesbian persons do not have happy, fulfilled lives? What factual information and multiple examples do I have to support this idea? Could this idea also apply to heterosexuals? In other words, are there heterosexuals who do not lead happy, fulfilled lives? Should it not stand to reason, then, that all people, regardless of their sexual orientation, can lead happy, fulfilled lives? What is the worst that can happen if I believe that gay, lesbian, bisexual, and transgender persons can lead happy, fulfilled lives?"

As another example, if you strongly disagreed with item 26, "I would attend a Gay–Straight Alliance meeting or event," you can reflect, "Why would I not attend? What fear or discomfort do I have that keeps me from attending a meeting? Where is this coming from? What factual information or multiple examples do I have that support my fear and discomfort? What do I achieve if I intentionally do not attend a GSA meeting? What message do I send if I decline an invitation to attend a meeting? What is the worst that can happen if I attend a GSA meeting or sponsored event?"

If your temperature reading on the thermometer is less than 75 and you want to adjust your beliefs, attitudes, and behaviors so that they are more favorable, you should begin to internalize the notion that gay and lesbian persons are valuable, contributing members of our society. To set this in motion, you can review some of the suggested resources outlined in chapter 12, and you should also read some books, journal articles, and periodicals or watch some movies or documentaries on the gay and lesbian community. You can also discuss with your colleagues how they have adjusted favorably toward gay and lesbian persons.

Gay and lesbian students will feel more accepted and supported if you apply the following recommendations in your classroom. These are categorized like items on a restaurant menu, with a pepper representing the amount of effort it will take to infuse these into your teaching repertoire—one pepper is mild (easy to implement), two peppers indicate spicy (takes effort to implement), and three peppers represent very spicy (takes considerable effort; have a support network handy). Some of these recommendations may be overwhelming, but depending on your teaching pallet (determined by how conservative or liberal you are), implement as many as you can, as best as you can, and to a degree and pace that is comfortable for you.

✎ Challenge Assumptions about Gay and Lesbian Persons

Teach your students that not everyone is heterosexual, and never assume that all of your students are, or come from homes where everyone is, heterosexual. You may have very few (or no) students who are openly gay or lesbian, but you probably have some who are struggling with their sexual identity. Some of your students may also have gay, lesbian, bisexual, or transgender parents, siblings, friends, aunts, uncles, and cousins. You may not even know, but some of your own coworkers or relatives might be gay or lesbian.

Do not assume that students who demonstrate affection to their same-gender friends are gay or lesbian. Allow students to label themselves, because sometimes they will suggest that they have same-gender attractions and/or sexual behavior, which does not mean that they have identified themselves as gay or lesbian. Also, do not assume that students are likely homosexual if they are harassed or assaulted because others perceive them to be.

✎ Avoid Stereotypes about Gay and Lesbian Persons

Remember that gay and lesbian persons are a heterogeneous group and consequently do not have the same experiences or share the same beliefs about their sexuality—some may be prideful about their sexual orientation, and others may be more reserved. While some gay men may demonstrate some feminine characteristics and some lesbians masculine ones, you should not make generalizations about the gay and lesbian community. Some common stereotypes to avoid are as follows:

- Gay men tend to be florists, fashion designers, nurses, or beauticians;
- All lesbians are skilled at mechanics, home improvement, and sports and are likely to pursue careers in construction work, truck driving, coaching, tennis playing, and the armed forces;
- Gay and lesbian persons molest children;

- A limp wrist means that a person is gay;
- A person is most likely gay or lesbian if he or she dresses in drag for Halloween;
- A person can become gay or lesbian if a person of the same gender makes a pass at him or her;
- All gay and lesbian persons just need to have good sex with the opposite gender to be cured of their homosexuality;
- Gay men die from AIDS;
- Gay men are drawn to glamour; and
- Gay men want to be women, and lesbians want to be men.

✒ Use Sexual Orientation Instead of Sexual Preference

As noted in chapters 5 and 7, the phrase *sexual preference* strongly suggests that persons have a choice—in other words, they prefer one sexual orientation over another in the matter of their sexuality. Most gay and lesbian persons agree that they do not have a choice; their sexual orientation is inherent. When you use *sexual preference* instead of *sexual orientation*, you perpetuate the myth that persons choose being homosexual over being heterosexual.

✒ Use Neutral, Non-Gender-Specific Language in the Classroom

Use words like *partner, spouse, parent, lover, date, significant other,* and *longtime companion* as forthright as you would use any other word that conveys a serious relationship. Instead of asking a boy, "Do you have a girlfriend?" you can ask, "Are you seeing anyone?" or "Did you have a date this weekend?" Instead of saying, "The illustrator lived in New York City and never married," you can say, "The illustrator lived with her partner for 30 years" or "English historians now believe that he and his longtime companion traveled through Europe before settling in the States."

✒ Familiarize Yourself with the Gay, Lesbian and Straight Educator Network (GLSEN) Website

The GLSEN website offers a range of services, from daily news about gay and lesbian youth to lesson-plan ideas and practical information for immediate implementation. The more you visit the site, the more information you will likely learn and apply in your classroom and share with your colleagues and your students. Should a gay or lesbian student ever come to you for advice or support, you can then talk to them about what they are experiencing, refer them to the school counselor, and suggest they explore the site's links for additional support.

✍ Learn about Other Local or National Organizations That Cater to Gay and Lesbian Youth

In addition to familiarizing yourself with the GLSEN website, take the time to become acquainted with organizations that provide information and support for gay and lesbian youth. (Some of these organizations are found in chapter 8.) Each fills a niche in a spectrum that ranges from how to deal with a bully to finding the right gay pen pal. The more familiar you are with these organizations, the more knowledge you will have about the population, especially in terms of current events and how they impact gay and lesbian youth. Imagine how accepting you will seem when you promptly provide the organizations and Web addresses to a youth who has come to you in their time of dire need.

✍ ✍ Use the Words Gay, Lesbian, Bisexual, and Transgender in a Positive Way

Use these words in your daily routines in a matter-of-fact mode without causing the students to become distracted. As a conversation starter, you could say, "I heard that one of the fathers on the sitcom *It's All Relative* is gay in real life," "The gay and lesbian community has contributed so much money to AIDS research," or "Some historians believe that Eleanor Roosevelt was lesbian." You simply want to give your students the impression that you are not prejudiced toward gay and lesbian persons.

✍ ✍ Ask Your School Librarian to Purchase Books and Other Resources on Gay and Lesbian Issues

Students often do not have access to accurate information on gay and lesbian issues in their school libraries. This generally tends to give all students the impression that the accomplishments and contributions of the gay and lesbian community are minimal or negative, which further contributes to feelings of isolation among gay and lesbian youth. To lessen the degree of this isolation and to increase students' understanding of gay and lesbian persons, recommend that the librarian purchase books and videos about gay and lesbian persons or their community. The nonfiction work and documentaries can range from historic (e.g., the history of homosexuality, a biography on Walt Whitman) to contemporary issues (e.g., the gay-and-lesbian-rights movement; guides for gay and lesbian youth). The nonfiction pieces and videos can include material about or with gay and lesbian characters. Be sure that gay and lesbian magazines are in the same holdings as the other magazines. Students should not have to get special permission to view the magazines, and they should not have to endure added attention by having someone get the magazine for them from a secluded section.

✐ ✐ ✐ Include Gay and Lesbian Persons in Your Discussions about Diversity

Whenever discussions about diversity, civil rights, tolerance, or multicultural education emerge, be sure to address gay and lesbian persons among the African Americans, Latino Americans, Asian Americans, people with disabilities, women, and so forth. You can speak of how social misconceptions have led to their oppression in history, how heterosexism precludes them from enjoying and benefiting from the privileges that heterosexuals have, how they are often targets of hate crime, how they are mistreated in current times, and so forth. Convey that hateful, harmful, and hurtful comments and actions toward any group or person are not tolerated in our society, and communicate that any form of prejudice or discrimination based on a person's race, ethnicity, gender, age, cognitive or physical ability, or sexual orientation is unnecessary and wrong.

✐ ✐ ✐ Have Visible Gay and Lesbian Role Models in Your Classroom

Purchase or make posters that convey the acceptance of gay and lesbian persons. Display pictures of positive historic or contemporary gay and lesbian persons and the contributions they have made to society. You can also post in your classroom the various symbols associated with the gay and lesbian community (e.g., pink triangle, rainbow flag, lambda figure) with the word *Safe* beneath the symbol. You can use your bulletin board to teach your students about gay and lesbian issues such as heterosexism, the impact of hate crimes on the gay and lesbian community, the oppression of gay and lesbian persons in history, and so forth. You can also post catchy phrases in your room such as the following: "Regardless of who you are—black or white, short or tall, male or female, rich or poor, gay or straight—you are accepted in my classroom"; "It's not a gay thing; it's not a straight thing; it's a friend thing"; "The characteristics that make you whole are as rich as the contributions you make in this world"; or "Like the varying colors of gumballs in a vending machine, life is more spectacular when we let our true colors shine."

✐ ✐ ✐ Foster the Inclusiveness of Gay and Lesbian Persons in Your School Community

Recommend that the school decision makers designate "safe" persons (e.g., the counselor and other popular teachers) and "safe" places (e.g., the counselor's office or community room). A safe person is generally one who is willing to listen to any student, faculty, or staff member that wants to talk about any issue based on sexual orientation or identity. The safe person is confidential but directs self-endangerment and other serious cases to the proper channels. When an issue becomes too large to handle or resolve, he or she generally refers the student to a trained counselor or therapist.

Be sure that signs are posted in prominent places around the school so that all students know where these safe persons and places are. Any student who finds they need help, support, or information about gay and lesbian issues can then meet with these persons in a secure location without fear of retribution. Some students may not have the courage it takes to go to the school library and check out books on gay and lesbian issues, and it is therefore important to have pamphlets available featuring supportive organizations, lists of reading material, hotlines, websites, health information, and so forth.

Be a member of the curriculum and/or textbook committee and voice how the curriculum should accurately and positively portray gay and lesbian persons. For instance, the history or psychology textbooks should address the gay and lesbian movement; in English, students should be reading the work of gay and lesbian authors; and in health, students should learn about safe-sex practices for homo- and heterosexual persons. Also, join or organize a tolerance-building committee at your school and brainstorm how to augment the textbooks, curriculum, and other instructional resources so that students learn more about the gay and lesbian community. Suggest that the school hold a biography, history, or multicultural fair and ensure that gay and lesbian persons are represented; perhaps invite guest speakers to address gay and lesbian issues.

Recommend that the school sexual-harassment rules, behavior code, or bullying policy cover antigay verbal and physical assaults (see chapter 11). Have these posted in prominent places throughout the school, and remind students that you strictly follow these guidelines and will not tolerate any form of intimidation, harassment, or bullying. Recommend that the school spend time at the beginning and end of each year reviewing the policy and what constitutes these behaviors (e.g., graffiti, spreading rumors, name-calling) and teaching students about their rights and how to report such events. Recommend that faculty and staff receive professional-development training on how to create a learning community that is responsive to the needs of gay and lesbian students and is safe for and inclusive of all groups of students regardless of their personal composition.

What Lessons Could I Implement in My Classroom?

Students rightfully deserve to know about diverse sexual orientations (Owens, 1998). As difficult as it may be, you are obligated to impart the knowledge associated with diverse sexual orientations and then support students as they synthesize the information and draw their own conclusions about gay and lesbian persons. As it stands today, the knowl-

 Application

Which of these recommendations do you already implement in your classroom, and which recommendations could you implement the soonest?

edge that students receive at school about homosexual, bisexual, and transgender persons is minimal. Often the school curriculum rarely directs teachers to teach about gay and lesbian issues, and consequently,

- content-area teachers do not incorporate gay and lesbian issues into their lessons;
- discussions regarding oppressed groups, tolerance, equity, social justice, and cultural issues often forsake gay and lesbian persons;
- many textbooks disregard gay and lesbian rights, history, and movements;
- school libraries have few resources about gay and lesbian issues;
- discussions about gay and lesbian persons are generally in the context of sex and diseases in the health classes; and
- teachers rarely discuss the topic.

Moreover, when teachers have school-district consent to teach about gay and lesbian issues, many choose not to, and others misrepresent the community with inaccurate facts and myths (Harris & Bliss, 1997).

Given that gay and lesbian issues are prevalent in the media (e.g., the headline for the Friday, June 27, 2003, issue of the *Chicago Tribune* read, "Supreme Court strikes down laws against homosexual sex" and featured a 6 x 8 photo of a male couple embracing, and the July 7, 2003, issue of *Newsweek* ran the headline "Is Gay Marriage Next?" with a lesbian couple as their cover photo), your students are undoubtedly aware of some gay and lesbian issues. Any one of your students who has access to TV, magazines, or newspapers knows that gay and lesbian persons (and communities) exist. For most youth, whatever knowledge they have about gay and lesbian persons is derived from what they synthesize from the media or from conversations they have with peers and adults who do not have factual information about or correct understanding of gay and lesbian persons. These notions are consequently naive, negative, stereotypical, or false. Read the following examples and contemplate the affect the comments might have:

1. Mandy and Ty are best friends and fans of the sitcom *Will & Grace*. While watching an episode, Mandy says, "Gay men never find long-term relationships. Just look at Will and Jack. They can't meet a guy and settle down."
2. After hearing that Rosie O'Donnell has entered a lawsuit against her former publisher, Jaime's mother says, "That's the way lesbians are. They're just like men, ambitious and determined to win."
3. Holding a brief conversation about homosexuals in the military, Ken tells Jon, "My dad was in the army, and he says that gay men just want to be in the military so they can be around other men and watch them when they shower, dress, or sleep.

And when someone is down, like in combat, the gays will do sexual things to them when they're out."

4. A science teacher shows a video on the destruction of the 1989 earthquake in San Francisco, to which Ani remarks, "At least it killed a couple of faggots."

These types of comments drive youth to formulate new notions about gay and lesbian persons or confirm the notions they already have. In short, some myths and stereotypes are perpetuated, which can have unfortunate repercussions. First, youth who believe that gay and lesbian persons are substandard or idiotic are likely to discriminate against them or trivialize their accomplishments, making it difficult to teach youth to respect, accept, or tolerate them individually or as a whole. Second, some closeted gay and lesbian youth become fearful or depressed that they will fulfill some of the myths (e.g., not finding a long-time companion), or they experience shame because they belong to a group associated with such "revolting" attributes and "deserve to die."

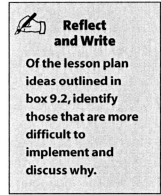

Reflect and Write

Of the lesson plan ideas outlined in box 9.2, identify those that are more difficult to implement and discuss why.

You can counter such repercussions and foster an inclusive learning community by teaching your students about topics central to the lives of gay and lesbian persons. Many teachers are uncomfortable with this idea because they believe that the lessons have to be about the physical aspects of same-gender sex. However, the lessons should be more powerful than discussions about sex. Consider preparing and teaching lessons in four modes. As a starting point, develop and teach lessons based on respect, acceptance, and tolerance. Then, depending on your comfort level, transition to gay-and-lesbian-specific topics, issues pertinent to the content areas, and sexual health issues. Some ideas for lesson plans are found in box 9.2. The lesson plan ideas in the first mode are relatively easy to design and implement. The ideas in the remaining modes require more design time (for research) and a stable comfort level when teaching the lesson.

There are many commercial curricula available that detail lesson plans about gay and lesbian persons (see appendix B), and the GLSEN website certainly offers an array of lesson plans and ideas. Consult these resources when developing your lessons, and refer to the *Guidelines for Comprehensive Sexuality Education* by Sex Information and Education Council of the United States (SIECUS, in press) for additional guidance. The guidelines serve as a basis for program planning and evaluation, training, research, and so forth, but most importantly they ensure that sexual health programs cover the topics critical for contemporary youth. The guidelines are divided into key concepts and are further categorized into topics and developmental messages that are age and grade appropriate. The messages found in box 9.3 address sexual identity and orientation. See these for more specific lesson-plan ideas centered on same-gender sexual development, romance, and attractions.

BOX 9.2. LESSON PLAN IDEAS

Mode: Respect, Acceptance, and Tolerance

Topic	Possible Lessons
Diversity in society	Different groups of people exist in society. Diversity is a cornerstone in our society. Differences and similarities exist among people.
Respect for individuals and groups of people	Respect and its importance in the classroom and in society; how respect is manifested. Respect for all groups of people regardless of their cognitive or physical ability, race and ethnicity, religion, language, gender, sexual orientation, and appearance. Every person is entitled to an opinion and can respect and fully disagree with the opinions, choices, etc. of others.
Social inequity	Inequities exists for some groups of people in our society. Oppressed groups exist in our society; review some groups' history and plight. Importance of empathy for and understanding of others.
Biases and prejudice	People have biases and should learn to challenge them. Stereotypes in society and their effect. Effects that biases have—prejudice, discrimination, and hate. Some negative attitudes toward people's ability, race and ethnicity, religion, language, gender, sexual orientation, and appearance.
Resisting discriminatory behavior	Devastating effect of name-calling, jokes, exclusive behaviors, and physical violence. Benefits of befriending and including others who are different. Extending to those who are different. Self-esteem and confidence building.
Cultural groups	Showcase the contributions of various groups (e.g., people with disabilities, African Americans, Latino Americans, women, gay and lesbian persons).

Mode: Gay and Lesbian Specific

Topic	Possible lessons
Gay, lesbian, bisexual, and transgender persons exist in society	Although most persons are heterosexual, a percentage of the population is gay, lesbian, bisexual, or transgender. Define gay, lesbian, bisexual, or transgender.

(Continued)

BOX 9.2. LESSON PLAN IDEAS (Continued)

Prejudice toward gay and lesbian persons	Famous gay and lesbian persons in history.
	Specific contributions of the gay and lesbian community.
	Heterosexism and homophobia.
	Oppression encountered by gay and lesbian persons.
	Challenge the biases and stereotypes of gay and lesbian persons.
	Myths about gay and lesbian persons (e.g., it's a "phase," a person's outward appearance dictates his or her sexual orientation).
	Harassment and hate crimes toward gay and lesbian persons.
	Combat discriminatory behavior such as name-calling, jokes, exclusive behaviors, and physical violence.
	Nonjudgmental language.
Significant events and associations	Gay and lesbian historical timeline.
	Contemporary issues: same-gender marriages, adoption by same-gender couples, gay and lesbian persons serving in the military, hate-crime legislation, civil rights protection, reparative therapy, and so forth.
	Significance of the symbols associated with the community (e.g., pink triangle, rainbow flag).
	Terms associated with the community, such as *closeted, coming out, sexual orientation* vs. *sexual preference.*

Mode: Gay and Lesbian Persons/Issues in the Content Areas

Topic	Possible Lessons
English	Read selected works of gay, lesbian, bisexual, or transgender authors; discuss how the author's message and his/her sexual orientation influenced the piece.
	Read short stories, poems, and novels about gay, lesbian, bisexual, and transgender characters; explore how the characters are portrayed; discuss their plight and how the character or premise compares to real life; discuss how the piece perpetuates or dispels some common myths or stereotypes; determine gender roles and their part in the piece.
Social studies: history, government, sociology, psychology, economics, etc.	Major gay and lesbian figures in history (by eras) and their contributions.
	Historical events that shaped the gay and lesbian rights movement.

(Continued)

BOX 9.2. LESSON PLAN IDEAS (Continued)

	How various cultures regard gay and lesbian persons.
	Homosexuals and the Holocaust.
	Debate current social/political issues (e.g., same-gender marriages, adoption by same-gender couples, gay and lesbian persons serving in the military, hate-crime legislation, civil rights protection, reparative therapy).
	Current gay and lesbian activism.
	The contemporary gay and lesbian identity and community (i.e., their buying power, gentrification, and so forth).
	Relationship of gender roles and sexism to sexual orientation.
	Oppression of homosexuals in societies.
	Homophobia and hate crime in society.
	Heterosexual privilege.
	Homosexuality in the Bible.
Math and sciences	Scientific origin and causes of homosexuality.
	Nature vs. nurture of homosexuality.
	Homosexuality in other species.
	Notable contributions of gay and lesbian figures to math and sciences.
	Testosterone and estrogen—have students dispel the myth that gay men have a lack of testosterone and that lesbians have a lack of estrogen.
	Develop math problems based on student surveys (e.g., harassment in your school, homophobia in your schools).
	Use gay and lesbian persons in math problems and examples when appropriate.
Performing and visual arts	Introduce notable gay and lesbian artisans; discuss how their sexual orientation may have influenced their pieces.
	Explore how sexual orientation is captured in art and dramas.
	Create projects that reflect diverse sexuality.
	Perform dramas that involve gay and lesbian characters or themes.

Mode: Gay and Lesbian Sexual Health Issues

Topic	Possible Lessons
Gay, lesbian, bisexual, and transgender behaviors	Scientific origins of same-gender behavior. Sexual behavior, experimentation, and fantasies do not dictate sexual orientation/identity.

(Continued)

BOX 9.2. LESSON PLAN IDEAS (Continued)

	Sexual myths about gay and lesbian persons (e.g., one has to play the dominant role, and the other the submissive role; someone who does not want to have sex with the opposite gender is bound to be homosexual).
Coitus	Protection from HIV and other STDs—"No" or "Know" to sex.
	Sexual-judgment skills and risky behaviors (e.g., using alcohol or drugs while having sex, engaging in anonymous sex, having sex with someone who seems "clean," having sexual partners who are older or have more sexual experience).
	Sexual options for gay and lesbian persons—making the best and responsible decision.
	Assertive skills to counter attempted rape or sexual abuse.
Emotional health	Stressors related to same-gender sexual orientations and where to get help.
	Self-esteem building to counter the emotional distress.
	Suicide prevention.
	Substance use and abuse to escape/cope with the stressors associated with being gay, lesbian, bisexual, or transgender.
	Establishing alliances with other gay, lesbian, bisexual, and transgender youth.
	Dating, long-term commitments, and civil unions.

Keep in mind several key points when you prepare and implement your lesson plans. First, be sure that the content is age appropriate. For instance, you would not introduce the terms gay, lesbian, bisexual, or transgender to kindergarteners, but you could certainly talk about how families are different. If you are uncertain about a lesson's appropriateness, discuss these with your colleagues or administrators and invite their feedback. Second, make certain that your lesson is based on factual, accurate information. Research various print and nonprint resources to support your content, and cross-reference your findings. If you are unfamiliar with a gay and lesbian topic, be sure to substantiate what you believe is accurate. Third, ensure that your lesson satisfies your state's content standards. Since all of your lessons satisfy your state's grade-level scope, sequence, and standards, you are less likely to risk professional admonishment when you can show that the lesson plans fulfill your state standards. Fourth, teach the lessons in a straightforward, nonjudgmental fashion. Students follow your lead; if you take the matter seriously, they will too. Last, your instructional delivery is likely to be more successful as long as you know the subject matter thoroughly, pre-

BOX 9.3. SIECUS GUIDELINES FOR COMPREHENSIVE SEXUALITY EDUCATION, KINDERGARTEN–12TH GRADE

Messages for Young People Ages 5 through 8

Human beings can love people of the same gender and people of the other gender.

There are men and women who are heterosexual, which means they can be attracted to and fall in love with someone of the other gender.

There are men and women who are homosexual, which means they can be attracted to and fall in love with someone of the same gender.

Homosexual men and women are also known as gay men and lesbian women.

People deserve respect regardless of their sexual orientation.

Making fun of people by calling them gay (e.g., "homo," "fag," "queer") is disrespectful and hurtful.

Messages for Young People Ages 9 through 12

Sexual orientation is a person's physical, emotional, and/or spiritual attraction to an individual of the same and/or opposite gender.

There are men and women who are bisexual, which means they can be attracted to and fall in love with people of either gender.

Sexual orientation is one part of who we are.

Gay men, lesbian women, bisexuals, and heterosexuals are alike in most ways.

The origin of people's sexual orientation is not known.

Some people are afraid to share that they are gay, lesbian, or bisexual because they fear they will be mistreated.

Gay, lesbian, or bisexual people's relationships can be as fulfilling as heterosexual people's relationships.

Gay men, lesbian women, and bisexual people can adopt children or have their own children.

Messages for Young People Ages 12 through 15

Every culture and society has people who are gay, lesbian, bisexual, and heterosexual.

People do not choose their sexual orientation.

Understanding one's sexual orientation can be an evolving process.

There are many theories about what determines sexual orientation, including genetics, prenatal and sociocultural influences, psychosocial factors, and a combination of all these.

Many scientific theories have concluded that sexual orientation cannot be changed by therapy or medicine.

Having discussions about sexual orientation can be difficult for some people.

Teenagers who have questions about their sexual orientation should consult a trusted and knowledgeable adult.

(Continued)

People's beliefs about sexual orientation are based on their religious, cultural, and family values.

When a gay, lesbian, or bisexual person tells another person his/her sexual orientation, it is known as "coming out."

Sometimes one's sexual orientation is disclosed without his/her consent. This is known as being "outed."

Coming out or being outed can be difficult because people may fear or experience negative reactions.

People who are gay, lesbian, or bisexual engage in many of the same sexual behaviors as heterosexual people.

There are young people who have sexual thoughts about and experiences with people of the same gender but do not consider themselves to be gay, lesbian, or bisexual.

There are young people who have sexual thoughts about and experiences with people of the other gender but do not consider themselves to be heterosexual.

Gay men, lesbian women, bisexuals, and heterosexuals can establish lifelong committed relationships.

Marriage between two people of the same gender is currently being debated in the United States.

There are organizations that offer support services, hotlines, and resources for young people who want to talk about sexual orientation.

Messages for Young People Ages 15 through 18

Sexual orientation is determined by a combination of a person's attractions, fantasies, and sexual behavior.

The understanding and identification of one's sexual orientation may change over the course of one's lifetime.

There are many states that ban discrimination against individuals because of their sexual orientation.

While the Internet offers a wide range of information about sexual orientation, some of it is inaccurate.

There are places on the Internet where gay, lesbian, and bisexual individuals can find and join communities for friendship and support.

While chatting or meeting people online can be fun, it is important to be cautious because it can be unsafe.

If you or someone you know is being intimidated, harassed, or harmed because of a perceived sexual orientation, it is important to tell a trusted adult, school official, or law enforcement authority.

Your school's bullying/harassment policy is _____. (fill in)

Civil rights for gay men and lesbian women are being debated in many states and communities across the United States.

Source: Sexuality Information and Education Council of the United States (SIECUS). (in press). *Guidelines for Comprehensive Sexuality Education: Kindergarten–12th Grade* (3rd Ed.). Sexuality Information and Education Council of the United States, 130 West 42nd Street, Suite 350, New York, NY 10036, www.siecus.org. Reprinted with permission.

sent the material in interesting and varied ways, allow the students to construct their own knowledge about the matter, connect the lessons to the students' community and lives, and connect the lessons to various subject areas.

What Is a Gay–Straight Alliance, and Should I Sponsor One?

A Gay–Straight Alliance is a student-run club that any youth—straight, gay, lesbian, bisexual, transgender, or questioning—can join who has a keen interest in building and promoting a finer understanding of the issues surrounding sexual orientation. Blumenfeld and Lindop (1999) elaborate, "The groups are designed to meet the needs of students who are interested in addressing issues related to sexual orientation and antigay prejudice and to address the concerns of lesbian and gay students and their friends" (p. 168). GSAs generally meet in safe zones and have faculty advisors who are safe persons. GSA agendas vary according to their school climate and the club's independent goals (Massachusetts Department of Education, 2004), but most meetings cover topics such as homophobia in school, gender roles, coming out, relationships, and so forth. Many GSAs raise gay-and-lesbian-awareness issues by sponsoring events such as Day of Silence, a Pride rally, antigay-bias training for teachers, and so on, and often members will plan for a dance, a group outing, or a political march. Box 9.4 outlines some ideas for GSA meetings.

Not all clubs for and about gay and lesbian issues are designated Gay–Straight Alliances. Some students have created clever club names such as GASP! (Gay And Straight People), HUGS (Helping Unite Gays and Straights), and LeSGab (Lesbian, Straight, Gay, and Bisexual) that embrace the GSA common purpose. Other clubs bear names such as PRISM (People Respecting Important Social Movements), TAP (Teens Against Prejudice), and DIRE (Diversity Is Reason Enough) and include gay and lesbian issues in their advocacy for social justice, but they largely focus their attention on the oppression of various groups in society.

Schools often offer their students a gay and lesbian support group, which has a mental-health nature that is administered through a school's wellness program, health center, or counselor's office. The support group, much like empowerment programs for pregnant students, students with health impairments, or those with self-esteem challenges, provides gay, lesbian, bisexual, transgender, or questioning students with opportunities to problem solve their challenges under a trained counselor. Some support groups are social and afford students with occasions to interact in an informal setting (e.g., watch a video, play board games) but are not likely to meet in a publicized setting or sponsor a gay-and-lesbian-themed event. Other schools offer their gay and lesbian students a support club where students gather in safe places to socialize and build mutual friendships. The clubs vary accordingly, as some are more visible and vocal than others.

BOX 9.4 IDEAS FOR A GSA MEETING

After a GSA mission statement, governance structure, ground rules, and general agenda have been created, a GSA could . . .

Discuss

Discuss the many myths and stereotypes about gay, lesbian, bisexual, and transgender persons and determine their effect on society.

Discuss the answers to the top ten questions most likely asked about diverse sexuality.

Discuss a contemporary social event and determine its impact on gay, lesbian, bisexual, and transgender youth.

Discuss and plan for what to include on your bulletin board.

Discuss and plan for a one-day or afternoon in-service about gay and lesbian youth for teachers.

Discuss how teachers could include gay and lesbian persons in their lessons, and recommend these to the respective teachers.

Discuss homophobia in your school and strategize how to combat it.

Discuss each member's personal challenges (e.g., coming out, family intolerance, harassment) or achievements (e.g., accepting an uncle's boyfriend, sending a congratulations card to a same-gender couple on their recent child adoption, being accepted by a best friend) with regard to sexuality.

Discuss, "If I could change one thing about society's beliefs about gay and lesbian persons, I would . . ."

Discuss specific instances of prejudice and discrimination (at school) toward gay and lesbian students and then strategize what to say or do if the situation reoccurs.

Discuss an admired gay, lesbian, bisexual, or transgender person in history and explain that person's accomplishments.

Discuss how effective the school's nondiscrimination and antiharassment policy is.

Create

Create a series of skits (or a play) about acceptance to present to the student body.

Create posters about acceptance and hang them up around school (but get permission first).

Create a list of books, magazines, journals, and videos for the school librarian to purchase.

Create a survey of homophobia, acceptance, gender roles, or stereotypes and disseminate it to your peers. Use the findings to sponsor a series of "understanding" workshops for the student body.

Create and play a board game that allows members of the club to contemplate their feelings (e.g., you can land on squares that say "Get five points if you can come up with a one-sentence compliment about a person's sexual orientation" or "Get 10 points if you can come up with a way to counter the word *faggot*" or "Your aunt just left you $20,000 that you have to spend to reduce homophobia in your school. Come up with three ways to spend the money" or "You just met a person you really love but who does not believe in the need to practice safe sex. What do you do?"

(Continued)

BOX 9.4 IDEAS FOR A GSA MEETING (CONTINUED)

Invite

Invite a GSA from another school and cosponsor an event.

Invite openly gay and lesbian adults to discuss issues they have encountered in their lives.

Invite a GSA from a university to discuss what university life is like as a GSA member.

Invite members of PFLAG, ACLU, GLSEN, or other similar organizations to discuss their initiatives.

Invite a health expert and a social worker to speak about sexual health and emotional issues.

Invite students and faculty to discuss some of their biases toward gay and lesbian persons, and then have members address their concerns.

Invite the superintendent or his/her associates to strategize how to include gay and lesbian issues in the curriculum.

Invite community members to discuss issues such as hate crimes (e.g., a police officer), legal issues (e.g., a gay-rights attorney), gay and lesbian persons in the media (e.g., a professor of radio, television, and film), historically oppressed groups (e.g., a history professor), coming out to a parent gracefully (e.g., a parent of an openly gay child), homosexuality in the Bible (e.g., a priest or pastor), and so forth.

Have

Have a picnic where members come as a famous gay or lesbian person in history.

Have an academy-award party where members come dressed as a favorite "out" actor or character from a movie.

Have a movie night featuring themes related to the club's agenda.

Have a board- or card-game afternoon.

Have a volunteer/community-service day (e.g., work at a Special Olympics event, work at a city-sponsored outdoor event, adopt a road/highway stretch, sing Christmas carols at a nursing home).

Have a car wash to raise funds (and awareness).

Have an arts-and-crafts afternoon (e.g., making scrapbooks).

Sponsor Events

Sponsor a gay-pride event (e.g., have divisions make posters of famous gay and lesbian persons and hang these up in the school hallways).

Sponsor a Day of Silence (i.e., no speaking for a full day, April 16).

Sponsor a hallway parade of civil-rights groups (and their courageous battle in history) and then design miniature floats.

Sponsor a masquerade ball where partiers come dressed as their favorite gay or straight historical person.

Sources: Massachusetts Department of Education. (2004). *Out and about: Other activities.* Retrieved January 30, 2004, from http://www.doe.mass.edu/hsss/GSA/OutAbout.html; Massachusetts Department of Education. (2004). *Top ten GSA meeting ideas.* Retrieved January 30, 2004, from http://www.doe.mass.edu/hssss/GSA/Meeting.html; GLSEN. (2001). *20 Ways Your GSA Can Rock the World!* Retrieved January 30, 2004, from http://glsen.org/cgi-bin/iowa/all/library/record/371.html.

Gay–Straight Alliances (and clubs similar in their mission) are found in urban, rural, and suburban school districts, as well as in private and parochial schools. The first GSA started in 1989 in Massachusetts (American Civil Liberties Union, 2003). GSAs were few in the beginning, but their numbers climbed rapidly from 99 in the summer of 1998 to 600 in 1999 (Jones, 1999) to over 1,000 in 2002 (Melendez, 2002). Some speculate that the national attention focused on the litigation of the students in Salt Lake City and Orange County against their respective school districts for banning GSA formations (see chapter 4) led to this rapid growth. The heavily publicized cases informed students across the country that clubs for gay and lesbian students existed and that students could ask for and legally form GSAs. Nearly 20,000 students nationwide were involved in GSA activities in 2001, and it is likely that the membership will continue to grow.

The rapid growth in this short time, however, is not indicative of full acceptance and support in schools. Despite the seemingly large numbers of Gay–Straight Alliances, only 1 out of 15 high schools has them, and members often report hostility and resistance from administrators and faculty members. Unsurprisingly, members find a lack of support from faculty and the local community, and very few resources are available for them in school libraries and public libraries (GLSEN, 2001a). Such accounts should be no surprise, considering that one research study found that 55% of secondary school health teachers indicated that a gay and lesbian support group would not be supported at their school (Telljohann, Price, Pourselami, & Easton, 1995).

Administrators and faculty members who believe that Gay–Straight Alliances are troublesome and unnecessary should recognize them as true alliances that work to advance a greater understanding of differences and similarities among students. Through their social interactions, club members learn that, despite their sexual-orientation differences, they all share a common bond: thriving in adolescence. This leads them to treat one another as they would want to be treated—with respect. When the heterosexual students in a GSA model respectful behavior toward gay and lesbian students, others begin to do the same, giving way to a safer school climate. GSAs also afford gay and lesbian students an opportunity to gather together and feel accepted, valued, and supported by their homo-, bi-, and heterosexual peers, thereby reducing feelings of isolation. According to GLSEN (2000), GSAs

- provide a safe environment for students to address issues of sexual orientation, gender identity and gender roles;
- focus on core school values for LGBTQ [Lesbian, Gay, Bisexual, Transgender, and Questioning] students to learn and grow;
- build a partnership between LGBTQ and straight-identified students;
- encompass the broadest range of students including "real or perceived" sexual orientation and gender identity;

- recognize outstanding contributions in the school environment;
- help the school establish effective anti-harassment and discrimination policies;
- educate the school and local community on LGBTQ issues; and
- promote safe schools where diversity is accepted and harassment is condemned. (p. 2)

Students generally start a Gay–Straight Alliance because they see the need for one. GSAs are student organized, led, facilitated, and initiated, and you may be asked to sponsor one if students think you would be supportive of the club. Your duties as a sponsor would be no different than those assigned to sponsors of other clubs. You would generally serve in an ancillary role where you would be likely to do the following:

- Assist in facilitating the meetings—giving advice about the GSA's governance structure, ground rules, meeting logistics, and so on.
- Offer ideas for the club meetings.
- Support students—encouraging appropriate behavior, remaining positive when the club morale may be low.
- Recommend how members might educate others about sexual-orientation issues.
- Invite faculty members to the meetings.
- Alleviate distressing moments.
- Publicize sponsored events in the teachers' lounge or other strategic locations.
- Talk to members or their parents if concerns should arise.
- Update your administrators about the club's progress.
- Retrieve resources (e.g., books, information) to help the cause.
- Mediate conflicts during meetings and sponsored events.

If these responsibilities seem overwhelming or if you simply lack the interest to sponsor a GSA, then decline the invitation. Explain that you are honored to have been asked but that you cannot at that time. Indicate that they can invite you to future meetings or events and then wish them success with the club. You can say something to this effect:

> I really can't at this time. I have such a full plate this year at school and at home, and I don't think I could give you the attention I think your club deserves. I'm flattered that you asked me. If you have a hard time finding a sponsor, come back and see me, and we'll brainstorm who else you might ask. Keep me posted, and if you invite me to a meeting or event, I'll try to come. Let me know if you have any problems starting up the club so I can put in a good word for you. Good luck.

If the idea of sponsoring a GSA sounds to your liking, then accept the invitation with honor. Tell the students that you realize it is a challenge to start a club but that you intend to work hard so that the club is successful. You can finish by asking how they would like you to help. Your acceptance conversation might sound like this:

> I'm so honored you asked me. I would love to, and I will work hard with you so that it is a benefit for everyone. It might not be easy to get this club going or keep it afloat, but we can work together to overcome our barriers. We all need to remember our mission and stay positive when others try to demoralize us with negative comments or hurtful names scribbled on our posters or bulletin boards. Let me know what the next step is for me and how I can help. I'll be at the first meeting.

By the time students have approached you about serving as a Gay–Straight Alliance sponsor, they should have followed the school's or district's policies for starting a club. If they have not, you should recommend that they follow the club guidelines immediately. The students are responsible for finding potential club members, informing the administrators about their intentions to start a GSA, finding a place to meet, advertising meeting dates and times, planning the meetings, establishing ground rules, and planning for future meetings (GLSEN, 2004). You and your students should visit the GLSEN website and download three excellent resources to help establish a GSA: *Q & A about Gay–Straight Alliances*, *Gay–Straight Alliance Handbook*, and *10 Steps Toward Starting a GSA*. The Gay–Straight Alliance network (www.gsanetwork.org) also has resources for GSA members to use immediately (e.g., *How to Have a Kick-Ass GSA*, *Fun Things to Do with Your GSA*, and sample mission statements).

As a Gay–Straight Alliance sponsor, you should keep the following in mind:

- Let the students run the meetings and plan the events.
- Offer assistance when asked or when you see that the students need guidance.
- Read over the club's mission statements and governance structure carefully and offer to modify these if you see the need. Be sure to explain why certain items should be rewritten.
- Ensure that the club rules stress confidentiality of the members and guests and that any personal information shared at the meetings should not be disseminated.
- Be positive and encouraging, especially when other teachers and students have offended club members.
- Strategize with the members on how to handle offensive remarks or the defacing of the club's posters and bulletin board.
- Ensure that members and guests who want to talk openly about their sexual orientation can do so, and that those who do not want to are not pressured to do so.
- Encourage students to collaborate with other clubs.

- Reaffirm that members should not make assumptions about the sexual orientation of other members or guests.
- Have meetings even though only a few students attend them.
- Remind students of the club's mission and help facilitate discussion of issues pertinent to the mission.
- Talk to the sponsors of GSAs in other schools and determine what has worked for their club, how they have overcome their obstacles, and so forth.
- Talk to your colleagues about the club. Let them know what the club is doing and what happens at the meetings. Their fear, distrust, and uneasiness is likely to lessen when they learn that students are talking about diversity, social justice, and antiharassment issues.
- Be a source of emotional support. Tell students that you are there for them.
- Find opportunities (e.g., public lectures, pride rallies) that allow the club to collaborate with the community.

Lastly, because your sexual orientation does not matter in the eyes of the Gay–Straight Alliance, you are likely to be invited to attend a meeting or sponsored event. If your schedule allows, try to attend one of their meetings despite your level of discomfort. There is nothing so offensive or painful that a group of students could encumber you with in one of their meetings. In fact, if you disagree with a meeting's subject matter or with the comments that are made, respectfully share your ideas with the group. The members are likely to reflect on your ideas, contemplate how others perceive the issues at hand, and respond accordingly. In short, the meetings and sponsored events become a learning experience for members and guests alike.

Summary

By now you already know that your gay and lesbian students have many challenges in their lives. Many of them fear being different, harassed, and losing friends or family members, and most do not have access to "special programs, task forces, after-school discussion groups, [or] openly gay teachers" (Pollack, 1998, cited in Tharinger & Wells, 2001, p. 168). As a result, many gay and lesbian youth feel isolated and alone. One student described his situation, "There was no one in my school for me to talk to about my issues. I felt completely alone and unsupported. I had nowhere to unload the burden I was feeling unless I ended it" (YouthPride Inc., 1997).

What a world of difference it would have made for this student (and many others) had a teacher taken the initiative to speak out against any disparaging language and harmful

remarks made about or to gay and lesbian students, to present a neutral-to-positive attitude toward gay and lesbian persons, and to understand the issues that confront them. The
student would have felt accepted, supported, and included, and the idea of suicide could
have been erased from his mind. When you choose to remain silent, to not address gay and
lesbian issues, or to not challenge antigay bias and discrimination, you inadvertently make
the situation worse for gay and lesbian youth. Your message speaks volumes—the lives of
gay and lesbian persons do not matter. As a consequence, some of the most vulnerable students are left behind.

You may not have the personality or convictions it takes to be the kind of teacher who
sponsors a Gay–Straight Alliance or who emotionally supports all gay and lesbian youth as
they make sense of their sexual orientation, but you can certainly be the type of teacher
who challenges assumptions about diverse groups of people; avoids stereotypes; and is
willing to teach students about inequity in society, biases and prejudice, and so forth. When
you make this effort, you give all students a sense of belonging that ultimately leads to a
school climate of acceptance, tolerance, safety, and support for all groups of students.

Idea File

1. Have your students count the number of times they hear homophobic remarks or
   slurs in a given day. Then plan for what you will tell them if the incidence is high.
2. Surf the Internet and find detailed lesson plans based on the lesson ideas found in
   box 9.2.
3. Identify other ideas you would recommend to a GSA and add them to the list
   found in box 9.4.
4. Imagine yourself at a first GSA meeting in your school. What would you like to see
   happen? Plan for a one-hour meeting.
5. Read the following scenario and role-play how you plan to handle the situation.

   > Jose grabs Tyson's portable CD player, and Tyson replies, "Give it back, you silly
   > fag." You begin to explain that such words are unacceptable, and Tyson
   > defends, "Well, Coach calls us football players 'queers' and 'faggots' all the time.
   > Why don't you tell him that he's out of line? If he stops using these 'unaccept-
   > able' words, then I'll stop. Until then, Jose is a big faggot."

References

American Civil Liberties Union. (2003). *Where we are: The annual report of the ACLU's nationwide work
    on LGBT rights and HIV/AIDS*. New York: Author.

Blumenfeld, W., & Lindop, L. (1999). How to start a gay/straight alliance. In L. Mitchell (ed.), *Tackling gay issues in schools: A resource module* (pp. 168–86). Watertown, CT: GLSEN Connecticut.

GLSEN. (2000). *Gay–straight alliance handbook: A resource of student pride USA*. Retrieved January 30, 2004, from http://www.lgbthistorymonth.org/binary-data/GLSEN_ATTACHMENTS/file/32-1.pdf.

GLSEN. (2001a). *GLSEN tallies 1,000 gay–straight alliances*. Retrieved January 29, 2004, from http://www.glsen.org/cgi-bin/iowa/all/libarary/record/863.html.

GLSEN. (2001b). *The 2001 national school climate survey: The school related experiences of our nations lesbian, gay, bisexual and transgender youth*. New York: Author.

GLSEN. (2004). *10 steps towards starting a GSA*. Retrieved January 29, 2004, from http://www.glsen.org/cgi-bin/iowa/all/library/record/12.html.

Harris, M., & Bliss, G. (1997). Coming out in a school setting: Former students' experiences and opinions about disclosure. *Journal of Gay and Lesbian Social Services, 7*(4), 85–100.

Jones, R. (1999). "I don't feel safe here anymore": Your legal duty to protect gay kids from harassment. *American School Board Journal, 186*(11), 26–31.

Lambda Legal Defense and Education Fund. (1998). *Defending gay/straight alliances and other gay-related groups in public schools under the Equal Access Act*. Retrieved January 23, 2004, from http://www.lambdalegal.org/cgi-bin/iowa/documents/record?record=251.

Massachusetts Department of Education. (2004). *Gay/straight alliances: A student guide*. Retrieved January 30, 2004, from http://ww.doe.mass.edu/hssss/GSA/Intro.html.

Melendez, M. (2002). *Schools face challenges as more teens come out*. Retrieved February 25, 2002, from http://www.glsen.org/templates/news/record.html?section=12&record=1151.

Mitchell, L. (1999). *Tackling gay* issues in school: A resource module*. Watertown, CT: GLSEN Connecticut.

Owens, R. (1998). *Queer kids: The challenges and promise for lesbian, gay, and bisexual youth*. New York: Harrington Park Press.

Pollack, W. (1998). *Real boys: Rescuing our sons from the myth of boyhood*. New York: Random House.

Sanelli, M., & Perrault, G. (2001). "I could be anybody": Gay, lesbian, and bisexual students in the U.S. schools. *NASSP Bulletin, 85*(622), 69–78.

SIECUS. (1998). *Filling the gaps: Hard to teach topics in sexuality education*. New York: Author.

SIECUS. (in press). *Guidelines for Comprehensive Sexuality Education: Kindergarten–12th Grade* (3rd Ed.). New York: Author.

Sivertsen, W. D., & Thames, T. B. (1995). *Each child that dies: Gays and lesbians in your schools*. Retrieved July 18, 2002, from http://www.outproud.org/article_each_child.html.

Telljohann, S., Price, J., Pourselami, M., & Easton, A. (1995). Teaching about sexual orientation by secondary health teachers. *Journal of School Health, 61*(1), 18–22.

Tharinger, D., & Wells, G. (2000). An attachment perspective on the developmental challenges of gay and lesbian adolescents: The need for continuity of caregiving from family and schools. *School Psychology Review, 29*(2), 158–72.

Todd, C. (1999). *Taking the lead: How school administrators can provide the leadership necessary to creating schools where all people are valued, regardless of sexual orientation*. Retrieved July 18, 2002, from http://www.glsen.org/templates/resources/record.html?section=14&record=384.

YouthPride Inc. (1997). *Creating safe schools for lesbian and gay students: A resource guide for school staff*. Retrieved July 20, 2001, from http://members.tripod.com/~twood/guide.html.

School Counselors and Their Gay and Lesbian Students

"REASON ENOUGH TO BE OUT," PAIGE, 15, OF HOUSTON

When people meet me, they can't tell that I am a lesbian. They know me before they know my sexual orientation; thus I show them that those who are "different" are really quite the same.

Because of this, I originally decided to attend my high school in Houston as a "straight" student. But I quickly found a group of people who were like me, along with a girl to call my own. I'm a sophomore and she was a senior, beautiful, and a great friend. And we dated for a short time at the beginning of this school year before she killed herself. She had talked to me about doing it—afraid of what her family and other friends would do or say if they found out she was a lesbian—and we both thought she was over it. But she wasn't.

Because of my girlfriend's death, I finally knew what I stood for and who I was, so I decided to do what she couldn't—come out to everyone. I made new friends and joined my school's gay-straight alliance club. I started coming out gradually and sticking up for the gay community. When some guys at my lunch table started talking about a "fag" I immediately spoke up. And when one of my teachers told me that I had to stop talking about my relationships because they were not "school-appropriate" I decided to talk about them anyway. Now he lets me "get away with it."

Coming out has been smooth for me; I just wish everyone were as lucky. Yes, our community has accomplished a great deal, but we still have a long way to go. We are still widely regarded as "different," but isn't everyone? Maybe when society realizes this, not as many of us will feel we have to kill ourselves.

Source: The Advocate Report. (2004, March 16). Generation Q: Reason enough to be out. *The Advocate, 910,* 18. Reprinted with permission.

Overview

The counseling profession is constantly evolving to meet the needs arising from societal changes (CACREP, 2001). As you have learned thus far, addressing the needs of gay and lesbian youth in schools is a relatively new phenomenon, one that has emerged primarily in the last decade. In fact, school counseling programs in the past did not offer training for candidates to effectively respond to gay and lesbian youth issues, which unfortunately left many school counselors unprepared to work with gay and lesbian students or those questioning their sexuality.

Research has found that many school counselors do not fully understand the context in which these youth survive. McFarland and Dupuis (2001), for instance, noted that school counselors alluded to the fact that there are no gay students in their schools, and others perceived education on gay and lesbian issues "as subversive attempts by homosexuals to take over schools" (p. 172). Researchers have also found that a significant number of school counselors would not find it gratifying to work with gay and lesbian students (Price & Telljohann, 1991), some have negative attitudes and feelings about gay and lesbian persons (Sears, 1992), and some would be uncomfortable working with gay or lesbian clients (Bailey & Phariss, 1996).

In reality, you may have students like Paige (in the vignette) who seek your help as they work through others' reactions to their coming out or who seek help with the issues associated their sexuality. This chapter is designed to help a wide range of counselors, with varying degrees of experience, effectively counsel gay and lesbian youth and those questioning their sexual orientation. However, many of the ways counselors develop good therapeutic relationships with gay and lesbian youth involve basic common skills and techniques reflective of good practice. This chapter addresses the following questions:

- What can I do so that gay and lesbian students feel safe to come see me?
- What should I consider when I counsel gay and lesbian students or those questioning their sexual orientation?
- What should I know about coming out?
- How do I help parents who seek consultation about their gay or lesbian child?

> **Reflect and Write**
>
> As a school counselor, what initiatives do you make to inform your student body that gay and lesbian students (and those questioning their sexual orientation) are invited and welcome to come see you?

What Can I Do So That Gay and Lesbian Students Feel Safe to Come See Me?

Gay and lesbian students are increasingly seeking guidance and direction from their counselors. One of the earliest studies on school counselors and gay and lesbian youth found that 71% of the counselors had counseled at least one gay or lesbian student (Price & Telljohann, 1991), and in a study of junior high and high school counselors conducted six years later, the percentage had increased to 93% (Fontaine, 1998). As their visibility in schools increases, your role as a school counselor is to be more responsive to their needs and to work toward enhancing a supportive and inclusive school environment. Many school-based organizations now strongly recommend that school counselors and social workers master the knowledge associated with sexual-orientation issues, be available for gay and lesbian youth, and counsel them in a practice that leads them to develop a positive sexual identity. (See box 10.1 for the American School Counselor Association positions on sexual minority youth.) The American Counselor Association (1995), for instance, outlines in their position statement the need for supporting gay and lesbian youth and reducing hostility directed toward them. The National Education Association (1992) clearly states,

> All persons, regardless of sexual orientation, should be afforded equal opportunity within the public education system. The Association further believes that every school district should provide counseling by trained personnel for students who are struggling with their sexual orientation. (National Education Association, 1992, p. 27)

 BOX 10.1. AMERICAN SCHOOL COUNSELOR ASSOCIATION POSITION ON SEXUAL MINORITY YOUTH

The American School Counselor Association does not knowingly engage in or support activities which discriminate on the basis of race, color, sex, religion, national origin, affectional or sexual orientation, disability, or age.

The Professional School Counselor and Sexual Minority Youth (Adopted 1995)

The members of the American School Counselor Association are committed to facilitating and promoting the fullest possible development of each individual by reducing the barriers of misinformation, myth, ignorance, hatred, and discrimination, which prevent sexual orientation minorities from achieving individual potential, healthy esteem, and equal status. School counselors are in a field committed to human development and need to be sensitive to the use of inclusive language and positive modeling of sexual orientation minority equity. ASCA is committed to equal opportunity regardless of sexual orientation.

The Rationale

Identity is determined by a complex mix of nature and nurture. Developmentally, the literature clearly states that sexual orientation is firmly established by age five and much research indicates such establishment occurs even earlier.

(Continued)

Many internal and external, as well as interpersonal obstacles exist in school and society that inhibit students from accurately understanding and positively accepting their sexual orientation. Counselors need to become accurately informed and aware of the ways verbal/nonverbal and conscious/unconscious communication limit the opportunities and infringe upon the healthy development of sexual orientation minorities' self-acceptance and healthy esteem solely because of their identity. Harm is perpetrated against sexual minorities through language, stereotypes, myths, misinformation, threat of expulsion from social and institutional structures and other entities, and from beliefs contrary to the reality of their identity.

Sexual orientation minority youth begin to experience self-identification and the "coming out' process, both essentially cognitive activities, during adolescence. Such identification is not indicative of sexual activity.

The Professional School Counselor's Role

The school counselor uses inclusive and non-presumptive language with equitable expectations toward sexual orientation minority individuals, being especially sensitive to those aspects of communication and social structures/institutions which provide accurate working models of acceptance of sexual minority identities and equality. Counselors must become vigilant to the pervasive negative effects of stereotyping and rubricizing individuals into rigid expressions of gender roles and sexual identities.

The professional school counselor is sensitive to ways in which attitudes and behavior negatively affect the individual. School counselors are called to provide constructive feedback on the negative use of exclusive and presumptive language and inequitable expectations toward sexual orientation minorities. The school counselor places emphasis on a person's behavioral choices and not on their unalterable identity and uniqueness. Demonstrations of sexual orientation minority equity also includes fair and accurate representation of sexual identities in visible leadership positions as well as role positions.

Summary

ASCA is committed to the inclusion and affirmation of sexual orientation minorities. ASCA supports conscious-raising among school counselors and increased modeling of inclusive language, advocacy and equal opportunity for participation among sexual orientation minorities' identities. This is done in order to break through individual, social and institutional behaviors and expectations which limit the development of human potential in all populations.

Source: American School Counselor Association. (2003). *The professional school counselor and sexual minority youth.* Retrieved February 13, 2004, from http://www.schoolcounselor.org. Reprinted with permission.

The time is now to support this population of students and prepare for their forthcoming. As one schoolteacher emphasized, waiting until a gay or lesbian student needs support is egregious:

> We cannot leave the burden of creating a safe environment on the shoulders of the students who need it. These things need to be approachable, very safe . . . gay support should be proactive, not reactive. If we wait until there is an obvious need, we have waited too long. How is a kid going to summon up the courage to jump out of the closet when there is no visible safety net out there? Educators need to be supportive of homosexuality, even though we have no students who are out of the closet. Part of creating a supportive atmosphere is not only being there for gay teens, but being there educating straight ones. (Rhode Island Task Force on Gay, Lesbian, Bisexual, and Transgendered Youth, 1996)

Gay and lesbian youth are like most students. Some will visit a school counselor because they need help with the challenges presented in their lives and believe that a counselor can help them resolve their problems without judgment or prejudice. Others will deal with their challenges as best as they can, sometimes consulting with a friend or family member or choosing to restrain their emotional issues. Often these youth avoid school counselors because they are fearful or skeptical of mental-health assistance and believe that the counselor will notify their parents, suggest reparative therapy, or recommend that they change their behavior. Some gay and lesbian youth simply may not be aware that a school counselor is available for them, and others may find it too difficult to discuss their issues.

As a mental health professional, you are the likely person on your campus to help gay and lesbian youth. You are best skilled to alleviate the repercussions that anxiety, fear, stress, isolation, depression, and feelings of worthlessness can have on gay and lesbian youth, and you can prevent some of them from engaging in self-destructive behaviors. Students who come to see you evidently perceive the need for mental-health assistance. With your training in listening skills, mental-health assessment, problem solving, and so forth, you can counsel them through a range of issues central to their sexual orientation and guide them through other challenges common among youth (e.g., parents' divorce, unpopularity at school, school failure, stature issues). The opportunities to do so are limited if they do not know that your services are available for them. There are many ways that you can make a concerted effort to welcome these students into your office or center. So that gay and lesbian students feel safe to come see you, consider implementing the following strategies.

"Can someone help me? I'm late for my next class."

The Physical Environment

Make sure your student body knows that counseling is available for gay, lesbian, bisexual, transgender, and questioning youth. The materials about your services or resources in your office or center will best convey this if they appear "gay friendly" and strongly suggest that counselors will not judge students, discriminate against them, punish them, betray their confidentiality, or trivialize matters associated with their sexual orientation. The following are some steps you can take to indicate that your office or center is a safe place for gay and lesbian students:

- Post flyers around the school informing students that you are available to talk about a host of issues, including sexual orientation.
- Place brochures outside your office informing students about sexual-orientation issues such as coming out, harassment, and what it means to be gay, lesbian, bisexual, transgender, or questioning.
- Post a "safe person, safe place" sign (with an inverted pink triangle) outside your office/center door.
- Hang posters outside the school office that convey that you are open to discuss sexuality issues (see box 10.2 for a list of commercially available posters on gay and lesbian issues).
- Display a bulletin board with "gay friendly" messages (e.g., "Be a friend to someone who has come out to you" or "Famous gay and lesbian persons").
- Post symbols commonly associated with the gay and lesbian community outside or around your office (e.g., rainbow flags with "friendly" inscribed in the center, the inverted pink triangle with "ally" written across it).
- Distribute bookmarks to the student body, with one side giving information about your services and times you are available, and the other side displaying a catchy phrase about your commitment to students' mental, physical, sexual, cognitive, and social well-being.
- Display a list of available books, magazines, articles, and videos concerning various sexual-orientation topics (include contemporary issues, gay and lesbian characters in fiction, and nonfiction pieces).
- Display a list of local or Web-based organizations and hotlines that support gay and lesbian persons (e.g., Parents and Friends of Lesbians and Gays [PFLAG]).
- Have a library of books and magazines (fiction and nonfiction) and videos (movies and documentaries) available for checkout.

BOX 10.2. POSTERS COMMERCIALLY AVAILABLE THAT CONVEY ACCEPTANCE OF DIVERSE SEXUAL ORIENTATIONS

Source	Poster(s) and Cost
University of Oregon LGBT Educational and Support Services Program (541) 346-1134 http://uoregon.edu/~program/posters.html	"What Is So Scary About This Couple?" "What is Wrong with This Family?" "How Could Anyone Hate their Love?" Initial set free; additional orders are $2.00 each.
Indiana Youth Group www.indianayouthgroup.org/buy.html	"This is a safe place to talk about . . ." $5.00 each
Wingspan Ministries 100 N Oxford Street St. Paul, MN 55104-6540 (651) 224-3371	"This attraction is in your neighborhood." "What can you do? Your best friend has just told you, 'I'm gay.'" "Cool, your parents are gay! Why didn't you tell me?" "One of Life's Discoveries" $8.00 each
Coalition for Positive Sexuality www.positive.org/Home/posters.html	"It's not a fad. We've got a different spin on sexuality." $5.00
Northwest Coalition for Human Dignity Freida Takamura (253) 756-7062 www.safeschoolscoalition.org/ssc_order .htm	"All Families Welcome" Free
Donnelly Colt Progressive Resources PO Box 188 Hampton, CT 06247 www.donnellycolt.com	"Unfortunately, History Has Set the Record a Little Too Straight." $12.00

The Personal Connection

In addition to materials and resources that convey that you are available for students, remind teachers and other school personnel that you are open to counseling gay and lesbian youth and are sensitive to their needs. In short, make the rounds on campus and pitch your services to teachers and the student body. You can do the following:

- Visit classrooms and announce that you enjoy talking to students who stop by. Mention a litany of topics that you are eager to discuss and include sexual-orientation issues.
- Provide flyers to teachers and have them announce the various services that are available through your office or center.
- Visit with different student clubs and teach a minilesson on tolerance, harassment, and support of gay and lesbian students.
- Write an editorial in the school newspaper informing students about your services, or write a piece on the challenges associated with growing up gay and lesbian in contemporary times.
- Announce at your school's PTA meeting that you enjoy and are open to collaborating with parents as they deal with their children's sexuality and relationship issues. Mention that you provide services to students exploring their sexuality.
- Talk to the Gay–Straight Alliance in your school and ask members if there are topics they would like to explore (e.g., what to do when a friend rejects you), personal skills they would like to strengthen (e.g., self-esteem, confidence building, and conflict-resolution skills), or help they need in making the school environment less hostile for them.
- Sponsor a faculty workshop on diverse-sexuality issues.

Application

How might you address a principal, school official, or parent who opposes your "advertising" your availability for gay and lesbian youth?

What Should I Consider When I Counsel Gay and Lesbian Students or Those Questioning Their Sexual Orientation?

Your gay and lesbian students may share commonalities, but they have unique needs. Some students may seek your services with pride and certainty about their sexuality, others may be more ambivalent and unsure about theirs, and others may consider the topic too overwhelming to even approach you. Some will walk through your door feeling confident and clear about the help they need; others may appear uneasy as they skirt around the issues; and others will exhibit shameful, fearful, or depressed behaviors. Box 10.3 demonstrates the range of emotions, topics students may want to explore, and self-destructive behaviors you are likely to encounter.

To ascertain what to consider when you counsel gay and lesbian students or those questioning their sexual orientation, read the following examples of questions your students may have for you and situations that may require your assistance. Deliberate on the following questions as you read:

**BOX 10.3. RANGE OF CHARACTERISTICS AND TOPIC EXPLORATION
MANIFESTED AMONG GAY AND LESBIAN YOUTH**

Students may struggle with: self-perception, self-acceptance, self-monitoring, self-image/identity, adjusting to sexuality, hostility from others, personal expectations, exploring/defining their sexuality, self-esteem/worth.

Students may feel: anxious, lonely, rejected, scared, isolated, eager, depressed, pride, ostracized, guilt, confident, ambitious, suicidal, shame, popular, grief, confused, hopeless, helpless, alienated, fear, accepted, supported, eager, trivialized, hopeful, enthusiastic, suicidal, spiritual.

Student may need your help with issues related to: family difficulties, starting a GSA, sexual experimentation, HIV/AIDS, harassment and violence, suicide, alcohol and substance abuse, running away, relationships, academic difficulty, coming out, complaints of nonacceptance, dropping out, organizing a gay march.

A lack of support, being a victim of or witnessing antigay harassment, and hearing/seeing homophobic/heterosexist messages can lead many gay and lesbian youth to feel that the weight of the world is on their shoulders.

- What is your initial response?
- How would you plan your counseling session?
- What other questions would you ask to evaluate the student's situation?
- What are some preliminary ideas for direction, development, and client-derived decisions?
- How will you help the student manage the issue outside of the counseling session?
- What else would you consider?

Students with Homosexual and Bisexual Issues

1. I think I might be gay. What should I do next?
2. Everyone in the school knows that I'm a lesbian, and after I made out with one of the girls on the volleyball team, she started to ignore me. Why is she being like that?
3. I don't want to be lesbian. How can I fix it so that I'm not lesbian anymore?
4. I'm scared people are going to find out that I am gay. What should I do?
5. Sometimes I have crushes on guys, and sometimes I have crushes on girls. Am I bisexual or am I going to be a lesbian?
6. I had sex with an older gay guy that I met at that mall. I want to see him again. Do you think that's OK?
7. I'm the worst 17-year-old in the whole wide world. I know I'm going to hell because I'm gay. Does God hate me, and will I die of AIDS?

8. I'm gay even though I have a girlfriend. I don't think that's fair to her. Should I break up with her?
9. My father kicked me out of the house last night because he found my gay magazines. What am I supposed to do now?
10. I feel like I'm OK being a lesbian, but why does everyone think I'm weird? How do I tell them that I'm not?
11. No one wants anything to do with me because I'm gay. I want friends so bad. How can I make a friend with at least one person in this school?
12. My girlfriend broke up with me last week because she says she's not a lesbian anymore. How can I make her become lesbian again?
13. How can I meet other gay and lesbian students like me?
14. I want to tell my best friend that I am gay. Should I? And what do I say?
15. I have a crush on my best friend. Do you think he'll freak out when I tell him that I'm gay and that I like him, or do you think he'll like me right back?
16. My mom said that if I ever become lesbian she will kick me out of the house. I think I might be. I'm scared she'll find out. What should I do?
17. One of the teachers keeps using words like "faggot" and "dyke" in the classroom. I don't think that's right, especially since I'm gay. I want you to stop him from saying things like that.

Students with Questioning Issues

1. I like things that girls typically like to do. Does that mean that I'm gay?
2. Sometimes I have dreams that I'm wearing men's clothes. Does that mean that I'm a lesbian?
3. Everyone calls me dyke. I don't think I am. Or am I? What do they know that I don't?
4. When I was nine years old, a neighbor molested me. Does that mean I'm going to be gay?
5. How do you know for sure if you're gay?
6. I know I'm in a phase right now. I know I'll be back to straight. What are some things I can do so that I don't become gay?

Students with Transgender Issues

1. Even though I'm a girl on the outside, I feel like a boy in the inside. I know I'm not lesbian. I want to be a boy. What should I do?
2. I'm a girl, damn it. Why does everyone still refer to me as he, his, or him? What's wrong with everybody?

3. Everyone keeps reminding me that I'm a boy, and I get tired of it. I want to be a woman, though. Do you think it'll cause a big commotion if I were to come to school dressed as a girl from now on?

4. Someone told me that there are some people that will pay for operations. If I want to have a sex-change operation, who could I contact so that they pay for the surgery?

Heterosexual Students with Gay and Lesbian Issues

1. Is it wrong to still be friends with someone who tells you that they're gay?

2. I have friends that are gay and lesbian, and my dad told me that if I didn't stop being friends with them I was going to go to hell too. He told me that I was a sinner for condoning their behavior, and then he said that he would cut me off if I continue being friends with them. I don't want to stop being their friend. What should I do?

3. When my family found out that my sister is a lesbian, they told her so many mean things. They said they didn't want anything to do with her anymore. They told me I couldn't see or contact her anymore. I really love her, and she's not an evil person. I want to see and hug her so bad. How can I get in touch with her without my parents finding out? What do I tell her? It's so sad at home right now. How can I make it better?

4. I think my best friend is gay. Do you think he'll get mad if I ask him if he's gay? And what do I do if he says yes?

5. The kids keep making fun of me because my mom is a lesbian. They say I'm going to be a lesbian too. What do I say to them so that they stop?

6. The guys on the baseball team keep harassing me because I went to the GSA meeting. I only went because my girlfriend told me to, and now they think I'm gay even though I'm not. What should I do? They rag on me all the time, and I'm getting sick of it.

7. Is it wrong to date someone who's bisexual? My friends say that it's not a good idea because he'll just go to the other gender when he gets tired of me. What do you think?

8. I have a crush on a guy who is gay. I know that if I have sex with him I can change him back to straight. What are some ways to get him interested in straight things again?

9. I'm so ashamed of the fact that my brother is gay. I can't stand him and want to kick his ass. We don't talk, and if he even looks at me I cuss him out. I need some help because I think about this all the time.

This range of questions demonstrates that the issues youth have with sexual orientation are often beyond the dimension of sex. The issues can be complex, and students seeking your guidance are likely to need help working through the emotional, cognitive, and social issues that accompany the conflict they may be having with their sexuality or their sexual or gender identity. As a school counselor, you will help students work through the range of feelings, emotions, attitudes, and behaviors they are experiencing.

Reflect and Write

What are some gay and lesbian issues that your students have had?

You are professionally and ethically bound to foster a climate of comfort, trust, openness, exploration, and understanding so that they are successful in resolving the conflict in their lives (Mallon, 1994). Box 10.4 outlines your responsibilities to the students you counsel as agreed upon by the American School Counselor Association (2000). The following discussion addresses essential elements for a counselor to work toward with a student: finding the source of a conflict, talking through feelings and emotions, developing possible solutions, choosing appropriate resolutions, guiding the application, and evaluating its effectiveness. Box 10.5 shows a visual representation of the essential elements.

BOX 10.4. ETHICAL STANDARDS FOR SCHOOL COUNSELORS, AMERICAN SCHOOL COUNSELOR ASSOCIATION

The school counselor:

1. Has a primary obligation and loyalty to the pupil, who is to be treated with respect as a unique individual.
2. Is concerned with the total needs of the pupil (i.e., educational, vocational, personal, and social) and encourages the maximum growth and development of each counselee.
3. Informs the counselee of the purpose, goals, techniques, and rules of procedure under which she/he may receive counseling assistance at or before the time when the counseling relationship is entered. Prior notice includes the possible necessity for consulting with other professionals, privileged communication, and legal or authoritative restraints.
4. Refrains from consciously encouraging the counselee's acceptance of values, lifestyles, plans, decisions, and beliefs, that represent only the counselor's personal orientation.
5. Is responsible for keeping abreast of laws relating to pupils and ensures that the rights of pupils are adequately provided for and protected.
6. Makes appropriate referrals when professional assistance can no longer be adequately provided to the counselee. Appropriate referral necessitates knowledge about available resources.
7. Protects the confidentiality of pupil records and releases personal data only according to prescribed laws and school policies. The counselor shall provide an accurate, objective, and appropriately detailed interpretation of pupil information.

(Continued)

BOX 10.4. ETHICAL STANDARDS FOR SCHOOL COUNSELORS, AMERICAN SCHOOL COUNSELOR ASSOCIATION (Continued)

8. Protects the confidentiality of information received in the counseling process as specified by law and ethical standards.
9. Informs the appropriate authorities when the counselee's condition indicates a clear and imminent danger to the counselee or others. This is to be done after careful deliberation and, where possible, after consultation with other professionals.
10. Provides explanations of the nature, purposes, and results of tests in language that is understanding to the client(s).
11. Adheres to relevant standards regarding selection, administration, and interpretation of assessment techniques.

Source: American School Counselor Association. (2000). *The professional school counselor and sexual minority youth.* Retrieved March 29, 2004, from http://www.schoolcounselor.org. Reprinted with permission.

BOX 10.5. ESSENTIAL ELEMENTS THAT ENHANCE COUNSELING GAY AND LESBIAN YOUTH

1. Monitor your attitudes, biases, and beliefs.
2. Have compassion for gay and lesbian students.
3. Create a safe space.
4. Maintain confidentiality.
5. Respect gay and lesbian students.
6. Assume gay and lesbian students can overcome their challenges.
7. Know gay and lesbian youth matters.
8. Work toward positive outcomes.
9. Advocate for gay and lesbian students.

With your student:

- Find source of conflict.
- Talk through feelings and emotions.
- Develop possible solutions.
- Choose appropriate resolution(s).
- Guide the application.
- Evaluate application effectiveness.

Essential Element 1: Monitor Your Attitudes, Biases, and Beliefs

Sexual orientation is not the easiest of topics to discuss with youth. In fact, the idea of affirming a student's homo- or bisexual identity can make the best of school counselors uncomfortable and anxious. As a mental health professional, you are ethically bound to examine your own attitudes, biases, assumptions, and beliefs toward gay and lesbian persons (Tharinger & Wells, 2000), and to demonstrate a high degree of self-awareness whenever you work with youth who have diverse sexual orientations (Reynolds & Koski, 1995). An honest self-examination is critical because your values and beliefs manifest in your mannerisms, behavior, and discussions, which ultimately affect the outcome of a student's counseling experience with you.

Explore the following questions to determine your level of comfort and how it might affect a gay or lesbian student that you are counseling:

- What do I generally believe about gay and lesbian persons (including youth)?
- What assumptions do I make about gay and lesbian persons?
- What assumptions have I made in the past about gay and lesbian persons (including youth)? Were these appropriate or positive?
- What language do I use when I discuss gay and lesbian persons (including youth)? What have I said to others? What have I said about them?
- How knowledgeable am I about gay and lesbian youth issues?
- How knowledgeable am I about gay and lesbian community issues?
- How supportive am I of the gay and lesbian community?
- How comfortable am I counseling students who have sexual-orientation issues or sexual- or gender-identity issues?
- How satisfying would I find it to work with students who have sexual-orientation issues or sexual- or gender-identity issues?
- How comfortable am I with guiding a student toward an affirmed sexual orientation in general, and how does this change, if it does, when that orientation is different from mine?
- How comfortable am I with researching gay and lesbian topics (including buying gay and lesbian books, magazines, videos) and connecting with organizations that serve the gay and lesbian community?
- How knowledgeable am I in counseling a gay or lesbian student toward a resolution?

If you conclude that you would find it uncomfortable or unsatisfying to work with gay and lesbian youth or if you simply do not want to become involved in their matters, then you have determined that you are not best suited to meet their unique needs. If this is the case, which is fine if it is, then simply refer the student to another counselor on campus who is more comfortable with counseling such a student. If another counselor is unavailable, then approach your district administrator about helping you locate a counselor (or social worker) who can work with you to guide the student. You may need to establish your own support network of counselors who have dealt with similar matters. Ask counselors in other districts or in private practice how they handle similar matters and if they are willing to assist you or if they are available for referral.

If you do not have the option of referring the student to another counselor, then as you interact with your students, be mindful so that your attitudes and beliefs do not convey a lack of support, insensitivity, unpleasantness, or unwillingness to help. Attend to the student as you would any other and incorporate these essential elements into your sessions. It is imperative that you "refrain from consciously encouraging the (student's) acceptance of values, lifestyles, plans, decisions, and beliefs that represent" only your personal views (American School Counselor Association, 2000). You clearly violate professional ethics when you suggest that intense therapy (e.g., reparative or "change" therapy) is a viable option for gay and lesbian youth (Owens, 1998).

Essential Element 2: Have a Compassionate Demeanor and Attitude

Chances are that you chose the mental-health profession because you have compassion for others and want to help them through the challenges presented in their lives. Gay and lesbian students (and those questioning their sexual orientation) who come to see you are likely to be uncomfortable, sensitive, and unsure whether counseling will help or hinder their situation. It is therefore critical that compassion is evident in your demeanor and attitude. The surest way to encourage these youth to come to your office is to show them that you are an approachable, caring professional. To this end, habitually greet students, smile at them, and convey that you take counseling seriously and that you are confident in your guidance ability. Much of the latter can be accomplished by posting your diploma and credentials in your office and by posting the times you have designated for counseling.

When students come to you and you suspect they want to talk about a sexual-orientation matter, demonstrate that you are concerned about their well-being. You can start the conversation, as you would with all students, with encouraging questions such as the following:

- How are things going for you?
- How is everything at home? School? With your friends?
- What's been going on lately?
- Has something been bothering you lately?

- What would you like to talk about?
- How can I help you?
- I'm open to talking about anything you want; do you have something on your mind?

As the student speaks, have a relaxed body posture, smile often, look directly at them, and remain attentive. Students are perceptive and will recognize a disinterested counselor. Because humans naturally desire comfort in difficult situations, most students, especially those struggling with their sexual orientation, will avoid a counselor who is stoic, uptight, disinterested, and hurried.

As the student describes the conflict in his or her life remain calm, nonconfrontational, and nonjudgmental. While you may feel some degree of shock, bewilderment, disappointment, panic, or outrage, try not to react in a derogatory manner when the student begins to explain his or her situation. Do not jump to any conclusion (e.g., that the student is engaging in self-destructive behaviors like using drugs, having unprotected sex, and so forth) or convey that being homo- or bisexual is a problem. Limit your interruptions and allow the student to do most of the talking. Use expressions that convey sensitivity and support. Follow the student's responses with smiles, nods, eye contact, and "I see" or "That's OK" if students become visibly upset. Ask exploratory questions that are inviting and positive, which will vary according to the issue at hand. (Undoubtedly, many of the counselor's questions will make some student feel defensive, but reflective listening, supportive statements, and good contact will help them to explore both sides of their dilemma, generate various options, and so forth.)

Review how two counselors handle the incident of a student who explains, "I want to tell my best friend that I am gay. Should I? And what do I say?" School Counselor A answers the student directly with his opinion and advice without taking the student and his needs into account:

> No. I don't think that's a good idea. You're just opening up a can of worms that I don't think you can deal with at your age. Plus, you never know if he'd turn on you. Do you honestly think you could cope with him telling others and with their spreading rumors about you? It could turn ugly. You have so much to worry about right now. You have state finals coming up. You have the SAT and ACT. You've got to raise your GPA. You don't need this on your plate right now. If I were you, I would just stay put and wait until college to start coming out. That way, when it starts to get messy, you can hide among a bigger student body. I hope that helps. Come back and see me if you have any other questions.

While School Counselor A may have had the student's best interest in mind, may have believed he totally understood the situation, and may have helped the student dodge some unpleasant episodes, the student was never given the opportunity to talk through the situation, arrive at any conclusions on his own, or make his own choices about coming out to his best friend. The student was talked to and told what was right for him, which can have long-lasting effects. He may have taken the counselor's response to mean that his idea was not a good one, as it was quashed by a "helping" professional. The possibility that his best friend would turn on him was reinforced. He was told that his sexuality was not a priority. And lastly, he was told that sexual-orientation disclosure has negative consequences and that he will probably not handle coming out well. Even though the student may have had some level of pride and self-acceptance of his sexuality before the session, he may have left feeling more anxious about his future and uncertain about his social support. How else do you suppose the student felt after his session with the counselor?

School Counselor B, on the hand, begins with conflict exploration in a gentle, positive style:

> I'm so glad you're sharing this with me. Let's see how we can work this out together. It sounds like you're comfortable being gay, and that's good, but the most pressing issue for you right now is whether you should tell your best friend that you are gay and how you should go about doing it. Does that sound right? . . . Let me ask you, how have others handled it when you have told them that you were gay?

She listens to the student carefully and follows up with open-ended questions and invitations to discuss the issue:

- "Tell me your thoughts about why you would like to share with your best friend that you're gay."
- "How accepting has he been of other people (or students) who are (or are believed to be) gay or lesbian?"
- "You know him best; how do you think he'll react?"
- "What has he mentioned in the past that has lead you to believe that he would want to know whether you are gay or not?"

She continues the conversation with honesty and acceptance:

> You and I know that there's nothing wrong with being gay. There are many successful people in society who are gay or lesbian. We also know that some gay and lesbian persons are accepted easily in some communities, but not in others. You have to be prepared for what your best friend might say and do if you tell him that you're gay, and you have to consider how will you react. Some friends will be very accepting when they hear the news and will continue to be your friends, but others may react negatively and have a hard time dealing with it. They may never associate with you again. We'll talk some

more about you telling your best friend that you are gay, but first let's take a few minutes to role-play. Let's pretend that I'm your best friend and that you are about to tell me that you're gay. We'll start with the more negative reactions and work toward the more positive ones, okay?

School Counselor B continues role-playing with the student and helps him to explore the different potential reactions that he may experience. In this way, the counselor helps him better understand the situation and the possible repercussions associated with coming out to a friend. The one-hour session comes to an end, and the counselor plans for the next meeting:

> Our session is about over. I am available to explore this with you some more if you would like to before you tell your best friend. If you decide that this is something you want to do, we can set up another time to meet. Then we can further work toward your goal of finding some effective ways of telling him. I hope you'll come back next week because I also want to hear how you're handling being gay. It sounds like it's going well, and that comforts me, but I just want to know if there are any other issues that we can work through. Is there anything else you'd like to add before we end for today? Feel free to come again.

School Counselor B was warm and comforting in her interactions with the student. She listened to him carefully. She was honest in her discussion, and the questions she asked the student were purposeful—she encouraged him to talk freely and to define and assess the situation, which enabled her to ascertain a direction for future meetings that was appropriate to the student's needs. Through her sensitive and engaging style, the student was given ownership of the situation and the decision making. The student likely left the session feeling better about himself and the situation. Even though there were no clear answers to his initial question, someone listened to him, someone took the time to work with him, someone affirmed his sexual orientation, and someone cared enough to invite him back.

A compassionate and caring school counselor generally provides comfort to students in their time of need. Such counselors have a positive attitude toward gay and lesbian students (and those questioning their sexual orientation). They make a concerted effort to accept, empathize with, encourage, and understand their students. Their behavior is sensitive and gentle. In their interactions with gay and lesbian students, they listen, support, affirm, and engage in honest, open-minded discussions.

Essential Element 3: Create a Safe Space

Ideally, your office or the location where the counseling takes place will convey safety and security, and it will be as warm, comfortable, and inviting as your demeanor and attitude. It is good practice to inform the student that the location is a designated safe place to talk about any issue without judgment, discrimination, or retaliation. A simple poster in your office that reads "Safe Person/Safe Place" can decrease some discomfort that a student may be having.

Some students will scrutinize your office to determine exactly how private your offices are. Privacy can be a significant issue for the student who works to keep his or her sexual orientation concealed, and he or she may examine the following aspects of the office and ask the following questions:

- How accessible the office is—"Is there high traffic nearby?" or "Will other students see me entering/exiting the office?"
- The layout of the waiting room—"While I'm in the waiting room, will others be able to see me?" or "Will others see me standing in the hall waiting to be seen by the counselor?"
- How enclosed the office is—"Will he counsel me with door open?" or "Will the blinds be open or closed when I'm being counseled?" or "Will others be able to see me when I'm being counseled?"
- Who else works in the office—"Are they all counselors, or are there student workers as well?" or "How often are the student workers around, and if they see me will they tell others?"
- How students are scheduled for counseling—"Is my appointment with the counselor written someplace where others will know why I'm there?"
- Whether the office is soundproof—"When I am outside of the office, can I hear other conversations going on inside?"
- Whether there are information boundaries—"Have I ever overheard this or other counselors in this office discussing private matters about other students?" or "Is information about other students in my view when I'm in the office?"

Counselors are responsible for ensuring that a student cannot be identified while in session. As a general practice, close your door and blinds. (Some students may appreciate being asked if they prefer them open or closed during the session.) You also want to keep their wait time to a minimum. Ideally, schedule your sessions with 15-minute breaks in between to limit the amount of time students must wait for you. This also prevents students from seeing one another enter or exit the office.

If you have student workers, be sure that they are not scheduled to be in your office when you have counseling sessions. Students can feel very awkward and uncomfortable explaining to their peers why they were waiting to see the counselor. You also want to ensure that the conversations in your office cannot be overheard in the hallways or outer

"I have no idea why more good students like you don't come see me about their concerns."

offices and that the session is free from distractions. Although this is often not in a school counselor's control, your office should be quiet, and your attention to the student should be undivided—do not accept phone calls, overhead announcements, knocks at the door, or student messenger deliveries during your counseling time. Lastly, keep your office neat and organized, with all files and other material regarding clients kept away from other students' view. This will assure students that any written information about them is kept confidential and stored away from others' access.

Essential Element 4: Convey Confidentiality

Your relationship with students becomes one of substance when, over time, students realize they can trust you. One of the best ways to develop trust is to respect students' privacy through confidentiality at all times (Reynolds & Koski, 1995). Explain your guidelines of confidentiality in the initial counseling session. Be clear in an age-appropriate manner about what information you are required to share or will share, and with whom, as well as what information you will not share with the student's parents, teachers, or peers unless the student gives you explicit permission to do so (Stevens & Morgan, 1999). Let students know the areas in which they have complete control to determine who knows their affairs. When a student comes to see you, you can start with

> Maria, I want you to know right away what my limits to confidentiality are. In most areas, everything you tell me will be kept in confidence. With a few exceptions, I won't discuss anything you share with me with anyone else—not my colleagues, not your peers or your teachers, not your siblings, and especially not your parents. I will only share information with others if you tell me that you want me to, but we'll talk through your situation for some time before coming to that decision. In other words, you have the right to determine who knows what about your situation. I also want you to know that if I think that you are in danger of being hurt, by yourself or by someone else, or that you might hurt someone else, I have to report it to the proper authorities. Okay? . . . Let's talk a little bit about what your questions and thoughts are regarding this . . ."

Essential Element 5: Respect the Students

Gay and lesbian students, like all other students, have the right to respect and dignity while being counseled. Respect is manifested in each of these essential elements, and it is certainly imparted when a student is spoken to in a compassionate and caring manner, is provided a safe place to talk, and is informed about and ensured appropriate levels of confidentiality. More specifically, a student is treated with respect and dignity when your counseling is free of antigay bias or judgment (Mallon, 1994) and when you accept students for who they are and where they are in their quest through their sexual-orientation realization.

At no time suggest that it is wrong, sinful, inappropriate, disgusting, illegal, or the like to be gay, lesbian, bisexual, transgender, or questioning of their sexuality. Never tell students that they should not or could not be the sexual orientation that they believe they are, that they are just going through a phase, or that you have misgivings about their self-realization. Moreover, do not propose that students have to, should, or can change their sexual orientation through reparative therapy to overcome their sexual-orientation issues (Owens, 1998). (Current research and reputable youth-advocacy organizations largely denounce reparative therapy.) Instead, communicate that you understand the emotions they are experiencing with statements that imply that their issue can be resolved and that their feelings can change. Consider the following examples. After assessing that a student is frustrated because he lives a closeted life, you can say

> I can guess that it must be frustrating for you. Most persons would be angry that they have to go around passing for someone they are not. I would be angry too if I couldn't tell the people closest to me a significant part of who I really am. Let's work this through some more, because I think we can help you develop some skills so that you're not as frustrated or angry because you currently have to be in the closet.

When another student comes to you because she hates the fact that she is lesbian, you might be able to say something like

> I can understand why you hate being lesbian at this age. You may have a lot to deal with from people who don't understand gay and lesbian persons or issues. [The counselor can stop here and invite the student to share relevant information. Then give referrals to support resources or acknowledge how it may be difficult for her if there is no support network or social outlet.] Let's work through some of these things and the feelings you have about them. I know that you may hate being lesbian now, but it will probably not always be that way.

Lastly, respect students by taking your time when working with them through their issues. Never rush students toward sexual-orientation acceptance or a premature resolution of their issues (McFarland, 1993). Convey that it is fine to be at the point where they are, that they can work toward resolution at their own pace, and that they can adjust their solutions accordingly. For instance, if a student tells you he thinks he might be gay, you could say, "It's OK that you think you might be gay, and it's also OK if you change your mind later and decide that you're not. I'm available if you'd like to enlist my support for working through this." As you acknowledge and process their feelings or concerns about their sexual orientation, let the student's comfort level establish the pace.

Essential Element 6: Believe That Students Can Overcome Their Challenges

Many gay and lesbian students function in a world filled with stresses. They not only contend with the issues common in adolescence, but dealing with homophobia and heterosexism at school and at home is a fixed part of their lives. Consequently, many will have adjustment issues, self-monitoring issues, self-esteem and self-image problems, emotional conflicts, and so forth as they plod along toward understanding who they are, what they believe, and the role they have in their social world (Callahan, 2001).

Never lose sight of the fact that the albatross for these youth can be a large one. But more importantly, work against perceiving gay and lesbian youth as "problems" or as having problems with their sexual orientation. When you view their issues or sexual identity as problems, you may lead some of them to interpret their sexual orientation as a long-lasting hardship, when in fact it is not. Being gay or lesbian is not a life sentence to unhappiness and misery, that is, a life filled with related "problems." Being gay or lesbian in contemporary society often means living successfully with a positive sexual identity and not being affected negatively by the opinions (e.g., antigay bias) of others. That is the direction to work toward with your gay and lesbian students, although they may not reach this critical point as an adolescent.

Regard all of their issues as accepted conflicts within the context of their sexual development and assume that they are challenges that can be overcome. Take the following example: When Lance believed that his romantic interest, Ramon, was also gay, he approached him about the possibility of experimenting. Ramon, however, was clear that he was not gay. Upset with the situation, Lance approached his counselor. School Counselor A took the "problem" route:

> Of course he would react that way, Lance. What were you thinking? All guys fight back when another guy tells them they have a crush on them. I can't believe you. You've got yourself in a big mess. I don't know how you're going to get yourself out of this one.

The counselor's tone was brash and unsupportive, and because Lance's issue was defined as a problem, he was likely to believe that he was in an insurmountable situation. Lance could easily interpret the remarks to mean that being gay is bound to cause him problems, especially when he comes out to other males.

School Counselor B, on the other hand, viewed Lance's issue as a challenge that he could overcome:

> I'm sorry to hear what happened. It doesn't matter whether you're gay or straight, sometimes others don't like us back as romantically as we hoped. That happens to adolescents and adults all over the world. That's why they call them crushes, because your heart is bound to get crushed by the one that you are smitten with. I like to tell students that

"I've rid the albatross, now if I can work on the crow and the finch."

when someone doesn't like you back, like Ramon, it's not that he's rejecting you as a person; it's that he's not interested in you romantically. That's pretty hard on the best of us. And remember, this may not be the last time this happens. Let's talk this through, because I want to know (1) how you can best handle this for now, (2) how you will handle this if it happens again, and (3) how you will handle it when someone tells you that they have a crush on you but it's not mutual . . .

School Counselor B had a much more supportive tone as she conveyed that Lance would be able to work through this issue and future episodes of unrequited love. Lance likely ended the session knowing that unrequited love is a natural part of relationships and that he was not necessarily rejected because he was gay.

Essential Element 7: Be Knowledgeable about Gay and Lesbian Youth Issues

Students with sexual-orientation issues summon much courage to approach you for guidance, which obliges you to provide them with clear, accurate, and adequate information (Mallon, 1994). They should not have to educate you about gay and lesbian issues. As the professional, it is your responsibility to find and stay current with the information, laws, print and electronic resources, and counseling interventions apropos to gay and lesbian youth.

The range of issues that these students have is undoubtedly broad, yet it is imperative that you have a correct understanding of the challenges unique to gay and lesbian youth and how to work with them toward appropriate resolutions. Familiarize yourself with the issues central to the following topics: the coming out process, homophobia and harassment, attractions, fear of being discovered or rejected by peers and family, self-identification and self-acceptance, social isolation, relationship and sexual experiences, pressures to conform to heterosexuality, the risk of HIV and STDs, and so forth (Owens, 1998; Minnesota Department of Education, 1994). Among these there are critical matters to consider.

Foremost, know and convey that homo- and bisexuality are natural, healthy, and acceptable manifestations in the human sexuality framework. If this goes against your personal beliefs, it will be important that you work to deal with your bias in a responsible way so that it does not interfere with your ability to counsel these youth. If this is not possible, seek consultation with your peers or supervisors or refer the student to another counselor. Gay and lesbian youth are not sick, abnormal, or unnatural—do not treat them as such. Some of your students will be sexually active with same-gender peers, others will have experimented sexually, and many will desire same-gender intimacy. Some will even believe that their only course for same-gender socialization is sexually based, and they will pursue clandestine sex with strangers in an attempt to deal with feeling lonely. Because their behavior and desires are counter to the expectations placed upon them by parents, peers, significant adults, and society, they are likely to feel guilty, ashamed, or embarrassed when they first approach you. Normalize their sexual feelings and identify issues related to their sexual-identity development, but explain that they should abstain from sex until they have entered a stable, committed relationship and are mature enough to handle the consequences associated with having sex. Because the reality is that youth have sex, take the time to inform them about safe sex and the untoward repercussions of risky, unsafe sex.

Second, provide a greater context and long-term perspective in which they can view their current challenges, because some youth will preoccupy themselves with an issue to the point that it becomes all-consuming. Stress how sexual-orientation matters do not necessarily define one's whole being; such matters constitute one aspect of the personal and social continuum (e.g., a pottery enthusiast may also be a lesbian, or a gay student may enjoy bike racing, and both aspects are parts of who they each are). Their sexual orientation, moreover, is one part of their overall sexuality and sexual development. Other areas within their sexuality will be attended to in their lifetimes, such as developing meaningful relationships, making commitments, regulating intimacy, expressing love, and so forth.

Third, be cognizant that homophobia and heterosexism exist and have an indelible impact on all youth. Examine your level of homophobia, as well as the level of homophobia on your campus. Inform students that you are aware of its presence and its impact on their issues and that you work toward reducing antigay bias and discrimination. This awareness can help you structure some of the students' issues in the context of homophobia or heterosexism, which can help you facilitate the understanding that these students are not the cause or source of fault and do not deserve self or social censure. Take, for example, students who are experiencing a difficult time being openly gay at school. Rather than casting blame on them (or another source), frame their issue in the context of some of the other students' lack of understanding:

> It sounds like this is a tough topic for you. I gather that some of it may have to do with the fact that there are some homophobic students in this school. That's a scary feeling when we don't know how people are going to react to the news about being gay. We try to curb homophobia as much as we can here, but there are and will always be people who have different belief systems related to homo- and bisexuality. Even though it's uncomfortable, you have the opportunity right now to develop some skills for how to deal with these types of experiences and feelings, which will help you now as well as in the future.

Or,

> I can see why you're having such a tough time with this. The reason that you say it's so tough being a lesbian nowadays is that you don't see very many encouraging examples of people who are openly lesbian in this school.

Then explore if the student feels that she is to blame for the issues she is having and help her to assess the reality of this.

Fourth, seek factual information. Investigate any gay and lesbian matters that are foreign to you rather than basing your guidance on conjecture, stereotypes, or myths. Because many of the students' issues stem directly from the notions of others, it is also critical that you correct and clarify their assumptions about who they are and what they believe (Owens, 1998). Explain that gay and lesbian persons are heterogeneous and, despite their commonalities, do not all have the same experiences, emotions, values, and beliefs (Gay and Lesbian Educators of British Columbia, 2000). Take, for example, Kevin, a student who is having a difficult time understanding how he can be gay and masculine at the same time. He has the current notion that gay men fit a stereotypical mold, which is based on his observations. He starts,

> I'm gay, but I'm not like the gay guys on TV, or even some of the Nelly ones at this school. I don't go around like this [models a limp wrist]. I don't swish. I don't want to be a girl. I don't like girly things, and I don't want a guy like that either. I like sports. I like to lift weights, and I want to be a sportscaster. I want to be with a guy who's athletic like me. Do you think that when I start doing gay things I'm going to become all faggy too?

His counselor initiated exploration of Kevin's identified issue in a positive tone, asked some open-ended questions, and then responded with clarity:

> It sounds to me like you've accepted that you're gay, but you feel worried that you might become feminine.

The counselor allowed dialogue from Kevin to include confirmation, clarification, or correction of her assumption and then proceeded:

> As far as I know, Kevin, there is no shred of research that supports that you automatically become feminine as you explore being gay. Gay men are a heterogeneous group of people. There are some guys who are feminine, are comfortable being feminine, and enjoy activities that are considered feminine. On the other hand, there are gay men out there who are masculine and who enjoy things that are masculine. I'm sure there are many gay men out there who enjoy sports, who like to lift weights, and who are even sportscasters. In the future, I think you will be able to meet other gay guys who are just as athletic as you are. I heard you use words like *Nelly* and *faggy*. Let's talk a little bit about your personal prejudices and biases related to gay guys who are feminine . . .

Last, know when to refer a student to outside counseling services, especially for suicide ideation or attempts. Contact the appropriate agencies immediately if you believe that a youth is at risk for suicide (see the warning signs outlined on p. 22). Anytime that you or your colleagues on campus (or in the district) are unable to effectively meet students' needs, it is necessary that you find the appropriate agencies, programs, or private therapists that serve gay and lesbian youth (Marinoble, 1998). Get to know the therapists, their expertise, and their logistical information (e.g., hourly rates, clinical hours, locations) and become acquainted with those who specialize in working with youth who endanger themselves, who have ideas about or have attempted suicide, who abuse substances, who have survived sexual or physical abuse, and so forth.

Essential Element 8: Work toward Positive Outcomes for the Students

Counseling sessions are undoubtedly successful if students have resolved the conflict in their lives. For varying reasons, however, not all students will resolve their conflict under your guidance. For example, some students will graduate, others may fear a follow-up session, and some may abruptly end their sessions because they do not want others to know that they see a counselor. Some students never return because they are overwhelmed with academics and extracurricular activities, and others find it easier to ignore the situation altogether.

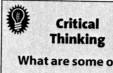 **Critical Thinking**

What are some of your greatest concerns (if any) with counseling and supporting gay and lesbian youth?

Bear in mind that a counseling session can be successful when you have listened to students discuss their feelings and emotions central to the issue, have validated their conflict, and have enriched their understanding that the issue can be resolved. The session is beneficial and worthwhile when it is a positive one and when the outcome leaves students feeling, among other things, (a) better about themselves; (b) more hopeful that their situation will improve; and (c) satisfied knowing that a willing, broad-minded professional affirmed where they are in terms of their sexual-orientation acceptance. Strive to develop positive outcomes for your gay and lesbian students in all of your sessions. To achieve positive outcomes consider the following.

Evaluate the Whole Student

In your initial meeting with a student, you certainly want to address his or her primary concerns, but do not lose sight of the fact that he or she may have others issues that extend beyond sexuality or sexual orientation. At some point in the consultation, evaluate all aspects of the student's life. Start with general questions that are appropriate for the individual student, and then get accordingly specific. Probe into the student's

- personal perceptions (e.g., self-image, self-esteem, coping skills, confidence):
  - How did you determine that you are lesbian?
  - How do you feel about being gay?
  - What is the hardest part about being open (or closeted)?
  - What gives you strength?
  - What do you do for fun?
  - Who provides you with the most support?
  - Who are your role models?

◆ How have you handled most issues in your life?

◆ How do you handle being gay now?

◆ What information and resources do you have about gay and lesbian matters?

◆ Are there times when you feel depressed?

◆ What makes you the happiest?

- home life (e.g., relationships between parents and siblings, family conflicts, parents' expectations):

  ◆ How are things at home with your parents and siblings?

  ◆ What are your relationships like with your parents and siblings?

  ◆ How accepting and supportive are they of your interests?

  ◆ What do your parents expect of you after high school?

  ◆ Who in your family knows or suspects that you are a lesbian?

  ◆ How supportive have they been?

  ◆ How do they regard gay and lesbian persons?

  ◆ How do you think they will react if they find out that you are gay?

  ◆ Have any of your family members given you a hard time?

- school life and peer dynamics (e.g., social network, popularity issues, academic standing, extracurricular activities, romantic interests and relationships):

  ◆ How are things at school? What are your grades like? What extracurricular activities are you involved in?

  ◆ Do you like school? What is your favorite class?

  ◆ Are you satisfied with your grades?

  ◆ What is the best part of the school day for you? The worst? Why?

  ◆ What are your plans for after high school?

  ◆ Are you dating anyone? Are you infatuated with anyone?

  ◆ Who else do you talk with about issues like these?

  ◆ Who is most supportive of you at school?

  ◆ Who are your friends, and what do you all do for fun?

  ◆ Who of your friends knows that you are lesbian?

  ◆ How have your friends reacted to your news?

  ◆ How do you think they will react to the news?

  ◆ Have you had sex?

  ◆ Have any teachers or students given you a hard time?

- workplace, if applicable (e.g., relationship with supervisors and coworkers):

  ◆ How are things going for you at work?

  ◆ Do you enjoy work?

- Are you out at work, or do you plan on telling anyone that you are gay?
- How accepting and supportive are your coworkers?
- How do you think they would react to your news?
- Is there anyone at work who gives you a hard time?
- How does work help you deal with your issue?

Listen

Give your students opportunities to do most of the talking. Listen as they describe their feelings and emotions. Most students come to counselors longing for a genuine, sympathetic listener, not someone who interrupts, does all the talking, or gives them quick thoughtless answers to their questions. Many students will appear initially quiet and shy because they are not comfortable discussing an issue they have kept hidden for so long. They will need some encouragement, to which you can reply, "This is what I hear so far . . . Talk to me about how . . ." Reflect upon their responses, and after they have finished talking, ask specific questions that compel them to elaborate and open up, which can help clarify their issues.

Affirm

In your discourse, communicate that you understand their situations and issues and the feelings and emotions associated with them. You can say,

- "I understand how hard it must be . . ."
- "I would be upset too . . ."
- "I can see why this is confusing . . ."
- "Most persons would find it frustrating . . ."
- "It's OK that you're feeling this way . . ."
- "You get lots of different messages, which would drive anyone crazy . . ."
- "That's a lot to take in; most youth your age would feel the same way . . ."

When students hear you make statements such as these, they learn that whatever conflict they have is valid. The comments help them understand that they are not necessarily unstable, irrational, and insane. Emphasize that it is fine to have sexuality issues and a mental-health professional with whom to talk these through. You can mention, "It's OK that you're going through this. Many youth and adults across the country share similar situations. You're neither the first person nor the last that this has happened to. I'm glad you've chosen to talk with me." Such remarks can promote the feeling that students are not alone or abnormal with their issues.

Many students will have a hard time accepting their sexual orientation because of the negative effects of homophobia and heterosexism. Some students are likely to experience shame, guilt, self-contempt, and grief because they know that their sexual orientation is a stigma in their world (Owens, 1998). Whether students know they are homo- or bisexual, are in a questioning phase, or are in denial, you have to help them work toward developing a positive and healthy sexual identity (Mallon, 2001; Owens, 1998; Reynolds & Koski, 1995). Emphasize that their sexual orientation is not a choice, a character flaw, or an illness (Owens, 1998).

In students' journey through adjustment and acceptance, portray gay and lesbian persons positively. Tell students that upstanding gay and lesbian persons exist in our society. Mention some contemporary and historical figures and celebrities and explain their contributions to society. Then discuss that there are many talented, creative, successful, and happy gay and lesbian citizens in our country. Underscore that being gay or lesbian is not a life sentence of misery and confinement, that students can venture into any profession, be involved in any social activity (e.g., politics, sports, cultural affairs), or pursue any hobby as a gay or lesbian person. These types of discussions enhance their understanding that their sexual orientation is not their whole identity, but just one aspect of the personal and social continuum.

As you discuss the positive qualities associated with gay and lesbian persons, ascertain the negative stereotypes, myths, and rumors students believe are factual. Then clarify the notions they have about being gay or lesbian. In a sensitive and caring manner, ask students,

- How do you know that you're gay?
- What does being lesbian mean to you?
- What do you know about gay and lesbian persons?
- What do you know about the gay and lesbian community?
- How do you suppose gay and lesbian persons feel about their sexual orientation?
- How do you think gay and lesbian persons get their support?
- How do you suppose gay and lesbian persons enter and maintain relationships?
- What are some of the expectations you have about the gay and lesbian community?
- What do you think your future will look like as a gay person?

Capitalize on students' qualities to help them develop a positive identity (Mallon, 2001). Use their qualities that manifest internally (e.g., a student is ambitious, kindhearted, spiritual, altruistic, dedicated, loyal, problem solver, or academically gifted) and externally (e.g., a student writes poetry, sings, plays a musical instrument, or illustrates) to work through and overcome their challenges. Suggest that these qualities can enhance their attitude toward their identity or situation, and ask how they can apply these to their benefit. Offer some examples if their ideas are limited:

- A spiritual student might design a prayer, mantra, or meditation procedure specifically for his or her conflict and then contemplate its future use among other gay and lesbian persons.
- A poetic student might write a poem about his or her conflict, compare it to another poem, and then contemplate how that poet might have resolved her conflict.
- An altruistic student might design an organization that serves gay and lesbian persons in need and then reflect on how it would help his own conflict.
- A student who plays a musical instrument might find and play one piece that captures the heart of her conflict and then find another that she intends to play to signify her resolution.
- An ambitious student might develop a business or political plan for the gay and lesbian community and then consider its benefits in future implementation.
- A student who illustrates might draw a comic book for gay and lesbian students that depict characters who have resolved their conflict.

Use Familiar Language

Use terminology that the students are familiar with. Because some students are not comfortable vocalizing words that describe their sexual orientation, they will not use them in their discussions. Many students will indicate that they have same-gender attractions, feelings, and erotic pleasure, but they may never say the words *gay*, *lesbian*, or *homosexual*. Other students may not know the proper terminology and use words or phrases they are familiar with, which are often the pejorative, such as *faggot*, *lesbo*, and so forth.

Initially, pay close attention to students' language and follow their lead, using the language that they use, and then introduce correct terminology (Project 10 East, 2002). Explain what the terms mean, and if students indicate that these accurately describe their feelings and situation, then use them in your consultation. If students appear uncomfortable after the explanation, then use safe, neutral phrases that describe same-gender or same-sex feelings and behaviors. For example, you can say to a lesbian student, "You seem to have developed feelings for girls . . .," or to a gay student, "You seem to have many crushes on boys . . ."

Do not use language that makes assumptions about students' sexual orientation (Reynolds & Koski, 1995). A gay student does not necessarily have a boyfriend or have sex exclusively with other gay youth, and the same applies to lesbians. A lesbian youth can have a girlfriend and still have occasional sex with men. Rather than asking her if she has a girlfriend, instead ask, "Are you seeing anyone?"

Teach Coping Skills

Students will increasingly confide in you as your relationship with them develops into a meaningful and trusting one. As this occurs, you will have opportunities to help them cope with their challenges. But, because you are not always available for them and because many gay and lesbian students do not entrust sensitive matters with friends, parents, siblings, or other significant adults, you should teach them coping skills to manage their issues outside of the counseling session.

Coping skills are as unique as the students and issues themselves, and they should be designed according to individual student's strengths and needs. For instance, the coping skills you design with your lesbian student who is angry that she is verbally harassed will differ from the coping skills you conceive with your bisexual male student who is saddened that he has no friends to talk with. The lesbian student may only need the skills to cope with her bursts of anger, while the bisexual male may need skills to cope with feeling sad and isolated.

In designing coping skills with students, ascertain the following:

- The severity of their issue (e.g., How severe is the issue? Should we work on coping skills in the first session or wait until subsequent sessions?)
- The degree to which the issue affects their emotional, cognitive, and social status and the ways in which it does so (e.g., How does the issue manifest? What areas of the student's life are most affected?)
- The frequency with which they fixate on the issue (e.g., How often does the student dwell on the issue? Is it all consuming or is it something that occurs at home only?)
- The manner in which they contend with the issue and how effective it is (e.g., How does the student deal with the issue outside of counseling, and is it working for them? How does the student cope with other challenges?)

Then problem solve how the student's strengths can be used to design and apply coping skills. Contemplate the following:

- What are the student's cognitive strengths? (e.g., is the student expressive, logical, able to reason, and good at interpersonal communication?)
- What are the student's emotional strengths? (e.g., is the student perceptive of others' motivations, self-aware, and confident?)
- How can the student's internal and external qualities be used?

Have the student analyze his or her strengths and conjure up some coping mechanisms as well. You can say, "Let's come up with some ways to help you deal with this, because there will be times when there is no one around that you trust enough to discuss this with. What are some approaches that might help you cope in times when you feel . . . ?" As you collaboratively develop coping skills, have the student describe the application process. Offer suggestions to enrich the skills, and make plans to evaluate how effective they are. Some coping skills can have students do the following: apply "define, judge, consider, decide" messages (i.e., define the feeling or conflict, judge the conflict's short- and long-term effects, consider options and their short- and long-term effects, and decide on an option); keep a reflective journal; communicate "I" messages (e.g., "I feel [describe the feeling] whenever [describe the situation], and I would appreciate [describe circumstances to improve the situation]"); role-play with inanimate objects; and so forth. (See box 10.6 for some examples.) Students are likely to need coping skills to deal with a range of personal and social conflicts (Mallon, 1994, p. 87).

BOX 10.6. SOME COPING SKILLS IN ACTION

1. Marcia and her counselor thought that "define, judge, consider, and decide" might help her cope with feeling guilty for having lesbian thoughts. On a Wednesday afternoon, she applied the process:

    Define the feeling: "I'm starting to feel bad about myself because I shouldn't think about girls that way."
    Define the conflict: "I have these natural feelings, which contradict what I have been taught all my life—it is wrong to be lesbian, and I should want to be with a man."
    Judge the conflict's short- and long-term effects: "Short—I can feel bad about myself all day; long—I can let the feelings take over everything I do and limit the things I could be exploring."
    Consider my options: "I could sit here feeling bad about myself and waste the day away, or I could finish reading *Annie on My Mind*; or I could create a collage that captures who I am, what I'm good at, and what I like to do; or I could write a letter to Dear Abby describing how I'm feeling."
    Decide on the option: "I'll continue reading *Annie on My Mind*, and when I finish I'll go to the bookstore and look at their gay and lesbian lifestyle section. I'll see if there are any magazines specifically for lesbians."

    What might have happened to Marcia this afternoon had she not had this coping skill?
2. Jay and his counselor thought keeping a reflective journal might help him cope with the challenges in his life. This is Jay's initial entry:

    (Continued)

BOX 10.6. SOME COPING SKILLS IN ACTION (Continued)

March 23, 2004

Dear Scruff,

It's Saturday afternoon, and I am feeling pretty bored right now. I've gone through all the cable channels, and there is nothing to watch. I don't want to do homework. And we don't have the Internet. No one is around. I'm feeling sad and lonely and wish there was someone to talk to. And I wish that he was gay. My counselor said that when this happens to just go ahead and write to you, and the only thing I can think of to do is to tell you the kind of guy that I would like to be my best friend. He would definitely be gay. He would look a lot like me but would have brown hair and brown eyes. I think I would want him to be Latino, and he would be fluent in Spanish or French. He would be funny, and he would always have suggestions for things for us to do. He would be tall and know a lot about movies. He would have a long name like Winston Theodore Winchester, but he would want me to call him Ted. He would be a genuine guy. I could tell him everything, and he would never judge me. He would be very talented and know how to write poetry, play the guitar, and dance. He would be smart, smarter than me even, and together we would go to an Ivy League college. I've gone through some magazine pages, and here is a picture of what Ted would look like. I like the glasses-and-turtleneck look on him. I wonder what Ted would do on a boring afternoon. Got to run; mom just came in.

L8R,

Jay

How did the reflective journal help Jay cope with his feelings of isolation and boredom?

3. Eric and his counselor thought that "I messages" might help him cope at home when his older brother tells him that he should act more masculine. Eric's brother often calls him "wimpy," "girly," and "faggy," and he questions why Eric "can't be more like a normal guy who's into sports, girls, and rock 'n' roll." As Eric was looking through a men's fashion magazine, his brother responded, "You should be reading *Sports Illustrated*, not this queer stuff. I've got to shake the girl right out of you." Eric replied in an "I message":

I feel (describe the feelings associated with the situation): "Alex, every time I hear things like that, they don't help me; they just make me feel worse about myself. It's bad enough that I hear things like that at school. This is just the way I am. I know you wish that I could change and be more like you and your friends, but that's just not me. This is the way I am, and this is what I like to do. I might change in the future, but that will be because I want to."

Whenever (describe the situation): "Whenever you use those words to describe me, they are mean and hurtful. Even though you might be horsing around, I really get offended. And I feel like I'm not living up to your expectations, so it makes me feel even worse."

I would appreciate (circumstance to improve the situation): "Please don't use words like that to describe me or the things I like to do. Things might change, but I don't know if I will ever be like you. If you want, I'll try to take an interest in what you do, but you should also take an interest in what I do. I'll ask you about sports, but you should also ask me about how the drama club is going, or what this magazine has to say about men's fashion."

If Eric and his counselor had not conceived this coping skill, what might have happened instead? How might Eric's brother react to the "I message"?

Foster a Positive Sense of Self-Worth

Understandably, the stresses and challenges that gay and lesbian youth experience leave many of them feeling devalued and lacking a positive self-esteem, which can have devastating effects if left unaddressed and unattended. Researchers have long supported the notion that a positive sense of self-worth is associated with good mental health (Hershberger & D'Augelli, 1995), implying that time (within the session) should be devoted to help students feel better about themselves. Some students are sure to require more assistance than others, but when the primary focus for your student is to cultivate a positive sense of self-worth, consult resources on self-esteem. (See box 10.7 for books intended

BOX 10.7. BOOKS TO HELP COUNSELORS UNDERSTAND AND IMPROVE THEIR CLIENT'S SELF-ESTEEM

Bloch, D. (1993). *Positive self-talk for children: Teaching self-esteem through affirmations: A guide for parents, teachers, and counselors.* New York: Bantam Books.

Bohensky, A. (2002). *Self esteem workbook for teens.* New York: Growth Central, LLC.

Borba, M. (1989). *Esteem builders: A K–8 self-esteem curriculum for improving student achievement, behavior, and school climate.* Rolling Hill Estates, CA: Jalamar Press.

Borba, M., & Borba, C. (1993). *Self-esteem: A classroom affair.* San Francisco: HarperSanFrancisco.

Branden, N. (1987). *The psychology of self-esteem: A revolutionary approach to self-understanding that launched a new era in modern psychology.* San Francisco: Jossey-Bass.

Branden, N. (1987). *How to raise your self-esteem: The proven action-oriented approach to greater self-respect and self-confidence.* New York: Bantam Books.

Branden, N. (1994). *Six pillars of self-esteem.* New York: Bantam Books.

Burns, D. D. (1993). *Ten days to self-esteem: In 10 exciting steps you will learn how to defeat depression, develop self-esteem, discover the secrets of joy in daily living.* New York: Quill.

Clemes, H., & Bean, R. (1981). *Self-esteem: The key to your child's well-being.* New York: Putnam.

Fennell, M. (2001). *Overcoming low self-esteem.* New York: New York University Press.

Jones, A. E. (1998). *104 activities that build esteem, teamwork, communication, discovery and coping skills.* Richland, WA: Rec Room Publishing.

Lipson, G. B. (1997). *Self-esteem.* Carthage, IL: Teaching & Learning Co.

McKay, M., & Fanning, P. (2002). *Self-esteem: A proven program for assessing, improving and maintaining your self-esteem.* New York: MJF Books.

McKay, M., Fanning, P., Honeychurch, C., & Sutker, C. (1999). *The self-esteem companion.* Oakland, CA: New Harbinger Press.

Peterson, J. S. (1995). *Talk with teens about feelings, family, relationships, and the future.* Minneapolis, MN: Free Spirit Publishing.

Sherfield, R. M. (2004). *The everything self-esteem book: Boost your confidence, achieve inner strengths, and learn to love yourself.* Avon, MA: Adams Media.

Sorensen, M. J. (2001). *Low self-esteem misunderstood & misdiagnosed.* Sherwood, OR: Wolf Publishing.

Sorensen, M. J. (2002). *The personal workbook for breaking the chain of low self-esteem.* Sherwood, OR: Wolf Publishing.

to help mental-health professionals improve their client's self-esteem.) Michele Borba's (1989) self-esteem curriculum, for instance, offers many ideas that promote a student's sense of belonging or relatedness, including friendship-making skills.

You help improve students' self-esteem when you practice these essential elements, which are inconspicuous but supportive pillars of the self-esteem foundation (e.g., building a trusting relationship, having a positive and caring environment). But you should also develop students' awareness that their mindset affects their daily life and their issue resolution. Heighten this understanding by reinforcing the following for your students:

- They are valuable and have unique qualities. Help them appreciate their inherent and physical qualities and the contributions they make at school and home.
- They have a purpose and aim in life. Help them comprehend that they can become motivated with life when they set and work toward achieving realistic goals.
- They are successful individuals. Help them recognize their competencies and achievements, accept their weaknesses, and learn from their mistakes. Introduce self-praise. (Borba, 1989)

Consider Starting a Gay and Lesbian Peer Support Group

Peer support groups allow students with common challenges to gather and support one another. Many districts offer peer support-group programs for students with disabilities, students with asthma, students whose parents are divorcing, and so on to afford students with opportunities to talk openly in a safe environment, without fear of being judged or ridiculed. As students share their challenges, the counselor and other group members validate what they are experiencing, offer solace, clarify faulty assumptions, and assist with problem solving, and this process normalizes the feelings and emotions associated with the students' challenges (McFarland, 1993). If you counsel a sizeable group of gay and lesbian students, consider starting a peer support group for them.

A support group gives gay and lesbian students opportunities to interact with others who have similar interests and concerns, which can lessen feelings of isolation and loneliness, and it provides the counselor ample occasion to educate group members about gay and lesbian matters. Information shared among group members can also be critical to the counselor, who can make plans to address common sources of members' challenges. If, for instance, members consistently report that the faculty makes antigay comments, the counselor can make plans to offer a professional-development workshop. Or, if members mention that a bully targets feminine boys, then the counselor can bring this to the attention of the vice principal of student affairs.

Many gay and lesbian students will not take interest in a support group because they do not want others to know that they are homo- or bisexual. But if you feel that a student would benefit from a support group, ask if he or she would like to participate. Assure them that

- support-group meetings are not announced to the general school population;
- membership is by invitation of the counselor(s) only;
- a membership list is not distributed for public knowledge;
- every member agrees to confidentiality, and nothing personal about another student is shared outside of group time;
- meetings are held during noninstructional times in a private, safe place;
- members do not have to talk during group time and do not have to engage in in-depth personal exploration; and
- members have to commit to the group, attending all meetings and supporting and respecting one another.

In the support-group meetings, members can discuss individual conflicts they have at school or at home, the challenges associated with coming out, the effects that political and social issues have on their lives, and so forth. You can start your group meeting with a "check-in" time, during which members briefly (for two to three minutes) discuss how they have been doing in general since the last meeting time. After check-in, you can do the following:

1. Ask members if they desire some time to talk about an event that has happened since the last meeting: "Now that we've had check-in, is there anyone who needs some time to discuss an event or situation that has happened since the last time we met?"
2. Use a prominent issue that has surfaced in check-in as the focus of the discussion: "In check-in, I heard a recurring message about prom. Let's talk about some of the feelings you have about prom."
3. Have a topic in mind for the meeting: "Some of you keep saying that you're scared that you're never going to meet your ideal person. Let's talk about that a bit."

Support-group meetings are generally conducted with the students and the counselor sitting in a circle. Some counselors choose a round-robin approach to give everyone a chance to speak; other counselors have students hold an object (such as a ball, rain stick, or stuffed animal) that signifies a member's time to address a personal issue. The meeting structures, however, can vary. Some counselors have meetings while members engage in a project, such as creating a mural or acting out a drama, and other counselors conduct their meetings while students play board or card games. These types of structures are more informal and social in nature but nonetheless afford members a support network that a counselor can monitor and guide.

Essential Element 9: Advocate for the Students

Helping gay and lesbian students work through their current challenges is undoubtedly the crux of your responsibility; however, you also have to advocate on their behalf. When the need presents itself, speak on behalf of a student to critical professionals: thoroughly explain the student's situation to out-of-district services if a referral is being made, and then follow up on the student's progress; raise safety concerns with school officials without breaking students' confidentiality (e.g., inform the principal that particular students continuously harass, intimidate, or bully gay and lesbian students); and talk to a student's teachers or parents about his or her issues, but only if the student has given you permission to do so.

Being an advocate also means that you educate district officials, faculty, staff, and the student body about accepting and tolerating gay and lesbian youth in schools. Be resourceful about gay and lesbian youth matters. Conduct professional-development workshops for your faculty on how to work effectively with gay and lesbian youth, and teach them about heterosexism, homophobia, and how to combat a hostile learning environment. Create your own library of books, videos, magazines, and journals on gay and lesbian matters and make these available for checkout. Ask the school librarian to purchase resources to complement your own lending library, and speak to the curriculum committee about including gay and lesbian persons and issues in texts and in the curricula. Help teachers, principals, school board members, and parents understand that gay and lesbian youth are not a "social problem," but that being gay or lesbian is a natural phenomena and a natural part of the sexual-development framework.

What Should I Know about Coming Out?

As mentioned in chapter 3, there are varied reasons that some students remain closeted and others choose to come out (see p. 51). Students generally come out to family and/or friends because they no longer want to pass for heterosexual, and they believe that more meaningful relationships will develop when others know their actual sexual orientation. Consequently, you may have students who will need your guidance with coming out, and they may ask the following questions:

- "Should I come out to my . . . ?"
- "When do you think would be a good time to come out to my . . . ?"
- "How do I come out to my . . . ?"
- "What do you think will happen when I come out to my . . . ?"

Rather than answering their questions directly, work with them to explore whether they are ready to come out. Help them do the following:

- Determine whether they are emotionally prepared to come out (e.g., "If you tell your best friend and she says she no longer wants to talk to you, how will you handle losing her friendship?").
- Determine their motivations for coming out (e.g., to whom and why, "Why do you want to come out to your coach? What do you think this will accomplish?").
- Plan their coming out (e.g., identify their options—when, where, and how).
- Role-play their coming out (e.g., "Let's pretend that I'm your mother. Tell me how you will respond to my different reactions").
- Reevaluate whether the timing is appropriate for coming out (e.g., "Now that we've had a chance to explore some of the rewards and risks of coming out, how do you feel now? Do you still want to pursue coming out?").
- Contend with the consequences of having come out (e.g., "Let's talk about what happened when you told your aunt. What did she tell you?").

Help the student understand the full range of consequences related to coming out, and together determine whether the student is emotionally capable of handling rejection, including being kicked out of his or her home. Most importantly, you want students to learn that rushing to come out, feeling pressured to come out, coming out in a moment of excitement, or coming out to intentionally hurt or shock others can have devastating results. Underscore that there is no certainty in how someone will react to the initial news that a student is gay or lesbian. Some persons will be warm and accepting, and others will be cold and rejecting. Some may even resort to violence or verbal abuse. And just because a friend in a clique accepted the news well does not mean the others will too. In some families, one parent (or sibling) accepts a youth's sexual orientation, but the other parent (or sibling) does not.

Prepare students for varied reactions, especially for those in which a person challenges, insults, or rejects them. A student may leave your office ready, able, and confident to come out but return feeling shocked, vulnerable, sad, and angry because the comments they received were unwelcoming at best and mean-spirited at worst. Teach students how to handle unpleasant reactions. Students, for instance, should know how to respond to the following:

- Parents who exclaim, "You're too young and stupid to know what's good for you. How can you possibly know that you're gay? It's that *Will & Grace* show you watch that made you gay. And your school counselor is making you gay, and you don't even know it. That's how dumb you are. Get out of my face, you freak."
- Friends who reply, "That's so disgusting. You'd better not be lesbian, because that means that you're going to hell, and I won't be friends with someone who goes

against what the Bible says. God doesn't love lesbians. You'd better think twice about being lesbian or you're going to end up all alone."

Help students understand that some persons make hurtful comments because everything they know about diverse sexual orientations is negative, and a youth who comes out will invariably seem like a disappointment to them. Persons receiving the news may change their attitude with time, but assure the student that at the moment of disclosure it is fine to do any of the following:

- Become visibly upset and cry.
- Say, "I'm sorry that you feel that way."
- Be quiet and let the person talk or ask questions.
- Address the person's concerns and clarify assumptions (e.g., "No, mom, not all gay men die of AIDS" or "No, I don't want to be a man, and I don't want to dress like or act like one. Being lesbian means that I just like girls. That's all. It doesn't mean anything about changing my body" or "I'm not gay because you and Dad divorced").
- Leave the room if that seems more comfortable or if the person asks to be left alone.
- Explain that coming out has not changed their personality, virtues, and so on.
- Give the person resources (e.g., websites, school counselor's information, fact sheets, and so forth) to help cope with the news.

Reflect and Write

What do you believe are some pressing issues for parents who discover that their child is gay or lesbian?

Unfortunately, some persons will never accept gay and lesbian persons, no matter how hard the student or others try to influence them. Work with those students who were rejected and reinforce that they will not always be rejected by people they come out to.

How Do I Help Parents Who Seek Consultation about Their Gay or Lesbian Child?

Most parents will not be accepting and enthusiastic when they learn that their child is gay or lesbian. The fact is that most parents will experience shock, denial, disbelief, grief, sadness, anger, disappointment, and so forth when they hear, "I'm gay." Many parents will be at a loss for what to say and do and will instinctively do the following:

- Refuse to accept their child's sexual orientation—"I don't want to hear it. I never want to hear you talk about it again."

- Believe that their child is going through a phase—"You can't be lesbian. You have too many boyfriends. You have no idea what you're talking about" or "It's just a phase you're going through. How can you possibly know that you're gay at your age? You just haven't met the right girl; that's all."
- Blame themselves or others for their child's sexual orientation—"Your father made you lesbian because he encouraged you to play sports," "I knew I shouldn't have taught you how to bake. That's what made you gay," "It's because you've been hanging around that tomboy down the street," or "You're gay because you watch *I Dream of Jeannie* and *Bewitched*."
- Wish that their child was heterosexual—"I wish you weren't lesbian," "I wish you had never told me," or "I wish you had never been born."
- Demand that their child change his or her sexual orientation—"You've got to stop being gay. I'm not going to tolerate it. And as long as you live in this house you will never act gay. You are a boy and you like girls. Got it?" or "You can change as long as you pray to God" or "I'm going to find a therapist that can change you."
- Shame and criticize their child—"You should be ashamed of yourself. There's nothing good that can come out of being gay, you filthy fag. I'm embarrassed that I gave birth to you. Now I've got to tell everyone that I have two daughters. You know that you're going to die of AIDS, right?"

Many parents will scream, others will cry, and some will become ill simply because the news is overwhelmingly disappointing to them. Most parents will remain distressed for an extensive period of time because they believe that their child is a member of a community they know little about. And what they know about gay and lesbian persons is generally negative, most of which being impressions based on stereotypes and myths. Many parents will mourn the passing of their former heterosexual child and all the dreams and goals they had for their child's future (e.g., a traditional marriage, family in the suburbs); be embarrassed and fear that others will discover the news; and feel disgraced because their religious beliefs condemn gay and lesbian persons.

After time passes, however, some parents will make an effort to better understand their gay or lesbian child and will seek you out for some consulting. Reassure parents that their child can have a happy, successful, fulfilled life as a gay or lesbian adult as long as they love, accept, and support their child. Explain that adjusting to the news will take time, and acknowledge that they are entitled to feel the pain, worry, and disappointment associated with the news. As you talk with them, clarify any misconceptions they have and explore the following with them.

1. Their Primary Concerns

Many parents will believe that their child has a mental disorder that can be changed through therapy. Assure them that being gay or lesbian is not a disease or mental illness, but a natural form of sexuality. Explain that parenting styles, people, and the media do not influence or make a child gay and that it is fine to struggle with the acceptance. Also address some of the fears they have for their child. Ask parents the following questions:

- How are you accepting the news that your child is gay?
- What are your biggest concerns about having a child who is gay?
- What is the hardest part of accepting that your child is gay?
- What are some of the fears that you have for your child?
- How would you like me to help you?

2. Their Understanding of What Being Gay or Lesbian Means

Ascertain their knowledge about gay and lesbian matters and determine whether they fully understand their child's sexual orientation. Explore their ideas and images of how their child should behave (e.g., fulfilling traditional gender roles), and together come up with ways they can accept their child's behavior and individual expression. You can even encourage parents to make an effort to learn more about gay and lesbian matters and persons. You can ask questions such as the following:

- What are some of the impressions you have about lesbians?
- How does your daughter conform to those impressions?
- What do you want for your daughter now?
- What do you think life is like for your daughter now?
- What do you think your daughter's future will be like as a lesbian?
- How have your expectations for your daughter changed since she came out to you?
- How would you like me to help your child?

3. Their Progress in Supporting Their Child

Help parents understand that, despite the seeming loss of a heterosexual child, they have a deeper understanding of the child they have now. Affirm that they can be upset or angry, and then probe together how derogatory communications such as yelling, insults, or criticism can affect their child. Work with parents to conjure up ways they can convey their love to their child directly (e.g., with statements such as "I will always love you no matter what," embraces, or asking their child to describe the support he or she wants) and indirectly (e.g., driving the child to a gay and lesbian youth-group meeting). Propose that they ask their child nonjudgmental questions, listen to his or her responses in a respectful manner, and accept when he or she chooses not to respond. Also, help parents appreciate their child's worth by asking them questions such as the following:

- What are some of the qualities that you love about your child?
- What are his strengths?
- What are the biggest differences you have noticed in your child since he came out to you?
- What do you think your child needs most from you at this time?
- What are your dreams and goals for your child?
- How do you think you can support your child so that he develops into a healthy, secure adult?

4. Their Support Structure

Examine where parents go for support. When parents consult with persons who have negative and hateful assumptions about gay and lesbian persons, they will continue to perceive their child as a problem and be unsympathetic and hostile toward his or her circumstances. Suggest that parents associate with persons or organizations that serve and support gay and lesbian allies, such as Parents and Friends of Lesbians and Gays (PFLAG) because they will need their own support network to help them cope with issues associated with having a gay or lesbian child. Provide the parents with literature (such as Kevin Jennings's [2003] text, *Always My Child*), videos, or websites that promote their understanding of having a gay or lesbian child. Explore their support structure with questions such as the following:

- How are you coping with the news that your child is gay?
- How are other members of the family handling the news?
- Who have you talked to for additional support?
- Who gives you the most support?
- Have you considered approaching your religious leader for guidance?
- What resources on gay and lesbian matters do you have access to?

Summary

If you have not yet counseled a gay or lesbian youth, you will eventually. Times are changing, and gay and lesbian students and those questioning their sexual orientation will seek counseling for matters associated with their sexuality if you appear inviting, concerned, and willing to help. The range of their possible issues is vast and complex, which obligates you to know as much as you can about the concerns they have in contemporary times.

As you counsel students, work with them to resolve their conflict and to develop a positive and healthy sexual identity. Accomplish this with compassion, respect, and care in a safe environment and with the belief that students can overcome their challenges. Many of the examples addressed in this chapter may seem unnecessarily negative, but the fact remains that gay and lesbian youth generally have unpleasant experiences that stem directly from the homophobic and antigay behavior and messages they witness at school and at home. Advocate on their behalf to combat some of the hostility directed toward them. Educate faculty, parents, students, and school officials about gay and lesbian persons and insist that they be included in the curricula and represented in the school library. In this endeavor, you ultimately improve the conditions for future generations of gay and lesbian youth.

Idea File

1. Choose one of the statements found on pages 252–54 and plan for the student's counseling session.
2. List the organizations and therapists in the community that serve gay and lesbian youth and distribute it to other counselors in the district.
3. Make a list of discussion topics for gay and lesbian support-group meetings.
4. Write your announcement to the faculty, students, and parents about your availability to discuss gay and lesbian matters.
5. Implement a "backpack for checkout" program, which allows students to check out backpacks that have five or six books, articles, or videos on sexual-orientation issues in them. A student can review these at his or her leisure, and when he or she returns for a counseling session, you can raise questions about the matters addressed in the material.

References

American Counselor Association. (1995). *Position statement: The school counselor and sexual minority youth.* Alexandria, VA: Author.

American School Counselor Association. (2000). *Ethical standards for school counselors.* Alexandria, VA: Author.

Bailey, N., & Phariss, T. (1996). Breaking through the wall of silence: Gay, lesbian, and bisexual issues for middle level educators. *Middle School Journal, 27*(3), 38–46.

Borba, M. (1989). *Esteem builders: A K–8 self-esteem curriculum for improving student achievement, behavior and school climate.* Torrance, CA: Jalmar Press.

Callahan, C. (2001). Protecting and counseling gay and lesbian students. *Journal of Humanistic Counseling, Education and Development, 40*(1), 5–10.

Council for Accreditation of Counseling and Related Educational Programs (CACREP). (2001). *The 2001 Standards.* Washington, DC: Author.

Fontaine, J. (1998). Evidencing a need: School counselors' experiences with gay and lesbian students. *Professional School Counseling, 1*(3), 8–14.

Gay and Lesbian Educators of British Columbia. (2000). *Challenging homophobia in schools. A K to 12 resource for educators, counsellors and administrators to aid in the support of, and education about lesbian, gay, bisexual, transgender youth and families.* Vancouver, BC: Author.

Hershberger, S., & D'Augelli, A. (1995). The impact of victimization on the mental health and suicidality of lesbian, gay, and bisexual youths. *Developmental Psychology, 31*(1), 65–74.

Jennings, K. (2003). *Always my child: A parent's guide to understanding your gay, lesbian, bisexual, transgendered or questioning son or daughter.* New York: Fireside.

Mallon, G. (1994). Counseling strategies with gay and lesbian youth. In Teresa DeCrescenzo (Ed.), *Helping gay and lesbian youth: New policies, new programs, new practice* (pp. 75–91). New York: Harrington Park Press.

Mallon, G. (2001). *Lesbian and gay youth issues: A practical guide for youth workers.* Washington, DC: Children's Welfare League of America Press.

Marinoble, R. (1998). Homosexuality: A blind spot in the school mirror. *Professional School Counseling, 1*(3), 4–7.

McFarland, W. (1993). A developmental approach to gay and lesbian youth. *Journal of Humanistic Education and Development, 32,* 17–29.

McFarland, W., & Dupuis, M. (2001). The legal duty to protect gay and lesbian students from violence in schools. *Professional School Counseling, 4*(3), 171–79.

Minnesota Department of Education. (1994). *Alone no more: Developing a school support system for gay, lesbian, and bisexual youth.* St. Paul, MN: Office of Service Design and Collaboration.

National Education Association. (1992). *The 1992–93 Resolutions of the National Education Association.* Washington, DC: Author.

Owens, R. (1998). *Queer kids: The challenges and promise for lesbian, gay, and bisexual youth.* New York: Harrington Park Press.

Price, J., & Telljohann, S. (1991). School counselors' perceptions of adolescent homosexuals. *Journal of School Health, 61,* 433–38.

Project 10 East. (2002). *The Project 10 East GSA handbook: Some definitions.* Retrieved July 18, 2002, from http://www.project10east.org/handbook.html.

Reynolds, A., & Koski, M. (1995). Lesbian, gay, and bisexual teens and the school counselor: Building alliances. In G. Unks (Ed.), *The gay teen: Educational practice and theory for lesbian, gay, and bisexual adolescents* (pp. 85–93). New York: Routledge.

Rhode Island Task Force on Gay, Lesbian, Bisexual, and Transgendered Youth. (1996). *School shouldn't hurt: Lifting the burden from gay, lesbian, bisexual, and transgendered youth.* Retrieved on February 13, 2004, from http://members.tripod.com/~twood/safeschools.html.

Sears, J. (1992). Educators, homosexuality, and homosexual students: Are personal feelings related to professional beliefs? In K. M. Harbeck (Ed.), *Coming out of the classroom closet: Gay and lesbian students, teachers, and curricula* (pp. 29–79). Binghamton, NY: Harrington Park Press.

Stevens, P., & Morgan, S. (1999). Health of lesbian, gay, bisexual, and transgender youth. *Journal of Child and Family Nursing, 2*(4), 237–49.

Tharinger, D., & Wells, G. (2000). An attachment perspective on the developmental challenges of gay and lesbian adolescents: The need for continuity of caregiving from family and schools. *School Psychology Review, 29*(2), 158–72.

CHAPTER 11

The School Administrator and the Protection of Gay and Lesbian Students

"MEET THE PRESIDENT," MORGAN, 17, OF MEDFORD, MASSACHUSETTS

When I moved from Colorado to Massachusetts two years ago, I never expected to become what I am today. My new school, Brighton High—an inner-city school in Boston—was nothing like my suburban school out west. But despite some predictable homophobia, I was accepted as an openly gay teen. I showed my fellow students that I am proud of who I am, and I ended my junior year surrounded by friends.

Coming back as a senior in 2003, I was intrigued to learn that every year the seniors elect class officers. I decided to run on an ostentatious whim—it was amusing to think of myself as class president, and I enjoyed the idea of competing for the job. Within two days I had my campaign in full swing. I handed out fliers, put up posters, and gave an impassioned speech to a receptive audience.

Running as an openly gay candidate was surprisingly uneventful. I overheard comments such as "Shit, I'm not gonna vote for that faggot!" But overall my campaign was received very positively, and by the end of the week, amazingly, I was president.

When they announced my name on the intercom, I leaped up and ran screaming and laughing down the hallways. Someone called me "fruit" and I spun around and yelled back at them. "Yes, I am!" I said. "But guess what? I am also your president!" It was one of the most beautiful moments of my life.

My achievement shines as proof of a changing world. Queer youths can survive today—and maybe even flourish. And a typical white kid can become the first openly gay class president at a Boston high school.

Source: The Advocate Report. (2004, February 17). Generation Q: Meet the president. *The Advocate, 908*, 18. Reprinted with permission.

Overview

Indeed, the world is changing, and so are school campuses nationwide. Many school administrators cannot imagine having their student body elect an openly gay class president. Morgan, however, is testimony that an openly gay student can become a prominent member of his or her senior class. Fortunately, his school climate, despite a few snide remarks, is one that has evidently accepted him. There may be no openly gay or lesbian youth at your school, but the reality is that you most likely have some students who are closeted, who are questioning their sexual orientation, or who are perceived to be gay or lesbian. It is up to you as the school leader to foster a climate where they are respected, accepted, and safe under your watch.

All youth, for that matter, need a safe, caring environment that is free from harassment, intimidation, and other aggressive actions. This chapter uses the Lesbian, Gay, Bisexual, and Transgender Students' Bill of Rights, modified by Out for Equity of Saint Paul Public Schools (n.d.) to explain how school administrators can create a climate that is inclusive of gay and lesbian students, and one where they feel safe and comfortable to attend. A discussion ensues on critical elements to consider in your school antiharassment policy and on how to address gay and lesbian students' complaints of harassment, intimidation, threats, and so forth. This chapter answers the following questions:

- As an administrator, what can I do to establish a school climate of respect, tolerance, and acceptance of gay and lesbian youth?
- What key components should a nondiscrimination and antiharassment policy include?
- As an administrator, how should I handle and respond to gay and lesbian youth's allegations of discrimination and harassment?

As an Administrator, What Can I Do to Establish a School Climate of Respect, Tolerance, and Acceptance of Gay and Lesbian Youth?

In the mid-1980s, Virginia Uribe, a Los Angeles school-teacher, created a support program for the gay and lesbian students in her school and called it Project 10. Project 10 later became a model program and was adopted by many Los Angeles schools. During the course of this time, Project 10 stakeholders wrote the Lesbian, Gay, Bisexual, and Transgender Students' Bill of Educational Rights to help school administrators, teachers, and staff understand their role in fulfilling the needs of gay and lesbian youth. An adapted version is found in box 11.1. Use this Bill of Educational Rights as a framework for establishing a school climate of respect, tolerance, and acceptance of gay and lesbian youth.

> **Application**
>
> What is your school district's policy on sexual harassment, discrimination, and harassment? Is sexual orientation included in the policy? Describe how well your students know the policy.

BOX 11.1. LESBIAN, GAY, BISEXUAL, TRANSGENDER STUDENTS' BILL OF EDUCATIONAL RIGHTS

- The right to fair and factual information about sexual orientation in textbooks and other classroom materials.
- The right to unbiased information about the historical and continuing contributions of lesbian, gay, bisexual, and transgender people in all subject areas, including art, literature, science, sports, and history.
- The right to positive role models, both in person and in the curriculum; the right to accurate information about themselves, free of negative judgment, and delivered by trained adults who not only inform lesbian, gay, bisexual, and transgender students, but also affirm them.
- The right to attend schools free of verbal and physical harassment, where education, not survival, is the priority.
- The right to attend schools where respect and dignity for all students, including lesbian, gay, bisexual, and transgender students, is a standard set by the Superintendent of Public Instruction, supported by the board of education, and enforced by every principal and classroom teacher.
- The right to be included in all support programs that exist to help teenagers deal with the difficulties of adolescence.
- The right to legislators who guarantee and fight for constitutional freedoms, rather than legislators who reinforce hatred and prejudice.
- The right to a heritage free of crippling self-hate and unchallenged discrimination.

Source: Saint Paul Public Schools. (n.d.). *Out for equity/Out4good safe schools manual.* St. Paul, MN: Author. For more information visit www.spps.org/outforequity. Reprinted with permission.

As a school leader, you have the training, expertise, and authority to transform a seemingly hostile learning environment into one where gay and lesbian youth feel safe to attend. Even if you are not convinced that meeting the specific needs of gay and lesbian youth is worthwhile, recognize the following.

These Youth Exist on Your Campus (Either Openly or Closeted) and Are Entitled to Resources and Services That Affirm the Lives of Gay and Lesbian Persons

The first three items in the Lesbian, Gay, Bisexual, and Transgender Students' Bill of Educational Rights address gay and lesbian students' access to factual, unbiased information in the classroom, school library, and counseling office. Administrators often assume that there are no gay or lesbian students on their campus because they have never seen or heard of any. It is unlikely, however, that gay and lesbian students will parade around campus with a sign, banner, or T-shirt declaring their sexual orientation, especially in a seemingly unsupportive environment. The uncertainty of being accepted is risky, which leaves many gay and lesbian youth closeted, and those who are comfortable with their sexuality come out to those they are closest to.

Despite your belief that there are no (or only one or two) gay or lesbian youth on your campus, you should still advocate that your campus have impartial, unbiased, and factual information and resources on gay and lesbian persons and their historical and contemporary contributions. By doing so, you help open and closeted youth feel better about themselves and less isolated; you help all students better understand gay and lesbian persons (e.g., parents, siblings, family members, close friends, and those in society); and you help your learning community comprehend that gay and lesbian persons are not monsters to be feared, avoided, or discriminated against.

To facilitate the acquisition of such information and resources, arrange that your faculty and staff receive professional-development training on gay and lesbian youth matters. Such training is effective when research finds that

> in schools that had undergone faculty training on gay issues, 54 percent of students said that gay students felt supported by teachers and counselors, while in schools that had not undergone faculty training only 26 percent of students said gay students felt supported. (Cahill, Ellen, & Tobias, 2003, p. 113)

Find district personnel (e.g., counselors or teachers knowledgeable in the topic), community organizations (e.g., GLSEN or PFLAG), and students (e.g., Gay–Straight Alliances) to conduct a series of workshops for your faculty and staff in two general strands:

1. Diversity issues, in which school personnel examine

   - culture and diversity in society;
   - diversity in the learning community;
   - their own attitudes, biases, and prejudices toward others;
   - their own understanding and knowledge of stereotypes, oppression, privilege, and the like;
   - isms such as racism, sexism, heterosexism, and the like; and
   - strategies to reduce hate, prejudice, discrimination, and so forth.

2. Harassment and gay and lesbian youth issues, in which school personnel learn how to

   - identify and respond to antigay harassment, homophobia, discrimination, and hate-based behaviors;

- report and prevent such behaviors;
- solicit assistance and resources to contend with such behavior;
- fulfill gay and lesbian students' needs;
- imbed gay and lesbian affairs into lesson plans, discussions of diversity, and so forth; and
- support gay and lesbian student victims of harassment.

Then encourage your teachers to organize a committee that actively reviews the curriculum and textbooks and recommends how to augment these with information about gay and lesbian matters. Oblige the school librarian as a member of the committee who can procure complementary materials (e.g., books, videos, magazines, journals) that accurately portray gay and lesbian persons.

Your Learning Community Has to Understand That These Youth Are Equally Valuable in the Learning Community and Do Not Deserve Discrimination or Harassment

The second two items in the Lesbian, Gay, Bisexual, and Transgender Students' Bill of Educational Rights consider gay and lesbian students' entitlement to school environments that are safe and conducive to learning, where everyone, regardless of his or her background or ability, is treated with respect and esteem. No student should fear harassment, intimidation, or bullying while at school. To borrow a popular catch phrase, it will take your whole village (i.e., you, your faculty, staff, and students) to turn a hostile learning environment into an amiable one, but you must enforce that harassment of any kind is not welcome or tolerated on your campus.

Stress upon your faculty to report and discourage any form of harassment, intimidation, or bullying. Start faculty meetings or distribute general e-mails with statements such as the following:

- "We cannot have harassment at this school. If we all work together we can eradicate all forms of harassment, intimidation, and bullying and have a school environment that students want to come to and learn in. Please tell your students that we do not tolerate these kinds of behaviors, and if you see it happen, reprimand the student immediately."
- "I'm going to say this again and again; I need your help to stop harassment and bullying behaviors. No student learns in an environment that he or she is afraid to be in. If you do your part to convey that harassment, intimidation, and bullying are 'uncool' and that you do not appreciate it, then students will not engage in these

behaviors. If you see such behavior, refer the offender to my office. Don't excuse such behavior as harmless play. Let's work together to make our school safe for all students."

- "I know we all work to make this school environment a safer one. To help us, I'm going to start all faculty meetings with the number of reports I have received on harassing behaviors and the characteristics of students who were targeted. Let's work together to bring this number to zero. Last month I received . . . If you suspect that one of your students is being picked on, do something about it."

Then work your way to the students and their parents. Use assemblies, division and back-to-school orientations, club and class visits, and hallway encounters to inform students that you do not tolerate any form of harassment and that there are grave repercussions for those who undermine the code of conduct. Explicitly mention that no student should be targeted for abuse of any kind. You can say something to the effect that our society is made up of many different people and that this is an opportune time to learn to accept differences. If your learning community perceives the need for students to fully comprehend the repercussions of what they consider harmless play (e.g., "I didn't really mean it," "I was just joking around," and "We were just kidding"), then arrange that they receive training to understand what hate-based (including biased and discriminatory) behaviors are; what their effects on the learning community are; and how to instead engage in positive, considerate behaviors.

Encourage your faculty to teach students how to respect others, and outline your expectations for respectful behavior in the student handbook or on posters around the school. The Kansas City Public Schools (Kansas), as an example, elaborated in their student handbook the expectations that students exhibit honesty, respect, responsibility, compassion, self-discipline, perseverance, and giving. (See box 11.2 for the Kansas City Public School reference on respectful behavior.) In letters home or in PTA meetings, ask parents to talk to their children about the importance of respecting others and of behaving appropriately. Tell them that you do not take these types of behaviors lightly, and consider having a counselor or consultant instruct parents on what to say and how to say it to their children. You eventually want the students to receive consistent messages—from you, faculty and staff, peers, and parents—about the importance of respectful behavior in the learning community.

Work with your faculty and staff to develop and enforce a nondiscrimination and anti-harassment policy and procedures for handling infractions. Then announce what the policy is and how to report offenses. Include it in the student handbook along with a list of expectations for student behavior and a list of behaviors that are sure to land them a suspension or expulsion. (Box 11.3 outlines some unacceptable behaviors for the student

BOX 11.2. KANSAS CITY KANSAS PUBLIC SCHOOLS CODE OF CONDUCT EXPECTATIONS: RESPECTFUL BEHAVIOR

Treat each person as you should be treated.

Model positive behavior and language, which reflect cooperation with all members of the school community in order to realize opportunities for academic and personal growth.

- Exhibit a positive, cooperative attitude about school and learning.
- Respect the racial, gender, language, cultural and religious difference of others.
- Avoid profane and obscene language and gestures.
- Use a respectful tone of voice and body language.
- "Put-up," don't "Put-down."
- Resolve conflicts in a respectful, non-physical manner.
- Keep your school clean, don't litter or deface.
- Take turns when talking.
- Use manners and be polite (please, thank you).

Source: Kansas City Kansas Public Schools. (2004). *Student code of conduct expectations: A guide for student behavior,* p. 5. Kansas City, KS: Author. Reprinted with permission.

BOX 11.3. UNACCEPTABLE BEHAVIORS FOR A STUDENT HANDBOOK

Violence Is Unaccepted Behavior

Any student or a group of students who intentionally harms another student physically, emotionally, or socially is the perpetrator of violence.

Those who grossly disrespect another student and engage in any of the following behaviors (or comparable behavior), or encourage this type of behavior in others, are subject to disciplinary action. These behaviors are not tolerated on school grounds, at school-associated events, or on the way to or from school.

Verbal or written harassment: insulting remarks or gestures or usage of racial or homophobic slurs.
Verbal abuse: objectionable (vulgar) language, obscenity, profanity, libel, or slander.
Physical abuse: fighting, assault, battery, pushing, or hitting.
Sexual harassment: any form of unwanted sexual advances, vulgar language or gestures, or indecent exposure.
Endangerment through: intimidation, extortion, threats, or coercion.

Violence Can Start and End With You

handbook.) At some point in your discourse with your learning community, underscore that the policy is as significant as the sexual harassment policy (which should outline inappropriate behaviors) and that students who harass gay and lesbian students (or those perceived to be gay or lesbian) might be violating two distinct policies. Ultimately, when these types of policies are in effect, you help the learning community understand that despite inherent differences, everyone deserves to be treated with respect, and gay and lesbian students realize that they can attend school without the threat of being harmed.

Some Gay and Lesbian Youth Need Support in Dealing with a Range of Emotional Issues

Two of the remaining items on the Lesbian, Gay, Bisexual, and Transgender Students' Bill of Educational Rights imply that these students are entitled to supportive programs that empower them in their journey toward sexual-orientation self-acceptance. As mentioned throughout this text, gay and lesbian students experience an array of challenges and have no or very few persons with whom to discuss them, which compounds their feelings of loneliness and isolation. You can help these youth by identifying members of your leadership team or faculty as safe persons who provide emotional support and guidance and who advocate for those who feel unsafe. The safe persons should be open-minded, approachable, willing to listen to and guide gay and lesbian students in their time of need, capable of validating the challenges these youth have, inclined to affirm the students' sexual orientation, and trusting and confidential. Ensure that these safe persons get trained in crises management, conflict resolution, problem solving, and gay and lesbian youth matters. Then publicize that there are safe persons and safe places (e.g., their offices or classrooms) in the school. Inform faculty and students that these safe persons are trained to deal with sensitive issues, can be trusted with confidential information, and will not ridicule the matter or inform others (especially parents) about the situation unless the need presents itself.

Also see to it that your counselors are trained and skilled to work with gay and lesbian youth. Encourage them to promote their services, including counseling for sexual-orientation matters. If the need arises on campus, ask the counselors to visit individual classrooms to discuss and model respect, tolerance, acceptance, inclusive practices, and so on. And, when teachers are seemingly resistant to accepting gay and lesbian youth, rely on counselors to intervene and conduct professional-development workshops on diversity, social justice, hate, prejudice, discrimination, and so forth. Remember, counselors have the academic preparation and counseling experiences to work with gay and lesbian youth, their parents, and students and teachers who are having a difficult time accommodating youth with diverse sexual orientations.

Lastly, if members of the learning community want to start a Gay–Straight Alliance, allow them to. Legal precedent has firmly set a losing battle for any administrator who denies students the right to a GSA. GSAs can be wonderful tools for promoting a welcoming climate for all groups of students because club members educate the learning community about prejudice, antigay bias, homophobia, and so forth. Moreover, research is finding that GSAs (and clubs like them) have a positive effect on the student body (GLSEN, 2002; Uribe & Harbeck, 1992). And, if members of your learning community have a GSA, show your support by attending a meeting, commending the faculty sponsor(s), and ensuring the club has a safe place to meet.

Alliances with Out-of-Campus Organizations Are Beneficial

The remaining item in the Lesbian, Gay, Bisexual, and Transgender Students' Bill of Educational Rights addresses that these youth need committed persons who advocate on their behalf. Although you could certainly contact your local government representatives and voice your support for gay and lesbian youth, you can also make alliances with organizations that advocate for and serve them. Making alliances with PFLAG, GLSEN, or local organizations, for instance, helps you direct faculty, counselors, students, and parents to warehouses of information and resources, and these organizations can also recommend professionals who will train your faculty or serve as guest speakers. Alliances not only help you and your learning community, but they help the advocates' cause by validating that their services are needed, which gives them leverage to lobby legislators to support their programs. In the long run, alliances improve the circumstances for future generations of gay and lesbian youth.

What Key Components Should a Nondiscrimination and Antiharassment Policy Include?

Your district, school, or classroom policy on nondiscrimination and antiharassment should include key components that convey the importance of equity, safety, and respect for all students. To determine the necessary components of an effective policy, consider the language that professional organizations use in their position statements.

- American School Health Association—"All young persons should have an equal opportunity for quality education regardless of their sexual orientation.... School personnel should discourage any sexually oriented, deprecating, harassing and prejudicial statements injurious to students' self-esteem."

- Association for Supervision and Curriculum Development—"ASCD believes that schools should demonstrate respect for the dignity and worth of all students and that all students should be treated equitably. ASCD opposes discrimination and supports policies and programs that promote equity."
- National Education Association—"The National Education Association believes that all persons, regardless of sexual orientation, should be afforded equal opportunity within the public school system. . . . The NEA . . . calls upon Americans to eliminate—by statute and practice—barriers of race, color, national origin, religion, sex, sexual orientation, age, handicap, marital status and economic status that prevent some individuals, adult or juvenile, from exercising rights enjoyed by others, including liberties decreed in common law, the Constitution, and statutes of the United States. . . . The NEA deplores prejudice based on race, ethnicity, religion, sexual orientation, gender or size and rejects the use of names, symbols, caricatures, emblems, logos and mascots that promote such prejudice."
- National Association of School Nurses—"All students, regardless or sexual orientation, are entitled to equal opportunities in the educational system. The school health nurse should be involved in fostering a safe environment, demonstrating an acceptance of diversity."
- National Association of State Boards of Education—"State boards should provide leadership in eliminating the stereotyping and discrimination on the basis of sex, age, disability, race, religion, sexual orientation, ethnic background or national origin in curriculum materials, counseling methods and other education processes. In addition, boards should adopt statewide policies that promote equal educational opportunities."
- The National School Boards Association—"School boards should ensure that students are not subject to discrimination on the basis of socioeconomic status, race, color, national origin, gender, disability, or sexual orientation. Equitable access to and promotion of educational opportunity should be provided to all public school students regardless of factors such as race, gender, sexual orientation, ethnic background, English proficiency, socioeconomic status, or disability."

The pattern that emerges in this position-statement language speaks to four key components that should be included in your policy. Tailor these to reflect the needs of your learning community, but ultimately express that

> *All students must have an equitable opportunity to earn an education.* Indicate that all students, regardless of their background or ability, must have a fair chance at academic progression. Continue that all students must have equal access to school

activities designed to enhance talent and creativity, and that all students are entitled to fair treatment that leads to sound postsecondary preparation.

Respect for one another is critical. Explain that the diversity in the student body is appreciated and that respect for fellow citizens is an indispensable quality and fundamental basis of American citizenship. Emphasize that students, faculty, and staff should accept differences and treat one another with dignity.

Prejudicial behavior against personal attributes is not tolerated. Relate that students, faculty, and staff have a right to protection from discrimination. Include that discrimination-based or hate-motivated behavior toward a person's race, religion, creed, ethnicity, age, color, national origin, political beliefs, gender, mental or physical disability, English language skills, or sexual orientation (actual or perceived) is not tolerated. Some school policies do not include these characteristics, but underscore that no form of discrimination is tolerated—period. It is important, however, to outline some of these attributes to convey that persons do not deserve discrimination simply because they are different, and to give students (who know they are different) a sense of security from being targeted for prejudicial behavior.

Discriminatory and hate-motivated behaviors are discouraged. Mention that the learning community must be a safe, civil, and orderly one. Describe unacceptable behaviors and indicate that persons who engage in, condone, or collaborate in discriminatory and hate-motivated behavior will be disciplined accordingly. The statement should convey that all forms of harassment—verbal (e.g., slurs, name-calling, insults) and physical (e.g., shoving, pushing, physical attacks), intimidation and threats, and bullying—are taken and handled seriously.

Here are some policies found throughout the country. Examine how they incorporate the above components and contemplate how the policies meet the needs of their respective learning communities.

- An Illinois classroom—"In this room, I have the right to safety, to hear and be heard, to be happy, to be treated fairly, to be myself, to learn about myself, to express my feelings and opinions without being interrupted and/or punished, to learn according to my ability. I will not judge my peers on the color of their skin, their weight, their height, their gender, their sexual orientation, their ethnicity, their race, and their religion. We are for difference, for respecting difference, for allowing difference, until difference doesn't make any more difference."
- A California high school—"All students at Alta Loma are expected to respect others in word, deed and action. We do not tolerate language that insults any person on the basis of race, religion, gender, sexual orientation, disability or appearance. The

consequences for antislur violations at Alta Loma High School may be worth emulating. If a student violates the policy, that student is sent to the office and given a series of questions to answer." (Latham, 2000, p. 25)

- A Texas school district—"The Austin Independent School District does not discriminate on the basis of race, creed, color, national origin, age, gender, sexual orientation, disability, or English language skills in its programs and activities. The Austin Independent School District believes that a valuable element of education is the development of respect for all individuals, regardless of race, color, creed, national origin, age, gender, sexual orientation, disability, or other personal attributes." (Austin Independent School District, 2003, p. 2)

- The Rhode Island Board of Regents—"The Rhode Island Board of Regents for Elementary and Secondary Education recognizes that full access of all people and groups to educational opportunities and full participation in educational experiences should be the policy and practice of educational agencies. All individuals and groups must be afforded the opportunity to participate fully and thereby reach their maximum potential. Barriers to student participation that are based on sexual orientation must be identified and removed.

"Certain students, because of their actual or perceived sexual orientation, have been subject to discrimination through abuse, harassment or exclusion from full participation in educational activities. These conditions undermine the goals of Civil Rights activities in education, i.e., to remover barriers, promote nondiscrimination and support the provision of equal educational opportunities. The Board also recognizes that all students, without exception, have the right to come to school and feel safe.

"Therefore it is the Policy of the Board of Regents that no student shall be excluded from, discriminated against, or harassed in any educational program, activity or facility in a public school on account of sexual orientation or perception of same. The policy shall apply to admissions, guidance, recreational and extracurricular activities as well as all public educational programs and activities."

Reflect and Write

What aspects of these policies appeal to you the most? How would you modify the statement to meet your learning community needs?

Application

How would your school respond to a gay or lesbian student's allegations that he or she had been discriminated against or harassed?

As an Administrator, How Should I Handle and Respond to Gay and Lesbian Youth's Allegations of Discrimination and Harassment?

The process for handling and responding to gay and lesbian youth's allegations of discrimination and harassment vary according to your campus needs and leadership style. Because you and your leadership team have the responsibility of safeguarding students from harm, you should take all complaints of discrimination, harassment, or hate conduct very seriously. Emphasize to your learning community that you do not discount any form of harassment whatsoever. Student complaints that are handled earnestly decrease the probability that the student might be retaliated against, and the student body learns that it is not permissible or acceptable to harass others, which, in the long run, promotes a safe school environment.

Just because a student happens to be gay or lesbian or is perceived to be does not minimize the value of his or her complaint. Gay and lesbian students (and those perceived to be such) muster incredible courage to approach you and your staff with a complaint. Many gravely fear that the aftermath could be worse than the harassment itself (e.g., assailants could retaliate, friends might perceive them as a snitch, peers might have their suspicions "confirmed"), yet they still press onward with a complaint. At no time should you or your leadership team devalue or ignore their complaints or the incidents that have occurred. Even if you believe that an incident is inconsequential, the fact remains that it is not so for the student filing the complaint. So often what seems like harmless banter to adults can be a humiliating experience for adolescents.

If your school or district does not already have a set of procedures for handling and responding to complaints of discrimination and harassment, develop one. Use the example flowchart in box 11.4 as a model to formulate a procedure that complements your district code of conduct and satisfies your campus needs. You first want to ensure that all students, faculty, staff, and parents know that a nondiscrimination and antiharassment policy exists. This statement should be on signage in high-traffic areas in the school, in the student handbook, on letters to parents, and on assorted forms. Second, distribute the procedure for filing a complaint to students and parents at the beginning of the school year and review the policy with your teachers at your first faculty meeting of the year. The procedure should instruct students to take the following actions:

> *Get to safety.* Mention that students who feel that their physical safety is in jeopardy should leave the situation immediately (e.g., walk away, run, or yell for help) and contact a school authority. Encourage students to seek out adults who have the power to intervene in a crisis (e.g., a physical attack, verbal assaults). Identify members of your leadership team as safe, nonjudgmental persons that gay and lesbian

Ensure that the learning community knows the policy.
*Post signage, send letters home, distribute flyers,
discuss in faculty meetings, and include in the student handbook.*

Describe the process.
*Get safe.
Talk it over.
Report all incidents.
Submit a report form.
Follow up.*

Student just harassed:
*Administer first aid.
Calm the student.
Ask what happened.
Have student complete report form.
Interview witnesses.
Interview the alleged.*

Student with a report:
*Take report seriously.
Convey urgency to resolve the matter.
Read report form.
Interview student for details.
Interview witnesses.
Interview the alleged.*

Encourage student to see the counselor.

Evaluate case to determine policy violations.

Violated policy

Compliant with policy

Reprimand.
*Educate student.
Affirm what they did was wrong.
Warn about future violations.
Ask for written apology.*

Discipline.
*Reaffirm what they did was wrong.
Notify parents (and police if necessary).
Suspend or expel.
Transfer away from the harassed.
Recommend therapy-type counseling.*

Follow up.
*Justify evaluation in the investigative report.
Share with student who has filed report.
Inform student of appeal process.
Place report in appropriate files.
Monitor number of complaints.
Ensure that supervision is available where incident occurred.*

students can approach to report an incident of harassment or discrimination. Communicate that students should let these safe administrators handle the conflict or crises instead of taking matters into their own hands. If the students are uneasy about approaching the school authorities, supply the names and phone numbers of outside organizations that can contact the school on their behalf.

Discuss the incident with a trusted friend, adult, teacher, or counselor. Students who have been targets of discrimination or harassment can find it painful. All harassed students should be encouraged to consult with others who are supportive. The discussion should help them understand that they did not deserve the harassment; it is the offender who violated what the learning community upholds who is to blame.

Report any incidents of discrimination and harassment. Encourage students to report incidents of discrimination and harassment. Convey that discrimination, harassment, hate-motivated behaviors, and bullying cannot be addressed if administrators do not know that such problems exist. Emphasize that the information is supplied to impartial administrators and will be kept confidential and shared only with those involved in the incident.

Submit a report form. Encourage students to proceed immediately to your office if they risk impending harm, or to visit your office to discuss complaints of discrimination or harassment. Also explain that students should complete the discrimination-and-harassment report form that you (or your leadership team) will ultimately use in your investigation of the matter. The form, which should be available in prominent areas of the school (e.g., the front office, library, counselor's office, student clubs center), should include items to solicit the following pieces of information:

- background information on the student filing the report,
- a description of the incident, and
- solutions to remedy the incident.

See box 11.5 for an example of a nondiscrimination-and-harassment report form.

Follow up on the report. Inform the school community of the investigation timeframe. Let students know that after receiving the report form the matter will be investigated and resolved within a predetermined number of days. The fewer days between receipt of the form, initiation of the investigation, the investigation itself, and response to the student signals that you are serious about discrimination and harassment infractions. Share that if students are not satisfied with the investigation outcome they can appeal to a committee and continue the grievance process with the superintendent's office.

BOX 11.5. EXAMPLE OF A DISCRIMINATION AND HARASSMENT REPORT FORM

Clark Central High School

The Mighty Eagle

"We believe that all students are entitled to an education, regardless of their race, color, creed, religion, ethnicity, ancestry, sexual orientation, gender, or disability. Every student has a right to an environment that is safe, orderly, and civil to maximize his or her learning potential. We support, understand, and believe in diversity. We do not tolerate any form of harassment, intimidation, or bullying behaviors against any student, faculty, or staff member."

Complete this form if you were a target of harassment, intimidation, or bullying behavior or if you witnessed such behavior against another student. Any student who engages in offensive conduct by word (e.g., name-calling, hate language, slurs, obscene or vulgar language, profanity, threats, coercion, libel, slander, retaliation, any violent expressions) or deed (e.g., obscene or vulgar gestures, attacks, vandalizing personal property, pushing, shoving, hitting, any physical violence) toward another student while at school, on the way to and from school, or at a school-sponsored event threatens the safety and well-being of students, faculty, or staff and will be disciplined accordingly.

Be as specific, thorough, and clear as possible. The information you supply on this form will be kept confidential and will be shared only with the accused (if appropriate) and the school administrators who will conduct the investigation and disciplinary process.

I. Your Background Information

Name:_____   Date:_____
Homeroom teacher:_____   Grade:_____
How to best contact you: _____

II. The Incident

Date(s) of the incident or ongoing offenses: _____
Person(s) who committed the offense:

Where the incident(s) occurred:

(Continued)

BOX 11.5. EXAMPLE OF A DISCRIMINATION AND HARASSMENT REPORT FORM (Continued)

Names of persons who witnessed the incident(s):

Describe what happened; specify verbal and physical actions:

Describe your reactions to the person(s) who committed the offense:

III. Post-incident

Names of teachers you have discussed this with:

Your recommendations to resolve the incident:

Indicate if you would like to make an appointment with the counselor: Yes   No

Signature:_____   Date:_____

Attach additional sheets if needed. A school administrator will contact you within three school days to discuss the outcome of the investigation. If you remain unsatisfied with the course of actions taken, you can file an appeal with the Appeals Committee, chaired by a counselor and composed of faculty and staff. A copy will be provided to you.

If the student comes to you for safety (e.g., immediately after having sustained a physical attack), have the nurse administer first aid (if required) and then escort the student to a private room. The incident is humiliating enough; additional attention in a central location will only worsen matters. Ask what happened. The student will likely be upset, so patiently wait for an explanation. Request that a counselor consult the student while you or someone from your leadership team looks for the assailant(s). If a counselor is unavailable, offer the student some water, perhaps pat the student on the back (if this is your style), ask if he or she would like to call a family member or talk with a friend, and console the student with the following:

> You have every right to be upset. I would be too. I'm going out there to see if I can track them down and talk to them. When you feel a little better, I'd like you to fill out the discrimination-and-harassment report form so we can get started on the investigation.
>
> We're going to get to the bottom of this. I will not tolerate this one bit. I'm going to see if I can find the students who did this. When you're up to it, will you begin to complete the discrimination-and-harassment form?

As the student regains composure, begin to ask additional questions to determine the circumstances of the incident. The questions will vary, but they should generally include at least the following:

- What happened?
- Exactly what did the person do to you, or what did the person say to or about you?
- How did you respond?
- What was the response to your reaction?
- Has this type of incident happened before?
- Who witnessed the event?
- What did the witnesses say or do to encourage the behavior?
- Did anyone intervene?

In the conversations with the student, be prepared for a range of jokes, insults, vulgar language, and offensive gestures that were exchanged in the incident, and keep a calm demeanor. Do not laugh or smirk at a comment and do not stifle the student with such comments as

> "I don't want to hear that kind of foul language."
> "That's disgusting. I can't believe that you're sharing this with me."
> "If you think you can shock me with that gesture, you're mistaken. I'm here to help you."

Listen to the student in a sensitive, caring manner; do not assign him or her any blame (e.g., "None of this would have happened if you had just kept walking"); and never assume that the student is gay or lesbian even though he or she was insulted with anti-gay language.

HOW COULD THE ASSISTANT PRINCIPAL HAVE HANDLED THIS INCIDENT DIFFERENTLY?

In the matter of *Flores v. Morgan Hill Unified Schools District*, Alana Flores sought refuge in one of her school leaders. Read the following excerpt from the PFLAG April 10, 2003, press release and reflect on how the assistant principal could have handled the incident differently.

A female student, Alana Flores, found a pornographic picture taped to her locker. A handwritten note attached to the photo read, "Die, Die, Dyke bitch. Fuck off. We'll kill you." When Flores sought help from the school and asked for a new locker, an assistant principal said, "Yes, sure, sure, later. You need to go back to class. Don't bring me this trash anymore. This is disgusting."

Source: PFLAG. (2003). *PFLAG applauds groundbreaking decision proclaiming that schools must protect gay students from harassment.* Retrieved April 21, 2004, from http://www.pflag.org/press/030410.html.

Have the student complete the report form and mention that he or she will not have to confront his or her assailants. Do not bring the assailants to the student to comprehend the severity of the incident or to offer an apology. Talk to the assailants separately. You can explain the possibility that the assailants might be removed from the classes or extracurricular activities where the assailants and the victim regularly encounter each other. You can also ask the student if he or she would like to be temporarily excused from classes or activities where he or she encounters the assailants. As you finish your conversation, affirm that you (or someone from your leadership team) will handle the matter immediately, and encourage the student to make appointments with the counselor who can administer grief therapy or work on his or her self-confidence.

If students come to you with general complaints of discrimination or harassment, do not turn them away. As inconsequential as an incident might seem, still validate the complaint. Do not excuse an incident with any of the following:

"You're making a big deal out of nothing."
"Have you ever thought about what you did for them to act that way toward you?"
"I'm sure they were just playing around."
"They really didn't mean it."
"You need to lighten up—you take life too seriously."

Instead, assure the student that you take the report seriously. Honor the student with responses such as the following:

"I'm glad you came to me with this. It takes a lot of courage to come to this office to tell me. Fill out the discrimination-and-harassment report form, and I'll get right on it."

> "I appreciate your letting me know. Our administration can do nothing about bullies
> if we don't ever hear that they're on our campus. How are you handling this?"
> "You show such courage when you inform us that this happens. Thank you. You really
> are making this campus a safer one by coming here today. Fill out this form and . . ."

Reaffirm that any information supplied on the form will be kept confidential and that the student will not have to confront the assailants. Tell the student that as part of the investigation, he or she will be asked to elaborate on the incident.

Begin the investigation process immediately and do not let it straggle for more than three working days. So that each case investigation is as thorough as possible, develop an investigative format that documents the process. (Box 11.6 shows a checklist that investigators can use to guide their evaluation.) The initial stage of the investigation requires that you (or whoever conducts the investigation) read over the information on the report form and then begin the interview with the student. Ask questions similar to those you would ask a student who has just been harassed, and solicit recommendations for how the situation could be resolved. Proceed to interview the witnesses, if any, and determine if their perspective corroborates the information garnered from the interview and report form. Assure the witnesses that the information they supply is confidential and thank them for their testimony. Then locate the alleged assailants and inform them that you have received several complaints about their behavior on campus and would like to hear their side of the story.

BOX 11.6. FORM TO DOCUMENT POLICY VIOLATION INVESTIGATION

Discrimination and Harassment Policy Violation: Investigative Checklist

1. Investigator:_____ Date:_____
2. Date of receipt of the report form:_____
3. Persons involved in the incident (name, grade, homeroom):

4. Witnesses (name, grade, homeroom):

5. Type of discriminatory or harassing behaviors:

(Continued)

BOX 11.6. FORM TO DOCUMENT POLICY VIOLATION INVESTIGATION (Continued)

6. Date, time, and location incident occurred:

7. Restate the alleged incident and policy violation:

8. Background information on parties involved (retrieve data from student files):

9. Date of the interview with the complainant: _____
Additional information about the incident:

10. Date of the interview with the witnesses: _____
Additional information about the incident:

11. Date of the interview with the alleged: _____
Alleged's perspective and additional information:

12. Evaluation: Policy violation?   Yes   No
Justifications:

13. Recommended disciplinary actions:

14. Date final evaluation was reported to the complainant: _____

(Continued)

BOX 11.6. FORM TO DOCUMENT POLICY VIOLATION INVESTIGATION (Continued)

15. Complainant's response:_____ Considering appeal: Yes   No
Justification:

16. Dates and times to monitor the setting where incident occurred:

Signature:_____

Most cases of harassment, intimidation, bullying, and hate-motivated behavior are complex and will take much judgment on your part, but if you find that the alleged perpetrators have violated the policy, then determine the course of reprimand for the student. At no time should you yell at or insult the assailants or reprieve them in public. Foremost, make sure you do the following:

Educate them about the untoward effects the incident has. Ask assailants to explain why they were wrong to discriminate against or harass another student. Often assailants are unaware that the hateful comments, gestures, or behavior are fundamentally improper and disgraceful. You can ask what they had hoped to accomplish by engaging in such behavior and whether they know what their statements (e.g., "You big silly fag. I'm going to get you.") imply. Insist that they contemplate how their behavior was hurtful and harmful. Then explain that such behavior not only violates school policy but that it inhibits respect and acceptance of difference and destroys a safe school environment.

Reprimand and warn them. Tell the assailants point blank that their behavior was wrong and unacceptable. Convey serious appall instead of superficial disappointment. Explain that they will be disciplined and will face stern consequences (e.g., expulsion, suspension) if they continue with this behavior or retaliate against those filing the complaint.

Have them apologize. Instruct the assailants to write a formal letter of apology to the student and to those who witnessed the event. In the letter the student should
- apologize for the behavior,
- explain that the behavior was wrong and hurtful,

- mention how the incident must have felt to the student and others who witnessed the event,
- write how such behaviors ruin the safety of and morale among students, and
- indicate how he or she is working to change and will not engage in such behavior in the future.

Next, determine your disciplinary course of action, which will vary according to the severity of the incident and must conform to your district procedures for code-of-conduct violations. More severe cases of discrimination, harassment, bullying, and so forth will require that the assailants be suspended or expelled. Needless to say, meet with the assailants' parents and inform them of what has happened. In some cases, you may have to call upon the police or your local sheriff's office. If the incident is severe or recurring, transfer the offenders away from the harassed student if they attend the same classes or school activities. It may seem easier to transfer the harassed student to another campus, but it is not ethical or sound to do so. Removing the harassed student gives your learning community the impression that the harassed are punished with a transfer and that the harassers are rewarded with continued attendance at the school. Just ask yourself, "What student would want to report an incident of discrimination or harassment when they could be transferred away from familiar surroundings and friends?"

 Critical Thinking

Why is it not a good idea to have the assailant apologize directly to the harassed student and/or shake hands to signify a resolution?

As a consequence of their prejudicial behavior, plan that the assailants confront their biases in therapy types of activities. Brainstorm activities that compel the students to reflect on the impact their biases and behaviors have on the student body and society as a whole. The assailant could get professional therapy or tolerance training for severe offenses; meet with the counselor for regular sessions; read articles on diversity or hate crimes, for instance; respond to some statements on personal bias in a journal; or fulfill some community service. Lastly, convey your confidence in the assailants' ability to change their attitude to one that is accepting of individual differences, and emphasize that you will monitor their behavior on campus.

Write a report describing the outcome of your investigation and justifying your evaluation. Include how the investigation was conducted; who was interviewed; a copy of the letter of apology (if the assailant violated the policy); and the disciplinary course of action taken, if any. Summon the student who filed the form to share your findings and communicate that you, the members of your team, and teachers will closely supervise the area where the incident occurred. Explain that the student can appeal the decision to a committee if he or she is unsatisfied with the outcome of the investigation, or that he or she can file a complaint with the superintendent's office. Instruct the student to report any acts of retribution or similar incidents, and encourage him or her to see a counselor to discuss the matter further. At this point, ask the student if there is anything you can do to help him or her cope with the aftermath of the incident, such as having the student transfer to another homeroom, change lockers, move to a class offered at a different time or location, escorted between classes or monitored during lunch or study hall, and so forth. Then encourage the student to come back and meet with you to inform you of how things are progressing.

Finally, monitor the number of complaints your office receives. A complaint or two in a semester suggests that very few students do not respect individual differences. A large number of complaints (per your student population), however, unveils a larger problem of intolerance, which will require that you educate your learning community about respect for diversity, prejudice and bias, certain groups of students (e.g., Vietnamese students, if they are routinely insulted, or gay and lesbian students, if they are consistently harassed), and so forth.

Summary

As a school administrator, you have many responsibilities that all seem to hold priority. But the most critical of all is your obligation to ensure the safety of all students. Your community entrusts you with making sure that all students are and feel safe at school, at school events, and going to and from school. Ensure that your school environment is a safe, orderly, and caring one, because harassment or abuse of any kind creates a hostile learning environment, which negatively affects students' overall achievement. Display signage that reads "Safe School—No Harassment Tolerated" or "Safe Zone," and train your faculty and staff how to prevent discrimination and prejudicial behaviors, especially those toward gay and lesbian youth. In the event that harassment, intimidation, or bullying is a persistent and pervasive problem, lead a schoolwide effort to teach students how to respect individual differences in the wake of bias, prejudice, discrimination, diversity, and so forth. Develop a nondiscrimination and antiharassment policy and procedure statement, and ensure that students and faculty know and believe in the reporting procedure. Survey the students to evaluate how safe they feel at school, how well they know the reporting procedures, and how well offenses are handled by administrators and teachers.

Here is a short list of things you can do to create a safe school environment for gay and lesbian youth. It may not be easy to accomplish all of these, but it is certainly worthwhile that you do.

- Believe that all students deserve a safe environment free from verbal or physical abuse.
- Use every opportunity to inform students that you do no tolerate verbal or physical abuse.
- Encourage students to report harassment.
- Take students' reports of harassment seriously.
- Provide your teachers and staff with training on gay and lesbian youth matters.
- Create a committee of teachers to recommend lessons and resources on gay and lesbian history, persons, and social contributions.
- Insist that your librarian procure print and nonprint media on gay and lesbian issues.
- Provide training for teachers on how to intervene when harassment occurs.
- Encourage teachers to stop and report harassment.
- Identify safe persons that students can approach for support and guidance.
- Inform parents of gay and lesbian youth that counseling is available.
- Provide training for parents on how to teach their children to respect individual differences.
- Display "safe school" signage and your nondiscrimination and antiharassment policy.
- Promote your nondiscrimination and antiharassment policy.
- Firmly punish policy violators, not the victims.
- Support GSAs and commend their teacher sponsors.

Idea File

1. Make a poster that informs students about the nondiscrimination and antiharassment policy.
2. Invite students to create a classroom policy on respecting individual differences.
3. Plan for a series of workshops for parents on how to teach and model respectful behavior.

References

Austin Independent School District. (2003). *Austin independent school district student code of conduct.* Austin, TX: Author.

Cahill, S., Ellen, M., & Tobias, S. (2003). *Family policy: Issues affecting gay, lesbian, bisexual and transgender families.* Retrieved April 28, 2004, from http://www.thetaskforce.org/library/familypolicy.htm.

GLSEN. (2002). *The 2001 National School Climate Survey: The school related experiences of our nation's lesbian, gay, bisexual, and transgender youth.* New York: Author.

Latham, B. (2000). *The invisible minority: GLBTQ youth at risk.* Point Richmond, CA: Point Richmond Press.

Saint Paul Public Schools. (n.d.). *Out for equity/Out4good safe schools manual.* St. Paul, MN: Author.

Uribe, V., & Harbeck, K. M. (1992). Addressing the needs of lesbian, gay, and bisexual youth: The origins of PROJECT 10 and school-based intervention. In K. Harbeck (ed.), *Coming out of the classroom closet* (pp. 9–28). New York: Haworth Press, Inc.

CHAPTER 12

Resources for Schools

"LIVING OUTSIDE THE STEREOTYPE," SCOTT, 18, OF SAN JOSE, CALIFORNIA

I'm feeling like I don't fit in. At school or church I'm treated like "that gay guy." But I'm also treated just as differently at the Billy DeFrank gay community center in my hometown. While there, I've heard other gay people say, "Oh he's not really gay," or "What's he doing here?"

I don't fit the stereotype of a gay 18-year-old who runs around in tight-fitting Abercrombie & Fitch T-shirts and designer sunglasses talking about last night's episode of *Queer Eye for the Straight Guy*. But at the same time I don't talk about the winning touchdown from a football game or how I "nailed" some girl the other night. It's as if I'm not straight enough or gay enough for the world.

To me, the gay community is driven by sex. It's everywhere—on television, in advertising, in anything geared toward gays. At the San Jose pride festival this past June, I found myself surrounded by booths offering free lube and condoms, porn stars signing autographs, and leather boutiques featuring live "pleasure" performances. But I am not interested in having sex right now, so I asked myself, *What am I doing at this festival?*

Even though straight people in my generation have taken huge leaps toward full acceptance of gays and lesbians, I still have hard time fitting into the image they have selected for me. I don't have a straight girlfriend to go shopping with and give advice to on dating boys, and I definitely don't have any guy friends to whom I give style tips or help to understand woman's emotions. In fact, most straight guys still run when they hear the word "gay."

So why are we still driven by stereotypes? I hope that one day I will be accepted by all for being me. And I hope that future gay youth never have to face this problem.

Source: The Advocate Report. (2004, September 14). Generation Q: Living outside the stereotype. *The Advocate, 922,* 26. Reprinted with permission.

Overview

Scott in the vignette appears frustrated by the fact that he cannot seem to align his sexual identity with the images that he has seen in the gay community. He clearly feels equally out of place in the straight and the gay community. Many gay and lesbian youth are like Scott. They know they are not straight, but they also know that they are not like the gay and lesbian persons that are projected in the mainstream, which are often stereotypic, superficial images. This dissonance confuses many gay and lesbian youth and heightens feelings of isolation and loneliness because they believe that they have no group to genuinely identify and bond with or go to for moral support. But when youth explore books and videos that accurately discuss and depict the diversity within the gay and lesbian community, they realize that the community is far more significant than the images they have been exposed to.

This chapter itemizes resources to consider for your library. The resources can help you (a) better understand gay and lesbian issues, (b) recommend resources to others who are trying to understand gay and lesbian issues, (c) plan for lessons on gay and lesbian issues, and d) recommend resources to gay and lesbian students who are working to make sense of their sexual orientation. The questions answered in this chapter include the following:

- What books on gay and lesbian youth, persons, and issues are recommended for teachers, students, and parents?
- What videos, journals, and popular magazines are recommended for our school library?
- What hotlines/help lines and online organizations are available for youth?
- What websites can youth visit to learn more about gay and lesbian issues?

What Books on Gay and Lesbian Youth, Persons, and Issues Are Recommended for Teachers, Students, and Parents?

Many of the books that were consulted for this text are listed below. Some are ideal as references, and others are suited for pleasure reading. The books are divided into six sections: books resourceful to teachers, books to better understand gay and lesbian youth, books to better understand the community of gay and lesbian persons, books for parents, books for adolescents, and books for children. The author(s), year, title, and publisher information are provided to assist you in locating a book (or a description of it), and these books can be found on the Internet through Web-based bookstores (e.g., amazon.com). When these books are acquired for your school library, ensure that everyone has easy access to them instead of secluding them in areas that obligate students to ask for them, require that they have their parents' written permission, or require that students leave their school ID.

Books Resourceful to Teachers

The following books can help some secondary education teachers plan for lessons in the content areas. These books offer a historical and contemporary perspective on some of the issues central to the lives of gay and lesbian persons.

Aldrich, R., & Wotherspoon, G. (2003). *Who's who in gay and lesbian history: From antiquity to World War II.* New York: Routledge.

Bagemihl, B. (1999). *Biological exuberance: Animal homosexuality and natural diversity.* New York: Saint Martin's Press.

Brelin, C. (Ed.). (1997). *Outstanding lives: Profiles of lesbians and gay men.* Canton, MI: Visible Ink Press.

Clendinen, D., & Nagourney, A. (1999). *Out for good: The struggle to build a gay rights movement in America.* New York: Simon & Schuster.

Cowan, T. (1997). *Gay men and women who enriched the world.* Los Angeles: Alyson Publications.

D'Emilio, J., Turner, W., & Vaid, U. (2000). *Creating change: Sexuality, public policy, and civil rights.* New York: St. Martin's Press.

Duberman, M., Vicinus, M., & Chauncey, G. (Eds.). (1989). *Hidden from history: Reclaiming the gay and lesbian past.* New York: New American Library.

Fone, B. (2000). *Homophobia: A history.* New York: Metropolitan Books.

Hogan, S., & Hudson, L. (1998). *Completely queer: The gay and lesbian encyclopedia.* New York: Henry Holt and Company.

Jennings, K. (Ed.). (1994). *Becoming visible: A reader in gay and lesbian history for high school and college students.* Los Angeles: Alyson Publications.

Katz, J. (1992). *Gay American history: Lesbian and gay men in the U.S.A.* New York: Meridian.

Marcus, E. (1992). *Making history: The struggle for gay and lesbian equal rights 1945–1990.* New York: HarperCollins.

Miller, N. (1993). *Out in the world. Gay and lesbian life from Buenos Aires to Bangkok.* New York: Vintage Books.

Miller, N. (1995). *Out of the past: Gay and lesbian history from 1869 to the present.* New York: Vintage Books.

Murdoch, J., & Price, D. (2001). *Courting justice: Gay men and lesbians v. the Supreme Court.* New York: Basic Books.

Russell, P. (1995). *The Gay 100: A ranking of the most influential gay men and lesbians, past and present.* New York: Kensington Books.

Singer, B. (Ed.). (1994). *Growing up gay/growing up lesbian: A literary anthology.* New York: New Press.

Spencer, C. (1995). *Homosexuality in history.* New York: Harcourt Brace & Company.

Summers, C. (Ed.). (1995). *The gay and lesbian literary heritage: A reader's companion to the writers and their works, from antiquity to the present.* New York: Henry Holt & Company.

Books to Better Understand Gay and Lesbian Youth

Consult this next group of books to gain a better understanding of what some gay and lesbian youth experience. Some of these books approach the topic from a developmental perspective, some are fact based and conceptual, and others offer advice to help gay and lesbian youth surmount some of their challenges.

Baker, J. (2001). *How homophobia hurts children: Nurturing diversity at home, at school, and in the community.* New York: Harrington Park Press.

Bass, E., & Kaufman, K. (1996). *Free your mind: The book for gay, lesbian, and bisexual youth and their allies.* New York: HarperPerennial.

Bauer, M. (Ed.). (1995). *Am I blue? Coming out from the silence.* New York: HarperTrophy.

Brimner, L. (2000). *Being different: Lambda youth speak out.* New York: Franklin Watts.

Chandler, K. (1995). *Passages of pride: Lesbian and gay youth come of age.* New York: Random House.

D'Augelli, A., & Patterson, C. (Eds.). (2001). *Lesbian, gay, and bisexual identities and youth: Psychological perspectives.* New York: Oxford.

DeCrescenzo, T. (Ed). (1994). *Helping gay and lesbian youth: New policies, new programs, new practice.* New York: Harrington Park Press.

Due, L. (1995). *Joining the tribe: Growing up gay and lesbian in the '90s.* New York: Doubleday.

Gray, M. (1999). *In your face: Stories from the lives of queer youth.* New York: Harrington Park Press.

Harris, M. (Ed.). (1998). *School experiences of gay and lesbian youth: The invisible minority.* New York: Harrington Park Press.

Herdt, G. (Ed.). (1989). *Gay and lesbian youth.* New York: Harrington Park Press.

Huegel, K. (2003). *GLBTQ: The survival guide for queer and questioning teens.* Minneapolis: Free Spirit Publishing.

Mallon, G. (2001). *Lesbian and gay youth issues: A practical guide for youth workers.* Washington, DC: Child Welfare League of America Press.

Mastoon, A. (2001). *The shared heart: Portraits and stories celebrating lesbian, gay and bisexual young people.* New York: HarperCollins Juvenile Books.

Owens, R. (1998). *Queer kids: The challenges and promise for lesbian, gay, and bisexual youth.* New York: Harrington Park Press.

Perrotti, J., & Westheimer, K. (2001). *When the drama club is not enough: Lessons from the Safe Schools program for gay and lesbian students.* Boston: Beacon Press.

Pollack, R., & Schwartz, C. (1995). *The journey out: A guide for and about lesbian, gay, and bisexual teens.* New York: Puffin.

Reed, R. (1997). *Growing up gay: The sorrows and joys of gay and lesbian adolescence.* New York: W. W. Norton & Company.

Remafedi, G. (Ed.). (1994). *Death by denial: Studies of suicide in gay and lesbian teenagers.* Los Angeles: Alyson Publishing.

Ryan, C., & Futterman, D. (1998). *Lesbian and gay youth. Care and counseling.* New York: Columbia University Press.

Unks, G. (Ed). (1995). *The gay teen: Educational practice and theory for lesbian, gay, and bisexual adolescents.* New York: Routledge.

Walling, D. (1996). *Open lives, safe schools: Addressing gay and lesbian issues in education.* Bloomington, IN: Phi Delta Kappa Education Foundation.

Woog, D. (Ed.). (1995). *School's out: The impact of gay and lesbian issues on America's Schools.* Los Angeles: Alyson Publishing.

Books to Better Understand Gay, Lesbian, Bisexual, and Transgender Persons

This next group of books can help you understand the community of gay, lesbian, bisexual, and transgender persons. Some of these books provide an overview of diverse sexuality, others describe the challenges of the community, and others discourse on a specific topic in depth.

Blumenfeld, W. (Ed.). (1992). *Homophobia: How we all pay the price.* Boston: Beacon Press.

Bono, C. (1999). *Family outing: A guide to the coming-out process for gays, lesbians, & their families.* New York: Back Bay Books.

Bornstein, K. (1995). *Gender outlaw: On men, women and the rest of us.* New York: Vintage Books.

Boykin, K. (1997). *One more river to cross: Black and gay in America.* New York: Doubleday Books.

Brimner, L. (Ed.). (1997). *Letters to our children: Lesbian and gay adults speak to the new generation.* New York: Franklin Watts.

Brown, L. (Ed.). (1992). *Two spirit people: American Indian lesbian women and gay men.* New York: Harrington Park Press.

Clausen, J. (1997). *Beyond gay or straight: Understanding sexual orientation.* New York: Chelsea House Publishers.

Elkins, R., & King, D. (Eds.). (1996). *Blending genders: Social aspects of cross-dressing and sex-changing.* New York: Routledge.

Evelyn, J. (1998). *Mom, I need to be a girl.* Imperial Beach, CA: Walter Trook Publishing.

Feinberg, L. (1997). *Transgender warriors: Making history from Joan of Arc to Dennis Rodman.* Boston: Beacon Press.

Feinberg, L. (1999). *Trans Liberation: Beyond pink or blue.* Boston: Beacon Press.

Ford, M. (1996). *The world out there: Becoming part of the lesbian and gay community.* New York: The New Press.

Ford, M. (1998). *Out spoken: Role models from the lesbian and gay community.* New York: Beech Tree Books.

Griffin, P. (1998). *Strong women, deep closets: Lesbians and homophobia in sport.* Champaign, IL: Human Kinetics Publishing.

Helminiak, D. (2000). *What the Bible really says about homosexuality.* San Francisco: Alamo Square Press.

Jennings, K. (Ed.). (1994). *One teacher in ten: Gay and lesbian educators tell their stories.* Los Angeles: Alyson Publishing.

Lipkin, A. (1999). *Understanding homosexuality, changing schools.* Boulder, CO: Westview Press.

Louganis, G. (1995). *Breaking the surface.* New York: Random House.

Marcus, E. (1999). *Is it a choice? Answers to 300 of the most frequently asked questions about gays and lesbians.* New York: HarperCollins.

Merla, P. (Ed.). (1996). *Boys like us: Gay writers tell their coming out stories.* New York: Avon.

Mixner, D. (2000). *Brave journeys: Profiles in gay and lesbian courage.* New York: Bantam Books.

Moore, L. (Ed.). (1998). *Does your mama know? An anthology of black lesbian coming out stories.* Washington, DC: Redbone Press.

Russell, P. (1995). *The Gay 100.* New York: Kensington Publishing.

Sears, J., & Williams, W. (Eds.). (1997). *Overcoming heterosexism and homophobia: Strategies that work.* New York: Columbia University Press.

Weinberg, M., Williams, C., & Pryor, D. (1995). *Dual attraction: Understanding bisexuality.* New York: Oxford Press.

Books for Parents

You can recommend that parents of gay and lesbian youth read any of the books outlined in this chapter. However, the books below educate parents about sexual orientation and assist them in meeting their child's and their own needs.

Bernstein, R. (1999). *Straight parents, gay children: Inspiring families to live honestly and with greater understanding.* New York: Thunder's Mouth Press.

Borhek, M. (1993). *Coming out to parents: A two-way survival guide for lesbians and gay men and their parents.* Cleveland: Pilgrim Press.

Cantwell, M. (1996). *Homosexuality: The secret a child dare not tell.* San Rafael, CA: Rafael Press.

Fairchild, B., & Hayward, N. (1998). *Now that you know: A parents' guide to understanding their gay and lesbian children.* Fort Washington, PA: Harvest Book Company.

Griffin, C., Wirth, M., & Wirth, A. (1997). *Beyond acceptance: Parents of lesbians and gays talk about their experiences.* New York: St. Martin's Press.

Jennings, K. (2003). *Always my child: A parent's guide to understanding your gay, lesbian, bisexual, transgendered or questioning son or daughter.* New York: Simon & Schuster.

McDougal, B. (Ed.). (1998). *My child is gay: How parents react when they hear the news.* Chicago: Independent Publishers Group.

Savin-Williams, R. (2001*). Mom, Dad, I'm gay: How families negotiate coming out.* Washington, DC: American Psychological Association.

Books for Adolescents

The following books focus on gay and lesbian themes and are intended for adolescents. While a few are nonfiction, most are fiction and involve gay and lesbian characters and storylines. Heterosexual students can also read these books to learn about the issues that gay and lesbian youth experience. Visit the Gay, Lesbian, Bisexual, and Transgender Roundtable's website (www.ala.org/ala/glbtrt/welcomeglbtround.htm) for a complete description of these books.

Bantle, L. (1995). *Diving for the Moon.* New York: Atheneum Publishers.

Bauer, M. (Ed.). (1995). *Am I Blue? Coming Out of the Silence.* New York: HarperTrophy.

Bechard, M. (1999). *If it doesn't kill you.* New York: Viking.

Benduhn, T. (2003). *Gravel queen.* New York: Simon & Schuster.

Block, F. (1997). *Baby be-bop.* New York: HarperTrophy.

Block, F. (1998). *Girl goddess #9: Nine Stories.* New York: HarperTrophy.

Boock, P. (1999). *Dare truth or promise.* New York: Houghton-Mifflin.

Brett, C. (1990). *S. P. likes A. D.* Toronto, Ontario, Canada: Women's Press.

Brown, R. (1983). *Rubyfruit jungle.* New York: Bantam Books.

Brown, T. (1995). *Entries from a hot pink notebook.* New York: Washington Square Press.

Chambers, A. (1995). *Dance on my grave.* New York: Random House.

Crutcher, C. (2004). *Ironman.* New York: HarperTempest.

Donovan, J. (1969). *I'll get there: It better be worth the trip.* New York: Dell.

Donovan, S. (1994). *Dive.* New York: Dutton Children's Books.

Feinberg, L. (2004). *Stone butch blues.* Los Angeles: Alyson Publications.

Ferris, J. (2000). *Eight seconds.* New York: Harcourt.

Flagg, F. (1988). *Fried green tomatoes at the whistle stop cafe.* New York: Random House.

Fricke, A., & Fricke, W. (2002). *Sudden strangers: The story of gay son and his father.* New York: St. Martin's Press.

Garden, N. (1991). *Lark in the morning.* New York: Farrar Straus & Giroux.

Garden, N. (1992). *Annie on my mind.* New York: Farrar Straus & Giroux.

Grima, T. (Ed.). (1995). *Not the only one: Lesbian and gay fiction for teens.* Los Angeles: Alyson Publications.

Grimsley, J. (1997). *Dream boy.* New York: Simon and Schuster.

Hartinger, B. (2003). *Geography club.* New York: HarperTempest.

Heron, A. (Ed.). (1995). *Two teenagers in twenty: Writings by gay and lesbian youth.* Los Angeles: Alyson Publications.

Kerr, M. (1995). *Deliver us from Evie*. New York: HarperTrophy.

Kerr, M. (1998). *Hello, I lied*. New York: Trophy.

Koertge, R. (1988). *The Arizona kid*. New York: Avon Books.

Larson, R. (1997). *What I know now*. New York: Henry Holt and Company.

Levithan, D. (2003). *Boy meets boy*. New York: Knopf Books for Young Readers.

Marcus, E. (2000). *What if someone I know is gay? Answers to questions about gay and lesbian people*. New York: Price Stern Sloan.

McCauslin, M. (1992). *Facts about . . . Lesbian and gay rights*. New York: Crestwood House.

McClain, E. (1994). *No big deal*. New York: Lodestar Books.

Murrow, L. (1993). *Twelve days in August*. New York: Holiday House.

Murrow, L. (1997). *Blue Coyote*. New York: Simon & Schuster.

Myracle, L. (2003). *Kissing Kate*. New York: Dutton Books.

Peters, J. (2003). *Keeping you a secret*. New York: Megan Tingley.

Reynolds, M. (2001). *Love rules*. Buena Park, CA: Morning Glory Press.

Sanchez, A. (2003). *Rainbow boys*. New York: Simon Pulse.

Shannon, G. (1995). *Unlived affections*. Los Angeles: Alyson Publications.

Stark, E. (2000). *Shy girl*. Seattle: Seal Press.

Stoehr, S. (2003). *Tomorrow Wendy: A love story*. New York: Delacorte.

Van Dijk, L. (1995). *Damned strong love: The true story of Willi G. and Stefan K.* New York: Henry Holt and Company.

Warren, P. (1996). *The front runner*. Beverly Hills, CA: Wildcat Press.

Warren, P. (1998). *Billy's boy*. Beverly Hills, CA: Wildcat Press.

Waters, S. (2002). *Fingersmith*. New York: Riverhead Books.

Williams, B. (1998). *Girl walking backwards*. New York: Griffin Trade Paperback.

Wittlinger, E. (2003). *What's in a name?* Lincoln, NE: Universe, Inc.

Woodson, J. (1995). *From the notebooks of melanin sun*. New York: Scholastic.

Books for Children

This next group of books is intended for children. Some of the books explore gender stereotypes; others introduce gay and lesbian issues from a diversity perspective (e.g., people are different); and some of these books address gay and lesbian issues in an explicit manner and include characters who must contend with gay and lesbian persons.

Abramchik, L. (1996). *Is your family like mine?* New York: Open Heart, Open Mind.

Brown, F. (2000). *Generous Jefferson Bartleby Jones*. Los Angeles: Alyson Publications.

de Hann, L., & Nijland, S. (2004). *King & King & Family*. Berkeley, CA: Tricycle Press.

DePaola, T. (1979). *Oliver Buttons is a sissy*. New York: Voyager Books.

Elwin, R., & Paulse, M. (2000). *Asha's Mums*. Toronto, Ontario, Canada: Women's Press.

Fierstein, F. (2002). *The sissy duckling*. New York: Simon & Schuster.

Garden, N. (2004). *Molly's family*. New York: FSG Books for Young Readers.

Heron, A., & Maran, M. (1991). *How would you feel if your dad was gay?* Los Angeles: Alyson Publications.

Kennedy, J., & Canemaker, J. (1998). *Lucy goes to the country*. Los Angeles: Alyson Publications.

Newman, L. (1991). *Gloria goes to gay pride*. Los Angeles: Alyson Publications.

Newman, L. (2000). *Heather has two mommies*. Los Angeles: Alyson Publications.

Newman, L. (2004). *The boy who cried fabulous*. Berkeley, CA: Tricycle Press.

Skutch, R. (1998). *Who's in a family?* Berkeley, CA: Tricycle Press.

Valentine, J. (2000). *Two moms, the zark, and me*. Los Angeles: Alyson Publications.

Valentine, J. (2004). *The daddy machine*. Los Angeles: Alyson Publications.

Valentine, J. (2004). *The duke who outlawed jellybeans and other stories*. Los Angeles: Alyson Publications.

Valentine, J. (2004). *One dad, two dads, brown dad, blue dad*. Los Angeles: Alyson Publications.

Vigna, J. (1995). *My two uncles*. Morton Grove, IL: Albert Whitman & Company.

Willhoite, M. (1991). *Daddy's roommate*. Los Angeles: Alyson Publications.

Willhoite, M. (1996). *Daddy's wedding*. Los Angeles: Alyson Publications.

Willhoite, M. (2000). *Uncle what-is-it is coming to visit*. Los Angeles: Alyson Publications.

Zolotow, C. (1985). *William's doll*. New York: HarperTrophy.

What Videos, Journals, and Popular Magazines Are Recommended for Our School Library?

Some students, school personnel, and parents like to explore topics through the media of videos, journals, and magazines. To augment the books on gay and lesbian issues, consider acquiring the following resources. A committee of school personnel (including the school's safe person) should review the content of these resources to determine which are most appropriate for your learning community.

Videos

Below is a sample of videos and the contact information on their distributors. Some of these are documentaries that cover many issues from homophobia to homosexuals in the holocaust. Others are short films that range in topic from a relationship between two boys to the story of a gay boy who attempts suicide.

Beyond Media
7013 N Glenwood Avenue
Chicago, IL 60626
(773) 973-2280
www.beyondmedia.org
• *A Fish (Almost) Eaten by a Shark*

The Cinema Guild Inc.
130 Madison Avenue
New York, NY 10016-7038
(212) 685-6242
www.cinemaguild.com
- *Anatomy of Desire*
- *Coming Home*
- *Companions: Tales from the Closet*
- *Fiction and Other Truths*
- *Jim Loves Jack: The James Eagan Story*
- *Mama, I Have Something to Tell You*
- *The Man Who Drove with Mandela*
- *Not All Parents Are Straight*
- *Rules of the Game*
- *Our House: A Very Real Documentary about Kids of Gay and Lesbian Parents*

Film Ideas Inc.
308 N Wolf Road
Wheeling, IL 60090
(800) 475-3456
www.filmideas.com
- *Acting Out*
- *We Love Our Children: Parents of Gays Speak Out*

Frameline Distribution
145 Ninth Street, #300
San Francisco, CA 94103
(415) 703-8650
www.frameline.org/distribution
- *Coming to Terms*
- *Contact*
- *Homoteens*
- *Just Call Me Kade*
- *Kiss in the Snow*
- *Out Loud*
- *Queer Geographies: Mapping Our Identities*
- *Queer Son*

- *Safe Place*
- *Surfacing*
- *Waves*

Gay, Lesbian and Straight Education Network
121 W 27th Street, Suite 804
New York, NY 10001
(212) 727-0135
http://www.glsen.org/cgi-bin/iowa/home.html
- *Outside the Lines: The World of the Gay Athlete*
- *Teaching Respect to All*

Intermedia Inc.
1165 Eastlake Avenue East
Suite 400
Seattle, WA 98109
(800) 553-8336
www.intermedia-inc.com/main.htm
- *Speaking for Ourselves: Portraits of Gay and Lesbian Youth*
- *Trevor*

ITL Media Inc.
30 W 26th Street, 7th Floor
New York, NY 10010
(212) 255-6012
www.inthelifetv.org
- *Out in the Workplace*
- *Friends and Family*
- *Vital Discoveries*
- *History and Humor*
- *Movers and Shakers*
- *Pride*
- *Cultural Legacies*
- *Building Safe Havens*
- *Challenging Tradition*
- *From Rights to Reverence*
- *Supporting Youth: Their Education and Survival*

- *In the Life Goes Global*
- *June Pride 2000*
- *8th Season Premier*
- *Travel*

Lesbian and Gay Parents Association
6705 California, Suite 1
San Francisco, CA 94121
(415) 387-9886
- *Both My Moms' Names are Judy: Children of Lesbians and Gays Speak Out*

Northeastern Wisconsin In-School Telecommunications
2420 Nicolet Drive, IS 1040
Green Bay, WI 54311
(800) 633-7445
(414) 465-2599
www.uwgb.edu/newist
- *Hate, Homophobia and Schools*
- *Sexual Orientation: Reading Between the Labels*

Public Broadcasting System (PBS)
www.pbs.org
- *Frontline: Assault on Gay America*
- *Not for Ourselves Alone*

Water Bearer Films Inc.
20 W 20th Street, 2nd Floor
New York, NY 10011
(212) 242-8686
ww.waterbearerfilms.com/pages/454565/index.htm
- *Desire*
- *Silent Pioneers*

Wolfe Video
21640 Almaden Road
San Jose, CA 95120
www.wolfevideo.com
- *Gay Youth: An Educational Video*
- *Paragraph 175*

- *Southern Comfort*
- *The Celluloid Closet*
- *Brandon Teena Story*
- *Coming Out Under Fire*
- *Laramie Project*
- *West Coast Crones*
- *Times of Harvey Milk*
- *Straight from the Heart*
- *Not for Ourselves Alone*
- *Oliver Button Is a Star*
- *One Nation Under God*
- *Before Stonewall*
- *Common Threads: Stories from the Quilt*

Women's Educational Media
2180 Bryant Street, Suite 203
San Francisco, CA 94110
(415) 641-4616
www.womedia.org
- *Let's Get Real*
- *That's a Family: A Film for Kids about Family Diversity*
- *It's Elementary: Talking about Gay Issues in Schools*
- *Choosing Children: A Film about Lesbians Becoming Parents*

Women Vision
Transit Media Communications
PO Box 1084
Harriman, NY 10926
www.woman-vision.org
- *No Secret Anymore: The Times of Del Martin and Phyllis Lyon*
- *Straight from the Heart*
- *All God's Children*
- *De Colores*
- *Out for a Change: Addressing Homophobia in Women's Sports*

Journals

Haworth Press Inc. publishes the following journals. Their contact information is listed below with the titles of journals that are focused on sexual-orientation issues. While the journal content is more suited for college students and professionals engaged in research, the essays and articles have implications for school personnel.

Haworth Press Inc.
10 Alice Street
Binghamton, NY 13904
(800) 429-6784
www.haworthpressinc.com
 • *Harrington Gay Men's Fiction Quarterly*
 • *Harrington Lesbian Fiction Quarterly*
 • *Journal of Bisexuality*
 • *Journal of Gay and Lesbian Issues in Education*
 • *Journal of Gay and Lesbian Politics*
 • *Journal of Gay and Lesbian Social Services*
 • *Journal of Homosexuality*
 • *Journal of Lesbian Studies*

Popular Magazines

Mainstream magazines are often popular with students because they capture current news events, fashion, arts and entertainment, and so on from a pop culture perspective. Some of the magazines for and about the gay and lesbian community are listed below. While much of the magazines' content is appropriate for secondary education students, occasionally a photograph (e.g., partially nude models) or storyline is featured that is inappropriate for high school students. A designated committee (which includes a safe person/advocate for gay and lesbian youth) should review each magazine to ensure that the content is appropriate for your learning community. Descriptions of the magazines and contact information for their publishers follow.

The Advocate
6922 Hollywood Blvd., Suite 1000
Los Angeles, CA 90028
(323) 871-1225
www.advocate.com

The Advocate is one of the oldest magazines that feature issues critical to the gay and lesbian community. Their cover stories and reports range from politics to interviews with celebrities. The magazine offers special reports; arts and entertainment; and departments including "My Perspective," "Rants & Raves," "The Buzz," and so on. The magazine's website also features online exclusive stories.

Curve
1 Haight Street, Suite B
San Francisco, CA 94102
(800) 998-5565
www.curvemag.com

Curve is considered the best-selling magazine for lesbians. The magazine is published eight times a year, and each issue offers "lesbian-related celebrity interviews, news, politics, pop culture, style, travel, social issues and entertainment." In short, the stories and reports profile aspects important to the lesbian community. Their website archives articles, provides forums for the community, and features stories in departments similar to those found in the magazine.

GENRE
213 West 35th Street, Suite 402
New York, NY 10001
(212) 594-8181
www.genremagazine.com

GENRE is a gay men's magazine. The publisher maintains, "*GENRE* provides images and ideas that inspire, while shedding relevant insights on the various aspects of How We Live: career, culture, relationships, technology, finance, design, health, travel, transportation and personal style. *GENRE* acknowledges and respects the diversity of our readership with no intention of defining or restricting it."

Girlfriends
3415 Cesar Chavez, Suite 101
San Francisco, CA 94110
(415) 648-9464

Girlfriends is a magazine aimed at the readership of lesbian women. Each issue covers various culture, political, and entertainment topics from the lesbian perspective.

Metrosouce
180 Varick Street, 5th Floor
New York, NY 10014
(212) 691-5127
www.metrosource.com

Metrosource captures the culture and interests of the urban gay community. The magazine is published five times a year, but plans are being made to allow for bimonthly releases in 2005. The magazine features cutting edge stories; interviews; fashion; reviews of television, music, and books; interior design; health and fitness; and so on.

> *Out*
> 6922 Hollywood Blvd., Suite 1000
> Los Angeles, CA 90028
> (323) 871-1225
> www.out.com

Out magazine is published monthly and features an array of articles on current affairs and pop culture. *Out* features stories and reports under the rubrics OutFront (reviews of film, music, books, art and design, etc.); Voices (first-person analysis of concerning issues); Features (interviews, fashion spreads, etc.); and Essentials (upcoming events, fashion, advice, horoscope, etc.) Many of the features are informative (e.g., a review of the Stonewall Riots), but others address topics that some may find offensive.

What Hotlines/Help Lines and Online Organizations Are Available for Youth?

Some organizations sponsor hotlines/help lines for youth who need help in a time of crisis. Inform students of these phone numbers so they know that someone can offer support and guidance when school personnel are not available for them. Phone numbers and a description of the services they offer are categorized respectively: general support, AIDS/HIV concerns, suicide prevention, and runaway concerns.

General Support

> Gay and Lesbian National Hotline
> (888) THE-GLNH

The hotline offers callers free information, referrals, and consulting services. Callers remain anonymous as trained volunteers access a database comprised of over 18,000 listings that range from business to entertainment. If callers prefer, they can also e-mail the hotline website at www.glnh.org/home.htm.

> Indiana Youth Group (IYG), Gay & Lesbian Youth National Hotline
> (800) 347-TEEN

Based out of Bloomington, Indiana, IYG offers this hotline to gay, lesbian, bisexual, transgender, and questioning youth under the age of 21. Services are limited to Friday and Saturday, 7:00–10:00 p.m., CST.

> LYRIC Youth Talkline/Infoline for Lesbian, Gay, Bisexual, Transgendered, Queer and Questioning Youth
> (800) 246-PRIDE

LYRIC serves members of the San Francisco GLBTQ community who are younger than 23 years old. The LYRIC website, www.lyric.org, has an array of resources and links in addition to a description of the programs available through their offices. The talk line/info line is free and anonymous, and it offers peer support, health and sexuality information, and referrals.

AIDS/HIV Concerns

> AIDS Hotline for Teens
> (800) 234-TEENS

This national AIDS hotline was created by adolescents for adolescents. Members of Teens Teaching Aids Prevention educate callers with information that leads to the prevention of AIDS.

> CDC National AIDS Hotline
> (800) 342-AIDS

This national hotline advises callers on AIDS prevention, testing, and treatment and on what constitutes risky sexual behavior. Callers can also be referred to local organizations.

> The TeenAIDS Hotline
> (800) 440-TEEN

This hotline is operated by trained peers who encourage callers to abstain from sex and drugs. Peer counselors, however, will advise their sexually active callers on how to reduce their risk of becoming infected.

Suicide Prevention

> National Hopeline Network
> (800) SUICIDE

Administered through the Kristin Brooks Hope Center, callers can receive assistance through a network of certified crisis centers.

The Trevor Helpline
(866) 4-U-TREVOR

The helpline was created to coincide with the release of *Trevor*, a short film about a 13-year-old boy who attempts suicide after he is rejected by his friends because of his sexuality. The Trevor Project website, www.thetrevorproject.org, provides information on youth suicide (e.g., signs to look for, how to help, etc.) and background information about the project's initiative. The calls are free and anonymous, with professional counselors managing all calls.

Runaway Concerns

Covenant House Nine Line
(800) 999-9999

The Covenant House provides the Nine Line for youth who need immediate assistance and have nowhere to turn. Calls do not necessarily have to deal with runaway or homeless issues. Youth can talk to Covenant House workers and volunteers about any issue of concern any time of day or night.

National Runaway Switchboard
(800) 231-6946

Callers can receive free and confidential services 24 hours a day, seven days a week. Operators are trained in crisis intervention and will help callers "work through problems and find a plan of action" instead of giving advice. The website, www.nrscrisisline.org, is supplied with a wealth of resources that can be accessed through Web buttons: news and research, publications and materials, training and prevention, and the like.

What Websites Can Youth Visit to Learn More about Gay and Lesbian Issues?

There are many websites that extend their support and resources to gay and lesbian youth. Below are some websites that are sponsored by reputable organizations and are committed to meeting the needs of this population. While some cater to local communities, most post current news for and about youth with diverse sexualities, have links to other support networks, offer advice, provide a search engine to retrieve archived articles, or provide online magazines. Remind youth to limit the amount of personal information they disclose on the Internet since law enforcement officials have found that some adults disguise themselves as youth and prey on adolescents' naiveté.

Books for and about Gay/Lesbian Teens and Youth: http://www.softlord.com/glbbooks
Boston Alliance of Gay, Lesbian, Bisexual, and Transgender Youth: http://www.bagly.org
Café Pride—Chicago's Gay Friend, Youth Coffeehouse: http://www.cafepride.com
Cool Page for Queer Teens: http://www.bidstrup.com/cool.htm
Day of Silence Project: http://www.dayofsilence.org
Dignity USA: http://www.dignityusa.org
District 202—Creating Safe Space for Queer Youth: http://www.dist202.org
Financial Aid for Lesbian, Gay, and Bisexual Students: http://www.finaid.org/otheraid/gay.phtml
Gay Teen Resource: http://www.gayteenresource.com
Gayteens.org: http://www.gayteens.org
GLBT Years Book: http://www.gayyearbook.com
Go Ask Alice—Columbia University's health question and answer Internet service: http://www.goaskalice.columbia.edu/index.html
Iwannaknow.org: http://www.iwannaknow.org
Lambda Foundation: http://www.lambdafoundation.com
Lambda 10 Project: http://www.lambda10.org
Lambda Youth Project: http://www.gayprom.org/lypinfo.html
Lavender Youth Recreation and Information Center: http://thecity.sfsu.edu/~lyric
Mogenic: http://mogenic.com/index.asp
National Association of Lesbian, Gay, Bisexual, and Transgender Community Centers: http://www.lgbtcenters.org
Oasis Magazine: www.oasismag.com
One in Teen: http://www.members.tripod.com/oneinteen
Outminds.com: http://www.outminds.com/common/index.cfm
OutProud—Be Yourself: http://www.outproud.org
Out Youth Austin: http://www.outyouth.org/index.html
Positive Images: http://www.posimages.org
Pride Street: http://www.pridestreet.net/Community/youth.html
Pride Zone: http://www.pridezone.org/home.html
Queer America—Find Your Way: http://www.queeramerica.com
Queer Resources Directory: www.qrd.org
QueerToday.com: http://www.queertoday.com

Sex, etc.: http://sexetc.rutgers.edu
Sexual Minority Youth Assistance League: http://smyal.org/main.php
Soc.support.youth.gay-lesbian-bi: http://ssyglb.org
Soulforce: http://soulforce.org
Teenwire.com: http://www.teenwire.com/index.asp
True Colors: http://www.ourtruecolors.org
Wingspan's Youth Services: http://www.wingspanaz.org
Young Gay America: http://www.younggayamerica.com/index.shtml
Young Gay and Lesbian: http://www.avert.org/ygmt.htm
Youth Guardian Service: http://www.youth-guard.org
Youth.Org: http://www.youth.org
Youth Resource: http://www.youthresource.com

Summary

Provided in this chapter are some of the resources that can help you and your learning community better understand gay and lesbian persons and their unique contributions. When members of your learning community explore these topics, they are challenged to examine the biases and preconceived notions they have toward gay and lesbian persons, which enables them to learn that persons with diverse sexualities are deserving of respect. These resources and others like them are beneficial to all students, especially those who are gay, lesbian, bisexual, transgender, or questioning their sexuality.

Idea File

1. Designate a school committee (inclusive of a safe person) to review your school library's inventory of resources on gay and lesbian matters and to recommend other supplementary materials for acquisition.

2. Choose a topic on gay and lesbian issues. Then watch a video and read an article or book on the topic. Write a lesson plan on the topic and include a range of activities that engage students to further explore the topic.

3. Sponsor a book club for faculty, staff, and students and read some of the books outlined in the chapter.

4. Create a "backpack on loan" program. In each backpack, include pamphlets, books, videos, and articles on gay and lesbian issues and make these available for students to check out.

5. Continue to add to this chapter of resources.

Answers to the Quizzes

Chapter 5: Matching Quiz

1. h	6. b	11. d
2. m	7. c	12. e
3. o	8. j	13. n
4. a	g. g	14. k
5. l	10. f	15. l

Chapter 6: True/False Quiz

1. True	6. False	11. False
2. True	7. True	12. True
3. False	8. True	13. True
4. True	9. False	14. False
5. False	10. True	15. False

Chapter 7: Multiple-Choice Quiz

1. a	6. d
2. d	7. a
3. a	8. b
4. c	9. a
5. c	10. b

Chapter 8: *Jeopardy* Quiz

1. Who is Billy Bean?
2. Who is Jane Addams?
3. Who is Truman Capote?
4. Who is Willa Cather?
5. Who is Susan B. Anthony?
6. Who is Robert Reed?

7. Who is Oscar Wilde?
8. Who is Barney Frank?
9. Who is Chastity Bono?
10. Who is John Nash?
11. Who is Michael Stipe?
12. Who is Chris Radko?

Commercially Available Curricula That Promote the Inclusion of Gay, Lesbian, Bisexual, and Transgender Youth

Curricula That Deal Exclusively with Gay, Lesbian, Bisexual, and Transgender Youth Issues

Title: *Becoming Visible: A Reader in Gay and Lesbian History for High School and College Students*
Author: Kevin Jennings
Publisher: Alyson Publications, ISBN 1-55583-254-7
Cost: $13.95

Jennings, founder of the Gay, Lesbian and Straight Education Network and former high school history teacher, served as the editor for this book because he wanted readers to learn more about gay history, and he wanted teachers to have the resources to teach about it. Seventeen chapters present how gay, lesbian, bisexual, and transgender persons have been treated by past and contemporary cultures. Each chapter consists of a published essay (a historical reference on homosexuality) with questions and activities for follow-up. The chapters are divided into three parts: "Homosexuals before 'Homosexuality': Looking at 'Gay' People in Pre-Modern Societies"; "The Emergence of the Modern Gay Movement"; and "The Ongoing Struggle: Gays and Lesbians in the Eighties and Nineties."

Title: *Challenging Homophobia in Schools: A Handbook for Educators*
Producer: Gay and Lesbian Educators of British Columbia
           (Available through the GLSEN website)
Cost: $14.00

The unit's content is divided into six sections: "Introduction" (to the handbook); "Rationale" (for incorporating the content into British Columbia Schools); "Background" (information about the GLBT population); "Strategies" (to promote tolerance of GLBT youth); "Lesson Plans" (for primary, intermediate, and secondary grades); and "Resources." Although the material is geared for the British Columbia Schools, much of it is easily adaptable for American schools. Some of the lessons address the following:

- types of families,
- name-calling,

- stereotypes,
- famous gay and lesbian persons, and
- myths about gay and lesbian persons.

Title: *Lesbian, Gay, Bisexual, and Transgender Rights: A Human Rights Perspective*
Author: David M. Donahue
Publisher: Amnesty International USA,
            GLSEN, and
            The University of Minnesota Human Rights Resource Center
            ISBN 0-96-75334-2-2
            (Available through the GLSEN website)
Cost: $19.95

The content in this unit is divided into three parts. Part 1 provides teachers with background information about GLBT human rights, part 2 is composed of nine activities to be used with high school youth, and part 3 provides resources to augment the activities. The activities have students do the following:

- examine language about or toward people with diverse sexualities;
- investigate how the GLBT community lacks civil rights; and
- debate tolerance, same-sex marriages, homophobia, and so forth.

Title: *The Invisible Minority: GLBTQ Youth at Risk*
Author: Bob Latham
Publisher: Point Richmond Press
            PO Box 70554
            Point Richmond, CA 94807-0554
            (Available through the GLSEN website)
Cost: $10.00

This text is a compilation of resources and tips for teachers and administrators. A vocabulary section, a quiz on gay and lesbian issues, the etiology of homosexuality, famous homosexuals, facts about the population, and so forth are included in the appendices. Some assignments (p. 9) suggest that students do the following:

- research homosexual behavior among animals,
- research how other cultures view homosexuality, and
- research a famous gay or lesbian person.

Other recommendations (p. 27) include the following:

- implementing an activity to enforce a slur-free environment;
- having students reflect on a time they were "put down";
- holding essay contests with gay and lesbian issues as the theme (e.g.,"A gay person I admire . . .");and
- conducting a youth survey.

Title: *Out for Equity/Out4Good Safe Schools Manual*
Producer: Saint Paul Public Schools/Out for Equity,
            Minneapolis Public Schools/Out4Good, GLSEN, Outfront Minnesota
            (Available through the GLSEN website)
Cost: $15.00

Most of the material in the content is background information to facilitate a better understanding of GLBT youth. For instance, school board and association policies, definitions about the GLBT community, myths and facts, and sources of support precede the lesson ideas, and a resource section (local, national, and online) concludes the unit. The lesson ideas are appropriate for high school youth, and they include the following:

- "GLBT Teens: A Population At Risk"—In groups students conjure the risks they believe are associated with the population and then compare their results with actual statistics.
- "GLBT Famous People 20 Questions"—Students pin the name of a famous gay person on their backs and have others inform them about the person's accomplishments. The student then tries to guess the famous gay person.
- "Role Playing to Counter Harassment"
- "Power + Prejudice = Oppression"—Students deliberate about power and prejudice in their schools and discuss how to change prejudice to acceptance.
- "Riddle Scale"—students arrange in a continuum the comments generally made about GLBT persons.
- "Imagery"—Students imagine what it would be like to be straight in an all-gay world.

Title: *Preventing Prejudice: Lesbian/Gay/Bisexual/Transgender Lesson Plan Guide for Elementary Schools*
Authors: Martha Hawthorne, Eric Heins, Lynn Levey, and Terri Massin
Publisher: Lesbian and Gay Parents Association and
            Buena Vista Lesbian and Gay Parents Group
            (Available through the GLSEN website)
Cost: $22.00

The unit is composed of 15 lesson plans for youth in kindergarten through fifth grade. These lessons are divided into five themes: "Stereotypes and Gender Roles," "Respect for Diversity," "Coming Out," "Family," and "Community and Civil Rights." The lesson plans address name-calling, various ways that love is expressed, being open-minded, GLBT relationships and symbols, people in the community, family structures and dynamics, and so forth.

Title:	*The Shared Heart: Affirming Images of Lesbian, Gay, and Bisexual Youth*
Author:	Adam Mastoon
Publisher:	The Shared Heart Foundation
	264 Beacon Street, Suite 2F
	Boston, MA 02116
	(413) 637-4278
Cost:	$105.00

This curriculum, appropriate for high school youth, is composed of a CD-ROM of 35 portraits from the Shared Heart, a copy of the Shared Heart, another CD-ROM of lesson plans and a resource guide, and a Shared Heart poster. Some the 28 lessons have the students do the following:

- research gay rights,
- analyze stereotypes in society,
- research a gay or lesbian person in history,
- explore gay and lesbian celebrities, and
- explore bullying and harassment behaviors.

Title:	*Tackling Gay Issues in School: A Resource Module*
Editor:	Leif Mitchell
Sponsors:	GLSEN Connecticut; Planned Parenthood of Connecticut, Inc.
	(Available through the GLSEN website)
Cost:	$20.00

The content is divided into three sections: "Rationale," "Recommended Curriculum and Staff Development Activities," and "Recommended Extracurricular Activities and Resources." Over 25 lessons and activities (appropriate for junior high and senior high school youth) compose the curriculum section, including the following:

- "Getting the Facts: Homosexuality and Homophobia in Our Culture"—Students examine myths and stereotypes, brainstorm the various epithets directed toward GLBT persons, and so forth.

- "How We Reinforce Gender Roles:'Nice Young Ladies Don't'"
- "Guess What, Mom?"—Students role-play a girl coming out to her family during a holiday dinner.
- "What is Homophobia?"—Students define homophobia, discuss from where it is derived, and talk about whether it is a taught phenomenon.

Curricula with Lessons That Specifically Address the Topic

Title: *Filling the Gaps: Hard to Teach Topics in Sexuality Education*
Publisher: SEICUS
             130 W 42nd Street, Suite 350
             New York, NY 10036
             (212) 819-9770
Cost: $20.00
Pages: 133–46

The unit discusses how the *Guidelines for Comprehensive Sexuality Education* address sexual identity and orientation, and it also includes a fact sheet with permission to reproduce for the classroom. The following lessons address GLBT issues:

1. "Toward Understanding . . . Some of Us Are Lesbian or Gay"—Students reflect on homosexuality and their concerns if someone were to come out to them. Appropriate for senior high school youth.
2. "Heterosexuals in An Alien World"—Teacher reads a passage about a futuristic time when homosexuals dominate the planet, and students imagine what it would be like to be the alienated heterosexual. The students then strategize how to deal with oppression. Appropriate for junior and senior high school youth.
3. "Exploring Sexual Orientation"—Students answer 15 questions that are often asked about homosexuals but rarely asked of heterosexuals. Students then reflect on the exercise and learn about some of the stereotypes and misconceptions they have about sexual orientation. Appropriate for senior high school youth.
4. "Some of Your Best Friends Are"—Students are asked to imagine and reflect on how they would react if people they admired were gay, lesbian, or bisexual. Appropriate for junior and senior high school youth.
5. "Sexual Orientation: A Lesson with Parents"—Students are given a series of questions to ask their parents regarding their opinions about sexual orientation. Students reconvene to discuss how they felt about the assignment and the types of responses made by their parents. Appropriate for senior high school youth.

Title: *Open Minds To Equality: A Sourcebook of Learning Activities to Affirm Diversity and Promote Equity*

Authors: Nancy Schiendewind and Ellen Davidson

Publisher: Allyn and Bacon, ISBN 0-205-16109-X

Cost: $51.00

Pages: 276–77, 298–99

This 11-chapter book has a number of lessons and activities that help promote tolerance and affirm diversity among upper elementary and junior high youth. (The lessons can be easily adapted for high school youth and adults.) Although many of the lessons and activities lend themselves extremely well to the inclusion of GLBT persons, one lesson is exclusively devoted to GLBT issues. The lesson, "Speaking Out Against Bias in Schools," has students read an interview about two youth (whose mothers are lesbian) and how they dealt with homophobia in their elementary school.

Title: *Our Whole Lives: Sexuality Education for Grades 7–9*

Author: Pamela M. Wilson

Publisher: Unitarian Universalist Association
             (Available online at www.uua.org)

Cost: $75.00

Pages: 79–114

Our Whole Lives (OWL) is a comprehensive sex-education curriculum that ranges from modules appropriate for youth in K–1 to 10–12. In this OWL module, "Sexual Orientation and Gender Identity" is one unit among 11 other sexual themes such as body awareness, relationships, lovemaking, and so forth. The lessons on GLBT issues have the students do the following:

- read and reflect on a passage from the book, "One Teenager in Ten: Writings by Gay and Lesbian Youth,"
- learn about and discuss six underlying beliefs about GLBT persons,
- play the MythInformation Game, where they read a statement and determine if it is a fact or a myth.
- imagine that they live in a society where they are the sexual minority, and
- reflect on how they feel about what they have just learned.

Title: *A Place at the Table: Struggles for Equality in America*

Publisher: Tolerance.org
             A Web project of the Southern Poverty Law Center
             (Available online at www.tolerance.org)

Cost: Free
Pages: 130–39

This unit is composed of 12 narratives of Americans who have fought for social justice. Included among these is the story of lesbian teacher Wendy Weaver who fought a courageous battle to keep her Utah teaching job. A video and lesson plan accompany the story, which has the students deliberate questions, write a ballad about her struggles, write a news piece covering the events that led up to the court's decision, and so forth.

Title: *Sex, Etc.: A Newsletter by Teens for Teens*
Author: (Compiled by) Nora Gelperin
Publisher: Network for Family Life Education
             Center for Applied Psychology
             41 Gordon Road, Suite A
             Piscataway, NJ 08854
             (732) 445-7929
Cost: $25.00
Pages: 91–95

Articles from the *Sex, Etc. Newsletter* are used to approach sexual-orientation issues with an activity following each of the readings. Additional articles on sexual-orientation issues can be retrieved through their website. (The titles of these are found on p. 159.) The unit includes two articles and activities:

1. "Homophobia Hatches Hostility, Hate"—The article addresses beliefs about homosexuality and the insecurity often associated with these. The activity invites youth to reflect on why homophobia exists and to examine their own feelings toward gay men and lesbian women.

2. "Coming Out: A Gay Teen Talks about Telling"—The article discusses one teen's coming-out process with various responses from those closest to him. The activity requires students to think about a secret about themselves and to imagine what it would be like if others found out about it.

Title: *Sexuality & Relationships*
Author: Betty M. Hubbard
Publisher: ETR Associates
             PO Box 1830
             Santa Cruz, CA 95061-1830
             (800) 321-4407
Cost: $27.00
Pages: 74–84

Three lessons on sexual orientation are presented in one unit of 10 sexuality themes. The lessons include four activity sheets and information about sexual orientation for the "Instant Expert." The three lessons are

1. "The Facts about Homosexuality"—Students answer questions about homosexuality on an activity sheet titled "Fact or Fiction?" Students then read five facts about homosexuality and discuss how society's attitudes toward homosexuality often lack accurate information.
2. "A Continuum of Sexual Orientation"—Students discuss the Kinsey continuum of sexual orientation. No questions or prompts are available to facilitate the discussion.
3. "Homophobia in Our Society"—Students complete an activity sheet about the various forms of homophobia in society. Students then decide on an action to decrease homophobia and present this action and their rationale to other students.

Title: *Streetwise to Sex-wise: Sexuality Education for High-Risk Youth*
Authors: Steve Brown and Bill Taverner
Publisher: Planned Parenthood of Greater Northern New Jersey Inc.
            196 Speedwell Avenue
            Morristown, NJ 07960
            (973) 539-9580
Cost: $30.00
Pages: 15–18, 117–34

A profile of the population (with facts and critical messages) precedes the lessons on homosexuality. The two lessons on sexual orientation issues are

1. "Facts Are the Cure for Fear"—Three activities are available for the students: first, they reflect on and complete a sentence stem (e.g., "Gays, lesbians, and bisexuals are . . .") and then discuss their feelings toward the statements; second, they gather in groups and make a list of the advantages and disadvantages of being gay and conclude with a discussion; and third, they complete a worksheet on myths and facts about homosexuality and then review an explanation for each myth.
2. "The Invisible Minority"—Teachers are given guidelines for finding a gay or lesbian speaker to talk to students about what the gay/lesbian lifestyle is like. When a speaker is unavailable, students first discuss what they perceive it is like to grow up gay in contemporary society. Students then read and discuss a journal entry written by a real gay student. As a third activity, students are given a handout, "True Stories of Lesbian and Gay Teens," and then discuss the various entries.

Book with Poetic Pieces That Address Gay, Lesbian, and Transgender Issues

Title: *Cootie Shots: Theatrical Inoculations against Bigotry for Kids, Parents and Teachers*

Author(s): Norma Bowles with Mark E. Rosenthal

Publisher: A Fringe Benefits Book

Theatre Communication Group, New York

ISBN: 1-55936-184-0

Cost: $18.95

This collection of plays, songs, poems, and other powerful words is designed to eradicate intolerance based on race, class, gender, sexual orientation, and ability. The authors write, "These pieces ask children to acknowledge the bigotry and discrimination in their lives, while helping them to imagine and take responsibility for creating a world shaped by love and understanding." Their performance pieces are divided into four units:

1. "My Family Tree Is a Garden!"
2. "Get to Know Me!"
3. "Be Proud of Your Difference!"
4. "We Can Change the World!"

Although no lesson plans or guides are available, teachers can create lessons around the pieces that address gay and lesbian issues or use these to spark discussions. The following pieces directly address gay and lesbian issues:

- "A Different Family," p. 16—A young girl discloses that her father is gay.
- "That's a Family," p. 19—An excerpt from a girl who has two fathers.
- "Play Wedding," p. 26—A reflection on a gay wedding.
- "La Peluca de Su Mama," p. 41—A boy gets teased for putting on his mother's wig.
- "Doing the Right Thing," p. 45—A play about a girl who gets teased because her brother is gay.
- "Fair Play," p. 58—A boy degrades another for playing with a doll.
- "Anyone Double Dutch?" p. 61—Gender stereotypes and name-calling.
- "Mariposas," p. 71—A gay boy reflects on intolerance.
- "In Mommy's High Heels," p. 88—A boy gets comfort when he wears his mother's shoes.
- "The Princess Petunia," p. 97—A princess discusses how she is in love with another woman.

- "Just Because You're You," p. 105—A father comforts his son who has been called *maricon*.
- "Four Heroes," p. 120—Activist Harvey Milk is mentioned.
- "What's with the Dress, Jack?" p. 132—Two spirit; challenges "boys don't wear dresses."
- "America Didn't Crumble," p. 137—A young girl discusses what it's like to have two lesbian mothers.

Training Manuals for Schools or Educational Organizations

Title: *Ending Anti-gay Bias in Schools: A Training of Trainers Manual*
Publisher: GLSEN
        (Available through the GLSEN website)
Cost: $54.95
This manual is a two-day extension of the *Lunchbox* (see below) and is designed for experienced trainers "who wish to expand their local network of facilitators and develop an ongoing training initiative to reduce anti-gay bias in schools" (p. 4). The curriculum covers some of the same elements found in the *Lunchbox* ("Warm-up," "Setting the Stage," "Just the Facts," "Paying the Price," "Creating Change,""Taking Action," and "Wrap-up") and uses the same step-by-step approach with scripts that trainers can read to their audiences. The curriculum is complete with forms to disseminate to participants.

Title: *Fraternity and Sorority Anti-Homophobia: Train the Trainer Manual*
Authors: Shane L. Windmeyer and Pamela W. Freeman
Publisher: Lambda 10 Project, National Clearinghouse for Gay, Lesbian, Bisexual
        Fraternity and Sorority Issues
        (Available through www.lambda10.org)
Cost: $69.95
This curriculum is clearly appropriate for professionals who work closely with fraternities and sororities. The six modules have lessons and activities that are detailed and easy to implement, and they include handouts and transparencies to facilitate the sessions. The modules are as follows:

- "Coming out on Campus"—Participants learn about coming out from the GLB perspective.
- "Harms of Homophobia"—Participants learn the untoward effects of homophobia on GLB and heterosexuals.
- "Becoming an Ally for Gay Brothers and Sisters"—Participants learn how to support GLB persons.

- "Religion and Greek Life"—Participants learn how religion influences attitudes toward GLB persons.
- "Responding to Homophobia and Hate"—Participants learn how homophobia is manifested and strategize how to contend with it.
- "Creating a Climate of Acceptance"

Title:	*The GLSEN Lunchbox: A Comprehensive Training Program for Ending Anti-gay Bias in Schools*
Publisher:	GLSEN
	(Available through the GLSEN website)
Cost:	$79.95

This training program comes complete with a training manual, a how-to booklet that orients facilitators to the lunchbox, a video, and laminated exercise cards. The curriculum is very elaborate, with seven types of exercises that take participants from warm-up to wrap-up. The manual offers practical advice for trainers, with various activities and the tools necessary to implement them. The 25 activities include the following:

- "Sit Down If . . ."—Participants learn about "unearned privilege."
- "Attitudes toward Difference Survey"—Participants complete the survey and then discuss their scores and beliefs and how to facilitate better attitudes toward GLBT persons.
- "Passing the Glass Slipper"—Participants read a lesbian version of Cinderella.

Title:	*Making Schools Safe: An Anti-Harassment Training Program*
Publisher:	Lesbian & Gay Rights Project of the American Civil Liberties Union
	American Civil Liberties Union Foundation
	125 Broad Street, 18th floor
	New York, NY 10004-2400
Cost:	Free

This curriculum is divided into four sections: the manual (discusses the need for the Making Schools Safe program and addresses the preliminary work that must be conducted); the tools (what is needed to prepare for the program and all the background information that is needed to facilitate the workshop); the lesson plan (a step-by-step arrangement of the material to be presented, including the agenda, scripts, review of vocabulary, etc.); and the handouts.

Title:	*Strengthening the Learning Environment: A School Employee's Guide to Gay and Lesbian Issues*

Publisher: National Education Association
               (Available at http://www.nea.org/books)
Cost: $15.95
This guide provides general information about GLBT youth in terms of education, safety, health, and legal issues. Although no specific lesson plans, activities, or ideas accompany the issues, a list of resources is available in each of the issue subcategories (e.g., student achievement, staff development, curriculum).

Index

About the Author

David Campos is associate professor of education in the School of Education at the University of the Incarnate Word. His experiences include teaching second grade and conducting corporate training and development for Advanced Micro Devices and Guiltless Gourmet, Inc. He has supervised student teachers and taught undergraduate and graduate courses in special education, multicultural education, and curriculum methods. In addition to his duties as associate professor, he has served as assistant dean of academic affairs and as project coordinator for a Title II Teacher Quality Enhancement Grant. He has written books on sex education, diverse sexuality in schools, and English language learners, and he traveled to China in 2004 as a Fulbright Scholar.